CHILD PROTECTION AND THE EUROPEAN COURT OF HUMAN RIGHTS

Lessons from Norway in the Development and Contestation of Children's Rights

Edited by
Hege Stein Helland, Marit Skivenes
and Siri Gloppen

First published in Great Britain in 2025 by

Policy Press, an imprint of
Bristol University Press
University of Bristol
1–9 Old Park Hill
Bristol
BS2 8BB
UK
t: +44 (0)117 374 6645
e: bup-info@bristol.ac.uk

Details of international sales and distribution partners are available at policy.bristoluniversitypress.co.uk

Editorial selection and matter © the editors 2025; individual chapters © their respective authors 2025

The digital PDF and ePub versions of this title are available open access and distributed under the terms of the Creative Commons Attribution-NonCommercial-NoDerivatives 4.0 International licence (https://creativecommons.org/licenses/by-nc-nd/4.0/) which permits reproduction and distribution for non-commercial use without further permission provided the original work is attributed.

DOI: https://doi.org/10.51952/9781447371496

British Library Cataloguing in Publication Data
A catalogue record for this book is available from the British Library

ISBN 978-1-4473-7147-2 paperback
ISBN 978-1-4473-7148-9 ePub
ISBN 978-1-4473-7149-6 ePdf

The right of Hege Stein Helland, Marit Skivenes and Siri Gloppen to be identified as editors of this work has been asserted by them in accordance with the Copyright, Designs and Patents Act 1988.

All rights reserved: no part of this publication may be reproduced, stored in a retrieval system, or transmitted in any form or by any means, electronic, mechanical, photocopying, recording, or otherwise without the prior permission of Bristol University Press.

Every reasonable effort has been made to obtain permission to reproduce copyrighted material. If, however, anyone knows of an oversight, please contact the publisher.

The statements and opinions contained within this publication are solely those of the editors and contributors and not of the University of Bristol or Bristol University Press. The University of Bristol and Bristol University Press disclaim responsibility for any injury to persons or property resulting from any material published in this publication.

Bristol University Press and Policy Press work to counter discrimination on grounds of gender, race, disability, age and sexuality.

Cover design: Gareth Davies
Front cover image: Stocksy / Oleksandra Stets

Contents

List of figures and tables v
List of abbreviations vi
Notes on contributors vii
Acknowledgements xii
Preface xiii

1　Children's rights under pressure: Norway, the European Court　1
　　of Human Rights and the challenges to welfare state legitimacy
　　Hege Stein Helland, Marit Skivenes and Siri Gloppen

PART I　The European Court of Human Rights from a national perspective

2　Are the child welfare cases against Norway in the European　23
　　Court of Human Rights unique?
　　Marius Emberland
3　Child protection and the European Court of Human　45
　　Rights: the case of Finland and Article 8
　　Raija Huhtanen and Tarja Pösö
4　Children's rights and European Court of Human Rights　59
　　judgments' effects on Norwegian courts and jurisprudence
　　Kirsten Sandberg
5　Implementing international human rights case law at the　75
　　domestic street level: the case of Norwegian child protection
　　Hege Stein Helland
6　Representations of children in European Court of Human　98
　　Rights judgments
　　Katrin Križ and Daniela Reimer
7　Exploring ethnicity constructs in European Court of　116
　　Human Rights judgments
　　Daniela Reimer, Katrin Križ, Mary Burns,
　　Gabriela Serra and Kerry Shea

PART II　Transnational influence of the European Court of Human Rights

8　Prioritising the child's best interests: mixed messages in the　135
　　international human rights arena
　　Elaine E. Sutherland
9　Think of the children! Children's rights as the new frontier in　153
　　anti-gender contestation
　　Neil Datta
10　When 'bad friends' lobby the court against human rights　178
　　Asgeir Falch-Eriksen

| 11 | Mobilised interests, the European Court of Human Rights and children's rights
Rachel Cichowski and Elizabeth Chrun | 192 |

PART III The European Court of Human Rights and its jurisprudence

12	Children and rights to identity at the European Court of Human Rights *Jill Marshall*	211
13	Normative considerations about the guiding principles for the European Court of Human Rights allocating custody in child protection *David Archard and Marit Skivenes*	229
14	The relationship between the UN Convention on the Rights of the Child and the European Court of Human Rights in numbers *Claire Fenton-Glynn*	244
15	The European Court of Human Rights: an untapped source for advancing child rights? *Hege Stein Helland, Marit Skivenes and Siri Gloppen*	260

| Index | 272 |

List of figures and tables

Figures

7.1	The data about court cases	119
11.1	Annual number of amicus briefs filed in ECtHR judgments by key institutional reform to third-party intervention access, 1979–2022	196

Tables

1.1	An overview of Article 8 judgments relating to child protection in the ECtHR, from 1959 to 2022	7
1.2	The CoE member countries rank on the Lancet Child Flourishing Index and on the 2023 WJP Rule of Law Index	8
1.3	Countries subscribing to the ECtHR and key child protection information	12
2.1	Table of cases and outcome sorted by respondent state	28
3.1	ECHR and the ECtHR judgments in the Nordic context, 1959–2023	46
3.2	ECtHR judgments concerning Finnish child protection in 1990–2023	48
5.1	Coding frame	81
6.1	ECtHR judgments overview (Norway)	101
6.2	Categories, codes and code descriptions	105
6.3	The child as a subject and object	107
6.4	The child as a subject	108
6.5	The child as an object	110
9.1	Anti-gender organisation involvement in ECtHR cases about child protection	164
11.1	Norwegian children's rights ECtHR judgments and associated third-party interventions by state governments and interest groups from 2019 to 2022	197
14.1	Number of cases mentioning the CRC	248
14.2	Part of the judgment in which the CRC was mentioned	249
14.3	Level of engagement with Convention materials	249
14.4	Areas of law where the CRC has been cited	251
14.5	CRC Articles used in decisions	252
14.6	UN Committee General Comments	255

List of abbreviations

ADF	Alliance Defending Freedom
ADFI	Alliance Defending Freedom International
AIMMF	Associazione Italiana dei Magistrati per i Minorenni e per la Famiglia
AIRE Centre	Advice on Individual Rights in Europe
CEP	Child Equality Perspective
CM	Committee of Ministers of the Council of Europe
CoE	Council of Europe
CPS	child protection systems
CRC	The United Nations Convention on the Rights of the Child
CRC Committee	The United Nations Committee on the Rights of the Child
CSE	comprehensive sexuality education
CWS	child protection agencies
DGD	Days of General Discussion
ECHR	European Convention on Human Rights
ECHRdb	European Court of Human Rights Database
ECLJ	European Centre for Law and Justice
ECtHR	European Court of Human Rights
EEA	European Economic Area
GC	European Court of Human Rights' Grand Chamber
GCs	General Comments
KKN	Kristen Koalisjon Norge
ME	minoritised ethnic
MoA	margin of appreciation
NGOs	non-governmental organisations
NIM (NHRI)	Norges institusjon for menneskerettigheter [Norwegian Human Rights Institution]
NME	non-minoritised ethnic
NORDIS	Nordic Observatory for Digital Media and Information Disorder
NOU	Norges offentlige utredninger [Norwegian Official Report]
OPIC	Optional Protocol to the Convention on the Rights of the Child on a Communications Procedure
Ordo Iuris	Ordo Iuris Institute for Legal Culture
PACE	Parliamentary Assembly of the Council of Europe
SRHR	sexual and reproductive health and rights
WJP	World Justice Project

Notes on contributors

David Archard is Emeritus Professor of Philosophy and Applied Ethics at Queen's University Belfast, Northern Ireland. He is a leading applied moral philosopher, known for his extensive work on children's rights, parental duties and family ethics. Archard has taught at several universities, including Ulster, St Andrews and Lancaster. His research spans topics such as sexual consent, privacy, multiculturalism and education. He has served as Honorary Chair of the Society for Applied Philosophy and was a member of the UK's Human Fertilization and Embryology Authority for 12 years. Archard chaired the Nuffield Council on Bioethics and is a member of the Clinical Ethics Committee at Great Ormond Street Hospital. His contributions to ethical debates on contemporary issues, including the COVID-19 pandemic, have made him a respected voice in both academic and public policy spheres.

Mary Burns is a social worker for the Department of Children and Families in Massachusetts, USA. She is an Emmanuel College alumna, graduating with the class of 2023 with a Bachelor of Arts in Psychology and Sociology. Burns has worked as a research assistant to Dr Katrin Križ, studying child welfare cases found in the European Court of Human Rights. She also assisted Dr Križ and Dr Free's research on the lived experiences of working full-time college students, and Dr Mitchell's study of the impact of the COVID-19 pandemic on older adults' identity and purpose. Her interests are child welfare, lifespan development and identity formation.

Elizabeth Chrun is Assistant Professor of Political Science at the Université du Québec à Montréal, Canada. She received her PhD from the University of Washington. Her research focuses on governance and legal mobilisation using a comparative and international perspective. Her work is currently supported by the Fonds de recherche du Québec – Société et culture.

Rachel Cichowski is Chair and Professor in the Department of Political Science and Professor in the Law, Societies and Justice Department at the University of Washington, USA. Her primary research and teaching interests include international law and courts, legal mobilisation, comparative constitutionalism, human rights, women's rights and environmental justice. Key publications include *The European Court and Civil Society* (Cambridge University Press, 2007) and *Law, Politics and Society* (Oxford University Press, 2003). Her research is also published in journals such as *Law & Society Review*, *Comparative Political Studies* and *Journal of European Public Policy*.

Neil Datta is Executive Director and founder of the European Parliamentary Forum for Sexual and Reproductive Rights based in Brussels, Belgium. He has worked extensively on European policies related to sexual and reproductive health, focusing on anti-gender and anti-rights movements. Neil authored key reports, including *Restoring the Natural Order* (EPF, 2018) and *Tip of the Iceberg* (EPF, 2021), and co-authored a chapter on anti-gender contestation in the EU, featured in *The Christian Right in Europe* (Transcript, 2023). He received the Don and Arvonne Fraser Human Rights Award for his work in exposing anti-rights actors.

Marius Emberland is Professor of Law at BI Norwegian Business School, Norway, specialising in public and international law. He joined the BI faculty in 2023. In his capacity as attorney at the Office of the Attorney General for Civil Affairs he was the Norwegian Government's Agent before the European Court of Human Rights and the UN human rights committees 2012–2022 and he has inter alia held positions in the Ministry of Foreign Affairs and the Ministry of Justice and Public Security. His D.Phil. in law from Oxford University was published by Oxford University Press as *The Human Rights of Companies: Exploring the Structure of ECHR Protection* in 2006. He has his basic law degree from the University of Oslo and holds an LL.M. from Harvard Law School.

Asgeir Falch-Eriksen is Head of the academic unit Globalization and Social Sustainability at Oslo Metropolitan University, Norway. His professional expertise lies in the field of political science with a focus on democracy, the rule of law, policy analysis and social work, and with a primary aim to advance through theoretical contributions and policy analysis. Recent publications are *Generational Tensions and Solidarity within Advanced Welfare States* (Taylor & Francis, 2022), *Professional Practice in Child Protection and the Child's Right to Participate* (Routledge, 2022) and *Citizenship and Social Exclusion at the Margins of the Welfare State* (Taylor & Francis, 2023).

Claire Fenton-Glynn is Professor of Law at the University of Monash, Australia. She was previously the Professor of Child and Family Law at the University of Cambridge, and Director of Cambridge Family Law. Claire is on the Editorial Board of the *International Journal of Law, Policy and the Family* and is the Managing Editor of the *Australian Journal of Family Law*. Her research lies in the field of children's rights, comparative law and international human rights law. She has published on a wide range of issues including parenthood (especially international surrogacy), child trafficking and gender identity.

Siri Gloppen is Professor of Political Science in the Department of Government and Director of the Centre for Law and Social Transformation at the University of Bergen, Norway. Recognised for her theoretical and empirical socio-legal scholarship on law as political strategy, spanning legal mobilisation/lawfare and effects of mobilising the law in different fields, and the role of legal institutions in building, protecting and undermining democracy, her work has pioneered systematic, cross-regional studies in these areas across the global South. Publications include 'Legalised resistance to autocratisation in common law Africa' (*Third World Quarterly*, 2024); 'Butterfly judging' in *Litigating the Climate Crisis* (Cambridge University Press, 2023); and Queer Lawfare in Africa (PULP, 2022).

Hege Stein Helland is a postdoctoral fellow in political science at the Department of Government and the Centre for Research on Discretion and Paternalism, University of Bergen, Norway. Her research focuses on children's rights, child protection, government interventions, discretionary decision-making in public services and the courts, as well as population attitudes towards welfare state authorities and policies. Recent research is published in journals such as *The International Journal of Children's Rights* and *Social Policy & Administration*.

Raija Huhtanen, Professor Emerita of Public Law at Tampere University, Finland, specialises in administrative law, social welfare law and child welfare law. She has participated in law drafting and has served as a counsellor to the Constitutional Law Committee of Parliament. She has published articles on child welfare such as 'Removals of children in Finland: A mix of voluntary and involuntary decisions' in *Child Removals by the State* (edited by Kenneth Burns et al; Oxford University Press, 2017; together with Tarja Pösö) and 'Consenting to the taking of a child into care' in *Lakimies* (2020) (in Finnish).

Katrin Križ is Professor of Sociology at Emmanuel College Boston, USA, and a Professor II in the Department of Government at the University of Bergen, Norway. Her research aims to document oppressive social structures and analyse how they can be changed. She has published on child welfare programmes and policies for immigrant children and youth, migrant education and anti-poverty policies. Her books are *Child Welfare and Migrant Families* (Oxford University Press, 2015), *Protecting Children, Creating Citizens* (Policy Press, 2020) and *Children and Young People's Participation in Child Protection* (Oxford University Press, 2023).

Jill Marshall, Professor of Law, Department of Law and Criminology, Royal Holloway University of London, UK, co-directs the interdisciplinary Centre for the Study of Emotion and Law. She leads the Rights and Freedoms research cluster and postgraduate research within her department. She is a qualified lawyer. Her work focuses on the relationship between law, personal freedom and human flourishing, with a focus on girls' and women's human rights. She has written widely on these topics and is the author of three books and one edited collection, including: *Personal Freedom Through Human Rights Law?* (Brill Nijhoff Publishers, 2009); *Human Rights Law and Personal Identity* (Routledge, 2014) and *Personal Identity and the European Court of Human Rights* (Routledge, 2022).

Tarja Pösö, Professor Emerita in Social Work at Tampere University, Finland, has over 30 years of experience in studying social work, particularly child welfare, from various perspectives, with a keen interest in exploring methods and ethics in child welfare studies. She has published extensively in Finnish and English. Most recently, in 2024, she co-authored the report 'The protection and promotion of the rights of children in alternative care' for the European Network of Ombudspersons for Children.

Daniela Reimer is Professor of Childhood, Youth and Family at Zurich University of Applied Science, Department of Social Work, Switzerland. Her research is qualitative and focuses on foster care, residential care and child protection. She has published on participation, normality, culture and biographies with books and contributions in German, English and French. She is co-editor of special issues on 'The perspective of the child in child and youth welfare' (*Child and Youth Services Review*, 2023) and 'Professional love and diversity in foster care' (*Children & Society*, 2022).

Kirsten Sandberg is Professor of Law, University of Oslo, Norway. Sandberg was a member of the UN Committee on the Rights of the Child from 2011 to 2019 and the Committee's chairperson from 2013 to 2015. Her research interests include child law and children's rights. Relevant publications include 'Alternative care and children's rights', in *International Human Rights of Children* (edited by U. Kilkelly and T. Liefaard; Springer, 2019) and 'Grandparents' and grandchildren's right to contact under the European Convention on Human Rights' (*Family & Law*, 2021).

Gabriela Serra is a master's student of social work at Boston University and an Emmanuel College (USA) alumna with a Bachelor of Arts in Sociology with a concentration in Human Services. Throughout undergrad, Serra worked as a research assistant to Dr Katrin Križ, researching the perspectives of families portrayed in child welfare cases found in the European Court of Human Rights. She also assisted Dr Janese Free and Dr Križ in their research on the experiences of working college students. Serra's interests are child welfare, family culture and immigration.

Kerry Shea graduated from Emmanuel College, Boston, USA, with a degree in Developmental Psychology and Sociology in spring 2024. During undergrad, Kerry acted as a research assistant to Katrin Kriz to assist in research on child welfare cases ruled by the European Court of Human Rights. Kerry also completed research on the experiences of working college students and conducted interviews on the challenges and motivations behind being a working college student. Kerry continues to have research interests in child welfare, as well as in the systems used to support the behavioural health of children in the United States.

Marit Skivenes is Professor of Political Science at the Department of Government and the director of the Centre for Research on Discretion and Paternalism, University of Bergen, Norway. Skivenes is the Principal Investigator on several international research projects on child rights, child protection systems and welfare states, including a European Research Council Consolidator grant. Skivenes has published numerous scientific works on decision-making, government interventions, child protection systems and broader welfare issues, as well as being co-editor of *Oxford Handbook of Child Protection Systems* (Oxford University Press, 2023). Skivenes also led the government appointed committee on the rule of law and child protection that resulted in a Norwegian Official Report (NOU 2023: 7).

Elaine E. Sutherland is Professor Emerita of Child and Family Law at Stirling University Law School, Scotland, and Distinguished Professor of Law Emerita at Lewis & Clark Law School, Portland, Oregon. She has published widely, mainly on domestic, comparative and international child and family law; presents papers at national and international conferences; serves on Scottish Law Commission advisory groups and the Law Society of Scotland's Child and Family Law Committee; and is consulted regularly by the Scottish Government, the Scottish Parliament and non-governmental organisations.

Acknowledgements

This book is the result of an interdisciplinary and international research project on the contemporary legitimacy challenges facing welfare states in general, and children's rights and child protection systems in particular. We are grateful to the contributing authors, who shared their expertise and knowledge on various topics related to the book's overarching theme. The book has also greatly benefited from the research environment at the Centre for Research on Discretion and Paternalism, with insightful feedback and steadfast support from our colleagues.

The work was presented at two workshops in Bergen in 2022 and one in 2023. We are deeply indebted to the participants for the fruitful discussions during these meetings and, not least, for their thoughtful comments and input. We would also like to acknowledge the assistance provided by research assistants Suljo Corsulic and Layne Wetherbee with editing and formatting at various stages of the process, as well as by Zacky Dhaffa Pratama during the final editing round.

This project received funding from the Research Council of Norway under the Research Programme on Welfare, Working Life and Migration (VAM II) (grant no. 302042). Additional funding for this publication was provided by the Publication Fund for Open Access at the University of Bergen.

Preface

This book, *Child Protection and the European Court of Human Rights*, is a part of the Challenges Project, which examines the legitimacy challenges faced by Nordic welfare states, with a particular focus on Norway's child protection system. The Challenges Project received funding from the Research Council of Norway under the Research Programme on Welfare, Working Life and Migration (VAM II) (grant no. 302042) for the period 2020–2026. Professor Marit Skivenes is the Principal Investigator. The project set out to reveal conditions and mechanisms for sustaining legitimacy in societies in which there is a backlash on social and political right developments. The aim is to conduct empirical and critical examinaitons to understand the rationale behind what seem to be a strong citizen driven mobilisation against established institutions in democratic welfare states. The empirical foci on the Norwegian child protection system has its background in the harsh criticism from citizen groups as well as from religious and ultra-conservative groups. At the same time Norway is consistently ranked high on all types of measures on child rights, child well-being, rule of law and confidence in the government. The critics question the legitimacy of the child protection system and children's rights, but are simultaneously expressing a strong mistrust in legal institutions and the normative foundations of the Nordic welfare state model. An empirical foci on child protection and child's rights provides an in-depth approach to a general phenemenon.

The Principal Investigator for the book project that has resulted in the present volume is post-doc Hege Stein Helland. The edited book provides a critical and interdisciplinary exploration of how ECtHR judgments intersect with national welfare policies, children's rights and broader ideological debates. Through contributions from legal scholars, political scientists and social scientists, this volume bridges disciplinary divides to illuminate the complex interplay between international law and domestic policy. It underscores how Nordic welfare states must navigate global pressures while preserving their child-centric ethos. By addressing these challenges, this book provides invaluable insights for policy makers, advocates and scholars committed to advancing children's rights within robust and legitimate welfare systems.

1

Children's rights under pressure: Norway, the European Court of Human Rights and the challenges to welfare state legitimacy

Hege Stein Helland, Marit Skivenes and Siri Gloppen

Introduction

In the area of child protection and human rights, Norway presents a paradoxical case that challenges our understanding of welfare states and international law. Despite Norway's consistently high rankings in child well-being and rule of law indices, the country has faced an unprecedented number of European Court of Human Rights (ECtHR) judgments concerning child protection. As of December 2024, Norway holds the unfortunate record of being found in violation of human rights in more ECtHR judgments concerning its child protection decisions than any other country (Helland et al, in preparation). Violations of Article 8 of the European Convention on Human Rights (ECHR) have been found in 23 judgments – including two Grand Chamber judgments (Strand Lobben and Others v Norway and Abdi Ibrahim v Norway).[1] While these cases have attracted substantial attention in the legal community, academia and the public sphere, the conditions and mechanisms that gave rise to and facilitated the large number of Norwegian cases being admitted by the ECtHR remain largely unknown.

This paradox of the 'Norwegian case' raises critical questions about the gaps between legal frameworks and practice in child protection systems (CPS), even in high-performing welfare states. Parallel to the many ECtHR judgments on child protection, there is a current of attacks against especially Nordic child protection systems, with massive, international and seemingly coordinated protests (Bragdø-Ellenes and Torjesen, 2020). An illustration is the worldwide demonstrations against the Norwegian CPS – where it is often referred to by its Norwegian name, 'Barnevernet' (Norman, 2016). The critique reflects conservative family values movements and backlashes against minority group rights and state institutions in Europe, as well as in other parts of the world. The broader European conflicts over politics, rights and values also encompass the role and functions of supranational courts, raising discussions on state sovereignty and the relationship between politics and law. The massive critique of Norway's child protection system and parents claiming infringement on their right to family life[2] is not only challenging the legitimacy of Norway's CPS. It can be interpreted more broadly as a challenge to the Nordic welfare state model and its normative foundation. Child protection also addresses the universal challenge of drawing the border between state and family responsibilities, and between individual freedom and government restrictions. The social and legal criticism of the Norwegian child protection provides a unique lens through which to examine broader questions about the dynamics, effects and normative context of international litigation and mobilisation in matters concerning fundamental societal values. The current circumstances actualise several questions concerning the role of human rights and the ECtHR for child protection systems and for children's rights (Draghici, 2017).

With child protection as a focal point, the interdisciplinary team of authors in this book aims to uncover the conditions and mechanisms for sustaining legitimacy in welfare state institutions facing a backlash against children's social, civil and political rights. Through the investigation of domestic and international repercussions when the ECtHR scrutinises one country's practice, we aim to advance understanding of the role of supranational courts and discuss broader implications for children's rights in the country under scrutiny, Norway, and for other countries' policies and laws. By examining the ECtHR's role in the development of children's rights, as outlined in the Convention on the Rights of the Child (CRC), this book highlights discussions that are rarely addressed in international human rights and family-state literature. One ambition is to critically examine child and family rights litigation to the ECtHR in a multifaceted manner, investigating decision-making processes and contestation within the Court, as well as its interrelated relations with institutions, individuals and organisations in civil society, national governments and local authorities. We will shed some light on why so many child protection cases have been admitted to the ECtHR, and to understand the consequences – both on the Court and on its jurisprudence, and for the relevant laws and practices in the member states. Through this exploration, we seek to uncover the societal challenges and research questions surrounding children's rights, child protection and the ECtHR in contemporary Europe.

In the following sections, we expand on the main topics of the book, starting with an outline of the ECtHR and child rights, followed by a section on child rights and child protection. To better understand the European situation, we provide key information about the judicial conditions and the situation for children's welfare in the countries that subscribe to the ECtHR, followed by details about child protection systems in the member states. The final section introduces the outline of the book, consisting of Part I covering national perspectives, Part II discussing transnational perspectives, and Part III, studies of the ECtHR's decision-making.

The European Court of Human Rights and child rights

The ECtHR is one of the main entities of the Council of Europe (CoE), the leading human rights organisation on the continent, comprising 46 member states (47 until 2022, when Russia was expelled)[3] from Europe and beyond, which have all signed up to the ECHR. Established in 1959, the ECtHR is tasked with interpreting and monitoring the application of the ECHR among CoE member states and has developed into a court of the highest influence and importance. Every year, the Court delivers more than 1,000 judgments and processes over 50,000 applications. While often considered an effective human rights court (see, for example, Helfer, 2008), judgments from the ECtHR regularly create controversies, sometimes resulting in member states threatening to withdraw from the Court, as recent debates in the UK have demonstrated. Migration issues tend to be particularly contentious, and consolidated democracies like Denmark and the Netherlands have criticised the Court for being overly interventionist and overstepping the limits of domestic affairs (Stiansen and Voeten, 2020).[4] Others refer to this as anti-liberal backlash (Buzogány and Varga, 2018; Goetz, 2020; Guasti and Bustikova, 2023). This showcases the challenges that arise when there is a clash between states and international institutions in conceptions of sovereignty, value systems and ideology. Interpreting human rights in a dynamic, consistent and comprehensible way is a fundamental duty of the Court. Hence, it becomes crucial to analyse how they navigate this in practice when addressing the controversial area of child protection (see Sutherland, Chapter 8).

Child protection is a minor issue in the Court's overall portfolio. Of the 1,892 judgments concerning Article 8 delivered by the Court between 1959 and 2022, 112 judgments (5.9 per cent) are about child protection (ECHR, 2023; Helland and Skivenes, in preparation). Most child protection cases are brought under Article 8 of the ECHR, which outlines the right to protection of private and family life and which reads as follows:

1. Everyone has the right to respect for his private and family life, his home and his correspondence.
2. There shall be no interference by a public authority with the exercise of this right except such as is in accordance with the law and is necessary in a democratic society in the interests of national security, public safety or the economic well-being of the country, for the prevention of disorder or crime, for the protection of health or morals, or for the protection of the rights and freedoms of others.

Article 8 is a 'qualified right' under the Convention, meaning it can be interfered with to protect the rights of another person or to safeguard the wider public interest. It permits state interference when it is 'in accordance with the law, in pursuit of a legitimate aim and necessary in a democratic society' (Bueren, 2007, p 117) and when 'decisions are supported by relevant and sufficient reasons' (Kilkelly, 1999, p 297). In other words, states are required to justify the necessity of intervention (Draghici, 2017). In its examination of child protection cases, the Court must navigate the tensions between parents' and children's rights, as well as the interests of society as a whole (see Archard and Skivenes, Chapter 13). How this balance is ultimately struck depends on the interpretation of the ECHR and is grounded in the concept of the ECHR as a 'living instrument'. Accordingly, decisions reflect the evolving recognition of values that require protection and, therefore, when restrictions on individual rights are deemed necessary (Thomassen, 2004).

In Article 8 decisions, the ECtHR actively applies the doctrine of the 'margin of appreciation' (MoA). The MoA allows the Court to 'provide endorsement of the maintenance of cultural diversity' (Arai-Takahashi, 2002, p 249), serving the important purpose of preserving value pluralism (see Falch-Eriksen, Chapter 10). However, in doing so, the Court also grants great discretion regarding proportionality (Fenton-Glynn, 2021, pp 7–8). In other words, it provides judges with significant latitude when determining how to balance a legitimate aim against the interference it necessitates. For instance, one might ask whether the large complex of cases concerning Norway in the ECtHR– beyond the specific disputes at hand – also reflects the Court's effort to establish international jurisprudence while also addressing emerging lines of conflict in child and family matters across Europe (see, for example, Graham, 2020). Both national and international jurisprudence are shaped by normative assumptions about childhood, family and parental autonomy, and the protection of children often raises fundamental questions in how to balance parental and children's rights. As illustrated by the protests against the Norwegian CPS, family matters provoke controversies on moral, political and legal grounds that align with broader political and cultural divides (see, for example, Bragdø-Ellenes and Torjesen, 2020). The unusually high number of intervening parties in the Norwegian ECtHR may also reflect the emotionally and culturally sensitive nature of family and child protection matters (Emberland, 2018; Emberland, Chapter 2; Cichowski and Chrun, Chapter 11). These cases have involved both nation-states and civil society organisations acting as friends of the court, also known as amici curiae, supporting certain outcomes of a decision or attempting to influence the Court to make decisions that align with specific normative standpoints (see Falch-Eriksen, Chapter 10).

Child rights and child protection in the European Court of Human Rights

Driven by the children's rights movement, recent decades have brought children to the forefront of the legal and social agenda (Becker, 2020), including a widespread recognition of children's citizenship, individual autonomy and distinct interests. This includes recognising children as holders and beneficiaries of rights, as outlined in the CRC, and the UN Committee on the Rights of the Child (CRC Committee) states that children have economic, social and cultural rights, as well as civil and political rights, and that these rights are regarded as justiciable (see GC, 2003, p 3).

Under Article 1 of the ECHR, children enjoy the same rights as adults to the protection of their human rights and freedoms.[5] However, children were not a concern in the drafting of the Convention, and there are no specific provisions for children's rights in the main body of the ECHR.[6] The granting of rights to children under the ECHR is thus up to the discretion of the Court, and children's rights and interests were, for a long time, a peripheral concern of the Court (Kilkelly, 1999; Fenton-Glynn, 2021). When carrying out its mandate to interpret and monitor the ECHR, the Court has faced challenges in adjudicating children's rights, particularly in child protection cases (Kilkelly, 2001; Draghici, 2017). As children themselves rarely bring legal complaints, the question before the court is almost invariably concerned with the parents' right to family life. In recent years, however, children's rights have had a stronger hold in ECtHR jurisprudence (Fenton-Glynn, 2021), and the Court has adopted a more child-centric approach (Jacobsen, 2016; Skivenes and Søvig, 2016; Breen et al, 2020). The increasing child-centrism is evident in a stronger emphasis on the child's individual right to family life under Article 8 of the ECHR, as well as in the acknowledgement of the child as an autonomous and rights-bearing individual. However, this is now changing. The Grand Chamber decision on Strand Lobben and Others v Norway from 2019 is criticised as a setback for children's human rights:

> It is to be hoped that this case is nothing but an anomaly: a brief deviation from which the Court will soon recover – much like Neulinger in relation to the substantive requirements it set for parental child abduction. However, early indications are not good. In AS v Norway, decided three months after Strand Lobben, the Court had reverted to using the Johansen test of 'a fair balance' and 'depending on their nature and seriousness'. The term 'paramount' was not mentioned at any stage. (Fenton-Glynn, 2021, p 308)

While the ECtHR has been less concerned with children's individual interests and rights until relatively recently, children and child protection have been a matter for the Court for over three decades. Matters concerning child protection are brought to the ECtHR under a range of provisions, but, as mentioned, the majority of cases fall within the ambit of Article 8 (Fenton-Glynn, 2021; see also Skivenes and Søvig, 2016). A fluctuating, but overall low, number of child protection cases have been brought to the ECtHR yearly. However, in recent years, these circumstances have changed (see Table 1.1) and an unprecedented number of child protection cases have been admitted by the ECtHR. An overwhelming majority of these cases concern Norwegian child protection: during a nine-year period, from 2015 to 2024, a total of 78 cases concerning child protection were communicated by the ECtHR to the Norwegian state (see Emberland, Chapter 2).

Another implication that has been pointed out is the potential backsliding of children's rights. Recent developments in the Court's jurisprudence have been criticised for a lack of reasoning related to the best interest of the child regarding visitation (Søvig and Vindenes, 2020), and for impeding child-centric development (Mørk et al, 2022). Others explicitly state that the latest judgments represent a setback for children's rights, as mentioned earlier (Fenton-Glynn, 2021, p 308; Do Vale Alves, 2023). Furthermore, we are witnessing worldwide demonstrations against child protection. The protests are vocal and have garnered attention in both traditional news media and social media. So far, the demonstrations do not seem to reflect the general public opinion (Juhasz and Skivenes, 2017; Skivenes, 2021; Loen and Skivenes, 2023; Skivenes and Benbenishty 2022; 2023), but the long-term implications are yet to be seen. In a broader context, protests and criticism of child protection appear to be closely linked to the rise of conservative family values (Datta, 2021; Chapter 9), including the backlash against gender equality and women's rights in parts of European society (Pap and Juhász, 2018).

Rule of law and child flourishing

Rule of law is a foundational principle ensuring that public institutions operate within the constraints of law, in alignment with democratic values, fundamental rights, and under the oversight of independent and impartial courts. A key criterion for bringing a case about a country's violation of human rights to the ECtHR is that the citizen has pursued and exhausted all legal options in their country. In family and child protection cases, this typically entails the involvement of a court or judicial institution (Burns et al, 2017; Berrick et al, 2023). Member states subscribing to the ECtHR display clear variations in their adherence to rule of law principles, as indicated by the World Justice Project's (WJP) global ranking from 2023, with Norway at the top and Russia at the bottom (see Table 1.2). The WJP Rule of Law Index evaluates and ranks countries based on eight key indicators, including constraints on government powers, absence of corruption, open government,

Table 1.1: An overview of Article 8 judgments* relating to child protection in the ECtHR, from 1959 to 2022

Respondent country	Year					
	Total (violations)	1959–1990	1991–2000	2001–2010	2011–2020	2021–2022
Norway	21 (14)	0	1 (1)	2 (0)	10 (7)	8 (6)
UK	16 (9)	5 (4)	1 (1)	8 (4)	2 (0)	0
Sweden	10 (4)	2 (2)	3 (2)	1 (0)	3 (0)	1 (0)
Germany	9 (5)	0	0	5 (4)	4 (1)	0
Russia	8 (6)	0	0	1 (1)	6 (5)	1 (0)
Italy	7 (6)	0	3 (2)	0	4 (4)	0
Finland	5 (4)	0	1 (0)	4 (4)	0	0
Slovenia	4 (1)	0	0	0	3 (1)	1 (0)
Croatia	4 (3)	0	0	1 (1)	3 (2)	0
Ukraine	3 (3)	0	0	2 (2)	1 (1)	0
Romania	3 (1)	0	0	0	3 (1)	0
Austria	3 (3)	0	0	2 (2)	1 (1)	0
Spain	2 (2)	0	0	0	2 (2)	0
France	2 (0)	0	1 (0)	1 (0)	0	0
Czechia	2 (2)	0	0	1 (1)	1 (1)	0
Bulgaria	2 (0)	0	0	0	1 (0)	1 (0)
Netherlands	1 (1)	0	0	1 (1)	0	0
Moldova	1 (1)	0	0	0	1 (1)	0
Malta	1 (1)	0	0	0	1 (1)	0
Lithuania	1 (0)	0	0	0	1 (0)	0
Latvia	1 (0)	0	0	0	0	1 (0)
Iceland	1 (0)	0	0	0	0	1 (0)
Hungary	1 (1)	0	0	0	1 (1)	0
Total	108	7	10	29	48	14

Note: * Judgments only, not including 'Decisions'. Violations are in parentheses. N=108 judgments, here excluding four Grand Chamber judgments.
Source: Helland and Skivenes (in preparation)

fundamental rights, order and security, regulatory enforcement, civil and criminal justice systems.[7] There are 13 countries in the highest quartile, scoring between 0.9 (Denmark) and 0.77 (Lithuania), while five countries score below 0.5 (Ukraine, Albania, Serbia, Russia and Turkey). This suggests substantial variation in how well each member state secures its citizens' right to a fair trial and access to justice at the domestic level.

The ECtHR member states also display variation in how they provide for their children, meaning here prosperity for children, with Norway and the Netherlands at the top and Ukraine and Romania at the bottom (see Table 1.2). This is based on the WHO–UNICEF–Lancet Commission (Clark et al, 2020) that have ranked the performance of 180 countries

Table 1.2: The CoE member countries rank on the Lancet Child Flourishing Index and on the 2023 WJP Rule of Law Index*

The Lancet Flourishing Index (2020)			The 2023 WJP Rule of Law Index		
Rank	Country	Flourishing	Rank	Country	Overall Score
1	Norway	0.95	1	Denmark	0.90
3	Netherlands	0.95	2	Norway	0.89
4	France	0.95	3	Finland	0.87
5	Ireland	0.95	4	Sweden	0.85
6	Denmark	0.94	5	Germany	0.83
8	Belgium	0.94	6	Luxembourg	0.83
9	Iceland	0.92	7	Netherlands	0.83
10	United Kingdom	0.92	9	Estonia	0.82
11	Luxembourg	0.92	10	Ireland	0.81
13	Sweden	0.92	11	Austria	0.80
14	Germany	0.92	15	United Kingdom	0.78
15	Switzerland	0.92	16	Belgium	0.78
16	Finland	0.91	18	Lithuania	0.77
17	Spain	0.91	20	Czechia	0.73
18	Malta	0.91	21	France	0.73
19	Austria	0.90	22	Latvia	0.73
22	Portugal	0.90	24	Spain	0.72
23	Cyprus	0.90	27	Slovenia	0.69
25	Slovenia	0.89	28	Portugal	0.68
26	Italy	0.89	30	Malta	0.68
27	Estonia	0.88	31	Cyprus	0.68
28	Croatia	0.88	32	Italy	0.67
29	Hungary	0.88	34	Slovak Republic	0.66
30	Slovakia	0.87	36	Poland	0.64
31	Greece	0.86	40	Romania	0.63
33	Poland	0.85	45	Croatia	0.61

Table 1.2: The CoE member countries rank on the Lancet Child Flourishing Index and on the 2023 WJP Rule of Law Index* (continued)

The Lancet Flourishing Index (2020)			The 2023 WJP Rule of Law Index		
34	Montenegro	0.85	47	Greece	0.61
37	Latvia	0.84	48	Georgia	0.60
38	Bosnia and Herzegovina	0.84	57	Montenegro	0.56
40	North Macedonia	0.83	59	Bulgaria	0.56
41	Lithuania	0.82	64	Moldova	0.54
45	Bulgaria	0.80	67	North Macedonia	0.53
48	Serbia	0.79	73	Hungary	0.51
55	Moldova	0.75	75	Bosnia and Herzegovina	0.51
56	Armenia	0.75	89	Ukraine	0.49
60	Turkey	0.75	91	Albania	0.48
69	Albania	0.74	93	Serbia	0.48
76	Georgia	0.71	113	Russia	0.44
77	Azerbaijan	0.71	117	Turkey	0.41
79	Russia	0.71			
80	Romania	0.71			
91	Ukraine	0.66			

Note: * The table includes Russia, as it was a member of the CoE until March 2022 (see endnote 3). For the Lancet Index, the CoE countries Andorra, Liechtenstein, Monaco, San Marino and Czechia are not included in the index. For the Rule of Law Index, the CoE countries Andorra, Armenia, Azerbaijan, Iceland, Liechtenstein, Monaco, San Marino and Switzerland are not included in the index. Sorted from high (highest score is 1) to low (lowest score is 0).

Source: Clark et al (2020)

based on a Child Flourishing Index comprised of indicators on two dimensions: children's survival and thriving (which includes access to health services, educational achievement and protection from violence).[8] The overview, which includes CoE members only, shows that most CoE countries are in the top 25 per cent of the countries worldwide, with ten countries in the comparatively lower segment, ranked from number 48 (Serbia) to 91 (Ukraine).

Child protection and the member states of the European Court of Human Rights

The child rights development has not stood uncontested, and controversies and struggles persist over the nature and scope of children's rights (see, for example, Stalford et al, 2017). One contested right is the right to protection, which, in the case of child protection, underscores the need to consider the interdependent and interrelated nature of children's rights in relation to those held by parents and the family unit (Goonesekere, 2020). Under the ECHR and the CRC, European states have a positive duty to act to prevent and protect children from violence, abuse and neglect. The CRC Article 19 states this responsibility clearly:

1. States Parties shall take all appropriate legislative, administrative, social and educational measures to protect the child from all forms of physical or mental violence, injury or abuse, neglect or negligent treatment, maltreatment or exploitation, including sexual abuse, while in the care of parent(s), legal guardian(s) or any other person who has the care of the child.
2. Such protective measures should, as appropriate, include effective procedures for the establishment of social programmes to provide necessary support for the child and for those who have the care of the child, as well as for other forms of prevention and for identification, reporting, referral, investigation, treatment and follow-up of instances of child maltreatment described heretofore, and, as appropriate, for judicial involvement.

Through the child protection system, the state can intervene with or without consent from the involved parties to assume parental responsibility or terminate all parental rights when parents are unable or unwilling to perform their parental obligations. Child protection interventions represent an immensely strong state power, simultaneously challenging individual rights and freedoms as well as the privacy and autonomy of family life (Shapiro, 1999; Brighouse and Swift, 2007). Such decisions must therefore be of high quality and withstand public scrutiny (Habermas, 1996; cf Rothstein, 1998) and be accepted by citizens (Suchman, 1995; Zelditch, 2006). Decisions concerning child protection are both normatively and empirically complex, involving challenging cases that often involve different and sometimes conflicting interests and rights between the concerned parties. This means that those authorised with decision-making power must balance the various rights and interests against each other. The normative, emotional and private nature of these decisions makes contestation and disputes inevitable. When interpreting Article 8 of the ECHR, cited earlier, decision-makers must make predictions and weigh the considerations of protecting family life and a child's right to a healthy and caring upbringing. It is thus not surprising to find child protection described as 'the perfect exemplar of the difficulty governments face in setting boundaries between public and private life' (Holland and Scourfield, 2004, p 22) and in these cases the role of the ECtHR is to determine whether individual human rights are violated when drawing this boundary.

Albeit countries subscribing to the CRC have a similar obligation to establish systems that protect children against abuse, there are huge variations between countries in their policies and practices for *when* to intervene to protect children, and what purpose their systems serve. An indication of this is the number of children placed out of home by the CPS (see Table 1.3). In the child protection literature, the global typology of child protection systems (Berrick et al, 2023) is the most comprehensive theoretical platform to date. The typology comprises five *types* of child protection systems, based on the 'ambitions'[9] of the system regarding the protection of children in difficult life situations. At the bare minimum, a child protection system aims to protect children against exploitation, and at best, it aims to fulfil the obligations set forth in the CRC. The typology presents a detailed conceptualisation of child protection systems based on case studies of 50 countries, spanning all regions of the world (although skewed towards Western Europe) and in all stages of economic and welfare development. The typology formulates generalisations about the essential characteristics of child protection systems and arrangements, resulting in five systems: *Child exploitation-protective system*; *Child deprivation-protective system*; *Child maltreatment-protective system*; *Child well-being-protective system*; and *Child rights-protective system*. The countries that subscribe to the ECtHR include four types of child protection systems, as shown in Table 1.3, in which member states are *tentatively* classified.

Structure of the book

The book is divided into three parts. Part I examines the ECtHR from a national perspective, while Part II includes chapters that adopt a transnational perspective, and Part III focuses more narrowly on the Court's decision-making and jurisprudence.

The European Court of Human Rights from a national perspective

In the first part of this edited volume, six chapters examine the complex of child protection cases at the ECtHR from a national perspective, including Finland and Norway. Primarily, these chapters focus on various aspects of the Norwegian cases, analysing their unique nature, the assessment they receive from the Court, and their implications for Norwegian policy, law and practice.

In Chapter 2, Marius Emberland discusses the surge of child protection cases against Norway in the ECtHR over the last decade, often referred to as the Strand Lobben group of cases. He asks if this group of cases are, in fact, unique in a European context. Through a comparative analysis of ECtHR case law, he examines how the Court has dealt with child protection cases

Table 1.3: Countries subscribing to the ECtHR and key child protection information

Country	Out-of-home placements per 1,000 children	Children placed out-of-home in total (year)	Type of child protection system	Judgments in the ECtHR
Russia	23 ^	613,000 (2014) ^	Child deprivation-protective	8
Lithuania	17.4 #	8,752 (2017) #	Child deprivation-protective	1
Finland	16.5 ^	17,689 (2015) ^	Child rights-protective	5
Czechia	15.8 #	26,372 (2018) #	Child maltreatment-protective	2
Latvia	15.7 #	5,805 (2016) #	Child maltreatment-protective	1
Sweden	13.2 ^	29,473 (2015) ^ 21,051 (2015) #	Child rights-protective	10
Germany	10.8 #	145,949 (2016) #	Child well-being-protective	9
Switzerland	10.6 #	ND 2,665 (2016) #	Child well-being-protective	0
Poland	10.6 #	73,393 (2016) #	Child maltreatment-protective	0
Slovak Republic	10.4 ^	8,739 (2017) ^	Child deprivation-protective	0
Norway	10.3 #	11,612 (2016) #	Child rights-protective	21
Denmark	10.2 #	11,916 (2016) #	Child rights-protective	0
Estonia	10 #	2,599 (2016) #	Child maltreatment-protective	0
France	9.9 #	146,322 (2015) #	Child well being-protective	2
Belgium	9.6 ^	22,132 (2012) ^	Child well-being-protective	0
Netherlands	9.1 #	31,000 (2017) #	Child well-being-protective	1
Austria	8.7 ^	13,325 (2018) ^	Child well-being-protective	3
Northern Ireland	6.9 #	3,019 (2018) #	Child maltreatment-protective	16 (UK)
England	6.2 #	72,590 (2016–17) #	Child maltreatment-protective	16 (UK)
Ireland	5.1 #	6,116 (2017) #	Child maltreatment-protective	0
Portugal	4.9 #	8,673 (2018) #	Child well-being-protective	0
Spain	4.3 #	34,644 (2017) #	Child well-being-protective	2
Italy	2.6 #	26,420 (2014) #	Child maltreatment-protective	7
Greece	1.6 #	3,000 (2015) #	Child maltreatment-protective	0

Note: Including the type of child protection system, out-of-home placements (based on court order and/or parental agreement or abandonment), total and per 1,000 children total child population. Data from Switzerland is from three cantons. ND=no data. Sorted in decreasing order by out-of-home placements per 1,000 children (# = stock stat / ^ = flow). ECtHR judgments under Article 8 available in English.

Source: Helland and Skivenes (in preparation); Berrick et al (2023)

involving other member states during the same period (2017–2024). He also investigates whether the Norwegian cases have attracted disproportionate attention from other member states through the use of the third-party intervention mechanism before the Court.

In Chapter 3, Raija Huhtanen and Tarja Pösö examine the influence of the ECtHR and its case law on Finland's child protection law and practices following the Court's finding that the country had violated ECHR Article 8 in four child protection cases in the early 2000s. In their study, they elaborate on the four judgments and discuss their implications through an empirical analysis of national policy, the Supreme Administrative Court's decisions and the process that culminated in the Child Welfare Act of 2007. Pösö and Huhtanen note that, following the adoption of the new Child Welfare Act, Finland has not faced any cases before the ECtHR concerning child protection, and the analysis contributes to understanding why this is the case. They also provide a critical discussion of the consequences of the ECtHR influence for children in long-term care.

In Chapter 4, Kirsten Sandberg examines the ECtHR's criticism of Norwegian child protection decisions and discusses the effects of the Court's judgments on Norwegian Courts and jurisprudence. She focuses on the reunification goal as set out by the ECtHR in child protection cases, where Norwegian courts have been found to violate this goal by stipulating too limited contact between parents and children when a child has been placed in alternative care, without sufficient consideration of individual circumstances. She investigates the Supreme Court's adaptation of the signals from the ECtHR into the Norwegian context and discusses the dilemmas this adaptation raises regarding a child- or family-oriented approach to child protection and the understanding of the child's best interests.

In Chapter 5, Hege Stein Helland focuses on the domestic impact of the ECtHR judgments against Norway. Through interviews with local child protection managers, she investigates whether the judgments have led to actual adjustments in decision-making practices and routines at the 'street level' of the child protection system. By employing a bottom-up approach to policy implementation, the study examines the factors that have influenced the implementation of ECtHR case law in local child protection agencies. She critically discusses the findings in relation to legitimate child protection practices.

In Chapter 6, Katrin Križ and Daniela Reimer examine how the ECtHR portrays children in its assessments. They analyse 18 judgments decided between 2017 and 2022, in which the applicants raised complaints against the Norwegian state related to child protection, claiming violation of ECHR Article 8. The chapter aims to contribute to knowledge about the textual representation of children in international law by assessing how the Court's reasoning described the child(ren) in the case. Guided by a Child Equality

Perspective, they examine whether the judgments depict children as subjects or objects through a qualitative analysis of the Court's assessments.

In Chapter 7, Daniela Reimer, Katrin Križ, Mary Burns, Gabriela Serra and Kerry Shea critically examine the construction of ethnicity in the judgments of the ECtHR. Using the same data as the study in Chapter 6, 18 judgments from child protection-related cases against Norway, they explore how the language in judgment texts by the ECtHR portrays children's and families' 'ethnicity'. Through a qualitative text analysis, the authors analyse and compare the words and phrases used to describe children and families with minoritised ethnic and non-minoritised ethnic backgrounds in two sections of the judgment: the 'national case histories' and the Court's assessment, respectively.

Transnational influence of the European Court of Human Rights

In the second part of the book, the perspective shifts from the national to the transnational level, seeking to understand the international drivers and influences that shape the ECtHR's emphasis on child protection and the development of its child rights jurisprudence. The four chapters in this section scrutinise children's rights and the ECtHR within a broader context of international human rights norms and the transnational contestation surrounding these norms.

In Chapter 8, Elaine Sutherland examines the role of international human rights norms in European child protection. Specifically, she examines the priority accorded to the child's best interests in the child protection context when weighed against the rights and interests of others, particularly the child's parents. In her analysis, she explores whether the ECtHR, in its interpretation of the ECHR, and the CRC Committee, in their amplification of the CRC, are sending mixed messages to states parties about what is required of them and discusses how inconsistencies might be addressed.

In Chapter 9, Neil Datta investigates the role of global anti-gender actors in contemporary contestations around child protection. With a specific focus on Norwegian and Nordic child protection services, the study examines whether children's rights and child protection feature in anti-gender contestation, and if so, how. Are children the new frontiers of anti-gender contestation? He examines the role of prominent anti-gender actors in contesting issues related to children's rights, analysing their strategies, areas of focus and prominence within this arena, including how these actors work to influence human rights norms and decisions before the ECtHR.

In Chapter 10, Asgeir Falch-Eriksen examines the ECtHR's MoA doctrine and discusses its vulnerability to judicial lobbying by third-party interveners. While third-party interveners are typically considered *amici curiae* or friends of the court, not all interveners have good intentions, according to Falch-Eriksen. As such, he asks whether the flexibility of the MoA can be exploited by 'bad amici' who seek to influence court decisions in ways that do not align with a human rights ethos. Following the argument that without a solid theoretical foundation for decision-making, the ECtHR risks inconsistency in its decisions due to the influence of bad amici, this study explores how the MoA, understood through either legal positivism or discourse theory, can mitigate the risks of manipulation by interest groups.

In Chapter 11, Rachel Cichowski and Elizabeth Crun also address the topic of third-party interventions, also known as amicus curiae, in ECtHR cases. The study focuses on amicus curiae participation in Norwegian children's rights cases, examining how and why third parties intervene. Using data from the ECtHR Database, which identifies third-party interventions by states, individuals, organisations and interest activists from all ECtHR judgments from 1961 to 2022, they analyse the main content of the third-party brief through the summaries included in the ECtHR judgment and if the brief supports the applicant or the respondent state. The Norwegian cases are contextualised by including all third-party interventions in the ECtHR since 1979 through 2022 in the analysis.

The European Court of Human Rights and its jurisprudence

In Part III, the perspective shifts to the ECtHR itself, examining the Court's current jurisprudence on child rights and child protection – and its potential future development.

In Chapter 12, Jill Marshall examines how the ECtHR's development of a right to personal identity, arising from the right to personal identity under ECHR Article 8, has been interpreted in relation to children's lives and their sense of identity. With a specific focus on the tensions between children's and adults' identity rights and the moral assumptions underlying child protection, Marshall analyses ECtHR case law relating to children's lives. The chapter provides an analysis of how the right to personal identity has evolved as a protected right by the Court, examining the various ways this right has emerged for children and young people.

In Chapter 13, David Archard and Marit Skivenes deal with the ECtHR's understanding of custody and family life. They discuss key normative arguments for the custody of children and the allocation of custody. This framework is used to examine the guiding principles applied by the majority and the minority in the seminal ECtHR Grand Chamber judgment, Strand Lobben and Others v Norway (2019). The analysis shows how the child as property and attachment as biology are dominant in the majority's reasoning, and as such confirms that the ECtHR has taken a step back in terms of protecting child rights.

In Chapter 14, Claire Fenton-Glynn provides an empirical investigation of the relationship between the ECtHR and the CRC. Based on the argument that ECHR rights must be interpreted in light of the CRC, she aims to examine the progress, or lack thereof, in the engagement of the Court with children's rights. Investigating the Court's decision-making in various topics relating to children, Fenton-Glynn explores how the ECtHR relates to the CRC and the guidance of the CRC Committee through General Comments and Concluding Observations by mapping the frequency with which the CRC and its associated material is cited by the ECtHR, as well as in which subject areas and at what stage of the decision-making process.

In Chapter 15, the editors, Hege Stein Helland, Marit Skivenes and Siri Gloppen, summarise the main findings from the book and discuss the challenges to children's rights in Europe, as well as the role of the ECtHR in child protection cases. The ECtHR's judgments have significantly influenced domestic child protection practices, and highlight tensions between national systems and international human rights standards. Norway's record-high violations of Article 8 of the ECHR initiate debates about fair balancing of parental rights and children's best interests. Third-party interventions (amicus curiae) in ECtHR cases emerge as a possible double-edged sword: while they can promote children's rights, they are vulnerable to manipulation by actors with anti-rights agendas. A conclusion is to secure more transparency in ECtHR processes, including its use of the margin of appreciation doctrine. We call for further research into the Court's decision-making mechanisms and how grassroots mobilisation shapes litigation outcomes.

Notes

[1] Six cases have been determined inadmissible whereas no violation is found in four cases. Before this, Norway was found to violate Article 8 in a case concerning adoption in 1996 (Johansen v Norway).
[2] Pursuant to Article 8 of the ECHR.
[3] The current 46 member countries of the CoE are: Albania, Andorra, Armenia, Austria, Azerbaijan, Belgium, Bosnia and Herzegovina, Bulgaria, Croatia, Cyprus, Czechia, Denmark, Estonia, Finland, France, Georgia, Germany, Greece, Hungary, Iceland, Ireland, Italy, Latvia, Liechtenstein, Lithuania, Luxembourg, Malta, Republic of Moldova, Monaco, Montenegro, Netherlands, North Macedonia, Norway, Poland, Portugal, Romania, San Marino, Serbia, Slovak Republic, Slovenia, Spain, Sweden, Switzerland, Türkiye, Ukraine, United Kingdom.
[4] See also Sormunen's (2019) comparison of the ECtHR's best interest assessments in immigration cases versus child protection cases.
[5] Moreover, with reference to Article 14, the Convention's rights shall be granted to everyone without (age) discrimination.
[6] Children (minors or juveniles) are specifically mentioned in the main body of the ECHR's Articles 5 and 6.
[7] These are further broken down into 44 sub-factors that provide detailed insights into specific aspects of the rule of law, such as checks on executive power, freedom from corruption, access to justice and protection of fundamental rights.

[8] The indicators for Surviving are maternal survival, survival in children younger than five years old, suicide, access to maternal and child health services, basic hygiene and sanitation, and lack of extreme poverty, and for Thriving they are educational achievement, growth and nutrition, reproductive freedom, and protection from violence (Clark et al, 2020, p 640).

[9] A country subscribing to the CRC have at a formal level high ambitions for their child population, but the ability to protect child rights are influenced or determined by the realities of what is possible, for example in terms of resources, and of political will to prioritise child rights.

References

Arai-Takahashi, Y. (2002) *The Margin of Appreciation Doctrine and the Principle of Proportionality in the Jurisprudence of the ECHR*, Intersentia nv.

Becker, J. (2020) 'The evolution of the children's rights movement', in J. Todres and S.M. King (eds), *The Oxford Handbook of Children's Rights Law*, Oxford University Press, pp 33–48.

Berrick, J.D., Gilbert, N. and Skivenes, M. (eds) (2023) *Oxford Handbook of Child Protection Systems*, Oxford University Press.

Bragdø-Ellenes, S.C. and Torjesen, S. (2020) 'Diplomatisk hodebry: Internasjonale reaksjoner på kontroversielle avgjørelser i norsk barnevern [Diplomatic headache: International reactions to controversial decisions in Norwegian child welfare]', *Internasjonal Politikk*, 78(1): 1–31.

Breen, C., Krutzinna, J., Luhamaa, K., and Skivenes, M. (2020) 'Family life for children in state care: An analysis of the European Court of Human Rights' reasoning on adoption without consent', *The International Journal of Children's Rights*, 28(4): 715–747.

Brighouse, H. and Swift, A. (2007) 'Parents' rights and the value of the family', *Ethics*, 117(1): 80–108.

Bueren, G.V. (2007) *Child Rights in Europe: Convergence and Divergence in Judicial Protection*, Council of Europe.

Burns, K., Pösö, T. and Skivenes, M. (eds) (2017) *Child Welfare Removals by the State: A Cross-Country Analysis of Decision-Making Systems*, Oxford University Press.

Buzogány, A. and Varga, M. (2018) 'The ideational foundations of the illiberal backlash in Central and Eastern Europe: The case of Hungary', *Review of International Political Economy*, 25(6): 811–828.

Clark, H., Coll-Seck, A.M., Banerjee, A., Peterson, S., Dalglish, S.L., Ameratunga, S., et al (2020) 'A future for the world's children? A WHO–UNICEF–Lancet Commission', *The Lancet*, 395(10224): 605–658.

Datta, N. (2021) 'Tip of the iceberg: Religious extremist funders against human rights for sexuality and reproductive health in Europe 2009–2018', *European Parliamentary Forum for Sexual & Reproductive Rights*. Available from: https://www.epfweb.org/sites/default/files/2021-06/Tip%20of%20the%20Iceberg%20June%202021%20Final.pdf

Do Vale Alves, A. (2023) 'Children's religious identity in alternative care and adoption: The need to recentre the child's best interest in international human rights adjudication', *Human Rights Law Review*, 23(2): 1–22.

Draghici, C. (2017) *The Legitimacy of Family Rights in Strasbourg Case Law: 'Living Instrument' or Extinguished Sovereignty?*, Hart Publishing.

ECHR (European Court of Human Rights) (2023) 'Violations by article and by state'. Available from: https://www.echr.coe.int/documents/d/echr/Stats_violation_1959_2022_ENG

Emberland, M. (2018) 'Det norske barnevernet under lupen – del 3 [The Norwegian child welfare system under the microscope – part 3]', *Lov og Rett*, 57(10): 583–584.

Fenton-Glynn, C. (2021) *Children and the European Court of Human Rights*, Oxford University Press.

GC (General Comment) (2003) 'General measures of implementation of the Convention on the Rights of the Child (arts. 4, 42 and 44, para. 6)', *Committee on the Rights of the Child General Comment no. 5*.

Goetz, A.M. (2020) 'The new competition in multilateral norm-setting: Transnational feminists & the illiberal backlash', *Daedalus*, 149(1): 160–179.

Goonesekere, S. (2020) 'The interrelated and interdependent nature of children's rights', in J. Todres and S.M. King (eds), *The Oxford Handbook of Children's Rights Law*, Oxford University Press, pp 71–98.

Graham, L. (2020) 'Strategic admissibility decisions in the European Court of Human Rights', *International & Comparative Law Quarterly*, 69(1): 79–102.

Guasti, P. and Bustikova, L. (2023) 'Varieties of illiberal backlash in Central Europe', *Problems of Post-Communism*, 70(2): 130–142.

Habermas, J. (1996) *Between Facts and Norms: Contributions to a Discourse Theory of Law and Democracy*, translated by W. Rehg, MIT Press.

Helfer, L.R. (2008) 'Redesigning the European Court of Human Rights: Embeddedness as a deep structural principle of the European human rights regime', *European Journal of International Law*, 19(1): 125–159.

Helland, H.S. and Skivenes, M. (in preparation) 'Fair trial for children in the ECtHR? An analysis of all child protection judgements from 1959–2022'. Unpublished manuscript.

Holland, S. and Scourfield, J. (2004) 'Liberty and respect in child protection', *The British Journal of Social Work*, 34(1): 21–36.

Jacobsen, A.F. (2016) 'Children's rights in the European Court of Human Rights: An emerging power structure', *International Journal of Children's Rights*, 24(3): 548–574.

Juhasz, I. and Skivenes, M. (2017) 'The population's confidence in the child protection system – a survey study of England, Finland, Norway and the United States (California)', *Social Policy & Administration*, 51(7): 1330–1347.

Kilkelly, U. (1999) *The Child and the European Convention on Human Rights*, Ashgate.

Kilkelly, U. (2001) 'The best of both worlds for children's rights? Interpreting the European Convention on Human Rights in the light of the UN Convention on the Rights of the Child', *Human Rights Quarterly*, 23(2): 308–326.

Loen, M. and Skivenes, M. (2023) 'Legitimate child protection interventions and the dimension of confidence: A comparative analysis of populations views in six European Countries', *Journal of Social Policy*, 54(2): 1–20.

Mørk, A., Sandberg, K., Schultz, T. and Hartoft, H. (2022) 'A conflict between the best interests of the child and the right to respect for family life? Non-consensual adoption in Denmark and Norway as an example of the difficulties in balancing different considerations', *International Journal of Law, Policy and the Family*, 36(1): ebac019.

Norman, M.G. (2016) 'Massedemonstrasjoner mot norsk barnevern i 19 land [Mass demonstrations against Norwegian child welfare in 19 countries]', *Verdens Gang*, 1 September. Available from: https://www.vg.no/i/ejxPl

Pap, E. and Juhász, B. (2018) 'Backlash in gender equality and women's and girls' rights', *European Parliament (FEMM Committee)*. Available from: https://www.europarl.europa.eu/RegData/etudes/STUD/2018/604955/IPOL_STU(2018)604955_EN.pdf

Rothstein, B. (1998) *Just Institutions Matter: The Moral and Political Logic of the Universal Welfare State*, Cambridge University Press.

Shapiro, I. (1999) *Democratic Justice*, Yale University Press.

Skivenes, M. (2021) 'Exploring populations view on thresholds and reasons for child protection intervention – comparing England, Norway, Poland and Romania', *European Journal of Social Work*, 26(1): 92–107.

Skivenes, M. and Søvig, K.H. (2016) 'Judicial discretion and the child's best interest: The European Court of Human Rights on child protection adoptions', in E. Sutherland and L. Macfarlane (eds), *Implementing Article 3 of the United Nations Convention on the Rights of the Child: Best Interests, Welfare and Well-being*, Cambridge University Press, pp 341–357.

Skivenes, M. and Benbenishty, R. (2022) 'Populations trust in the child protection system: A cross-country comparison of nine high-income jurisdictions', *Journal of European Social Policy*, 32(4): 422–435.

Skivenes, M. and Benbenishty, R. (2023) 'Securing permanence for children in care: A cross-country analysis of citizen's view on adoption versus foster care', *Child & Family Social Work*, 28(2): 432–442.

Sormunen, M. (2019) 'A comparison of child protection and immigration jurisprudence of the European Court of Human Rights: What role for the best interests of the child?', *Child and Family Law Quarterly*, 31(3): 249–268.

Søvig, K.H. and Vindenes, P.H. (2020) 'Avgjørelser fra EMD i saker om vern av privat-og familieliv fra 2019–2020 [Decisions from the ECHR in cases concerning the protection of private and family life from 2019–2020]', *Tidsskrift for Familierett, Arverett og Barnevernrettslige Spørsmål*, 18(3–4): 173–209.

Stalford, H., Hollingsworth, K. and Gilmore, S. (eds) (2017) *Rewriting Children's Rights Judgments: From Academic Vision to New Practice*, Bloomsbury Publishing.

Stiansen, Ø. and Voeten, E. (2020) 'Backlash and judicial restraint: Evidence from the European Court of Human Rights', *International Studies Quarterly*, 64(4): 770–784.

Suchman, M.C. (1995) 'Managing legitimacy: Strategic and institutional approaches', *Academy of Management Review*, 20(3): 571–610.

Thomassen, W. (2004) 'Six years as a judge in the European Court of Human Rights 1998/2004: Highlights and frustrations', *Netherlands Quarterly of Human Rights*, 22(4): 675–689.

Zelditch, M. (2006) 'Legitimacy theory', in P.J. Burke (ed), *Contemporary Social Pscyhological Theories*, Stanford University Press, pp 324–356.

PART I

The European Court of Human Rights from a national perspective

2

Are the child welfare cases against Norway in the European Court of Human Rights unique?

Marius Emberland

What this chapter is about

This chapter deals with the surge of child welfare cases against Norway in the European Court of Human Rights (ECtHR) in recent years, often referred to as the Strand Lobben group of cases and explained further in what follows. This set of cases – decided by the ECtHR in the period 2017–2024 – appears to stand out comparatively speaking in both numbers and in the way in which the ECtHR has scrutinised domestic authorities' practice in this field. The cases have also attracted a particular form of engagement from Norway's fellow member states of the European Convention on Human Rights (ECHR), in that other states have notably intervened as so-called third parties in support of the individual complainants and against Norway's position. Such involvement is generally considered a rarity in the ECtHR's practice.[1]

The child welfare cases against Norway in the ECtHR comprise a human rights phenomenon that warrants attention for many reasons. Not all are considered here. The chapter has a modest goal: it interrogates the possible *uniqueness* of the Strand Lobben group. Uniqueness for the purpose of this study refers to what is unprecedented in the history of the ECtHR. It is apt to probe the singularity of the Strand Lobben group of cases because the phenomenon for the reasons explained further in what follows is remarkable, and the cases are perceived as such in the general discourse. But *how unique* are the cases upon closer inspection, and what is the uniqueness about?

The present chapter considers this question by a two-fold approach, the methodology of which is explained further in what follows. First, the analysis queries whether the ECtHR in the same period has scrutinised other ECHR member states' child welfare practices in the same manner as it has considered the Norwegian cases, in substance as well as in numerical terms. Second, the analysis asks whether the involvement of other states parties as third parties in this group really does stand out, quantitatively and substantively.

As will be shown, there are aspects of uniqueness on both points, but the material divulges nuances and – possibly – some surprising features. Whether the Strand Lobben group really is a unique phenomenon depends in part on how the ECtHR will consider child welfare cases against other states that are still pending, and what future research might tell us.

The Strand Lobben group of cases

On 1 December 2015, the ECtHR notified the Norwegian government of a complaint submitted under the procedure in Article 34 of the ECHR. A woman, Ms Trude Strand Lobben, alleged that Norwegian authorities' approval of her son being adopted by his foster parents violated her and her son's right to respect for family life guaranteed by ECHR Article 8. Norwegian child welfare authorities have been scrutinised by the ECtHR before. Five years prior, in Aune, the ECtHR delivered a judgment that was thematically fairly similar to the case subject to notification in 2015. Article 8 of the ECHR was not violated in that case. Aune was for its part preceded by the 1996 Johansen judgment, where Article 8 was violated. Neither judgment signalled any systemic failures in how Norway made use of its powers to forcibly interfere in family relations out of concern for children's well-being and development. Prior to 2015, the ECtHR had also occasionally refused to consider the merits of other child welfare applications as they appeared not to disclose any ECHR violations (Olsson in 1995, T.C. in 1998, Johansen no. 2 in 2002, and I. and U. in 2004). In December 2015 it was difficult to foresee what was in store.

Near four years later, on 10 September 2019, the Grand Chamber of the ECtHR – reversing its Chamber judgment of 30 November 2017 – by a majority held in favour of Ms Strand Lobben and found that Article 8 had been violated. The decision to allow the child's foster parents to adopt him, against the wishes of his mother, failed to meet the proportionality requirement in ECHR Article 8 § 2. The ECtHR, by a majority, reformulated a set of general requirements central to proportionality (paras 202–213 of the judgment). The government was ordered to compensate the mother EUR 25,000 for her immaterial loss (see further Skivenes, 2019).

By then, it was clear that the judgment, commonly referred to as Strand Lobben and Others v Norway, was no insulated matter; it marked a turning point in Norway's human rights record. The ECtHR had in the meantime decided three similar cases, with different outcomes (M.L. in 2017, and Jansen and Mohamed Hasan in 2018). Besides, an additional 22 other cases were pending before the ECtHR at that time, and more were to follow. As of 31 December 2024, the total of pending and decided child welfare cases against Norway originating after the Strand Lobben complaint had swelled to 80, with two pending cases, 49 cases found to be inadmissible on procedural grounds or on the merits, and 29 cases decided by a judgment either finding a violation or not finding a violation (Appendix 1 gives an overview of the child welfare cases against Norway as per 31 December 2024).

The volume itself warrants attention. A total of 76 judgments on the merits (a number which includes the child welfare cases) have been handed down against Norway since the first was delivered in 1990. From a Norwegian vantage point, the child welfare cases not only stand out in volume but also substantively, as they have significantly impacted Norwegian policy and legal practice, as further dealt with by Sandberg in Chapter 4, and in other ways too, see Chapter 5 by Helland. It fits into a broader picture: Norway's child welfare policies have simultaneously garnered massive attention in many corners abroad, including in the form of coordinated protests on a global scale (Haugevik and Neumann, 2021). Even diplomatic situations of various kinds have ensued (Rojkov, 2019).

In December 2019, the Committee of Ministers of the Council of Europe set in motion its enhanced supervision procedure in the Strand Lobben group of cases against Norway, and subsequent cases resulting in a violation have been included. Set forth in Rule 4 § 1 of the Committee's Rules for supervision of execution of judgments, the enhanced procedure is reserved for judgments where the ECtHR has identified 'a systemic problem' in the state in question. Adopted by the body comprised of the member states' governments that on a peer review basis oversees national implementation of judgments finding a violation, the decision of enhanced supervision reflects a general sentiment at the Council of Europe that there are structural shortcomings in Norway in the field of child welfare practices (Committee of Ministers, 2006).[2]

The cases have also attracted prolific use at the ECtHR of the so-called third-party intervention mechanism under ECHR Article 36. While the ECtHR is set up to decide disputes between two parties only, ECHR Article 36 permits formal involvement of other stakeholders in the proceedings as intervening third parties. The conditions are strict. The first paragraph grants the home state of an individual applicant the entitlement to take part in support of its own nationals. The second paragraph allows for *any* member state of the Council of Europe as well as 'any person concerned' to intervene if it is 'in the interest of the proper administration of justice'. While this condition may not appear strict, it is for the ECtHR to decide whether it is satisfied, and the ECtHR has set a high threshold for allowing the form of third-party intervention set forth in the second paragraph. Most interventions in the cases against Norway have come from conservative non-governmental organisations, typically Ordo Iuris, and, most importantly for the purpose of the present chapter, other Council of Europe member states in favour of the individual complainants and against Norway.

Interrogating two aspects of uniqueness: methodology

The first research question is whether the ECtHR in the same period as that of the Strand Lobben cases has scrutinised other member states' child welfare decisions in the same manner as it has dealt with the Norwegian cases, in numbers and in substance. This essentially *comparative* aspect, dealt with in the next section, has necessitated first a process of identifying child welfare cases against other states in the period in question, and second, examining them in terms of their reasoning and result. The ECtHR's online HUDOC database, which stores all judgments, reasoned decisions and communicated cases, has been consulted. HUDOC is generally reliable not only because of its near completeness. The ECtHR's decisions consistently and with detailed citations refer to prior leading cases in the same field; this is the style in which the ECtHR writes its case law. HUDOC searches, therefore, generally produce a high degree of search output accuracy in identifying similar cases.

Two search modes have been employed. For the first phase of the 'Strand Lobben era', which starts 1 December 2015 when Strand Lobben was communicated and ends with its landmark judgment on 10 September 2019, comparative material has been assembled by searching HUDOC for cases that refer to the then-leading Court authorities on child welfare measures under ECHR Article 8, notably the Grand Chamber judgments in K. and T. v Finland (2001) and Paradiso and Campanelli v Italy (2017), and the Chamber judgments in Y.C. v United Kingdom (2012) and Jovanovic v Sweden (2015). All cases in HUDOC that refer to them have been checked, and decisions that refer to these cases have, in turn, generated additional results. The second phase starts with the date of the adoption of the Strand Lobben Grand Chamber judgment and ends with the time the present chapter was completed (31 December 2024). As the ECtHR has subsequently regarded the Strand Lobben judgment as the leading case on the proportionality of child welfare measures under ECHR Article 8, regardless of the state involved, comparative material in this phase has been generated by simply searching HUDOC for cases citing it. The two-fold HUDOC search is apt to reveal whether the cases against Norway stand out numerically and whether the ECtHR has treated child welfare measures adopted by other states in the same fashion and with a similar scrutiny as done with Norway.

The second research question relating to the uniqueness of the Strand Lobben cases considers the form of *inter-state* action mentioned earlier, notably other member states confronting Norway directly at the ECtHR by the means of third-party intervention under ECHR Article 36 in support of complainants, whether they are nationals of the intervening state or not. This is considered in the penultimate section. Searching HUDOC is the methodological tool also applied here. The instances of inter-state confrontation in the child welfare cases against Norway are compared with the overall use of this mechanism – regardless of which state is respondent party and regardless of topic – in the case law of the ECtHR in the same period. The search terms used are variants of 'third-party' and (in French) 'intervenant' and 'Article 36'. Here, too, the period of interest is 1 December 2015 to 31 December 2024, but for reasons that will become clear, the search has not been confined to child welfare cases.

The comparative perspective: child welfare cases against other states from December 2015 to December 2024

Norway stands out in numbers

Let us first consider the comparative aspect of uniqueness. Does the Strand Lobben group of cases represent a singular phenomenon when seen in the light of how the ECtHR has handled child welfare cases against other Council of Europe member states in the same period?

The HUDOC search reveals that several other states have had their share of child welfare cases at the ECtHR; a total of 56 cases – 38 decided and 18 pending – against other states have been identified. Comparing that with the 78 cases against one single state – Norway – we can certainly conclude that the Strand Lobben group does stand out – numerically speaking – in a comparative perspective (Appendix 2 lists the judgments, decisions and pending cases against other states, and Table 2.1 presents these numbers in a table).

Sorted by country, Italy (18) and Russia (9) have the majority of cases, followed by Portugal (4) and Germany (3). Spain, Sweden, the United Kingdom, Iceland, France and Slovenia have two cases each, and there is one case per state as regards the Czech Republic, Latvia, Lithuania, Austria, Bulgaria, Romania, Serbia, Switzerland and Netherlands.

In terms of *outcome*, 38 of these 56 cases have been finally decided by the ECtHR, of which 14 have ended in the ECtHR finding a violation of ECHR Article 8. In order words, more than one third of the cases in the comparative material have resulted in a violation. Six of these are against Russia, four concern Italy, and Portugal and Spain have two violations each. The 24 cases of non-violation are distributed as follows: Italy (4), Russia (3), Germany (3), Portugal (2), Sweden (2), France (2), and Austria, Bulgaria, Iceland, the Czech Republic, Latvia, Romania, Slovenia and Lithuania with one each.

In contrast, the ECtHR has found a violation of ECHR Article 8 in 23 of the 78 decided cases against Norway, in other words also more than a third. The outcome in the cases against other states appears at this stage, then, to align with the Strand Lobben group of cases. From the perspective of the general outcome of the ECtHR's handling of child welfare cases, the Norwegian cases appear not to stand out.

Table 2.1: Table of cases and outcome sorted by respondent state

State	Number of cases	Decided/pending	Decision (violation/non violation)
Italy	18	8/10	4/4
Russia	9	9/0	6/3
Portugal	4	4/0	2/2
Germany	3	3/0	0/3
Sweden	2	2/0	0/2
Spain	2	2/0	2/0
United Kingdom	2	0/2	N/A
Iceland	2	1/1	0/1
Slovenia	2	1/1	0/1
France	2	2/0	0/2
Czech Republic	1	1/0	0/1
Latvia	1	1/0	0/1
Lithuania	1	1/0	0/1
Austria	1	1/0	0/1
Bulgaria	1	1/0	0/1
Romania	2	1/1	0/1
Netherlands	1	0/1	N/A
Serbia	1	0/1	N/A
Switzerland	1	0/1	N/A
Total other	56	38/18	14/24
Norway	80	78/2	23/55

It belongs to the realm of speculation how the ECtHR will conclude the pending cases. Some of them however share features with Norwegian cases in which the ECtHR has found a violation. One case in point is the oldest yet pending: van Slooten v Netherlands was communicated to Dutch authorities on 31 August 2020. It relates to a decision to divest the applicant of her parental authority over her young daughter some one and a half years after she had been taken into care and placed in a foster family. The ECtHR has asked the parties, with reference to paragraph 205 of the Strand Lobben judgment, 'what measures were taken to facilitate family reunification' (van Slooten v Netherlands, 2020). Further, in the first quarter of 2022, the ECtHR referred two cases against the United Kingdom (D.B. v United Kingdom, 2022; N.S. v United Kingdom, 2022). In D.B., the authorities granted adoption of a child that shortly after birth had been placed in foster care due to the parents' history of drug abuse. N.S. concerns adoption by foster parents after four years on and off public care due to the applicant's mental illness. Judging by what can be gleaned from the rendition of the facts that is publicly available, it would be noteworthy – in comparative terms – should the ECtHR decide that no violation has occurred in them.

Looking behind the numbers

A perusal of the totality of cases decided between December 2015 and December 2024 suggests that the Norwegian cases merely stand out in numerical terms. The ECtHR appears not to be particularly inclined to strike down child welfare measures disproportionately in cases against Norway. The outcome of the ECtHR's scrutiny does not support a view that there is a bias at the ECtHR towards Norway.

R.M. v Latvia may indicate that the ECtHR, at times, does not follow one singular and overall approach to such cases. In a judgment on 9 December 2021, a Court majority of six found that the temporary suspension of the applicant's parental authority of her son and his temporary placement in public care did not violate Article 8 of the ECHR. As is always the case, the majority's conclusion was based on a number of factors, and it is not an easy task to disentangle the driving forces leading to the outcome.

It is nonetheless striking that the ECtHR – which based its reasoning on the general principles of interpretation set out in Strand Lobben – stated that 'the case material reveals a particularly worrying trend in Latvia for dealing with emotionally vulnerable children with behavioural problems', as domestic authorities, as was the case here, appeared to 'place these children in psychiatric institutions as the first resort' and that such placement 'cannot be considered conducive to the well-being of the child or in his or her best interests in the absence of psychiatric illness'. The ECtHR went on to note that there was 'a lack of alternative out-of-family care arrangements', and that the institutions 'did not address individual behavioural issues' (para 113).

The ECtHR also observed that the domestic courts 'did not invite the applicant's son to express his wishes', despite his being of an age where that would otherwise be prescient, and regardless of the fact that domestic courts had concluded that 'his wish to stay with the applicant' (conveyed through expert opinion) had been 'unduly influenced by the applicant' (para 117). Domestic courts had also not ordered any 'fresh assessment' of the situation (para 119). What ultimately led the ECtHR majority to conclude that Latvian authorities nonetheless had acted within Article 8 was that the applicant mother had taken her son away from the institution, thus 'flagrantly disregarding the decision to suspend her parental authority' (para 114). Her lack of cooperation was, in other words, the decisive factor for the ECtHR's conclusion.

It is obviously impossible to know whether a similar case had led to this outcome had the applicant's complaint been addressed to Norway, not Latvia. The dissenting opinion indicates that another conclusion was entirely feasible. Building on extant Court jurisprudence, Judge Hüseynov had regard to the best interests of the child, the absence of giving the child the possibility to express his wishes, and that a parent's failure to cooperate cannot be decisive for the ECtHR in its assessment of proportionality. These are sentiments well-known to the jurisprudence applied in the Strand Lobben group of cases.

One should caution against inflating disparities between the Norwegian and non-Norwegian cases. Far from all applications against Norway in the Strand Lobben group of cases have led to the ECtHR to conclude with a violation: in fact, the majority of decided cases have ended with the ECtHR not finding a violation, either in a judgment stating this explicitly or in the form of a decision that the application is inadmissible on material grounds. For instance, the applicant parents have generally not succeeded in their claim that they have been the victim of a violation of Article 8 by Norway when domestic violence was the reason for intervening in the family. A case in point from the Strand Lobben segment is Mohamed Hasan. The ECtHR found no violation in respect of a mother whose daughters had witnessed violence perpetrated by their biological father and his relatives. Despite an extremely intrusive measure – the consent to the children being adopted by their foster parents combined with giving them a new identity permanently cutting all ties to the applicant – the ECtHR did not voice any doubt as to its conclusion. Other decided cases against Norway suggests a similar approach when domestic violence is at issue (see O.S., S.A. and Bodnariu).

Near-zero tolerance of physical violence is also evident in the comparative material. In Wetjen and Others and Tlapak and Others, both against Germany, the ECtHR found no violation of Article 8 in domestic authorities' handling of the withdrawal of parental authority. The measures were taken as the applicant parents were members of communities that condoned and practised corporal punishment against children.

The total material – the Norwegian cases as well as the cases against other States – also indicates that the ECtHR generally is not favourably inclined when adoption is the child welfare measure at issue or when measures thus far taken indicate future adoption. This is certainly so in the Strand Lobben segment, where most cases regarding adoption have resulted in a breach of Article 8. Both Grand Chamber judgments against Norway – Strand Lobben and Abdi Ibrahim – were about adoption, and the same is true for the Chamber judgments in the cases such as Pedersen, F.Z., M.L., L.S. and O.V., and E.H. But there are exceptions to this rule, as the outcome in Mohamed Hasan, I.M., S.P., and R.I. testifies.

While not entirely unison, most cases in the comparative material that relate to adoption and permanent deprivation of parental responsibility have also ended with violation of Article 8, including cases against Italy (I.M and Others., Fiagbe and D.M. and N.), Portugal (Manteigas, P.V. and Silva Justa), and Spain (Omorefe and Haddad). This seems to suggest that the ECtHR strictly scrutinises this very invasive form of interference in the relationship between biological parents and their children regardless of which state is the respondent party.

The inter-state perspective: the occurrence of third-party state intervention against Norway

We move now to the other aspect of uniqueness dealt with; the level of confrontational involvement from other states in the Strand Lobben group of cases through the third-party intervention procedure. As was mentioned earlier, states may intervene as third parties in two ways – either by means of ECHR Article 36 § 1 when the state operates in support of its own nationals, or by Article 36 § 2, when there is no such national link between the complainant and the intervening state. It is instructive to consider the two forms of intervention separately.

Home state intervention

Quite a few of the child welfare cases against Norway originate in applications from individuals who are citizens of other Council of Europe member states. This entitles their home states to intervene pursuant to ECHR Article 36 § 1. The home state has made use of this right in at least seven out of 13 decided cases: Poland (in A.S.), Romania (Bodnariu), Slovakia (A.L. and Others), Bosnia-Hercegovina (D.R.), Bulgaria and Armenia (E.M. and T.A.), the Czech Republic (E.M. and Others) and Turkey (F.K.). But frequently the complainants are not supported by their home state by means of third-party intervention: this includes Swedish (Hernehult no. 1, Hernehult no. 2, and S.E. and Others), Russian (O.S., A.G.) and Portuguese (H.L.) nationals.

In the same period HUDOC searches show that the ECtHR has decided more than 200 other individual cases (regardless of subject matter) where the home state (or home states) of the applicant(s) had been informed of their right to exercise third-party intervention pursuant to Article 36 § 1. None of them concern child welfare measures. In approximately 30 of those instances the ECtHR's decisions reveal that the applicant's home state did intervene. This gives us an approximate of 15 per cent home state third-party involvement in the comparative material.

The numbers thus suggest a slightly higher degree of third-party intervention pursuant to Article 36 § 1 in the Strand Lobben group of cases compared with other types of cases. Another striking observation is that most of the interventions in the comparative material have come in cases that are intimately connected with inter-state tensions in Eastern Europe after the dissolution of the Soviet Union, including conflicts between Azerbaijan and Armenia (Petrosyan v Azerbaijan, 2011; Makuchyan and Minasyan v Azerbaijan and Hungary, 2020; Saribekyan and Balyan v Azerbaijan, 2020; Badalyan v Azerbaijan, 2021; Khojoyan and Vardazaryan v Azerbaijan, 2021), Georgia and Russia (Berdzenishvili and Others v Russia, 2016; Dzidzava v Russia, 2016; Shioshvili and Others v Russia, 2016; Tchankotadze v Georgia, 2016; Sapondzhyan v Russia, 2017), Ukraine and Russia (Butkevich v Russia, 2018; Lazoriva v Ukraine, 2018; Popov and Others v Russia, 2018), and other former members of the Eastern European bloc (Mitrova and Savik v Macedonia, 2016; M.R. and D.R. v Ukraine, 2018; Makhmudova v Russia, 2020; Zoletic and Others v Azerbaijan, 2021; Savickis and Others v Latvia, 2022; Suslov and Batikyan v Armenia, 2022). Just a couple have concerned children (but not child welfare) (Severe v Austria, 2017; P.D. v Russia, 2022), while four other dealt with a variety of issues of no interest for the present purposes (D.L. v Austria, 2017; Romeo Castano v Belgium, 2019; T.I. and Others v Greece, 2019; Filkin v Portugal, 2020). The numbers suggest that child welfare cases against Norway have attracted home state intervention to a noticeable degree.

As was mentioned earlier, the Norwegian child welfare authorities have attracted international opprobrium. The prevalence of home state intervention in the Strand Lobben group of cases corroborates a general sentiment which is also reflected in some of the ECHR Article 36 § 1 submissions as they are found in the ECtHR's decisions: they reveal a noticeable affront towards the respondent state. In A.S., the Polish government in their written submissions referred to 'the context of the general concerns connected to the functioning of the child protection system in the respondent State' and weighed decisively and concretely into the specific circumstances of the case, considering it 'doubtful whether the authorities of the respondent State had done everything in their power to reunite the applicant and her son, in such a way as to guarantee the rights stemming from Article 8 of the Convention' (paras 55–56). The Slovak Republic's written submission in A.L. and Others, as referred to by the ECtHR, were couched in slightly more diplomatic terms, but the gist of it is nonetheless unmistakable: 'The Government of the Slovak Republic submitted that they had welcomed the ECtHR's judgment in Strand Lobben and Others v. Norway … which had been applied to subsequent cases concerning child welfare measures adopted by the authorities of the respondent State' (para 40). The Armenian intervention in E.M. and T.A. v Norway (paras 22–23) and the Czech government's submissions in E.M. and Others likewise convey a clear disagreement with Norwegian authorities' decisions (para 48).

States intervening as third parties regardless of a national link

The other form of confrontational third-party involvement in the cases against Norway come by using Article 36 § 2, where there is no national link between the intervener and the applicant. When states intervene in cases that do not concern their own citizens, they tend to do so *in support* of the respondent state (Dzehtsiarou, 2023). Thus, in the Grand Chamber stage of Strand Lobben, Italy, Denmark and the United Kingdom were permitted to submit submissions as third parties to voice some form of support of Norway's case (see paras 182–186 and 189–191 of the judgment). Denmark also intervened in support of the respondent State before the Grand Chamber in Abdi Ibrahim (see paras 110–112).

There has been a slight surge in this form of supportive state third-party intervention since the member states adopted the Copenhagen Declaration in 2018, which encouraged concerted involvement by states through this mechanism (para 40). My perusal of HUDOC shows that the ECtHR in the reference period used for the present study adopted judgments and decisions in slightly less than 300 cases (excluding cases against Norway) were various third party submitted interventions pursuant to Article 36 § 2. In less than 10 per cent of them states intervened, and in the great majority they support the respondent state.

It is however extremely rare for states to actively seek involvement as third parties under Article 36 § 2 *in support* of the individual applicant and, conversely, *against* the respondent fellow member state of the Council of Europe. In the reference material, I have found only three possible instances (of approximately 300 cases) where states have adopted such an approach. Two of them were against Bosnia and Herzegovina and concerned ownership of property following the respondent state's departure from Yugoslavia (Jakovljević and Others v Bosnia and Herzegovina, 2019; Apostolovski and Others v Bosnia and Herzegovina, 2022). The third concerned aspects of government control of Poland's judiciary (Grzęda v Poland, 2022).

The intervention practice in Strand Lobben group of cases deviates from this norm: in 22 of the cases states have been given leave to intervene as third parties pursuant to Article 36 § 2 of the ECHR in support of the applicant's position. The Czech Republic has been the most active, with written third-party observations submitted in 19 cases (Strand Lobben, Pedersen, Abdi Ibrahim, K.O. and V.M., Bodnariu, F.Z., A.L. and Others, M.F., O.S., E.M. and T.A., K.E. and A.K., S.A., R.O., C.E., S.S. and J.H., S.E. and Others, K.F. and A.F., M.A. and M.A., and D.R.). The Slovak government has been permitted to intervene in 12 decided cases (Strand Lobben, K.O. and V.M., Bodnariu, F.Z., M.L., M.F., O.S., E.M. and T.A., K.E. and A.K., S.A., E.M. and Others, R.O., C.E., S.S. and J.H., S.E. and Others, K.F. and A.F., M.A. and M.A., and D.R.). Both states have additionally sought intervention in a number of other cases without being granted permission by the ECtHR to do so; the Czech government made unsuccessful attempts in 13 additional cases (M.L., Jansen, Mohamed Hasan, A.S., H.L., Hernehult no. 2, R.A., A.H., E.H., D.J. and P.J., G.B., A.G., G.G., L.S. and O.V., and J.B. and E.M), while Slovakia was not permitted to intervene in ten (Hernehult no. 2, R.A., A.H., E.H., D.J. and P.J., G.B., A.G., G.G., L.S. and O.V., and J.B. and E.M.). An additional three other states have engaged in third-party intervention in support of the applicant: Belgium and Bulgaria were permitted to submit observations pursuant to Article 36 § 2 before the Grand Chamber in Strand Lobben (see paras 176–181 and 187–188 of the judgment); while Turkey acted as third party before the Grand Chamber in Abdi Ibrahim (paras 119–123) and was permitted to intervene in F.K.

A similar antagonistic tenor against Norway as that mentioned in home state interventions is visible in some of the third-party submissions made under Article 36 § 2. In Strand Lobben, the government of Slovakia, for instance, commented 'on international concern about child welfare measures adopted in the respondent State' (para 188); and both the Czech Republic and Slovakia in their interventions in K.O. and V.M. maintained that 'the granting of limited contact rights in the instant case was indicative of a systemic practice in Norway which was problematic' in the light of Article 8 of the ECHR (para 56). In Bodnariu, the Slovak Republic argued that 'the systemic character of the substantive issue at stake in the instant case could be taken into account in the ECtHR's examination of whether relevant remedies had been exhausted' (para 18).

From the viewpoint of Strasbourg insiders, the confrontational tone – whatever the glossing or the cautious language – is rare. Generally, states who avail themselves of the entitlement to support their own citizens do so cautiously so not as to unduly upset relations with the respondent state (Ciliz v Netherlands, 2000; Somogyi v Italy, 2004).[3] Confrontational submissions are generally restricted to cases where the intervening state and the respondent state more generally have strained relations, such as between Cyprus and Turkey (Demades v Turkey, 2003, para 28; Eugenia Michaelidou Developments Ltd and Michael Tymvios v Turkey, 2003, para 27), and Latvia and Russia (Slivenko v Latvia, 2003, paras 90–92; Sisojeva and Others v Latvia, 2007, paras 85–88). From this perspective the Strand Lobben group of cases stand out.

Conclusion

The present chapter has interrogated two aspects of uniqueness associated with the Strand Lobben group of cases concerning child welfare measures against Norway before the ECtHR.

First, it has mapped whether and to what extent other member states of the ECHR have experienced similar cases in the same period as that which characterises the Strand Lobben group – notably from December 2015 to December 2024. The search shows that Norway is singular in terms of the number of child welfare cases before the ECtHR in the period 2015–2024, with 80 cases in total as compared with a mere 56 cases against all other Council of Europe states combined. When it comes to the outcome, the numbers suggest that the ECtHR is not more inclined to conclude with a violation in cases against Norway compared with non-Norwegian cases. The material at hand may suggest individual elements of a certain bias at the ECtHR against Norway, but it is not possible to draw firm conclusions at this stage, as a number of cases against other states are still pending before the ECtHR.

The second aspect of uniqueness took an inter-state perspective. It has been shown that a particularly unique feature of the Norwegian child welfare cases in the ECtHR is the active and formal involvement of other Council of Europe member states against a fellow state. The ECtHR has rarely, if at all, seen the same degree of state involvement against a fellow state as in the Strand Lobben group of cases. The material seems to suggest that other states have regarded the Norwegian child welfare cases with a degree of human rights urgency that is normally reserved for cases that rise out of more general inter-state conflicts.

The purpose of the present chapter has been to bring data to the fore. It takes another format and other methodological tools to analyse whether the Norwegian cases genuinely stand out in terms of substantive law, that is, if they represent domestic decision-making in the field of child welfare measures that are more at odds with Convention requirements than what is the case in other states or whether the ECtHR in fact adopts a more stringent scrutiny of Norway than other Contracting Parties of the ECHR. It is also for others to seek to understand why the Norwegian child welfare cases have attracted such outstanding attention by the ECtHR and the outsized attention from Norway's peers. It cannot be denied, however, that the Strand Lobben group of cases have unique features the reasons for which deserve more analysis.

Appendix 2.1
List of all decided and pending child welfare cases against Norway (alphabetical order)

A.A. v Norway (no. 59082/19) [2021] ECtHR (10 June) (public care, access restrictions) (inadmissible).

Abdi Ibrahim v Norway [GC] (no. 15379/16) [2021] ECtHR (10 December) (adoption by foster parents) (violation).

Abdi Ibrahim v Norway (no. 2) (no. 41803/22) [2022] ECtHR (13 December) (adoption by foster parents) (inadmissible).

A.D. and Others v Norway (no. 56464/21) [2024] ECtHR (15 April) (public care, access restrictions) (inadmissible).
A.G. v Norway (no. 14301/19) [2023] ECtHR (11 July) (public care, no access) (inadmissible).
A.H. v Norway (no. 39771/19) [2023] ECtHR (11 July) (public care, access restrictions) (inadmissible).
A.L. and Others v Norway (no. 45889/18) [2022] ECtHR (20 January) (public care, very restricted access) (violation).
A.M. v Norway (no. 2287/22) [2024] ECtHR (4 June 2024) (care order) (inadmissible).
Å.N. v Norway (no. 12825/20) [2023] ECtHR (11 July) (public care, access restrictions) (inadmissible).
A.N. v Norway (no. 36588/22) [2024] ECtHR (26 March) (care order, access restrictions) (inadmissible).
A.S. v Norway (no. 60371/15) [2019] ECtHR (17 December) (public care, undisclosed location, no access) (violation).
A.T. v Norway (no. 56132/21) [2023] ECtHR (12 December) (public care, access restrictions) (inadmissible).
Aune v Norway (no. 52502/07) [2010] ECtHR (28 October) (deprivation of parental responsibility and authorisation of adoption by foster parents) (violation).
Bodnariu v Norway (no. 73890/16) [2020] ECtHR (17 December) (temporary public care) (inadmissible).
C.E. v Norway (no. 50286/18) [2021] ECtHR (1 July) (public care, access restrictions) (inadmissible).
D.J. and P.J. v Norway (no. 38105/19) [2023] ECtHR (12 September) (public care with no access) (violation).
D.R. v Norway (no. 63307/16) [2023] ECtHR (12 September) (public care, access restrictions) (violation).
E.H. v Norway (no. 39717/19) [2021] ECtHR (25 November) (adoption by foster parents) (violation).
E.M. and Others v Norway (no. 3471/17) [2022] ECtHR (20 January) (public care, deprivation of parental responsibility) (no violation).
E.M. and T.A. v Norway (no. 56271/17) [2021] ECtHR (30 September) (public care, access restrictions) (inadmissible).
F.K. v Norway (no. 51860/19) [2023] ECtHR (11 July) (no access) (inadmissible).
F.Z. v Norway (no. 64789/16) [2021] ECtHR (1 July) (adoption by foster parents) (violation).
G.B. v Norway (no. 38097/19) [2023] ECtHR (12 September) (adoption by foster parents) (violation).
G.G. v Norway (no. 45985/19) [2023] ECtHR (12 September) (adoption by foster parents) (violation).

Grefsrud-Halvorsen v Norway (no. 39661/22) [2023] ECtHR (23 May) (public care, participation of foster parents in proceedings initiated by biological father regarding lifting of care order) (inadmissible).

H.B. and Others v Norway (nos. 35858/21 and 28537/21) [2024] ECtHR (30 January) (public care, access restrictions) (inadmissible).

Hernehult v Norway (no. 14652/16) [2020] ECtHR (10 March) (public care, restricted access) (violation).

Hernehult v Norway (no. 2) (no. 20102/19) [2023] ECtHR (5 September) (access restrictions) (inadmissible).

H.H. v Norway (no. 27186/21) [2023] ECtHR (12 December) (public care, access restrictions) (inadmissible).

H.L. v Norway (no. 59747/19) [2023] ECtHR (11 July) (refusal to terminate public care) (inadmissible).

I. and U. v Norway (dec.) (no. 75531/01) [2004] ECtHR (21 October) (public care) (inadmissible).

I.D. v Norway (no. 51374/16) [2017] ECtHR (4 April) (public care, access restrictions) (inadmissible).

I.H. and Others v Norway (no. 19628/21) [2024] ECtHR (8 January) (public care, access restrictions) (pending).

I.L. v Norway (no. 28160/22) [2024] ECtHR (4 June) (public care, access restrictions) (inadmissible).

I.M. v Norway (no. 16998/20) [2023] ECtHR (11 July) (adoption by foster parents) (inadmissible).

I.O. and R.A. v Norway (no. 29789/21) [2024] ECtHR (16 April) (public care, access restrictions) (inadmissible).

Jansen v Norway (no. 2822/16) [2018] ECtHR (6 September) (public care, no access) (violation).

J.B. and E.M. v Norway (no. 277/20) [2023] ECtHR (11 July) (adoption by gay foster parents) (inadmissible).

J.K. and Others v Norway (nos. 24657/21 and 41323/22) [2024] ECtHR (8 January) (adoption by foster parents) (pending).

J.M.N. and C.H. v Norway (no. 3145/16) [2016] ECtHR (11 October) (public care, access restrictions) (inadmissible).

Johansen v Norway (no. 17383/90) [1996] ECtHR (7 August) (public care, deprivation of parental responsibility) (violation).

Johansen v Norway (no. 2) (no. 12750/02) [2002] ECtHR (10 October) (public care, deprivation of parental responsibility, authorisation of adoption by foster parents) (inadmissible).

K.E. and A.K. v Norway (no. 57678/18) [2021] ECtHR (1 July) (public care, access restrictions) (violation).

K.F. and A.F. v Norway (no. 39769/17) [2023] ECtHR (12 September) (adoption by foster parents) (violation).

K.O. and V.M. v Norway (no. 64808/16) [2019] ECtHR (19 November) (temporary public care) (violation).

L.S. and O.V. v Norway (no. 58880/19) [2023] ECtHR (12 September) (adoption by foster parents) (violation).

M.A. and M.A. v Norway (no. 48372/18) [2023] ECtHR (12 September) (adoption by foster parents) (violation).

M.A. and Others v Norway (no. 41172/20) [2023] ECtHR (11 July) (deprivation of parental responsibility, access restrictions) (inadmissible).

M.F. v Norway (no. 5947/19) [2021] ECtHR (25 November) (public care, access restrictions) (violation).

M.J.M. v Norway (no. 44412/21) [2023] ECtHR (12 December) (public care, access restrictions) (inadmissible).

M.L. v Norway (no. 64639/16) [2020] ECtHR (20 December) (adoption by foster parents) (violation).

M.L. v Norway (no. 2) (no. 43701/14) [2017] ECtHR (7 September) (public care) (no violation).

M.M. v Norway (no. 27182/21) [2023] ECtHR (12 December) (public care, access restrictions) (inadmissible).

M.N. v Norway (no. 19626/21) [2024] ECtHR (12 March) (public care, access restrictions) (inadmissible).

Mohamed Hasan v Norway (no. 27496/15) [2018] ECtHR (26 April) (adoption by foster parents) (no violation).

M.R. and K.G. v Norway (no. 36825/21) [2024] ECtHR (12 March) (public care, access restrictions) (inadmissible).

M.T. v Norway (no. 24148/22) [2024] ECtHR (4 June) (public care, access restrictions) (inadmissible).

Olsson v Norway (no. 20592/92) [1995] ECtHR (5 April) (public care, access restrictions) (inadmissible).

O.S. v Norway (no. 63295/17) [2021] ECtHR (30 September) (public care, access restrictions) (no violation).

Pedersen v Norway (no. 39710/15) [2020] ECtHR (10 March) (adoption by foster parents) (violation).

R.A. v Norway (no. 44598/19) [2023] ECtHR (11 July) (public care, no access) (inadmissible).

R.A. v Norway (no. 1461/21) [2024] ECtHR (13 February) (public care, access restrictions) (inadmissible).

R.I. v Norway (no. 7692/20) [2023] ECtHR (11 July) (adoption by foster parents) (inadmissible).

R.K. v Norway (no. 45413/20) [2023] ECtHR (11 July) (public care, access restrictions) (inadmissible).

R.O. v Norway (no. 49452/18) [2021] ECtHR (1 July) (public care, access restrictions) (violation).

S.A. v Norway (no. 26727/19) [2021] ECtHR (21 October) (public care, access restrictions) (inadmissible).
S.E. and Others v Norway (no. 9167/18) [2023] ECtHR (12 September) (adoption by foster parents) (violation).
S.G. and M.C. v Norway (no. 38082/21) [2024] ECtHR (26 March) (public care, access restrictions) (inadmissible).
S.G. and S.O. v Norway (nos. 18004/21 and 54072/21) [2024] ECtHR (4 June) (adoption by foster parents) (inadmissible).
S.P. v Norway (no. 54419/19) [2021] ECtHR (10 June) (adoption by foster parents) (inadmissible).
S.S. and J.H. v Norway (no. 15784/19) [2023] ECtHR (12 September) (adoption by foster parents) (violation).
Strand Lobben and Others v Norway (no. 37283/13) [2019] ECtHR Grand Chamber (10 September) (adoption by foster parents) (violation, 13–4).
T.C. v Norway (no. 29821/96) [1998] ECtHR (20 May) (deprivation of parental responsibility, no access) (inadmissible).
T.E. and J.E. v Norway (no. 4348/22) [2024] ECtHR (4 June) (public care, access restrictions) (inadmissible).
T.G. and Others v Norway (no. 4993/21) [2023] ECtHR (12 December) (public care, access restrictions) (inadmissible).
T.H. v Norway (no. 47015/21) [2023] ECtHR (12 December) (public care, access restrictions) (inadmissible).
T.H. v Norway (no. 2) (no. 42796/20) [2023] ECtHR (11 July) (public care, access restrictions) (inadmissible).
T.J. v Norway (no. 38014/22) [2024] ECtHR (21 November) (public care order) (struck out).
T.L. v Norway (no. 32874/22) [2024] ECtHR (21 May) (public care order) (inadmissible).
T.S. and J.J. v Norway (no. 14633/15) [2023] ECtHR (11 July) (public care, access restrictions) (inadmissible).

Appendix 2.2
List of child welfare cases against other Council of Europe member states (alphabetical order)

A v Slovenia (no. 53790/22) [2024] ECtHR (21 November) (placement in institutional care; contact restrictions) (struck out).
A. and Others v Iceland (nos. 25133/20 and 31856/20) [2022] ECtHR (15 November) (long-term placement in foster home) (no violation).
Achim v Romania (no. 45959/11) [2017] ECtHR (24 October) (temporary placement of children in public care) (no violation).
A.C.M.U. and Others v Italy (no. 9993/24) [2024] ECtHR (3 July) (public care order) (pending).

A.E. v France (no. 51944/22) [2024] ECtHR (23 May) (public care order) (no violation).

A.F. and M.F. v Italy (no. 44715/22) [2024] ECtHR (4 April) (public care order) (friendly settlement).

Á.F.L. v Iceland (no. 35789/22) [2023] ECtHR (communicated 20 June) (public care order) (pending).

Apadula v Italy (no. 4337/24) [2024] ECtHR (5 April) (public care order) (pending).

A.S. and M.S. v Italy (no. 48618/22) [2023] ECtHR (10 October) (contact restrictions) (violation).

Blyudik v Russia (no. 46401/08) [2019] ECtHR (25 June) (placement of daughter in closed educational institution for minors) (violation).

D.B. v United Kingdom (no. 43246/21) [2022] ECtHR (29 March) (adoption by foster parents) (pending).

D.G. and S.G. v Serbia (no. 61347/21) [2024] ECtHR (11 January) (public care order) (pending).

D.M. and N. v Italy (no. 60083/18) [2022] ECtHR (20 January) (public care and termination of parental responsibility) (violation).

Dragoni and Others v Italy (no. 12654/22) [2023] ECtHR (6 February) (adoption by foster parents) (pending).

E.C. v Italy (no. 82314/17) [2020] ECtHR (30 June) (public care) (no violation).

Ekoh and Ekoh v Italy (no. 43088/18) [2021] ECtHR (12 October) (temporary termination of parental responsibility) (no violation).

El Marradi v France (no. 827/24) [2024] ECtHR (17 October) (public care order) (no violation).

Fiagbe v Italy (no. 18549/20) [2022] ECtHR (28 April) (public care with adoption in mind) (violation).

Haddad v Spain (no. 16572/17) [2019] ECtHR (18 June) (pre-adoption foster placement despite father's acquittal for domestic violence) (violation).

Hatia v Italy (no. 31139/22) [2022] ECtHR (30 September) (public care with contact restrictions) (pending).

Hybkovi v Czech Republic (no. 30879/17) [2022] ECtHR (13 October) (public care placement in institution) (no violation).

I.M. and Others v Italy (no. 25426/20) [2022] ECtHR (10 November) (public care and termination of parental responsibility) (violation).

Jessica Marchi v Italy (no. 54978/17) [2021] ECtHR (27 May) (public care) (no violation).

Karovashkin and Aleksandrovna v Russia (no. 36701/13) [2019] ECtHR (10 December) (rejection of application for reinstatement of parental responsibility) (inadmissible).

Khusnutdinov and X v Russia (no. 76598/12) [2018] ECtHR (18 February) (refusal to return child in the care of her grandparents to her father) (no violation).

Kilic v Austria (no. 27700/15) [2023] ECtHR (12 February) (6–1 majority) (refusal to terminate public care) (no violation).

Kocherov and Sergeyevna v Russia (no. 16899/13) [2016] ECtHR (29 March) (restrictions on parental authority of father with intellectual disability) (violation).

Longo v Italy (no. 35875/23) [2024] ECtHR (communicated 1 February) (public care order) (pending).

L.Z. and D.Z. v Italy (no. 27379/24) [2024] ECtHR (communicated 25 November) (public care order) (pending).

Manteigas v Portugal (no. 22179/15) [2022] ECtHR (22 February) (public care with adoption in mind) (violation).

M.G.V. and Others v Italy (no. 39552/23) [2024] ECtHR (communicated 1 February) (public care order) (pending).

Nechay v Russia (no. 40639/17) [2021] ECtHR (25 May) (contact restrictions) (violation).

Neves Caratao Pinto v Portugal (no. 38433/19) [2021] ECtHR (12 October) (public care and refusal to terminate care) (violation).

N.P. v Switzerland (no. 52031/21) [2024] ECtHR (communicated 2 April) (public care order) (pending).

N.S. v United Kingdom (no. 38134/20) [2022] ECtHR (communicated 21 February) (adoption by foster parents) (pending).

Omorefe v Spain (no. 59339/16) [2020] ECtHR (23 June) (public care and subsequent adoption) (violation).

Paradiso and Campanelli v Italy [GC] (no. 25358/12) [2017] ECtHR (24 January) (removal of child into public care from a child born as a result of a surrogacy arrangement by a couple later found to have no biological link with the child (no violation, 11–6).

Pavel Shishkov v Russia (no. 78754/13) [2021] ECtHR (2 March) (refusal to terminate public care) (no violation).

P.S. and R.S. v Italy (no. 23691/22) [2023] ECtHR (14 September) (adoption) (friendly settlement).

P.V. v Portugal (no. 31253/18) [2020] ECtHR (8 December) (public care with adoption in mind) (inadmissible).

R.M. v Latvia (no. 53487/13) [2021] ECtHR (9 December) (temporary public care with access restrictions) (no violation).

Roengkasettakorn Eriksson v Sweden (no. 21574/16) [2022] ECtHR (19 May) (restricted access) (no violation).

Savinovskihk and Others v Russia (no. 16206/19) [2024] ECtHR (9 July) (public care order) (violation).

Silva Justa v Portugal (no. 29703/15) [2020] ECtHR (11 February) (public care with adoption in mind) (inadmissible).

S.J.P. and E.S. v Sweden (no. 8610/11) [2018] ECtHR (28 August) (public care with contact restrictions) (no violation).

S.S. v Slovenia (no. 40938/16) [2018] ECtHR (30 October) (withdrawal of parental rights of mentally ill mother) (no violation).

Stankūnaité v Lithuania (no. 67068/11) [2019] ECtHR (29 October) (temporary public care with contact restrictions and belated termination of care) (no violation).

Terna v Italy (no. 21052/18) [2021] ECtHR (14 January) (public care with contact restrictions) (violation).

Tlapak and Others v Germany (nos. 11308/16 and 11344/16) [2018] ECtHR (22 March) (taking into public care due to children subjected to corporal punishment) (no violation).

Van Slooten v Netherlands (no. 45644/18) [2020] ECtHR (communicated 31 August) (removal of parental authority) (pending).

Vassiliou v Romania (no. 57929/19) [2024] ECtHR (15 February) (adoption) (pending).

V.Y.R. and A.V.R. v Bulgaria (no. 48321/20) [2022] ECtHR (13 December) (adoption by foster parents) (no violation, 5–2).

Wetjen and Others v Germany (nos. 68125/14 and 72204/14) [2018] ECtHR (22 March) (taking into public care due to children subjected to corporal punishment) (no violation).

Wunderlich v Germany (no. 18925/15) [2019] ECtHR (10 January) (temporary placement of children in institution due to parents' refusal to send them to school) (no violation).

Y.I. v Russia (no. 68868/14) [2020] ECtHR (25 February) (termination of parental responsibility) (violation).

Zelikha Magomadova v Russia (no. 58724/14) [2019] ECtHR (8 October) (termination of parental responsibility; no access) (violation).

Notes

[1] The author served as the Agent of the Norwegian Government (2012–2022), including in the child welfare cases against Norway mentioned in this chapter for that period.

[2] Rule 4 § 1 of the Rule of the Committee of Ministers for the supervision of the execution of judgments and of the terms of friendly settlements, adopted by the Committee on 10 May 2006, states: 'The Committee of Ministers shall give priority to supervision of the execution of judgments in which the ECtHR has identified what it considers a systemic problem in accordance with Resolution Res(2004)3 of the Committee of Ministers on judgments revealing an underlying systemic problem.'

[3] See, typically, Hungary's third-party intervention briefly summarised in Somogyi v Italy, no. 67972/01, paras 59–60; and Turkey's intervention referred to in Ciliz v Netherlands, no. 29192/95, judgment 11 July 2000, paras 56–58.

References

Apostolovski and Others v Bosnia and Herzegovina (no. 28704/11) [2022] ECtHR (18 January).

Badalyan v Azerbaijan (no. 51295/11) [2021] ECtHR (22 July).

Berdzenishvili and Others v Russia (no. 14594/07) [2016] ECtHR (20 December).

Butkevich v Russia (no. 5865/07) [2018] ECtHR (13 February).
Ciliz v Netherlands (no. 29192/95) [2000] ECtHR (11 July).
Committee of Ministers (2006) *Rules of the Committee of Ministers for the Supervision of the Execution of Judgments and of the Terms of Friendly Settlements.* Available from: https://rm.coe.int/16806eebf0
Council of Europe (2018) *Copenhagen Declaration.* Available from: https://www.echr.coe.int/Documents/Copenhagen_Declaration_ENG.pdf
D.B. v United Kingdom (no. 43246/21) [2022] ECtHR (29 March). Subject matter and questions to the parties available from: https://hudoc.echr.coe.int/eng?i=001-217093
Demades v Turkey (no. 16219/90) [2003] ECtHR (31 July).
D.L. v Austria (no. 34999/16) [2017] ECtHR (7 December).
Dzehtsiarou, K. (2023) 'Conversations with friends: "Friends of the Court" interventions of the state parties to the European Convention on Human Rights', *Legal Studies*, 43(3): 1–21.
Dzidzava v Russia (no. 16363/07) [2016] ECtHR (20 December).
Eugenia Michaelidou Developments Ltd and Michael Tymvios v Turkey (no. 16163/90) [2003] ECtHR (31 July).
Filkin v Portugal (no. 69729/12) [2020] ECtHR (3 March).
Jakovljević and Others v Bosnia and Herzegovina (no. 51227/16) [2019] ECtHR (23 July).
Jovanovic v Sweden (no. 10592/12) [2015] ECtHR (22 October).
Grzęda v Poland (no. 43572/18) [2022] ECtHR (15 March).
Haugevik, K. and Neumann, C.B. (2021) 'Reputation crisis management and the state: Theorising containment as a diplomatic mode', *European Journal of International Relations*, 27(3): 708–729.
Khojoyan and Vardazaryan v Azerbaijan (no. 62161/14) [2021] ECtHR (4 November).
K. and T. v Finland [GC] (no. 25702/94) [2001] ECtHR (12 July).
Lazoriva v Ukraine (no. 6878/14) [2018] ECtHR (17 April).
Makhmudova v Russia (no. 61984/17) [2020] ECtHR (1 December).
Makuchyan and Minasyan v Azerbaijan and Hungary (no. 17247/13) [2020] ECtHR (26 May).
Mitrova and Savik v Macedonia (no. 42534/09) [2016] ECtHR (11 February).
M.R. and D.R. v Ukraine (no. 63551/13) [2018] ECtHR (22 May).
N.S. v United Kingdom (no. 38134/20) [2022] ECtHR (21 February).
Paradiso and Campanelli v Italy [GC] (no. 25358/12) [2017] ECtHR (24 January).
P.D. v Russia (no. 30560/19) [2022] ECtHR (3 May).
Petrosyan v Azerbaijan (no. 32427/16) [2011] ECtHR (4 November).
Popov and Others v Russia (no. 4456/11) [2018] ECtHR (27 November).

Rojkov, A. (2019) 'An international crisis over a little girl', *Die Zeit*. Available from: https://www.zeit.de/gesellschaft/2019-05/flucht-norwegen-sorgerecht-asyl-fluechtlinge-polen-staatsaffaere-english/komplettansicht?fbclid=IwAR2OKf14RBi8eqCv42V6KsE3rQGwfSvhxT-W7Rsxi-qxN4MeVSrUaRhTtvs

Romeo Castano v Belgium (no. 8351/17) [2019] ECtHR (9 July).

Sapondzhyan v Russia (no. 32986/08) [2017] ECtHR (21 March).

Saribekyan and Balyan v Azerbaijan (no. 35746/11) [2020] ECtHR (30 January).

Savickis and Others v Latvia [GC] (no. 49270/11) [2022] ECtHR (9 June).

Severe v Austria (no. 53661/15) [2017] ECtHR (21 September).

Shioshvili and Others v Russia (no. 19356/07) [2016] ECtHR (20 December).

Sisojeva and Others v Latvia (no. 60654/00) [2007] ECtHR (15 January).

Skivenes, M. (2019) 'Child protection and child-centrism: The Grand Chamber case of Strand Lobben and Others v. Norway 2019', *Strasbourg Observers*. Available from: https://strasbourgobservers.com/2019/10/10/child-protection-and-child-centrism-the-grand-chamber-case-of-strand-lobben-and-others-v-norway-2019/

Slivenko v Latvia (no. 48321/99) [2003] ECtHR (9 October).

Somogyi v Italy (no. 67972/01) [2004] ECtHR (18 May).

Suslov and Batikyan v Armenia (no. 56540/14) [2022] ECtHR (6 October).

Tchankotadze v Georgia (no. 15256/05) [2016] ECtHR (21 June).

T.I. and Others v Greece (no. 40311/10) [2019] ECtHR (18 July).

Van Slooten v Netherlands (no. 45644/18) [2020] ECtHR (31 August).

Y.C. v United Kingdom (no. 4547/10) [2012] ECtHR (13 March).

Zoletic and Others v Azerbaijan (no. 20116/12) [2021] ECtHR (7 October).

3

Child protection and the European Court of Human Rights: the case of Finland and Article 8

Raija Huhtanen and Tarja Pösö

Introduction

Finland first became a member of the Council of Europe in 1989 and ratified the European Convention on Human Rights (ECHR) in 1990 – almost 40 years later than the other Nordic countries (Council of Europe, 2023). The UN Convention on the Rights of the Child (CRC) was ratified the following year. As Finland ascribes to a dualistic model with regard to international treaties, the two conventions were implemented by means of national legislation in 1990 and 1991, respectively (Koulu, 2019). The ratifications were followed by the reform of fundamental rights in the Constitution of Finland in 1995 and the overall reform of the Constitution in 2000. These reforms and ratifications demonstrate a profound change in the Finnish legal culture with an increasing emphasis on human and fundamental rights in both the legislative process and the application of law by the courts and administrative authorities (Ojanen, 2012; Pellonpää et al, 2018).

Since its implementation, the ECHR has played an important role in many fields of Finnish law. The European Court of Human Rights (ECtHR) has issued almost 200 judgments concerning Finland, more than in any other Nordic country (Table 3.1). With regard to Finnish law-making, there are many references to the ECHR and ECtHR in government proposals as well as other legislative documents. Both Finnish supreme courts – the Supreme Court and the Supreme Administrative Court – have frequently referred to ECHR and ECtHR case law in their decisions. This especially concerns matters relating to Article 6 (the right to a fair trial), for instance, the length of proceedings, while the influence of Article 8 (the right to respect for private and family life) has most often been seen with regard to some family law matters and alien affairs (Pellonpää et al, 2018).

There are only a few ECtHR judgments (4) concerning Article 8 and Finnish child protection, which is different from Norway, for example (Skivenes and Tefre, 2021). Although the ECtHR case law has been

Table 3.1: ECHR and the ECtHR judgments in the Nordic context, 1959–2023

Country	The year of ratification of ECHR	Total number of judgments	Number of judgments with at least one violation of ECHR	Number of judgments with at least one violation of Article 8
Denmark	1953	70	25 (36 %)	8 (32 %)
Finland	1990	194	142 (73 %)	24 (17 %)
Iceland	1953	39	27 (69 %)	1 (4 %)
Norway	1952	75	48 (64 %)	26 (54 %)
Sweden	1952	159	62 (40 %)	10 (16 %)

Source: European Court of Human Rights (2023b; 2024)

explored by many Finnish researchers (for example, Sormunen, 2021), the particular influences on child protection have not been studied to our knowledge. In our tentative analysis, we will argue that the judgments have had a great – but not unproblematic – influence on Finnish child protection legislation and its application. The influence is most apparent in matters related to the duration of placements and termination of care, which were, in short, the violations recognised in those judgments. As a result, children should at the moment be placed into public care only 'for the time being' with the aim of family reunification. Although Finland shares many principles of child protection with the other Nordic countries as service-oriented child welfare systems (Gilbert et al, 2011; Berrick et al, 2023), the absence of the option of permanent placements distinguishes the Finnish child protection system from Sweden and Norway where the opportunity to consider a more permanent placement, or even adoption, exists on certain (exceptional) conditions (Svensson and Höjer, 2017; Helland and Skivenes, 2021).

In this chapter, we will first examine the four judgments by the ECtHR regarding Finnish child protection and the violations of Article 8[1] therein, and second the influences of ECtHR case law on the Finnish child protection in more detail. The sources explored for influences include the present Child Welfare Act (417/2007) and its preparatory works, the Supreme Administrative Court's decisions regarding child protection, as well as various policy papers concerning child protection, such as national reviews and reform programmes. All sources are official documents. In these, we have sought not only explicit textual justifications referring to Article 8 or ECtHR judgments but also more implicit references to the topic of permanent placements or the duration and termination of care. The sources and the methods used for our text analysis will be described in more detail in each subchapter.

The European Court of Human Rights judgments regarding Article 8 and Finnish child protection

In total, the ECtHR has issued 194 judgments concerning Finland and found at least one violation of the ECHR in 142 judgments (1959–2023). The total amount of judgments concerning Finland is large when compared with the other Nordic countries, as is the number of judgments finding at least one violation of the ECHR and the percentage of these judgments in all judgments (Table 3.1). The differences become even more apparent when considering the fact that Finland ratified the ECHR approximately 40 years later than the other Nordic countries. As regards Finland, Denmark, Iceland and Sweden, violations of Article 6 are the biggest group of judgments finding at least one violation of the ECHR, while in the case of Norway the biggest group in this respect consists of violations of Article 8 (European Court of Human Rights, 2023b; 2024).

The violations of Article 8 in 24 judgments concerning Finland are a heterogeneous group including, apart from child protection cases, cases concerning, for instance, child custody and access rights (for example, Hokkanen v Finland, 19823/92, 23.9.1994) and confidentiality of medical data (for example, Z. v Finland, 22009/93, 25.2.1997).

With regard to Finnish child protection, the ECtHR has altogether issued five judgments, which we sum up in short descriptions in Table 3.2.[2] In all of these judgments, there was a violation of the ECHR. We will focus on the four judgments relating to Article 8 and, therefore, exclude the first case from our analysis. The four judgments were issued in the early 2000s over a short period of six years (2001–2006). The violations concerned decisions made by child welfare authorities on grounds of legislation, especially of the Child Welfare Act (683/1983), and the discretionary powers the authorities used when applying this legislation. In three cases, the violation was exclusively or partially due to the authorities' failure to facilitate a possible family reunification – a failure that, according to the ECtHR, was proved by severe restrictions on contact reflecting the authorities' presumption of the need for long-lasting public care. For reasons of simplicity, we use the term 'duration and termination of care' in this chapter to cover these violations found by the ECtHR.

The first and the most important of the four judgments is K. and T., decided by the Grand Chamber (GC) in 2001. The issue at stake was the care orders concerning the applicants' two children and the implementation of these orders. The ECtHR found a violation of Article 8, first (by 14 votes to 3) in respect of the emergency care order related to the newborn baby J., and second (unanimously) by reason of the failure of the national authorities to take proper steps to reunite the family. As for the emergency care order, the ECtHR held that the situation was not an emergency in

Table 3.2: ECtHR judgments concerning Finnish child protection in 1990–2023

The case	The applicant(s)	The complaint	The article(s) applied by ECtHR	The violation(s) found by ECtHR
L. v Finland (25651/94) 27.4.2000	The father and the grandfather of two children born in 1985 and 1991 respectively.	Care orders concerning the children, continuation of care, the Court's refusal to hold an oral hearing when deciding on contact restrictions and prohibitions.	Art. 6 (Art. 8, Art. 13)	The lack of an oral hearing before the County Administrative Court in the proceedings concerning the contact restrictions and prohibitions.
K. and T. v Finland (25702/94) 12.7.2001 (GC)	The parents of two children born in 1988 and 1993 respectively.	Emergency and normal care orders concerning the children, continuation of the care, contact restrictions and prohibitions.	Art. 8 (Art. 13)	The emergency care order concerning the newborn baby, the authorities' failure to facilitate a possible family reunification.
K.A. v Finland (27751/95) 14.1.2003	The father of three children born in 1980, 1981 and 1986 respectively.	Care orders concerning the children, the implementation and continuation of care.	Art. 8.	The authorities' failure to facilitate a possible reunification of the applicant and his children.
R. v Finland (34141/96) 30.5.2006	The father of a child born in 1987.	Contact restrictions concerning the applicant and his child in care, continuation of care.	Art. 8 (Art. 6, Art. 13)	The authorities' failure to facilitate a possible family reunification, for instance by severely restricting the applicant's right to visit his child.
H.K. v Finland (36065/97) 26.9.2006	The father of a child born in 1990.	Emergency and normal care orders concerning the child, contact restrictions.	Art. 8 (Art. 6)	The authorities' failure to make any formal decision when placing the child in foster care and imposing contact restrictions despite the applicant's objection.

Source: European Court of Human Rights (2023a; 2024)

the sense of being unforeseen. The mother and the baby were in hospital at the time, and the authorities had known about the forthcoming birth months in advance and were well aware of the mother's mental problems. The reasons the national authorities relied on were insufficient to justify the serious intervention in the parents' family life. Even with regard to the national authorities' margin of appreciation, the making of the emergency care order and the methods used in implementing it were disproportionate in their effects on the parents' potential for enjoying a family life with their newborn child as from her birth. Therefore, the interference was 'not necessary in a democratic society' (para 168). As for the failure to facilitate the reunification of the family there had been only one effort on the authorities' part to that effect in the seven-year period during which the children had been in care. According to the ECtHR:

> The minimum to be expected of the authorities is to examine the situation anew from time to time to see whether there has been any improvement in the family's situation. The possibilities of reunification will be progressively diminished and eventually destroyed if the biological parents and the children are not allowed to meet each other at all, or only so rarely that no natural bonding between them is likely to occur. The restrictions and prohibitions imposed on the applicants' access to their children, far from preparing a possible reunification of the family, rather contributed to hindering it. (Para 179)

In the cases of K.A. and R. the national authorities had also failed to facilitate possible family reunification by restricting contact between the biological parent and his children in care and by not considering the reunification of the original family as a serious option but, instead, 'proceeding from a presumption that the children would be in need of long-lasting public care' by substitute carers (K.A., para 143). In the case of H.K., the ECtHR found two violations of Article 8 in respect of the decision-making procedure, as the authorities had made no formal decisions when placing the child away from the parent and issuing contact restrictions. As a result, the parent could not contest the restrictions, and no sufficient justification for that shortcoming had been provided.

Implications of the European Court of Human Rights case law on Finnish child protection

Implications for child welfare legislation

All the ECtHR judgments described in the previous section were based on decisions made under the previous Child Welfare Act (1983). It is noteworthy that there are no ECtHR judgments under the present Act (2007), suggesting prominent changes were introduced since the new Act. The reforms introduced by the present Child Welfare Act aimed at bringing the legislation up to date with regard to Finland's international treaty obligations (Tolonen et al, 2019). For example, a child's right to become involved in the decision-making concerning the child was strengthened in compliance with Article 12 of CRC regarding the child's participation rights (HE 252/2006 vp). With regard to the ECHR, the duration and termination of care were the issues most affected by the ECtHR case law. An important change in this respect was that the social worker responsible for the child's affairs must now assess the conditions for continuing the care when the client plan is reviewed, that is, at least once a year. This must also be done when a child or the custodian applies for termination of care or when it otherwise proves necessary. No such obligation was included in the previous Act when there was no option for permanent placements, either. In the preparatory works of the present Act, the change was justified by referring to, on the one hand, the four ECtHR judgments concerning Finland and, on the other, some real cases where the authorities had neglected to facilitate family reunification for many years (HE 252/2006 vp).

According to the present Act, taking a child into care is only valid for the time being. However, care must be terminated when the conditions prescribed by the Act are fulfilled. The conditions for discontinuing care are bound to those for taking into care, meaning that care must be terminated when the conditions for taking into care no longer exist. However, if the discontinuation is 'manifestly against the interests of the child', it is not permitted (section 47). Taken together with the obligation to regularly review the continuation of care, the provisions reflect the idea that placements in substitute care should be temporary in the first place. In addition, and due to the proposal by the Constitutional Law Committee of Parliament, the explicit aim of family reunification was added to the Act by the Parliament (PeVL 58/2006 vp). As one of the main principles of the Act, it is now prescribed that when providing substitute care, the aim of reuniting the family must be taken into account in a manner that accords with the child's best interests. Furthermore, a client plan for a child taken into care, as well as that for the parent, must set out how contact with the child will be organised, and how the aim of reuniting the family will be taken into account in a way that is in the child's best interests.

Accordingly, the present Child Welfare Act does not present any formal opportunity for a permanent placement. Adoption is not an option provided by Child Welfare Act nor is the deprivation of parental rights or the transfer of custody to the foster parents. Adoption is regulated by the Adoption Act (22/2012) and the custody of a child by the Act on Child Custody and Right of Access (361/1983). In both cases, the criteria, procedures, legal implications and decision-makers are different from those in child welfare.

Children who have been taken into care may be adopted by the Adoption Act, but this is rarely done (Eriksson and Pösö, 2021). Nevertheless, children stay in care for long periods and family reunifications are rare. There are very few studies examining the frequencies of family reunifications, but the statistical analysis based on the national child welfare register data highlights a very low frequency: in 2016, only 4.5 per cent of children who were in care through a care order decision had their order terminated in that particular year before they reached their adulthood (age 18) (THL, 2018, 10). Furthermore, when parents and children, aged 12 years or older, appeal decisions concerning the continuation of care, the administrative courts typically uphold the decisions made by child welfare authorities, meaning that the appeals do not usually lead to family reunification (Pösö et al, 2019).

Implications for the Supreme Administrative Court's decisions

Finnish law follows the Nordic legal system with Parliamentary Acts as the main source of law. Similar to Sweden, Finland has a system of general courts of law and administrative courts of law. The jurisdiction of administrative courts covers all administrative law cases, which also include child protection cases (Mäenpää, 2012; Pösö and Huhtanen, 2017). The Supreme Administrative Court is the court of last resort in administrative law cases with a task to grant judicial protection and guide the application of the law by precedent. It issues thousands of decisions yearly, the most important of which are published on the Court's web page (https://www.kho.fi/). While the legal-formal and doctrinal position of precedents is relatively weak in Finnish law, they still play a significant role (Husa, 2012).

At the time of writing, the Supreme Administrative Court has published 13 decisions regarding child protection with a reference to Article 8 ECHR and/or ECtHR case law.[3] The main topics of the decisions concern restricting contact or changing the substitute care place of the child in care, while some individual decisions, for example, concern the preconditions for taking into care. The majority of the references to ECtHR case law are very short and made in general terms only. In some cases, however, the Supreme Administrative Court has examined the ECtHR's reasoning more thoroughly and justified its decision by resorting to the principles developed by the ECtHR. Nonetheless, even in these decisions, the ECtHR judgments seem to comprise only an additional argument, while primary arguments are based on domestic legislation and, especially, the Child Welfare Act.

The aim of family reunification has played an important role in two Supreme Administrative Court precedents. In one of them, KHO 19.9.2000/2302, the issue was about changing the substitute care place of three children, aged eight, nine and 11 years, respectively, taken into care and placed in foster care six years earlier. The social welfare board rejected the parent's application for placing the children under their aunt's care as no remarkable shortcomings were found with regard to the original foster care place. The Court overruled the decision and returned the case to the board. It shortly referred to Article 8 and ECtHR case law and, apart from other arguments, held that placing the children under their aunt's care would facilitate reuniting the children with their biological parent. It was for the social welfare board to weigh this argument as well as other relevant considerations and decide the case anew.

The other case, KHO 2011:99, concerned the taking into care of a child of one year of age with a single mother with slight mental disabilities. The Court upheld the care order decision as the child's health and development had been seriously endangered due to the lack of care. According to the Court, the shortcomings found in the mother's caring skills were relevant with respect to a very young child but their relevance might decrease as the child grows older. They must therefore be reassessed later, and attention must then be paid to the ECtHR case law concerning a care order as a temporary measure to be discontinued as soon as circumstances permit. So, while the outcome was not directly affected by the ECtHR case law, the Supreme Administrative Court took advantage of the opportunity of guiding the application of law to be in harmony with it in the future.

In all, the Supreme Administrative Court has utilised ECtHR case law in few decisions regarding child protection. What is interesting is that in two decisions it explicitly referred to family reunification as the aim of substitute care. This might underline the precedential value of these decisions as they both only indirectly concerned duration or termination of care. Drawing any conclusions is, however, difficult, because of the age and small number of these decisions. While the more recent references to ECtHR judgments concern other issues – such as the notion of 'family life' in Article 8[4] – they still prove that these judgments are an important source of law in this area. This most probably also concerns the decision-making of the child welfare authorities as, due to the guidance by national authorities (via, for example, the online Handbook of Child Welfare), they are informed of the Supreme Administrative Court's precedents and the influence of the ECtHR judgments on them.

Child welfare policy and practice: permanent care orders or not?

Since the beginning of the 2010s, the policy and practice of child welfare have been the target of a variety of national reviews and reform programmes. Article 8 appears occasionally in the policy documents regarding children and child welfare. For example, the recent policy document, the National Child Strategy Committee report, published by the Finnish government in 2021, makes a clear reference to Article 8 when drawing the principles for policies regarding children's relations with other people (Finnish Government, 2022, p 29). The reference to Article 8 is not linked to child protection but addresses children's relations in a wider meaning. Child welfare policy documents seem to invite more frequently the recognition of CRC than that of ECHR. This does not, however, mean that the ECtHR judgments would be ignored; instead, their implications are more indirect as will be demonstrated by our examination of the pivotal policy review of the state of child welfare (STM, 2013) and its follow-up reports.[5] This review was run by an expert group established in 2013 by the Ministry of Social Affairs and Health and it was timed after the tragic death of a child known to the child welfare authorities, with a lot of media attention. The review resulted in 54 proposals for changes. Although the review lacked direct references to the ECtHR judgments, there was one recommendation which is relevant for this chapter. Recommendation number 19 states that the existing Child Welfare Act should be changed to make a permanent care order possible (STM, 2013, p 46).

According to the expert group, a permanent care order could be an option 'if there is a realistic reason to believe that parents or other custodians could not take care of the child's care and upbringing and no other options to secure the child's situation exist' (STM, 2013, pp 45–46). The temporary nature of a care order is seen as being a problem in those cases in which there is no real likelihood of family reunification. Therefore, the group argued that the existing regulation about care orders being only of a temporary nature should be changed.

The review was followed by an implementation plan for the period of 2014–2019, published again by the Ministry of Social Affairs and Health (STM, 2014). There the proposal about a permanent care order is among the recommendations *not* to be implemented, because of the serious criticism received. The criticism included concerns about the proposal's legitimacy from the point of view of the Constitution of Finland and human rights treaties (STM, 2014, p 35). Furthermore, there were also concerns about whether there would be any clear and uncontested criteria for those cases in which family reunification would not be a likely option. Despite the criticism, the plan documented that the proposal needed to be further elaborated regarding its relation to basic and human rights as well as to family reunification and practices abroad. However, in 2019, in another review of child welfare published by the Ministry, now as a part of a nationwide programme for child and family services, the conclusion was that that particular proposal of the review in 2013 had not been implemented as the views among authorities and stakeholders were not supportive of it (Kananoja and Ruuskanen, 2019, p 87).

As said, the series of these three policy documents, important in the Finnish child welfare context, do not make any direct reference to the ECtHR or

Article 8. It is, however, likely, in our view, that the sensitivity of the topic of permanent care orders is indirectly related to the ECtHR judgments and how they were nationally interpreted and manifested in the collective memory of stakeholders outside the law-making bodies: there were hesitations about whether permanent placements would be against human and basic rights, yet without any detailed exploration of the matter. A different and explicit frame for considering permanent placements is provided by the recent Government Programme, introduced in June 2023 by the newly elected government, as it includes a plan about considering adoption as an option for children in care for the best interests of the child (Valtioneuvosto, 2023, p 33). What is essential in this short formulation is that it is in a paragraph highlighting that childlessness affects one in five persons of fertile age whereas child protection issues are described in other sections. This may suggest a new emerging discursive frame for considering adoption with an emphasis on making families for adults to tackle childlessness, challenging the older hesitations about adoption or any other type of permanent placement being against basic and human rights.

Discussion and conclusion

We have seen in this chapter that since Finland ratified the ECHR in 1990 and CRC in 1991, the basic and human rights have been included in Finnish legislation, including the Child Welfare Act. We have also seen that the ECtHR, in the period of 1959–2023, has had more judgments regarding Finland than other Nordic countries, but only four ECtHR judgments about the violation of Article 8 ECHR in child protection in Finland. These judgments, focusing on the duration and termination of care, directly influenced legislation as the Child Welfare Act was reformed in 2007. As a result, social workers were required to carry out new procedures; for example, the continuation of placements needs to be assessed at least once a year, and the restrictions of contact between the child and parents, if needed, are time-limited and require a specific decision-making procedure. The judgments have also had indirect implications on child welfare policy, as we have seen in the policy reports analysed in the chapter: reluctance to examine permanent placements as options for children needing long-term care because of the perceived complexities concerning basic and human rights.

Consequently, at first glance, the right to respect for private and family life seems to be well guaranteed in Finland at the moment as there have been no ECtHR judgments regarding Article 8 and child protection since the reform of the Child Welfare Act in 2007. However, from a more robust point of view, the lack of permanent placements in Finnish child welfare may suppress the critical concerns some parties, parents especially, may have about child protection but it can be in conflict with the interests of those children needing long-term care. As formally no permanent care exists, children's everyday life is at stake at least once a year when a full assessment of their need for care is made. Sometimes there is no contact or the contact is not safe between the child and birth parents despite social workers' family reunification efforts (for example, Helavirta, 2016). In some case, children's sense of permanence and continuity, as well as their sense of belonging to a 'substitute family' may be threatened. As previously described, family reunifications are rare, as are adoptions from care. Children may stay in care for many years, even for their whole childhood, on 'a temporary basis'. Permanence consists of legal, residential and relational elements (Palacios et al, 2019) which are not well supported by the present legislation. Therefore, the consensus not to revise the Finnish legislation and policy about permanent placements may be problematic for some children.

Indeed, the case of Finland demonstrates that the role of ECtHR and its judgments can have multiple and even controversial influences on national legislation, policy and practice. Their implementation may eventually even exclude the interests of very vulnerable children needing long-term care if 'protection of family life' rests on the narrow concept of (birth) family only. Obviously, the question 'what is family' and whose standpoint is seen as being relevant in its definition is still highly topical in Finland and beyond (Pösö et al, 2021; Fenton-Glynn, 2021).

Notes

[1] Article 8 ECHR guarantees everyone the right to respect for his private and family life. As ECtHR has reiterated in numerous child protection cases, the mutual enjoyment by parent and child of each other's company constitutes a fundamental element of the family life protected by the ECHR (for example, Fenton-Glynn, 2021). Article 8 § 2 sets the preconditions under which any domestic measure hindering such enjoyment is permitted: the measure must be 'in accordance with the law', and it must be 'necessary in a democratic society in the interests of national security, public safety or the economic well-being of the country, for the prevention of disorder or crime, for the protection of health or morals, or for the protection of the rights and freedoms of others'.

[2] In addition to the judgments, ECtHR has issued 21 decisions regarding Finnish child protection (1990–2022). By the decisions, the application was declared inadmissible in 18 cases and struck out of the Court's list in three cases. See Art. 35 ECHR and https://hudoc.echr.coe.int/eng#{%22documentcollectionid2%22:[%22GRANDCHAMBER%22,%22CHAMBER%22]}. The data were collected from HUDOC by using different keywords ('public care', 'care order', 'child protection', 'child welfare') and reading the results in order to sort out the child protection cases from other, such as criminal law, cases (for example T. and others v Finland 34952/97, 14.10.1999). As these data are not directly available from the statistics published by the ECtHR, we cannot present corresponding figures regarding the other Nordic countries.

[3] The decisions were identified on the Supreme Administrative Court's web page by using keywords referring to Child Welfare Act and Article 8 ECHR. Since 1990, the Court has published altogether 103 decisions with reference to the Child Welfare Act. We may, therefore, say that a bit more than every ten of them also have a reference to Article 8. This

4   For example, the case of KHO 2021:22 concerning the foster carer's right to respect for her family life with the child placed under her care for five and a half years.
5   When analysing the review report and its follow-up reports, we have focused on three issues: whether the reports make any reference to Article 8 or, second, to the ECtHR judgments regarding the violations of Article 8, and third, whether they explore the topic of permanent placements or family reunification.

is, however, just a very rough estimate as the decisions differ from one another and some of them have only a loose connection to child welfare.

References

Berrick, J., Gilbert N. and Skivenes, M. (eds) (2023) *The Oxford Handbook of Child Protection Systems*, Oxford University Press.

Council of Europe (2023) 'Chart of signatures and ratifications of Treaty 005'. Available from: https://www.coe.int/en/web/conventions/full-list?module=signatures-by-treaty&treatynum=005

Eriksson, P. and Pösö, T. (2021) 'Adoption from care in Finland: currently an uncommon alternative to foster care', in T. Pösö, M. Skivenes and J. Thorburn (eds), *Adoption from Care. International Perspectives on Children's Rights, Family Preservation and State Intervention*, Policy Press, pp 103–120.

European Court of Human Rights (2023a) HUDOC. Available from: https://hudoc.echr.coe.int/eng#%20

European Court of Human Rights (2023b) 'Violations by article and by state 1959–2022'. Available from: https://echr.coe.int/Documents/Stats_violation_1959_2022_ENG.pdf

European Court of Human Rights (2024) 'Violations by article and by state 2023'. Available from: https://www.echr.coe.int/statistical-reports

Fenton-Glynn, C. (2021) *Children and the European Court of Human Rights*, Oxford University Press.

Finnish Government (2022) 'National child strategy: Committee report', Publication 16, Finnish Government.

Gilbert, N., Parton, N. and Skivenes, M. (eds) (2011) *Child Protection Systems: International Trends and Orientations*, Oxford University Press.

HE 252/2006 vp Hallituksen esitys eduskunnalle lastensuojelulaiksi ja eräiksi siihen liittyviksi laeiksi [Government proposal 252/2006 concerning the Child Welfare Act]. Available from: https://www.eduskunta.fi/FI/vaski/HallituksenEsitys/Documents/he_252+2006.pdf

Helavirta, S. (2016) 'Lapsen asioista vastaaminen huostaanoton jälkeen sosiaalityöntekijöiden kuvaamana [Being in charge of children's matters in care as described by social workers]', in R. Enroos, T. Heino and T. Pösö (eds), *Huostaanotto [Care Order]*, Vastapaino, pp 188–223.

Helland, H.S. and Skivenes, M. (2021) 'Adoption from care in Norway', in T. Pösö, M. Skivenes and J. Thoburn (eds), *Adoption from Care: International Perspectives on Children's Rights, Family Preservation and State Intervention*, Policy Press, pp 139–156.

Husa, J. (2012) 'Panorama of world's legal systems – focusing on Finland', in K. Nuotio, S. Melander and M. Huomo-Kettunen (eds), *Introduction to Finnish Law and Legal Culture*, University of Helsinki, pp 5–18.

Kananoja, A. and Ruuskanen, K. (2019) 'Selvityshenkilön ehdotus lastensuojelun toimintaedellytysten ja laadun parantamiseksi Loppuraportti [The expert proposal about increasing the conditions and quality of child welfare]', Report 4, Sosiaali- ja terveysministeriö.

Koulu, S. (2019) 'Children's right to family life in Finland: A constitutional right or a side effect of the "normal family"?', in T. Haugli, A. Nylund, R. Sigurdsen and L.R.L Bendiksen (eds), *Children's Constitutional Rights in the Nordic Countries*, Brill, pp 338–356.

Mäenpää, O. (2012) 'The rule of law and administrative implementation in Finland', in K. Nuotio, S. Melander and M. Huomo-Kettunen (eds), *Introduction to Finnish Law and Legal Culture*, University of Helsinki, pp 187–203.

Ojanen, T. (2012) 'The Europeanization of Finnish law: Observations on the transformations of the Finnish scene of constitutionalism', in K. Nuotio, S. Melander and M. Huomo-Kettunen (eds), *Introduction to Finnish Law and Legal Culture*, University of Helsinki, pp 97–110.

Palacios, J., Brodzinsky, D., Grotevant, H., Johnson, D., Juffer, F., Marninez-Mora, L., et al (2019) 'Adoption in the service of child protection: An international interdisciplinary perspective', *Psychology, Public Policy, and Law*, 25(2): 57–72.

Pellonpää, M., Gullans, M., Pölönen, P. and Tapanila, A. (2018) *Euroopan ihmisoikeussopimus [The European Convention on Human Rights]*, Alma Talent.

PeVL 58/2006 vp Perustuslakivaliokunnan lausunto hallituksen esityksestä lastensuojelulaiksi ja eräiksi siihen liittyviksi laeiksi [The statement of the Constitutional Law Committee of Parliament 58/2006 vp concerning the Child Welfare Act]. Available from: https://www.eduskunta.fi/FI/vaski/Lausunto/Documents/pevl_58+2006.pdf

Pösö, T. and Huhtanen, R. (2017) 'Removals of children in Finland: A mix of voluntary and involuntary decisions', in K. Burns, T. Pösö and M. Skivenes (eds), *Child Welfare Removals by the State: A Cross-Country Analysis of Decision-Making Systems*, Oxford University Press, pp 18–39.

Pösö, T., Toivonen, V. and Kalliomaa-Puha, L. (2019) '"Haluaa kotiin äidin luo". Erimielisyydet ja lapsen etu huostaanoton jatkamista koskevissa valituksissa ja hallinto-oikeuden ratkaisuissa ["Wants to be with her mother". Disagreement and the best interests of the child in appeals and administrative court decisions]', *Oikeus*, 48(3): 226–243.

Pösö, T., Skivenes, M. and Thoburn, J. (eds) (2021) *Adoption from Care*, Policy Press.

Skivenes, M. and Tefre, Ø. (2021) 'Errors and mistakes in the Norwegian child protection system', in K. Biesel, J. Masson, N. Parton and T. Pösö (eds), *Errors and Mistakes in Child Protection*, Policy Press, pp 115–134.

Sormunen, M. (2021) *The Best Interests of the Child in Human Rights Practice: An Analysis of Domestic, European and International Jurisprudence*, Helsingin yliopisto.

STM (2013) 'Toimiva lastensuojelu, Selvitysryhmän loppuraportti [Functioning child welfare. The final report]', Report 19, Sosiaali- ja terveysministeriö.

STM (2014) 'Toimiva lastensuojelu. Toteuttamissuunnitelma vuosille 2014–2019 [Functioning child welfare. The implementation plan for 2014–2019]', Report 19, Sosiaali- ja terveysministeriö.

Svensson, G. and Höjer, S. (2017) 'Placing children in state care in Sweden: Decision-making bodies, laypersons and legal framework', in K. Burns, T. Pösö and M. Skivenes (eds), *Child Welfare Removals by the State*, Oxford University Press, pp 65–88.

THL (2018) 'Kodin ulkopuolelle sijoitettujen lasten sijoitusten kestot 2016 [The length of placements out of home]', Statistical report 9, Terveyden ja hyvinvoinnin laitos. Available from: https://www.julkari.fi/bitstream/handle/10024/136279/Tr09_18.pdf?sequence=5&isAllowed=y

Tolonen, H., Koulu, S. and Hakalehto, S. (2019) 'Best interests of the child in Finnish legislation and doctrine: What has changed and what remains the same?', in T. Haugli, A. Nylund, R. Sigurdsen and L.R.L. Bendiksen (eds), *Children's Constitutional Rights in the Nordic Countries*, Brill, pp 159–84.

Valtioneuvosto (2023) 'Vahva ja välittävä Suomi Pääministeri Petteri Orpon hallituksen ohjelma 20.6.2023 [A strong and committed Finland. Programme of Prime Minster Petteri Orpo's Government]', *Publications of the Finnish Government 2023:58*, Valtioneuvosto. Available from: https://valtioneuvosto.fi/en/governments/government-programme#/

4

Children's rights and European Court of Human Rights judgments' effects on Norwegian courts and jurisprudence

Kirsten Sandberg

Introduction

The judgments by the European Court of Human Rights (ECtHR) against Norway in recent years concern the right to family life in cases where a child has been placed in alternative care. Since family life between a child and their parents is best served by their living together, the ECtHR strongly emphasises the goal of reuniting the child with their parents. The goal has consequences for decisions on contact and adoption, and a timely question is how it relates to children's rights.

In the Grand Chamber judgment in Strand Lobben v Norway (2019), the majority found that the decision to let the foster parents adopt the child violated the European Convention on Human Rights (ECHR) on procedural grounds. The evidence was insufficient, and the reasoning was unsatisfactory in that the child's interests should have been balanced with those of his parents. I will leave the procedural issues here and concentrate on the substantive shortcomings that subsequent ECtHR judgments have found regarding child protection practices in Norway. These were already highlighted by the minority among those judges who found a violation in the Strand Lobben case.

Under the Norwegian Child Welfare Act, the requirements for taking a child into public care are strict. Situations described in the Act encompass abuse, serious violence and serious neglect, including with regard to personal contact and security. Thus, the family situation of a child who is taken into care has been harmful and, due to the treatment the child has been exposed to, the child has a complicated relationship with its parents. Some children have not been able to form a stable attachment to their parents. I see this as an important backdrop for discussing the ECtHR judgments and their implications for decisions during alternative care in relation to children's rights.

The cases are brought to the ECtHR by the parents, and children's rights do not come to the forefront. This does not mean they are irrelevant in this context. Important rights that should be safeguarded by the child protection system are the right to protection, care and health, all of which are linked to the right to development. However, the child has a right to family life and not to be separated from its parents under the UN Convention on the Rights of the Child (CRC) as well. When harmonising the rights of the child, the best interests of the child is a useful concept, including the child's own views as an essential element. In reaching the final solution, the rights and best interests of the child should be balanced with those of the parents. In this balancing exercise, the weight of the child's best interests is of the essence.

In this chapter, I will start by outlining the reunification goal as set out by the ECtHR in cases against Norway over the last few years. Subsequently, I present the Norwegian Supreme Court's interpretation and adaptation of the judgments, followed by an account of more recent practice in these cases. A separate section will be dedicated to explaining children's rights in this area more in depth. I will go on to discuss the approach to the child's best interests by the ECtHR and Norwegian decision-makers, before concluding.

The European Court of Human Rights: the reunification goal and contact

The reunification goal implies that taking a child into care should be seen as a temporary measure to be ended as soon as reasonably feasible (Strand Lobben, 2019, para 205). Under Article 8 of the ECHR, no interference in family life is acceptable unless it is deemed necessary. When the grounds leading to placement are no longer present or no longer sufficiently strong to justify the placement of the child in alternative care, it is unproportional and thus unnecessary.

In order to facilitate the child's return to its parents, the authorities have a positive duty to take measures for this purpose. The duty weighs on the authorities with progressively increasing force from the beginning of the period of care (Strand Lobben, 2019, para 208). To uphold the reunification goal it is essential to facilitate contact between the parents and the child. This was emphasised in the concurring opinion of six judges out of the 13 that found a violation in the Strand Lobben case (Strand Lobben, 2019, concurring opinion by Judge Ranzoni et al, para 6).[1] While the majority of seven found a violation on procedural grounds, the concurring opinion went straight to the substantive issue of reunification and stated that the goal was absent from the outset of the domestic proceedings (Strand Lobben, 2019, concurring opinion by Judge Ranzoni et al, para 4). Only a few months after the care order, when the child was still less than six months old, the decision-making Board envisaged that the child would grow up in the foster home and that the foster parents would become the child's psychological parents. Contact with the biological mother should not disrupt the attachment process to the foster parents. Thus, the purpose of contact was not to 'establish a relationship with a view to the child's future return' (Strand Lobben, 2019, para 5).

In later judgments, the ECtHR has explicitly found a violation with regard to contact, see, for example, K.O. and V.M. (2019), M.L. (2020) and Abdi Ibrahim (2021). The amount of contact stipulated in these cases was four (or less) to six times a year, which 'rendered impossible the development of any meaningful relationship' (M.L., 2020, para 93), between mother and child and was seen by the ECtHR as 'a complete and definite severance of the ties' between them (Abdi Ibrahim, 2021, para 162).

Thus, the authorities may not presume at an early stage that the placement will be permanent or long-term and stipulate contact accordingly. Contact should be stipulated in support of the reunification goal. Furthermore, the decision should be based on an individual assessment of each case and not rely on a norm of a certain (limited) number of sessions per year. Regarding the frequency of sessions, the ECtHR has stated that intervals of weeks, or even months, between each contact session do not normally support the reunification goal (K.O. and V.M. v Norway, 2019, para 94).

The limit, according to ECtHR, is that contact may not expose the child to undue hardship (K.O. and V.M. v Norway, 2019, para 79). However, strong evidence and reasoning is needed if this is used to argue that the child cannot have more than a few contact sessions per year. A claim of undue hardship will often be related to the child's being particularly vulnerable. However, according to Strand Lobben, if the child's vulnerability is used as an argument, it has to be based on a proper assessment and analysis of the facts of the case (Strand Lobben, 2019, para 224). An expert evaluation may be needed, or an already existing one may need updating (Strand Lobben, 2019, paras 224–225).

The Supreme Court's interpretation and adaptation

The Supreme Court of Norway in March 2020 rendered three principled decisions concerning the interpretation and follow-up of the ECtHR judgments. The decisions emphasised the reunification goal while at the same time making clear that the goal is already reflected in Norwegian law, as a care order is supposed to be a temporary measure. However, the Court acknowledged that the goal does not appear clearly from practice in alternative care cases.

Importantly, the Court followed up the signals from the ECtHR regarding contact, stating that it should be determined on a case-by-case basis and not according to a norm. Moreover, the distinction between short- and long-term placements previously used as a guideline in relation to contact should no longer guide contact decisions. Norwegian authorities should not make contact dependent on the anticipated length of a care order. According to Norwegian practice up to the ECtHR judgments, in long-term placements the child would only need to have so much (or little) contact as to retain a knowledge of its parents. Based on psychological theory, to secure their emotional development, children without a proper attachment to their parents needed to form an attachment to their foster parents. In legal terms, the distinction between long-term and short-term placements and subsequent determination of contact was based on a Supreme Court judgment of 1998, reiterated by a judgment of 2012, which, according to the Supreme Court in 2020, had been misunderstood (Norwegian Supreme Court, 2019b).

A reservation is necessary with regard to what has just been said about not anticipating the duration of a placement. The Supreme Court has held that in choosing a placement for a child in alternative care, one may take into account that the placement probably will be long-term (Norwegian Supreme Court, 2019a). The possibility to find foster parents who are willing and able to keep the child for a longer time is important, as long as it does not influence the frequency of contact with the parents. Even in determining contact, the Supreme Court has stated that the duration of the care order is one of the elements that may be considered. Although not decisive, it is relevant (Norwegian Supreme Court, 2020a, paras 52–58).

Another reservation needs to be made regarding the ECtHR's discouragement of having a rule of thumb for how many contact meetings there should be. Under the Child Welfare Act, contact may only be strongly limited or totally denied where there are strong and special grounds (Child Welfare Act, 2021, section 7–2). This requirement was originally set out by the Supreme Court based on the ECtHR's term 'extraordinary circumstances' and is considered to have the same content. To know when the requirement is applicable, there is a need to establish the meaning of 'strongly limited' in the Child Welfare Act. In that regard, the Supreme Court has stated that the level of contact should be above eight times a year where the reunification goal is retained and the child's interests do not dictate less (Norwegian Supreme Court 2020b, para 56). Thus, a rule of thumb on how much contact there should be is made after all.

The criterion set out by the ECtHR that contact should not expose the child to undue hardship has been criticised for implying that it is acceptable for the child to be exposed to some hardship, which may not be in the best interests of the child. However, the Supreme Court clarified that the amount of contact should not be close to the limit of what is undue, because in no circumstance may contact be prescribed that will harm the child's health or development (Norwegian Supreme Court, 2019b, para

134). Later, the Supreme Court has stated that the contact arrangement, all things considered, should be in accordance with the child's best interests (Norwegian Supreme Court, 2020c, para 38). The latter approach holds the best interests as a positive goal to reach, rather than a bottom line of what a child should tolerate.

Another important clarification made by the Supreme Court concerns the possibility of abandoning the reunification goal. Based on the ECtHR's own jurisprudence, the Supreme Court has indicated three alternative situations where the goal may be abandoned. These may operate independently but also be intertwined. The three situations are: (1) where the parents are particularly unfit; (2) where a measure may harm the child's health and development; and (3) where considerable time has passed since the child was taken into care and the child's need for stability weighs more heavily than the aim of reunification (Norwegian Supreme Court, 2019a, paras 146–147).

Changes in practice

Two extensive research reports have been published on the practice of decision-making bodies after the ECtHR judgments and the Supreme Court's clarifications. The first of them, from November 2021 (Alvik, 2021), is a qualitative study of 37 decisions from the first instance court-assembling Child Protection Boards and 32 Court of Appeal judgments.[2] The decisions and judgments were all rendered in 2020, after the Supreme Court decisions that clarified the law as explained earlier. The second one, published in March 2023, combines the just mentioned text research with a survey to case managers in the child welfare services mapping the extent of visitation and how it was practised in 525 cases, a quantitative online study involving a questionnaire to children, parents and foster parents, and a qualitative case study with interviews with children, parents, foster parents, supervisors and case managers (Stang et al, 2023). The main impression from the reports is that practice has been adjusted according to the guidelines from the ECtHR as interpreted and adapted by the Supreme Court.

According to the studies, decisions no longer state that a placement will be long-term even where the facts indicate that it will be. The reunification goal is hardly ever explicitly abandoned, although the Supreme Court, based on the ECtHR's judgments, made an opening for doing that. If it happens, it is with a very thorough reasoning. The research also shows that contact is determined on a case-by-case basis and is much more frequent than before.

The latter report provides a much more complex picture of contact arrangements than what appears from the ECtHR decisions and the subsequent public debate. The general picture left by the ECtHR judgments is that very little contact is granted. However, there is in fact considerable variation in the frequency of contact and the ways in which contact is practised, and the survey results show that many contact arrangements seem to work well for children, parents and foster parents. Probably the researchers are right in assuming that where contact arrangements work well for all those involved, they are not brought to court (Stang et al, 2023, p 18). Thus, these types of cases will not reach the ECtHR.

Many of the children participating in an online study of contact arrangements in the same report said they wanted to be more involved in the formulation of the obligatory contact plan (Stang et al, 2023, p 19), which is where the contact arrangements are planned in more detail. This resonates well with a report from the Change Factory based on interviews with 100 children in care about contact with their parents (Forandringsfabrikken, 2021). One of the most striking features was that to children themselves, the details of the contact arrangements – where will we be, who will be present, what will we do – is much more important than the scope (frequency and length) of the contact sessions.

While the reports mainly praise Norwegian child protection decision-makers for having adapted to the signals from the ECtHR, they also express a cautious concern. On the positive side, they find that decisions on contact are thorough and specific to the individual case and that relevant considerations are taken into account and balanced in a fair way. Where the goal of reunification in a minority of the cases is abandoned, it is done with a reasoning that seems to be in line with ECtHR and Supreme Court decisions.

Nevertheless, a concern is raised regarding the fact that the reunification goal is abandoned in so few cases, although the facts of the case and the child's situation may point in that direction. In cases where the child's reactions to contact are strong, the child has developed a strong attachment to the foster family, or it seems obvious that the parents will not in the foreseeable future be able to care for the child, the researchers indicate that the requirements for abandoning the goal may have been satisfied (Alvik, 2021).

Another concern relates to the threshold for establishing that contact will expose the child to undue hardship, where there seems to be an uncertainty among decision-makers (Alvik, 2021). Yet, as the researcher says, it is neither possible nor desirable to set a clear, general limit, as all cases must be considered individually. Many factors are relevant and what seems to be undue hardship in one case may not be undue in another case. Clearly, the threshold of undue hardship should not be too high, and never so high that the child's health or development is harmed (Alvik, 2021, p 37). However, very few of the decisions examined problematise the relationship between the requirement of due hardship and the best interests of the child. In some decisions, the facts as described, including the child's reactions, views and the parents' ability to cooperate, give reason to believe that the contact prescribed is close to the limit of what the child can endure (Alvik, 2021, p 135). According to the Supreme Court, this should not be the case (HR-2020–662-S, para 134).

Where the child has been exposed to serious violence, this is given great weight in the determination of contact, at least by the Child Protection Boards, provided there has been a criminal conviction or another court decision establishing it as a fact. Where that is not the case, the Boards seem reluctant to discuss the occurrence of violence and whether the evidence is strong enough. If the Boards had discussed it and arrived at the conclusion that the child had been exposed to violence, the report suggests that it might have led to the reunification goal being abandoned (Alvik, 2021, pp 135–136). This is interesting in the light of the ECtHR being criticised for considering cases of physical violence differently (and as being more serious) than emotional neglect (NOU 2023: 7, para 2.2.8).

Children's rights in this context

Introduction

In the preceding discussion of the ECtHR judgments, Supreme Court decisions and changes in practice, there have been some hints of how the jurisprudence and practice relate to children's rights, although not explicitly. In this section, I will present the most relevant rights of the child in relation to alternative care, primarily based on the CRC.

As mentioned in the introduction, the backdrop to the cases before the ECtHR is a decision to place a child in alternative care. In Norway, it is generally considered to be in the interests of children, parents and society that children grow up with their parents (NOU 1985: 18, p 157). For this reason, and because children and parents have a right to family life, a decision to place a child in public care cannot be made unless strong requirements are fulfilled. Those requirements are laid down in the Child Welfare Act and have been accepted by the ECtHR as sufficient legal basis for intervening in family life under Article 8 (2). In the following, I will introduce the child's right to protection from all forms of maltreatment and their right to health and development, before presenting their right to family life. Finally, I will focus on the child's views and best interests.

Freedom from violence and right to care

The requirements in the Child Welfare Act are closely linked to the right of the child under the CRC to be protected from all forms of violence (see UN Committee on the Rights of the Child, 2011, title and paras 7(e), 71).[3] In the words of Article 19 (1), the state is under the obligation 'to protect the child from all forms of physical or mental violence, injury or abuse, neglect or negligent treatment, maltreatment or exploitation, including sexual abuse, while in the care of parent(s)'. The obligation includes taking 'all appropriate legislative, administrative, social and educational measures' for this purpose, further detailed in No. 2 of the same article. Thus, where there is no other measure that will provide the child with sufficient protection, the state may have an obligation to place a child in alternative care. And, consequently, the child should not be returned to their parents if it may expose the child to maltreatment once more. In relation to contact, it is a right of the child not to be exposed to any maltreatment during contact with parents or others.

The child also has a right under Article 3 (2) to 'such protection and care as is necessary for his or her well-being'. The provision is formulated in a positive way, implying that not only should the treatment of the child stay above a certain minimum level, it should also contribute to the child's well-being. The child should be able to enjoy life here and now. This is an important reminder in discussing the limits of contact. If contact with their parents exposes a child to a certain degree of hardship, it is acceptable in the eyes of the ECtHR as long as the hardship is not undue. However, will such contact contribute to the child's well-being? Similarly, when considering whether the reunification goal should be abandoned, the child's right under Article 3 (2) should be taken into account. Some children living with foster parents have a strong fear of being returned to their biological parents, or even of the issue being brought up.[4] In such cases, it might be more in line with their right to the care necessary for their well-being to abandon that goal.

Or perhaps adoption, which is mentioned in the CRC Article 20 as an acceptable form of alternative care, would in some cases provide the child with precisely what they need for their well-being. One might object that adoption is not about the 'care' necessary for their well-being, as they already are in the care of their foster parents who would then adopt them.[5] However, care is a broad term which includes the issue of stability and belonging. For some children, adoption is necessary to obtain that.

Right to health

Children's right to health under the CRC Article 24 deserves an obvious place in this picture. We already heard that parents are not entitled to contact, or any other measure, that would harm the child's health or development (see more about development in the remainder of the chapter) (Strand Lobben, 2019, para 207). The child's health includes physical and psychological aspects. The Committee on the Rights of the Child underlines the importance of a child rights approach to health, that all children have the right to opportunities to survive, grow and develop, within the context of physical, emotional and social well-being, to each child's full potential (UN Committee on the Rights of the Child, 2013).[6] Thus, psycho-social aspects that may affect the child's health are included. Among determinants to be considered, the Committee mentions those at work in the immediate environment of families (UN Committee on the Rights of the Child, 2013, para 17). Circumstances connected to the family situation while the child is in public care may well have effects on the child's mental health. This is not only about possible harmful contact with parents but may also be about the lack of contact with parents, siblings or other family members. Other factors affecting the child's health are conflicts between parents and foster parents, and the child's own feeling of being in a squeeze between them, feeling loyalty to both. Cooperation between all the adults in this picture – parents, foster parents and child protection services – is key to promoting the child's mental health in this situation (Barneombudet, 2023; Stang et al, 2023). Not least, it is essential to involve the child in shaping the contact arrangements.

Right to development

An overarching right in respect of the child's right to protection, care, health and so on is the right of the child to development. The right to life and development under Article 6 has been identified by the Committee on the Rights of the Child as one of the four general principles of the CRC (UN Committee on the Rights of the Child, 2003, para 12; 2009, para 2; 2013b, para 1), meaning that it should be taken into account in the interpretation and implementation of all articles in the Convention. One of the defining characteristics of childhood is that the child is in development. If the child's right to protection, care and health are not taking seriously, the long-term consequence may be that the child's development is undermined. True, the child as a being here and now, with their experiences and feelings, is important, yet developing is also an essential aspect of being a child. The child should not only be seen as 'becoming' but it should also not be overlooked, and General Comment No. 5 states: 'The Committee expects States to interpret "development" in its broadest sense as a holistic concept, embracing the child's physical, mental, spiritual, moral, psychological and social development. Implementation measures should be aimed at achieving the optimal development for all children.' Taking the child's development seriously does not run counter to the signals from the ECtHR. However, drawing the line by what is harmful to the child's development is not ambitious enough. Fulfilling the child's right to development is not just a question of avoiding harm, but of facilitating or even promoting that the child may develop in a positive way.

Right to family life

The child has a right to family life under Article 16, which is similar to Article 8 (1) of the ECHR. The preamble of the Convention emphasises the value for the child of growing up in a family, recognising that 'the child, for the full and harmonious development of his or her personality, should grow up in a family environment, in an atmosphere of happiness, love and understanding'. For this purpose, the preamble also states that the family, as the natural environment for the growth and well-being of children, should be afforded the necessary protection and assistance. Thus, it is not true, as held by some, that the CRC promotes the child as a person separated from their surroundings and is family unfriendly.

However, when the atmosphere in the family is not one of happiness as described in the preamble, the child has the right to protection and extra support as presented earlier. In certain instances, this may imply being removed from a detrimental family situation. Under Article 9 (1), the child has a right not to be separated from their parents unless certain conditions are fulfilled. The conditions for separating a child from their parents under Article 9 (1) are similar to those under Article 8 (2) ECHR. Such interference with family life must have a basis in law, it shall have the child's best interests as its aim, and it must be necessary for that purpose. If the child is separated from one or both parents, the child has the right under Article 9 (3) to maintain personal relations and direct contact with both parents on a regular basis. This is not unlike what the ECtHR has expressed in its judgments against Norway, but the CRC states it explicitly in the Convention text. Accordingly, the CRC is family friendly and there need not be a conflict between the ECHR and the CRC.

Also, growing up in a family does not necessarily mean the child's biological family. When the child has lived for some time in a foster family, they may have developed a family life with each other, which deserves respect under the conventions. Both Article 16 CRC and Article 8 ECHR recognise that a social or de facto family may be protected. The Committee on the Rights of the Child has interpreted the term family 'in a broad sense to include biological, adoptive or foster parents' (UN Committee on the Rights of the Child, 2013, para 59). According to the ECtHR, family life is 'essentially a question of fact depending upon the real existence in practice of close personal ties' (K. and T. v Finland, 2001). It depends on elements such as the time spent together, the quality of the relationship and the role that the adult has taken on vis-à-vis the child (Moretti and Benedetti v Italy, 2010, para 48). If they have developed a family life in this sense, it should mean that the reunification goal loses some of its strength. The family life between the child and its foster parents should be taken into account in considering whether to return a child to their biological parents and in decisions on adoption. However, there is little trace of this thinking in the ECtHR decisions in child protection cases against Norway.

Best interests and the child's views

Once a decision is to be made on these issues, the child's best interests shall be a primary consideration (see Article 3 (1)). This is one of the Convention's general principles. What is in the child's best interests has to be considered on an individual basis and with a number of elements taken into account, all of which should be assessed for this particular child in their specific situation. At the stage of deciding whether a child should go into alternative care, the child's right to protection and care will invariably be in conflict with the child's right to family life. However, rather than seeing this as a conflict impossible to solve, the decision-maker should consider how to safeguard the child while at the same time upholding the right to family life. If it is not possible to provide a child with adequate protection and care in the biological family, the right to family life of the child with that family will have to be implemented through contact sessions. Here, I speak about the child's rights. How they are to be balanced with the right to family life of the parents is the topic of section 'The ECtHR and the child's best interests'.

A crucial factor in making decisions affecting children, not least in assessing and determining the child's best interests, is the child's own views. Article 12 CRC, giving the child a right to express their views and have them duly taken into account, is another general principle of the CRC and thus important in implementing all of the rights of the child. Importantly, children should not only be heard but listened to. The hearing should not be tokenistic (UN Committee on the Rights of the Child, 2009). A common complaint from children is that adults want to hear their views but do not take them seriously. In relation to decisions within the child protection system, listening to children should be self-evident, as the decisions first and foremost concern those children's lives – at present and in the future. Contact arrangements will not work if they are decided without the child's views being heard and taken into account (see earlier paragraph on changes in practice). The child's own views are generally not given much attention in the ECtHR judgments.

In its 2023 report, a Commission appointed by the Norwegian government proposed that all children in child protection cases, before and during alternative care, should have an independent representative whose only responsibility would be the child and the child's interests. The representative should make sure that the child is heard in a proper way and assist the child in the process (NOU 2023: 7, 2023, chapter 7).

If a child living with foster parents wants to be reassured that this is where she will spend her childhood, it should be possible to give that reassurance, be it in the form of explicitly abandoning the reunification goal or more formally by giving the foster parents the parental responsibility for the duration of the child's childhood or even by adoption. Transferring parental responsibility to foster parents is possible in Sweden, but not in Norway at present. This was one of the proposals of the just-mentioned Commission (see NOU 2023: 7). Perhaps such a solution would be more acceptable to the ECtHR than adoption.

The European Court of Human Rights and the child's best interests

In the judgments of the ECtHR, the content of the child's best interests consists of two main components (see Neulinger and Shuruk v Switzerland, 2010).[7] On the one hand, to maintain the family ties, on the other to ensure the child's development in a sound environment and thus parents are not entitled to anything that may harm the child (Strand Lobben, 2019, para 207). The latter limitation is important; however, one may ask if the ECtHR sees the child's best interests as synonymous with avoiding harm. If that is so, it is too narrow an understanding. The term 'best interests of the child' aims at obtaining the 'best' or optimal solution from the perspective of the child, not just to avoid harm. Only after determining what is in the best interests of the child may those interests be balanced with those of the parents. Without a clear and correct view of how to assess and determine the child's best interests, the decision-maker is not able to do the balancing exercise in a proper way.

In that exercise, the child's best interests are weighted against the parents' right to family life in order to find a 'fair balance' between them. As for the weight of the best interests of the child, the ECtHR states at a general level that they should be paramount, which more than fulfils the requirement of Article 3 CRC that they should be a primary consideration. More specifically, the ECtHR holds that 'in cases involving care of children and contact restrictions, the child's interests must come before all other considerations' (Strand Lobben, 2019, para 204). However, looking more closely at the Court's concrete assessment of the cases, this general assumption seems hardly to be reflected. The requirements for restricting contact or accepting adoption are so strict that they are very difficult to fulfil, even where it may seem to be in the best interests of the child to make a decision contrary to the parents' wish.

It is hard to disentangle whether it is in considering the content or the weight of the child's best interests that the ECtHR downplays the rights and interests of the child. I already mentioned that avoiding harm does not do justice to the concept of the child's best interests. In addition, the Court takes as a starting point – regarding the content of the child's best interests – that only in very exceptional circumstances may family ties be severed. This makes me wonder whether the parents' right to family life spills over into the understanding of the child's best interests.

Norwegian practice before the ECtHR judgments may have gone too far in one direction, and this may be part of the explanation for the decisions against Norway. In its response, however, the ECtHR may have gone too far in the opposite direction. There is reason to ask whether Norwegian authorities (child protection services, boards and courts), in adjusting their practice, follow the signals from the ECtHR too strictly and thus end up placing too little weight on the child's rights and interests.

Conclusion

Based on the right to family life of both parents and children, the ECtHR has a family-oriented approach to child protection cases, its main goal being to optimise family life within the biological family. Yet, as explained earlier, the CRC also emphasises the family as being important to the child. At the outset there is no conflict between the two conventions in this regard or between the rights and interests of children and parents.

However, the ECtHR seems to presume that the parents and the child continue to share the same interests after the child has been taken into alternative care. This is not self-evident when the reason for taking a child into public care is the parents' abuse or serious neglect of the child, as required by Norwegian law. In these circumstances, the preconditions for optimising family life are no longer present. Because of the parents' treatment of the child, they cannot live together, at least for the time being. How is it possible, then, to assume that they share the same interest in being together as much as practicable? In all fairness, the ECtHR does not explicitly say that their interests are the same, as it speaks about 'balancing the interests'. However, the Court seems not to take into account the difficult relationship between the parents and the child, which was actually the reason for the child being taken into care. The Norwegian decisions have been criticised for focusing too narrowly on the child's interests (Strand Lobben, 2019).[8] One may ask if, rather, the ECtHR focuses too narrowly on the parents' interests, when the Court apparently does not recognise that the situation in these families is different from the situation in families where there has not been reason to take the child into care.

As child protection cases are brought before the ECtHR by the parents, it is their right to family life that is tried. Children's rights are under-communicated in the cases, and the child's best interests only appear in the proportionality assessment of whether the interference with the parents' family life is necessary. This is an unfortunate situation which may probably only be improved by Norwegian authorities emphasising children's rights more strongly than today. Along these lines, the Supreme Court has emphasised the national authorities' obligation to find a solution that is in the child's best interests at present and in the future. Recognising that their perspective is different, the ECtHR actually has accepted this (M.L. v Norway, 2020).[9] The child's right to protection, proper care, health and development might also be brought to the forefront more explicitly by Norwegian child protection services, boards and courts.

On a positive note, in 2024 the ECtHR published 20 decisions on child protection cases brought against Norway, dismissing all of them as manifestly ill-founded. The decisions were made by a committee of three members that only applied the principles already established by previous judgments. Still, by describing the facts of the cases and the reasoning in the Norwegian decisions, they shed light on the present legal status. As all the Norwegian judgments in question were rendered in late 2021 or 2022, for example, after Strand Lobben and the subsequent ECtHR cases, the dismissals show that the reasoning of the Norwegian courts was sufficient to convince the ECtHR judges that the interference with the family life of the parents was justified. This may not seem so surprising since, as mentioned, practice in Norway has been adjusted to the strong signals from the ECtHR and may even be going too far. However, in some of the recent decisions the ECtHR accepted that contact had been limited to a few hours six times per year, including in cases based on emotional neglect from the parents. In one decision the Court even accepted adoption, but in that case, there had been violence in the family which the Court has more easily accepted as a justification for interference in earlier cases as well. Encouragingly, explicit reference to the child's own view was made in some of the ECtHR decisions.

These decisions appear to be more positive to safeguarding the rights of the individual child than the previous ECtHR judgments. A gradual change in this direction, based on thorough documentation and careful reasoning by Norwegian authorities and courts, is a welcome development.

Notes

[1] The majority also criticises the limited contact, but only in relation to using the contact sessions as evidence of the poor relationship between them (Strand Lobben, 2019, para 221).

[2] The Child Protection and Health Boards (earlier called County Boards) have been considered by the ECtHR to fulfill the criteria of being a court under Article 6 ECHR (NOU, 2017: 8). Board decisions may be appealed to the City Court and then, provided leave is given, to the Court of Appeal (High Court).

[3] See UN Committee on the Rights of the Child, General Comment No. 13 (2011), title and paras 7(e), 71.

[4] Like the girl in HR-2022-2292-A where the reunification goal was not abandoned.

[5] In Norway, only those who are already foster parents of a child may adopt them.

[6] UN Committee on the Rights of the Child (2013) on the right of the child to the enjoyment of the highest attainable standard of health (Article 24), CRC/C/GC/15, para 1. The Committee refers to the World Health Organization's definition of health as a state of complete physical, mental and social well-being and not merely the absence of disease or infirmity, see UN Committee on the Rights of the Child (2013), para 4, with reference to the preamble to the Constitution of the World Health Organization as adopted by the International Health Conference, New York, 22 July 1946.

[7] In earlier judgments called 'limbs', see for example, Neulinger and Shuruk v Switzerland (Grand Chamber, 2010), para 136.

[8] Strand Lobben (2019), para 220, 'focused on the child's interests instead of trying to combine both sets of interests'.

[9] M.L. v Norway (2020), para 98.

References

Abdi Ibrahim v Norway [GC] (no. 15379/16) [2021] ECtHR (10 December).

Alvik, I. (2021) 'Samvær etter omsorgsovertakelse. En undersøkelse av praksis fra fylkesnemnder og lagmannsretter [Access after taking care of children. A survey of practice from county boards and courts of appeal]', *OsloMet skriftserie 4/21*, OsloMet – storbyuniversitetet. Available from: https://skriftserien.oslomet.no/index.php/skriftserien/article/view/753

Barneombudet (2023) 'Blod er ikke alltid tykkere enn vann [Blood is not always thicker than water]', Rapport om barn i fosterhjem.

Child Welfare Act (2021) *Lov om barnevern (barnevernloven)*, Barne- og familiedepartementet.

Forandringsfabrikken (2021) 'Det handler om oss. 100 barn 7–18 år om samvær i barnevernet [It's about us. 100 children aged 7–18 about visitation in child welfare]', Forandringsfabrikken Kunnskapssenter.

K. and T. v Finland [GC] (no. 25702/94) [2001] ECtHR 32 (12 July).

K.O. and V.M. v Norway (no. 64808/16) [2019] ECtHR (19 November).

M.L. v Norway (no. 64639/16) [2020] ECtHR (22 December).

Moretti and Benedetti v Italy (no. 16318/07) [2010] ECtHR 129 (27 April).

Neulinger and Shuruk v Switzerland [GC] (no. 41615/07) [2010] ECtHR (6 July).

Norwegian Supreme Court (2019a) *Judgment in the case HR-2020–661-S (No. 00–0000001SIV-HRET)*.

Norwegian Supreme Court (2019b) *Judgment in the case HR-2020–662-S (No. 00–000000SIV-HRET)*.

Norwegian Supreme Court (2020a) *Judgment in the case HR-2021–474-A (No. 20–140524SIV-HRET)*.

Norwegian Supreme Court (2020b) *Judgment in the case HR-2021–1437-A (No. 21–016374SIV-HRET)*.

Norwegian Supreme Court (2020c) *Judgment in the case HR-2021–475-A (No. 20–137359SIV-HRET)*.

NOU 1985: 18 (1958) 'Lov om sosiale tjenester m.v. [Act on Social Services etc.]', Norwegian Official Reports.

NOU 2017: 8 (2017) 'Særdomstoler på nye områder? [Special courts in new areas?]', Utredning fra utvalg oppnevnt ved kongelig resolusjon 7. mai 2015, Avgitt til Justis- og beredskapsdepartementet og Barne- og likestillingsdepartementet 9. mars 2017.

NOU 2023: 7 (2023) 'Trygg barndom, sikker fremtid – Gjennomgang av rettssikkerheten for barn og foreldre i barnevernet [Safe childhood, secure future – review of legal protection for children and parents in child welfare services]', Utredning fra et utvalg oppnevnt ved kongelig resolusjon 19. mars 2021, Avgitt til Barne- og familiedepartementet 20, mars 2023.

Stang, E.G., Baugerud, G.A., Backe-Hansen, E. and Rugkåsa, M. (2023) 'Samvær i praksis. En forskningsbasert undersøkelse av samværsordninger i barnevernet [Visitation in practice. A research-based study of visitation arrangements in child welfare]', Hovedrapport fra prosjektet 'Samvær etter omsorgsovertakelse', OsloMet skriftserie 1/23, OsloMet – storbyuniversitetet. Available from: https://skriftserien.oslomet.no/index.php/skriftserien/article/view/802

Strand Lobben and Others v Norway [GC] (no. 37283/13) [2019] ECtHR (10 September).

UN Committee on the Rights of the Child (2003) General Comment No. 5: General measures of implementation of the Convention on the Rights of the Child (arts. 4, 42 and 44, para 6), CRC/GC/2003/5.

UN Committee on the Rights of the Child (2009) General Comment No. 12: The right of the child to be heard, CRC/C/GC/12. Available from: https://www.refworld.org/legal/general/crc/2009/en/70207

UN Committee on the Rights of the Child (2011) General Comment No. 13: The right of the child to freedom from all forms of violence, CRC/C/GC/13. GE.11. Available from: https://www.refworld.org/legal/general/crc/2011/en/82269

UN Committee on the Rights of the Child (2013[[a]]) General Comment No. 14 on the right of the child to have his or her best interests taken as a primary consideration (art. 3, para 1), CRC/C/GC/14. Available from: https://www2.ohchr.org/english/bodies/crc/docs/gc/crc_c_gc_14_eng.pdf

UN Committee on the Rights of the Child (2013[[b]]) General Comment No. 15 on the right of the child to the enjoyment of the highest attainable standard of health (art. 24), CRC/C/GC/15. Available from: https://www.refworld.org/legal/general/crc/2013/en/96127

5

Implementing international human rights case law at the domestic street level: the case of Norwegian child protection

Hege Stein Helland

Introduction

The European Court of Human Rights (ECtHR) has become an increasingly relevant source of legal doctrine for European democracies. As the interpreter of the European Convention on Human Rights (ECHR), the Court is an authority in monitoring and correcting states' enforcement of citizens' human rights, including in child protection (Janis et al, 2008; Fenton-Glynn, 2021). From 2015 until the end of 2024, the ECtHR communicated 80 complaints concerning child protection to the Norwegian government.[1] Among these cases, 78 have been decided, and Norway has been found to have violated ECHR Article 8 on the right to private and family life in an astonishing 23 cases (see Emberland, Chapter 2). The collective criticism in these judgments signals a need for state action and systematic amendments to existing praxis. But, have the judgments led to actual changes in child protection practice in Norway?

While there is a generous scholarship on the implementation and impact of European law on administrative and bureaucratic action (Versluis, 2007; Treib, 2014; Martinsen, 2015; Dörrenbächer, 2017; 2018), of international case law on national legal order and policy (Conant, 2002; Anagnostou, 2013; Stiansen, 2021), and of case law's indirect or 'radiating effects' on policy makers, social actors or civil society (Galanter, 1983; Anagnostou and Fokas, 2015; Fokas and Anagnostou, 2019), less is known about the domestic impact of international courts' case law on public administration or bureaucracies (Treib, 2014; cf Greer and Iniesta, 2014; Szot, 2016; Martinsen et al, 2019). This study contributes to unpacking the black box of the impact of international judicial policy on street-level bureaucracies. Specifically, I investigate if the judgments from the ECtHR have led to adjustments in child protection practice and what factors have influenced the process of implementing this case law in local agencies, as experienced by 14 managers in larger child protection agencies (CWS) in Norway. The study employs a bottom-up approach to implementation and is theoretically informed by the literature on organisations and judicial impact (Canon and Johnson, 1999; Canon, 2004), as well as insights from street-level implementation theory (Lipsky, 1980; Winter and Nielsen, 2008).

The chapter is structured as follows: First, judicial impact is introduced as part of discretionary policy implementation, emphasising the crucial role of managers in this process. Then, judicial implementation is operationalised, and a theoretical framework is offered for understanding what shapes implementation in bureaucratic organisations. A presentation and discussion of the findings follow the methods. Lastly, a conclusion is provided.

Discretion and implementation of judicial policies

The domestic impact of international judicial decisions encompasses a broad spectrum of actions and events following a court judgment. It embodies both intended and unintended reactions and implications, such as behavioural or structural adjustments of those actors that fall within the ambit of the court decision (Kapiszewski and Taylor, 2013). In a narrow sense, such actions can be seen as 'the behaviour of lower courts, government agencies, or other affected parties as it relates to enforcing a judicial decision', denoting the process of judicial *implementation* (Canon and Johnson, 1999, pp 14–15). Canon and Johnson (1999, p 2) argue that '[a]lthough judicial policies differ from legislative actions and executive orders in their origin, they are also public policies: they too must be implemented before disputes or problems are resolved, and they have an impact on the public'.[2]

Judicial implementation, in other words, is similar to public policy implementation (Baum, 1976). When an international court issues a judgment regarding a specific agency or policy area, it relies on the national governments to enforce or implement its rulings. Following the logic of the bureaucratic 'chain of command', it is the national state apparatus and the judicial system that are responsible for interpreting the ECtHR and enacting corresponding actions. However, it is the street-level bureaucrats who are tasked with implementing changes and policies issued by a principal. As such, the final and necessary policy-making stage occurs at the bureaucratic street level, where social workers deliver services and make intrusive decisions based on the discretionary application of general rules in individual cases (Lipsky, 1980). Child protection managers and social workers have the power and freedom to shape and transform policies into service delivery – the policy output (Baum, 1976; Winter and Nielsen, 2008). They are the 'implementing population' of judicial policies or directives (Canon and Johnson, 1999). Therefore, policy implementation and output are best measured by investigating discretionary behaviour at the street level, specifically through managers – the agents whose interpretations, preferences and leadership abilities contribute to shaping policy outcomes (Lipsky, 1980; Brehm and Gates, 1997; Vinzant and Crothers, 1998; Canon and Johnson, 1999). As authoritative figures in the organisation, managers are in a vital position to facilitate organisational change at the street level. They mediate and control implementation, acting as attitudinal role models (Keulemans and Groeneveld, 2020).

Judicial implementation and change

As with all forms of policies, judicial policies are not self-implementing and depend on the interpretation and application of street-level bureaucrats (Spriggs, 1996). Canon and Johnson's (1999) framework for understanding the implementation of court judgments embodies three sets of bureaucratic reactive activities: (1) interpretation; (2) searching; and (3) change. In the first step, implementers interpret how judgments apply to their agency, what demands they set for change, and decide whether to accept or reject the decision. The second step builds on the initial interpretation, and implementers search for ways to meet or bypass the demands for change. This includes exploring alternative agency responses and their potential implications. The third step concerns agency change or adjustments to bureaucratic policies, procedures and praxis. Presumably, the agency's reaction to and decision to accept or reject the decision influences the implementation trajectory, although it is not the only factor that explains change or lack thereof.

On the one hand, I expect that the type of channels and clarity in which judgments are communicated to the frontline matter for how it is implemented and for what changes are initiated (Canon and Johnson, 1999). Communication is defined broadly as the transmission of judicial judgment(s) through domestic authoritative superiors' regulation and directives, understood as 'domestic signalling'; how political, administrative and judicial superiors signal their interpretation, content and importance of a judicial policy (Winter and Nielsen, 2008; Martinsen et al, 2019). Various studies have demonstrated that signalling can provide direction (Brehm and Gates, 1997) and limit the discretion of street-level decision-makers while implementing a policy (Banks and Weingast, 1992). Providing clear direction for interpretation reduces discretion and increases consistency in service delivery. This is particularly relevant as street-level implementation is found to be more influenced by immediate superiors, in other words, domestic authoritative institutions (May and Winter, 2009). Signals may include public statements, proposals for legislative reform (political superiors); guidelines, circulars, operational memoranda, directives, codes and oral instructions (soft law), educational seminars, regular monitoring of street-level decisions (regional or national administrative superiors); domestic courts or quasi-judicial bodies interpretations of ECtHR case law in their application ECHR doctrine to the facts of individual cases (judicial superiors). The role of domestic authorities and the judiciary in implementing change is thus assumed to be one of direct influence through legal interpretation (case law) and enforcement of new laws and regulations, as well as one of indirect influence by mitigating the distance between the ECtHR and the frontline through communication and signalling. The average street-level decision-maker lacks the time, expertise or interest in reading international case law, even when it directly concerns their policy field or decision-making area (Canon, 2004; Sossin, 2004). While managers may be more skilled, interested and professionally obliged to engage in interpretation, they are also expected to rely on others' interpretations.

On the other hand, I anticipate that factors endogenous to the organisation matter for implementation and bureaucratic adjustments. Forces related to organisational inertia, agency costs associated with change, preferences of key agency personnel (norms, attitudes and profession), as well as tensions between an agency's (or organisation's) defined goals and preferences and the policy issued by the Court, may affect agency responses. These aspects relate to perceptions of the judgments' legitimacy and the costs and benefits associated with implementing the policy (Canon and Johnson, 1999). Managers may find the judgments legitimate because the demands emanate from a legitimate source – the ECtHR – regardless of whether they disagree with the substance of its instructions. One might also accept instructions because their substance is considered legitimate. However, managers may also choose to ignore the judgments if implementation is associated with more costs than benefits for the agency, even if they perceive the demands as legitimate (Stover and Brown, 1975). Or vice versa, to implement judicial policies they find illegitimate if the costs of not doing so outweigh the benefits of ignoring them. According to Brodkin (2011), we may expect such discretionary utility calculations in street-level bureaucracies because workers need to adjust policies to their work conditions. Moreover, forces exogenous to the organisation are expected to shape bureaucratic discretion and behaviour (Hawkins, 2002). Most importantly, by responding to external pressures to change or retain the status quo.

The judgments in context

If the ECtHR finds that a state has failed to protect the individual conventional rights of a citizen, the state is obliged by Article 46(1) of the ECHR to abide by the final judgment. Although their binding force is limited to individual cases, states are not merely expected to provide individual remedies in single cases but to take necessary action to prevent future violations in similar cases (see Chapter 2).³ Strand Lobben and Others v Norway is the leading case for 15 repetitive cases⁴ and in their communication with the supervising organ for the execution of judgments, the Committee of Ministers (CM) of the Council of Europe (CoE), the Norwegian government summarises the violations in this group of cases as relating to the following three areas:

- The decision-making process, the weighing of conflicting interests (the balancing exercise between the interests of the child and its biological family) or the reasoning for decisions taken.
- The contact arrangements (regime) between children and their parents.
- The authorities' duty to work towards reunification of the child and the parents. (Council of Europe, 2022, point 1.1)

Several responses to the adverse judgments are initiated domestically. In March 2020, the Norwegian Supreme Court's Grand Chamber (GC) processed three child protection cases (HR-2020–661S; HR-2020–662S; HR-2020–663S) concerning possible violations of the right to family life in Article 8. The joint hearing of the three cases contained elaborations on the ECtHR's case law principles and was a follow-up from the ECtHR GC judgment in Strand Lobben and Others v Norway and subsequent ECtHR case law (Mørk et al, 2022; see also Chapter 4).⁵ The Supreme Court found no conflict between the ECtHR and the general substantive and procedural principles under the Child Welfare Act.

Furthermore, Norwegian authorities have submitted action plans and reports to the CM indicating the measures taken and envisaged for complying with the groups of cases led by Strand Lobben and Others.⁶ Measures include interpretative statements of the Supreme Court's GC judgment issued by the Ministry to municipalities (in June 2020), adjustments to soft law sources, such as the child protection circular for case processing, and the introduction of new national guidelines for contact assessments in 2022. Measures for skill development, as well as various courses, seminars and conferences on human rights, were offered to decision-makers in CWS agencies and the courts, focusing on the ECtHR's and the Supreme Court's judgments.

Although legislative action was not deemed necessary to meet the ECtHR's demands, the critique is nonetheless reflected in the new Child Welfare Act, implemented in 2023, and the amendments made to the previous Act of 1992.⁷ Legislative guidance and signals from the authorities given in the years preceding the enactment of the new law have likely influenced practice in the later years (see especially Prop. 133 L (2020–2021)), so has the CWS structure and quality reform from 2022. However, agencies were left without statutory guidance for years after the judgments. Therefore, the new law is expected to play a minor role in the agencies' implementation of the judicial policies issued by the ECtHR.

Methods

To improve our understanding of the ECtHR's impact on Norwegian child protection from the street-level perspective, I have conducted semi-structured interviews with 14 agency managers.[8] Interviews with 'insiders' such as managers are a recommended methodological strategy to facilitate analysis of case law's impact on bureaucratic action (Kapiszewski and Taylor, 2013). It allows us to move beyond observations of formalised responses ('law in the books') to reveal the *informal* responses ('law in action') to judicial decisions and provides an in-depth understanding of the relationship between international case law and bureaucratic adjustments. The interview guide was developed based on theoretical insights into the mechanisms of judicial impact and organisational change. Managers were asked questions about their experiences and interpretations of the judgments and the demands they carried, what they had meant for their agency and their decision-making practices, and what sources influenced agency behaviour and handling of the critique.

The 14 managers were recruited from agencies in municipalities with a population of >50,000; in total, 19 municipalities and 39 agencies were approached. Seven were agency managers, and another seven headed sub-departments responsible for following up on children in out-of-home care and their parents.[9] All 14 were female and trained as social workers or child protection pedagogues. They had between nine and 30 years of experience working in child protection (mean 17.7 years) and, on average, 5.6 years' experience as leaders.[10] The agencies had 80.2 positions on average.[11] Three agencies had legal advisors at the agency level, six had both a legal advisor and a lawyer at the municipal level, and six only had a lawyer at the municipal level.

Operationalisation and coding

The interview data is coded using an abductive approach utilising the data analysis software Nvivo 12. The coding frame (Table 5.1) is inspired by Canon (2004) and Canon and Johnson's (1999) operationalisation of reactive actions and steps of implementing judicially encouraged or mandated change in organisations, as outlined in the theory section. The reactive steps are adjusted for analytical purposes, and the coding frame consists of three categories: (1) 'reception', (2) 'interpretation' and (3) 'adjustment'. By combining thematic analysis with pattern matching, I reviewed the data and located themes within each category that represent 'some level of patterned response or meaning within the data set' (Braun and Clarke, 2006, p 82) and look for patterns across interviews and throughout the stages of the implementation process that answer if, why, how and what behavioural adjustments have or have

Table 5.1: Coding frame

Code description (criteria)	
Reception	The overall reception of the judgments, the general reactions to the decisions as an event that was welcomed or resisted, and the general attitude to the judgments as aligning or not aligning with the organisations' goals and ambitions, or as positive or negative for practice.
Interpretation	Includes 'searching' for information and alternative actions to make. Includes interpretations and reflections on the judgments' content, expectations and their possible impact; the sources of interpretation or signalling, including managers' identification and reflections on the top-down interpretations and directives; and own efforts of implementations, including incentives and reasons for acting as a process of the search for alternative (re)actions.
Adjustments	Includes descriptions of behavioural adjustments in policies, procedures and praxis in the agency that can be traced to the directives and content of the ECtHR case law.

not found place. Quotes are illustrative of the experiences of the managers as relating to the different categories and sub-themes.

Ethical considerations

The study is part of a larger research project assessed by the Norwegian Centre for Research Data (Sikt) to comply with ethical standards for processing personal data (project no. 373319). The study is reported to RETTE (System for Risk and Compliance in research projects), the University of Bergen's system for overview and control of the processing of personal data in research projects. The interview data and informant keys were stored and analysed on the secure desktop 'SAFE'.[12] Respondents received written information about the study prior to the interviews and gave oral consent to participate.

Findings and analysis

The findings indicate that the adverse judgments from the ECtHR have impacted bureaucratic decision-making behaviour and that adjustments are made to accommodate the critique from the Court. Judicial decisions that demand immediate response (or, at least, are interpreted as such) may 'telescope' the steps into one process (Canon, 2004), and I find that the stages of implementation, though mainly sequential, sometimes overlap or coincide in time. Implementation involves ongoing interpretative efforts and adjustments, creating a non-linear process in several agencies. Nonetheless, key findings are in the following discussed through the logic of the three steps of implementation: reception, interpretation and adjustments.

Reception: the disrupting and unwelcomed judgments

Overall, the judgments were not well received at the street level, and the initial reaction was characterised by professional resistance and tensions. Nearly all managers describe how the Court's demands were seen to not align with the organisation's goals, values, ambitions and practices. Reactions like *shock and disbelief* were mentioned by half, often accompanied by descriptions of a *chaotic* situation. The judgments caused insecurity, and some describe this as 'fumbling in the dark', confused about the Court's expectations and what the judgments meant for practice. The situation was disruptive.

> In the beginning, it was very negative, including for myself. Because there was a perception that, now, we are going back to the child protection system as it was 30 years ago. The first thought was that, now, it won't be possible to help; these children must just live in this because parental rights are strengthened. ... So, there was quite a lot of despair in the beginning. And a bit of anger too, why are there people far down in Europe who sit ... and why aren't there any Norwegian politicians standing up, or why, you know? (Interview 9)

Five managers describe how they perceived the critique from the ECtHR as *unfair*, not right, as personal attacks, or as being unfairly presented. Some also emphasise cultural differences and values, as illustrated by previous quote. Six managers describe *fear and despair* among the social workers in their agency, fear of making mistakes and misstepping, of criticism, and of being judged. As one manager put it: 'We were very, like, terrified of making mistakes in the beginning when all of this came, you know' (Interview 10). Some managers reported experiencing external pressure during the reactive stage, which led to sudden changes that contradicted their professional convictions and knowledge. These pressures came from various sources, including lawyers and judges who acted as gatekeepers. In some cases, agencies paused submissions of care orders and adoption cases to the Tribunal or court due to felt pressure from such actors.

Interpretation

Although the managers generally agree on the meaning and embedded expectations of the judgments, they slightly differ in the aspects of the critique they emphasise the most. In the following sections, we examine the implementation process from reception, through interpretation and searching, to decisions to change.

From reception to interpretation: decisions to accept the judicial policy

The agencies' initial reaction was characterised by resistance and negative attitudes. Nevertheless, the rejection of the judgments was temporary, and the judgments were followed by both immediate, temporary and long-term adjustments in the agencies. As the critique matured and the initial shock settled, the judgments were essentially accepted in all agencies. The judicial policies embedded in the ECtHR's jurisprudence were welcomed by all managers, albeit at different rates.

The future threat of judicial sanctions influenced the decision to accept the judgments, and four managers considered adherence mandatory. To avoid or minimise costs associated with future appeals and ensure that cases would get approved in the judicial system, managers initiated pre-emptive actions, for example, increasing contact frequency. The process followed the principles of 'utility theory' (Stover and Brown, 1975) as it involved assessing the costs and benefits of implementing, partially implementing or not implementing the policy while simultaneously searching for solutions that matched the agency's preferences (Spriggs, 1996; Canon, 2004; Brodkin, 2011). At the same time, while the initial motivation for change may have been to avoid future costs, it eventually evolved into an accepting attitude towards the judgments, as one manager reported:

> [T]he motivation changed from being a bit like: Now we have to do everything right, or else we'll end up in court. … Whereas today, I feel that there is more of an understanding that this is actually a good way of working. … But I find that everyone understands why one. … Why this might be a good idea. That our attitudes have changed a bit along the way, for all of us. (Interview 8)

This was a process of maturing which involved stepping back and becoming accustomed to 'the idea'. To varying extents, all managers actively familiarised themselves with the criticism and demands conveyed by the judgments. They evaluated the applicability of the judgments and assessed the possible implications of implementing the embedded judicial policy. As part of the process, managers reflected critically on past practices. For example, regarding contact assessments and documentation, where there was a tendency to be less rigorous, overly general, or to act in a habitual or cursory fashion: 'Previously, they, in a way, used to … we sort of lightly skipped over the part about contact. They didn't discuss it so thoroughly' (Interview 1). All managers acknowledged that (parts of) the Court's critique was warranted, legitimate and necessary in some areas. They agreed with the broad lines of the critique and recognised that it pointed out weaknesses and poor practices that needed improvement. The managers all provided accounts of how the judgments contributed to improving their quality of work in some way, as illustrated by the following excerpt:

> I am happy that we have gained a professional field with a nuanced picture of assessments related to contact, the scope of contact. I think that's good. In a way, I think that it [the judgments] has pushed us to think in way less in general terms and more related to the individual child and the individual parent. And this has pushed us onto a much better path in relation to follow-up of biological parents. (Interview 1)

While the costs of implementing the policies raised concerns, particularly with the potential harm more frequent contact could have on children, the overall sentiment was that implementing the judgments would improve current practices. This positive evaluation influenced their implementation strategies, and cost-benefit analysis emerged as a prominent feature of their interpretation process (Spriggs, 1996), at least in hindsight, as demonstrated by the statement of one of the managers:

> [I]f I'm going to be completely honest about it, it's a bit of a process, isn't it? So, in the beginning, one is a bit shocked like, 'Don't we – isn't everything fine with us – we have such a good child protection system,' right? ... But as you delve into it and become a bit more accustomed to thinking about it or seeing those sides of it, I think that quite a few positive things have come out of it. Especially concerning the way we assess things, we are much more thorough now than we were just a few years ago, so there has been a direct consequence that I believe is positive. (Interview 5)

Sources of interpretation: the importance of signalling from legal actors and authorities

The findings suggest that communication from legal actors and authorities is the most important source for interpretation. First, local judicial resources and municipal or agency lawyer(s) are identified as indispensable partners and sources of interpretation by all but one manager. They play a crucial role in interpreting Supreme Court judgments and are perhaps the most significant source of interpretation.

Second, and following from the first point, almost all managers underscore the importance of the Supreme Court's GC judgments from March 2020 as a source of interpretation. This aligns with the expectation that implementers depend on judicial superiors (Martinsen et al, 2019). Managers also tend to prefer the Supreme Court's decisions over the ECtHR's, and signals from immediate superiors appear to have a more substantial influence on implementation (May and Winter, 2009). In multilevel contexts such as this, the implementing population evaluates which legal source is most legitimate (Dörrenbächer, 2017). Managers were positively inclined towards the Supreme Court's judgments due to the legal clarity they provided and their 'cultural adaptation'. Some managers consider the Supreme Court's translation to the Norwegian context a particularly valuable element, as it re-established the legitimacy of specific normative and professional ideas related to the child's best interest, thereby reinstating the position of the 'Norwegian way' of child protection. About half of the managers consider the ECtHR's criticisms culturally relative, seeing it as partly motivated or grounded in culture, for example, by pointing to the judges' constellation in the GC. Therefore, they perceive the national legal authority as more legitimate, and the national adaptation allowed them to maintain some of their original attitudes and values. This, in turn, increases moral alignment with agency goals and bureaucrats that are loyal to the legal source (Tyler, 2006), as illustrated by this manager's recounting of her experience:

> I feel that perhaps the ECtHR provides certain guidelines that the Supreme Court incorporates and attempts to adapt to the Norwegian system. So, in that sense, I believe that the guidance issued by the Supreme Court is perhaps a bit more influential than that of the ECtHR because they have connected it more closely to Norwegian practices and society and how we perceive children. Meanwhile, I think that the judges ... those who serve in the ECtHR, often have a slightly different perspective on this matter, particularly concerning family matters, among other things. (Interview 8)

Third, external legal forces were found influential by most. The managers note that the increased focus of municipal lawyers, the Tribunal, and the courts on meeting judicial demands and criteria led to the sidestepping of assessments of the child's needs and interests, acting as barriers to 'good practice'.[13] Considering CWS managers' frequent and recurring interactions with the judicial system, they may be characterised as 'repeat-players' (Galanter, 1974) with an ongoing relationship with the Tribunal and the Courts. The prospect of future interactions may thus influence their cost-benefit assessments of adhering to their demands, and, unsurprisingly, their interactions with the judicial system contribute to shaping their practices

Administrative authorities: an insufficient source of interpretation

Communication and signalling from political and administrative authorities were perceived as insufficient and subsidiary by managers. A few also felt abandoned by the political leaders, and that they were using them as scapegoats in public instead of providing clarity and support. While some managers were content with the guidance they received and, frankly, grateful that the authorities did not do anything hasty, many managers felt that they were left to do the interpretative work themselves, as they did not receive sufficient guidance or instruction on what the judgments meant and how to implement them accordingly. After the Strand Lobben GC judgment in December 2019, there was a considerable delay before the administrative authorities reacted. The managers felt there were few signals, and that the guidance was sluggish, insufficient and sometimes even non-existent. One manager expressed her dissatisfaction with the situation: 'Yes, I don't think we've received much support from others – from other public entities – it's just the Supreme Court' (Interview 12).

Half of the managers had trouble remembering if they received any guidance or instructions at all, and if they did, they could not recall what they consisted of. However, all managers mentioned some form of external guidance, such as courses with lawyers or brief written instructions from the directorate. At the same time, most managers said it was too late when formal guidance, instructions and support finally came. It felt superfluous as they had already carried out the interpretation and implemented the adjustments. When external guidance is slow, SLB managers and decision-makers have no option but to either wait or make their own decisions and arrangements (Kaul et al, 2022).

> But what we eventually received was some professional recommendations from Bufdir (the Directorate) on collaboration, but they came much later, way later. We can't wait for that. It takes far too long, you see. It's like, what's supposed to help contribute to these changes in practice only arrives much later, so that's why we have to address it ourselves as a service. (Interview 13)

Another manager describes how guidance was wanted but arrived after pre-emptive efforts were initiated:

> But, you see, the child protection services do request assistance from the Directorate: 'Hello, we need help!' And then it arrives one and a half years later. And then we're like, 'but now we've been dealing with it.' So, we haven't received much help from the government, we haven't. It's the Supreme Court rulings, and we've figured things out on our own. (Interview 12)

For others, the guidance, although delayed, confirmed that they were doing the right thing. Therefore, this support was considered an additional aid to implementation, although the changes were already in process: 'But as I said, we already had. ... It didn't add much; it was just a sort of repetition for us. And it's not a bad thing, but by then, we were already in the process of making changes in terms of how we think and changing attitudes' (Interview 3). Some directly relate the question of authoritative guidance to the urgency of the tasks at hand in a CWS agency and how their need to unbox the expectations from the judgments and to implement, or at least react to, new judicial policies is immediate: '[T]here's this sort of mismatch, if you understand, between what comes and the expectations that we'll encounter it in the next case. We're going before the Tribunal right, and then all this other stuff comes much later. It's quite classic, to put it that way' (Interview 13).

Without structural measures limiting local managers' discretionary efforts, their autonomy to interpret the judgments becomes significant. This is evident from their reports on how they identified and interpreted the expectations for behavioural adjustments and implemented them by creating new policies, routines, practices and processes. This required significant discretionary effort. Although the agencies were not instructed to make immediate organisational changes to accommodate the issues addressed by the ECtHR, the disruptive impact of the judgments, coupled with the urgent nature of child protection work, led managers and decision-makers to act and make 'reactive changes' (Pierce et al, 2001).

Adjustments

All the managers report behavioural adjustments in practice, culture, policy or procedures in response to the judgments. These adjustments largely correspond to the content and expectations that managers identify as embedded in the judgments of the ECtHR. Adjustments are found in various thematic areas and at different organisational levels, implemented with varying degrees of formality and intentionality. Adjustments are broadly categorised as relating to (a) adjustments in the organisational (decision-making) culture, including attitudes, awareness, focus and understanding, (b) adjustments to procedures, and (c) practical adjustments, professional change, work methods and decision-making tools. For each of these categories, there are subsets of specific adjustments mentioned by the managers. The adjustments are interrelated and sometimes overlapping in their intention and consequences. For example, procedural adjustments (b) may lead to more thorough and systematic assessments (c) and heightened awareness among workers (a).

Culture

Ten managers describe how informal processes, such as shifts in attitudes and focus, have been important in achieving change. Some managers actively work towards changing aspects of the agency culture and adjusting the ways of thinking. For others, it is more closely tied to a process in which policies mature within the agency and among the staff.

> [W]hen we looked at it about a year later, in 2021, we saw that internally among us, attitudes had changed quite significantly. … It's a maturation process, and it was a process we actively worked on. People gradually started to see different perspectives and consider the parents' side more. … That change in attitude, the shift in how we work, has been a focus of our guidance sessions. (Interview 4)

Procedures

Nearly all managers mention adjustments to procedures. This concerns introducing new or adjusted templates, formal routines, checklists and plans in specific decision-making areas such as parental follow-up after-care orders, assessment of contact frequency and quality, and reunification.

> Now we follow up birth parents after a care order almost as extensively as you do before a care order. … We didn't have a plan, for example, for the follow up of birth parents in the past. Now we have a plan in all cases of what kind of follow-up, with distinct goals in a way, for what it takes to make reunification possible, you know, which areas need to change. (Interview 9)

In many instances, the adjustments adhere to several of the critical points embedded in the ECtHR's judicial policy at the same time. For example, introducing routines for documenting individual assessments in matters such as contact and parental follow-up. Adjustments are made to standardise and improve documentation procedures, structure decision-making procedures and establish regularity in assessments by introducing plans, including follow-up after-care orders and the participation of birth parents in decision-making practice. Several mentioned that this change is formal in that it is 'not like they did not do these things before'; they were just not put in writing.

> Among other things, the way we carry out assessments. We do it much more thoroughly now, being more thorough from the very beginning. And do it thoroughly in writing. Previously, there were a lot of oral discussions about cases, but now there's a clear emphasis on documenting it in writing. And everyone is expected to do these things, weighing the considerations against each other. (Interview 5)

The procedures are often described as internally developed and independently implemented, but some find inspiration and guidance from the official guidelines that have emerged as a response to ECtHR judgments. Indirectly referring to the delayed nature of the administrative signals, this manager explained: 'And then we have also received very good templates for assessing contact – "contact tools." As it is, we were probably a bit ahead of it. Bufdir has released some now, quite recently, and it's not that different from what we developed in 2020' (Interview 4).

Practical and professional

All managers mention some form of practical changes ('how things are done') as a direct result of the judgments made by the ECtHR. These emerge from organically occurring shifts in praxis, such as increased awareness of areas where the practice has been critiqued, or from adjustments to formal routines and procedures. Some changes, such as heightened thresholds for care orders, adoption and the minimum amount of contact, appear accidental and have arisen as an indirect consequence of the implemented changes and from interpretations of the critique in the agency's external environment.

All managers describe adjustments to their decision-making behaviour that have improved the quality of their assessments: 'But I do see a shift in that we, we are better at arguing professionally in each individual case than we were before, right, before the judgments from the ECtHR' (Interview 10). How care orders are followed up is another area that many managers mention. They describe a more extensive and active approach to engaging with parents. This heightened awareness and focus on interacting with parents appears to be related to increased attention towards continuously revisiting the reunification process.

Concluding discussion

The Norwegian child protection frontline has adjusted its behaviour in response to the adverse judgments from the ECtHR. The agencies initially rejected the judgments due to tensions between the agencies' preferences and the policy issued by the ECtHR but were eventually accepted as legitimate in most respects. Implementing the judgments was a non-linear process influenced by forces both exogenous and endogenous to the organisation, such as signalling, professional values and legal resources, and fuelled by the urgency of child protection work and utility analysis.

What happened, why and what happens now?

The eruptive situation described by managers implies that the judgments constituted a *disruptive* or *galvanising* event (Kanter, 1984; Shaw, 2018). Stemming from the organisation's exogenous environment, the entirety of the critique and high-impact single judgments (especially Strand Lobben) constituted an exogenous shock to Norwegian child protection; an unanticipated, low-probability, potentially high-impact event (Chakrabarti, 2015). In this case, the judgments called 'the legitimacy, adequacy, or appropriateness' (Edelman et al, 2010, p 671) of the CWS agencies' existing culture and practice to question. As such, the negative reception is not surprising as change imposed by an exogenous shock is often opposed by those inside the organisation (Donahue and O'Leary, 2012). According to Lewin's (1943) theory of change, organisations are likely to experience immediate resistance when they encounter shocks due to the human desire to maintain equilibrium. At the same time, shocks also have the capacity to launch change processes, but this depends on the presence of enabling factors that challenge the status quo and cause existing practices to 'unfreeze' (Donahue and O'Leary, 2012). Thus, to move beyond the status quo, resistance must be 'tamed' and perceptions managed for change to occur. The disruptive nature of the ECtHR judgments appears to have caused institutionalised behaviour to unfreeze (Lewin, 1943; Heikkila and Isett, 2004) and prompted critical assessments of the agencies' existing child protection practices, procedures and policies. The agencies essentially found motivation for change to avoid sanctions, but most importantly, by accepting that the judgments and critiques they conveyed were legitimate and that implementing them would benefit child protection work. Besides the 'shock effect', the mechanisms that contribute to explaining the case law implementation process and its outcomes are, as expected, domestic signals, discretion, and forces internal and external to the organisation, but also temporal factors and bureaucratic self-governance.

Although domestic signalling was influential for implementation in the frontline, it was not entirely in line with our expectations. As anticipated, given the legal nature of the matter, the Norwegian Supreme Court's transmission of the ECtHR's judgments was of great importance for local implementation and behavioural adjustments. However, the influence of administrative and political authorities was minor. This is mainly explained by the delayed nature of government instructions and guidance to the frontline, making it a subsidiary source of interpretation. Governmental management tools and legislative measures have likely shaped current practices. However, the government has not managed to control the implementation of the judgments at the street level.

The analysis shows that bureaucratic (re)actions are shaped by the interplay of urgency, delay and shock. The consequences of the communication delay appear to have been amplified by the urgency of child protection work. In situations where social workers and managers felt compelled to act quickly, as they were confronted with the realities of ongoing cases affected by the judgments, they were interpreting policies and crafting responses within wide scopes of discretion. In Norway, the principle of self-governance is strong, and municipal child protection enjoys rather extensive discretionary autonomy in policy implementation. The lack of administrative guidance enhanced this autonomy, and it is beyond doubt that a vast number of adjustments to policies and praxis have emerged through bottom-up incentives without clear instructions from domestic administrative or political authorities. The lack of timely response from administrative authorities may reflect a reluctance to implement the judgments, or the delegation of discretion to local bureaucrats may be strategic, rooted in blame avoidance (Meers, 2019). It may also indicate a limited understanding of child protection work and the necessity of prompt action. First, the CWS needed to calibrate day-to-day activities to meet the new demands of the judicial system, a system that was also grappling with new policies and trying to adjust to the critique. Second, the continuous urgency of child protection work. There is no pause in child protection, as children do not cease to need help and protection during times of legal and political uncertainty. However, we cannot rule out that the delay may also be a result of the complexity inherent in the critique (Anagnostou and Mungiu-Pippidi, 2014). In this case, the adverse judgments, as a minimum, required a shift in judicial interpretation and systemic adjustments (see Emberland, Chapter 2), and the extent of remedial measures needed to comply may have delayed transposition. Nonetheless, the consequence is a highly discretionary implementation of the judicial policies from the ECtHR.

While partly necessary, discretionary implementation is potentially problematic for several reasons. First and foremost, there is insufficient democratic control over the changes implemented locally. Bureaucratic implementation of judicial policies can result in an imperfect translation of Court opinions into agency policies (Baum, 1976; Spriggs, 1996). Reactive changes entail the risk of being hurried. Although implemented policies can be altered, there is the danger that initial policy responses can become fixed policies to which an agency may cling for reasons of inertia or pride (Canon, 2004). This scenario cannot be dismissed, given the managers' confidence in their local processes. Whereas this study is not oriented towards revealing misapplied policies, the findings show signs that thresholds for care orders, adoption and contact have changed due to misinterpretations, external pressure and fear – not formal instructions. In the utmost consequence, the protection of children's well-being and their rights may be compromised. Public scandals tend to trigger pendulum swings in child protection policy, oscillating from child safety to family preservation. The lack of control over the implementation process may induce the pendulum's momentum. Now, it appears to swing towards an overzealous focus on family preservation and reunification at the expense of children's need for stability in care. In the last few years, children in out-of-home care have been returned to their parents at a higher rate compared to previous years (NOU, 2023). Additionally, the frequency of contact granted to parents and their children has increased substantially (Alvik, 2021; Ruiken, 2022). There has also been a marked reduction in child protection provisions. Adoption rates have plummeted, in-home child protection services have sharply decreased, and the number of care orders per year has halved between 2017 and 2021. These changes are not anchored in national policies or judicial precedent, suggesting that other forces influence practice. The question is whether adjustments to current practice depend on another shock to unfreeze or if agencies will find something close to equilibrium as time passes.

We should not overstate the concerns related to the lack of administrative signals, as the frontline was not without authoritative guidance. The Supreme Court's judgments, although arriving some months after the precedential Strand Lobben, were influential, and the managers do not appear to hold widely different interpretations of what was expected of them. However, uneven implementation across the country is still likely to be the outcome, as different agencies have unequal resources to allocate to the implementation process (Herd et al, 2023). By leaving the agencies to undertake the better part of the interpretative and implementation work, the government imposed a substantial administrative burden on street-level workers and managers (Burden et al, 2012). Seeing how vital local legal resources were for interpretation and guidance, placing this burden locally can lead to disparate outcomes in people's access to fundamental rights. The implemented changes have also led to an increased workload for the social workers, without additional resources being allocated to the agencies. There is a risk that the agencies become overburdened with the additional tasks arising from the new policies, which could also affect agencies of varying robustness, capacity and size differently. Future research should aim to include data on medium- and small-sized municipal agencies to further explore the question of implementation disparities.

This study contributes to an increased understanding of what mechanisms are essential for implementing judicial policies from a micro and bottom-up perspective. It illustrates how international human rights case law of a certain magnitude can function as an exogenous shock to the domestic street-level bureaucracy, causing reactive changes that depend on timely authoritative signalling to avoid predominantly discretionary implementation. The temporal dimension is revealed as a crucial mechanism for understanding the bottom-up implementation of international jurisprudence and law. While other studies have found that communication and signalling matter, but may also be ignored (Martinsen et al, 2019; Kaul et al, 2022), the presence and relevance of time lags, and how this affects implementation and degrees of discretion are less explored and often overlooked. Future research should further investigate this mechanism by including multilevel and longitudinal data.

Limitations

The conclusions drawn from this study are limited to agencies with specific capacities and resources associated with larger entities. Notably, the agencies included in the study had legal advisors available at the agency or municipal level. There is also a potential sample bias, as agencies with an active stance towards the ECtHR judgments agreed to participate in the study. Moreover, the narrow focus on managers and a limited number of interviews means the findings cannot be generalised. However, the results indicate how managers in larger agencies handled the judgments, providing insights into similar events. Lastly, causality is a common challenge in judicial impact studies (Kapiszewski and Taylor, 2013). While the landslide of cases in the ECtHR put massive pressure on the Norwegian child protection system to reform and redress the identified human rights violations, the judgments also arrived at a point where the Norwegian child protection system – 'Barnevernet' – was already in the international spotlight and where national systemic reforms were about to be implemented. We cannot control which sources have direct or signalling effects on the work at the street level or establish a definite cause-and-effect relationship between ECtHR case law and the effectuated changes.

Notes

[1] As per December 2024.
[2] Judicial policy making is also a Norwegian phenomenon (Waltenburg et al, 2015).
[3] See Emberland (Chapter 2) on the systemic nature of the problems identified in the Strand Lobben group of cases and the Committee of Ministers of the Council of Europe enhanced supervision procedure for these cases.
[4] When a case pertains to a recurring structural or systemic issue that has already been brought before the court, it is considered repetitive. The case that first brought these issues to light is known as the leading case, and the repetitive cases are usually consolidated with it. The 15 cases are: A.L. and Others; A.S.; Abdi Ibrahim; D.R. and Others; E.H.; F.Z.; Hernehult (1); K.E. and A.K.; K.F. and Others; K.O. and V.M.; M.F.; M.L.; Pedersen and Others; R.O.; S.S. and J.H.
[5] See Sandberg (Chapter 4) for a thorough examination of the influence of the ECtHR judgments on Norwegian Courts' practice, especially the section on the Supreme Court interpretation and adaption.
[6] A detailed overview of initiated measures is found in the aforementioned execution document from June 2022.
[7] See paragraphs 1-5, 7-2, 7-6, 12-5, 14-20 and 8-3 of the Child Protection Act 2021.
[8] The interviews were conducted digitally and audio recorded.
[9] One interview was conducted with the agency and department manager together, and in one agency both the agency and department leader were interviewed (separately).
[10] Information on one respondent is missing for the descriptives.

[11] Based on national statistics for 2022 (SSB, 2022, tables 12305 and 12605).
[12] In 'SAFE', the University of Bergen's solution for storing sensitive data used in research.
[13] Private party lawyers have also been influential, as managers experience that they are using the judgments to argue for reunification, pushing for new court cases.

References

Alvik, I.F. (2021) 'Samvær etter omsorgsovertakelse: En undersøkelse av praksis fra fylkesnemnder og lagmannsretter [Visitation after taking care of children: A survey of practice from county boards and courts of appeal]', *Skriftserien*, 217–217. Available from: https://skriftserien.oslomet.no/index.php/skriftserien/article/view/753

Anagnostou, D. (2013) *European Court of Human Rights: Implementing Strasbourg's Judgments on Domestic Policy*, Edinburgh University Press.

Anagnostou, D. and Mungiu-Pippidi, A. (2014) 'Domestic implementation of human rights judgments in Europe: Legal infrastructure and government effectiveness matter', *European Journal of International Law*, 25(1): 205–227.

Anagnostou, D. and Fokas, E. (2015) 'The "radiating effects" of the European Court of Human Rights on social mobilisations around religion in Europe – an analytical frame', *SSRN Electronic Journal*.

Banks, J.S. and Weingast, B.R. (1992) 'The political control of bureaucracies under asymmetric information', *American Journal of Political Science*, 36(2): 509–524.

Baum, L. (1976) 'Implementation of judicial decisions: An organizational analysis', *American Politics Quarterly*, 4(1): 86–114.

Braun, V. and Clarke, V. (2006) 'Using thematic analysis in psychology', *Qualitative Research in Psychology*, 3(2): 77–101.

Brehm, J. and Gates, S. (1997) *Working, Shirking, and Sabotage: Bureaucratic Response to a Democratic Public*, University of Michigan Press.

Brodkin, E.Z. (2011) 'Policy work: Street-level organizations under new managerialism', *Journal of Public Administration Research and Theory*, 21(Supplement 2): i253–i277.

Burden, B.C., Canon, D.T., Mayer, K.R. and Moynihan, D.P. (2012) 'The effect of administrative burden on bureaucratic perception of policies: Evidence from election administration', *Public Administration Review*, 72(5): 741–751.

Canon, B.C. (2004) 'Studying bureaucratic implementation of judicial policies in the United States: Conceptual and methodological approaches', in M. Hertogh and S. Halliday (eds), *Judicial Review and Bureaucratic Impact: International and Interdisciplinary Perspectives*, Cambridge University Press, pp 76–100.

Canon, B.C. and Johnson, C.A. (1999) 'The implementing population', in *Judicial Policies: Implementation and Impact*, CQ Press, pp 62–91.

Chakrabarti, A. (2015) 'Organizational adaptation in an economic shock: The role of growth reconfiguration', *Strategic Management Journal*, 36(11): 1717–1738.

Conant, L.J. (2002) *Justice Contained: Law and Politics in the European Union*, Cornell University Press.

Council of Europe. *Strand Lobben and Others v. Norway – European Court of Human Rights Case No. 37283/13 – Consolidated Action Plan June 2022*. Strasbourg: Council of Europe, 2022. DH-DD(2022)659. https://rm.coe.int/0900001680a6f064

Donahue, A.K. and O'Leary, R. (2012) 'Do shocks change organizations? The case of NASA', *Journal of Public Administration Research and Theory*, 22(3): 395–425.

Dörrenbächer, N. (2018a) 'Europe at the frontline: Analysing street-level motivations for the use of European Union migration law', *Journal of European Public Policy*, 24(9): 1328–1347.

Dörrenbächer, N. (2018) 'Frontline uses of European Union (EU) law: A parallel legal order? How structural discretion conditions uses of EU law in Dutch and German migration offices', *Journal of Public Policy*, 38(4): 455–479.

Edelman, L.B., Leachman, G. and McAdam, D. (2010) 'On law, organizations, and social movements', *Annual Review of Law and Social Science*, 6(1): 653–685.

Fenton-Glynn, C. (2021) *Children and the European Court of Human Rights*, Oxford University Press.

Fokas, E. and Anagnostou, D. (2019) 'The "radiating effects" of the ECtHR on social mobilizations around religion and education in Europe: An analytical frame', *Politics and Religion*, 12(S1): S9–S30.

Galanter, M. (1974) 'Why the haves come out ahead: Speculations on the limits of legal change essay', *Law & Society Review*, 9(1): 95–160.

Galanter, M. (1983) 'The radiating effects of courts', in K.O. Boyum and L.M. Mather (eds), *Empirical Theories About Courts*, Longman, pp 117–142.

Greer, S.L. and Iniesta, M.M.A. (2014) 'How bureaucracies listen to courts: Bureaucratized calculations and European law', *Law & Social Inquiry*, 39(2): 361–386.

Hawkins, K. (2002) *Law as Last Resort: Prosecution Decision-making in a Regulatory Agency*, Oxford University Press.

Heikkila, T. and Isett, K.R. (2004) 'Modeling operational decision making in public organizations: An Integration of two institutional theories', *The American Review of Public Administration*, 34(1): 3–19.

Herd, P., Hoynes, H., Michener, J. and Moynihan, D. (2023) 'Introduction: Administrative burden as a mechanism of inequality in policy implementation', *RSF: The Russell Sage Foundation Journal of the Social Sciences*, 9(5): 1–30.

Janis, M.W., Kay, R.S. and Bradley, A.W. (2008) *European Human Rights Law: Text and Materials*, Oxford University Press.

Kanter, R.M. (1984) *Change Masters*, Simon & Schuster.

Kapiszewski, D. and Taylor, M.M. (2013) 'Compliance: Conceptualizing, measuring, and explaining adherence to judicial rulings', *Law & Social Inquiry*, 38(4): 803–835.

Kaul, M., Comstock, M. and Simon, N.S. (2022) 'Leading from the middle: How principals rely on district guidance and organizational conditions in times of crisis', *AERA Open*, 8.

Keulemans, S. and Groeneveld, S. (2020) 'Supervisory leadership at the frontlines: Street-level discretion, supervisor influence, and street-level bureaucrats' attitude towards clients', *Journal of Public Administration Research and Theory*, 30(2): 307–323.

Lewin, K. (1943) 'Defining the "field at a given time"', *Psychological Review*, 50(3): 292–310.

Lipsky, M. (1980) *Street-Level Bureaucracy: Dilemmas of the Individual in Public Services*, Russell Sage Foundation.

Martinsen, D.S. (2015) 'Judicial influence on policy outputs? The political constraints of legal integration in the European Union', *Comparative Political Studies*, 48(12): 1622–1660.

Martinsen, D.S., Blauberger, M., Heindlmaier, A. and Thierry, J.S. (2019) 'Implementing European case law at the bureaucratic frontline: How domestic signalling influences the outcomes of EU law', *Public Administration*, 97(4): 814–828.

May, P.J. and Winter, S.C. (2009) 'Politicians, managers, and street-level bureaucrats: Influences on policy implementation', *Journal of Public Administration Research and Theory*, 19(3): 453–476.

Meers, J. (2019) 'Discretion as blame avoidance: Passing the buck to local authorities in "welfare reform"', *Journal of Poverty and Social Justice*, 27(1): 41–60.

Mørk, A., Sandberg, K., Schultz, T. and Hartoft, H. (2022) 'A conflict between the best interests of the child and the right to respect for family life? Non-consensual adoption in Denmark and Norway as an example of the difficulties in balancing different considerations', *International Journal of Law, Policy and the Family*, 36(1).

NOU (2023) *NOU 2023:7 Trygg barndom, sikker fremtid [Safe Childhood, Secure Future]*, Barne- og familiedepartementet.

Pierce, J.L., Gardner, D. and Dunham, R.B. (2001) *Management and Organizational Behavior: An Integrated Perspective* (1st edition), South-Western College Pub.

Ruiken, B. (2022) *Fylkesnemndenes avgjørelser om omsorgsovertakelser av barn og unge: Kartlegging fra årene 2021, 2018, og 2008 [County Boards' Decisions on Taking Children and Young People into Care: Survey from the Years 2021, 2018, and 2008]*, Centre for Research on Discretion and Paternalism, University of Bergen.

Shaw, M. (2018) 'Unplanned change and crisis management', in A. Farazmand (ed), *Global Encyclopedia of Public Administration, Public Policy, and Governance*, Springer International Publishing, pp 6058–6063.

Sossin, L. (2004) 'The politics of soft law: How judicial decisions influence bureaucratic discretion in Canada', in M. Hertogh and S. Halliday (eds), *Judicial Review and Bureaucratic Impact: International and Interdisciplinary Perspectives*, Cambridge University Press, pp 129–160.

Spriggs, J.F. (1996) 'The Supreme Court and federal administrative agencies: A resource-based theory and analysis of judicial impact', *American Journal of Political Science*, 40(4): 1122–1151.

SSB (Statistics Norway) (2022) Table 12305: 12305: Man-years in Child Welfare Services (M) 2015–2024. Available from: https://www.ssb.no/statbank/table/12305

Stiansen, Ø. (2021) 'Directing compliance? Remedial approach and compliance with European Court of Human Rights judgments', *British Journal of Political Science*, 51(2): 899–907.

Stover, R.V. and Brown, D.W. (1975) 'Understanding compliance and noncompliance with law: The contributions of utility theory', *Social Science Quarterly*, 56(3): 363–375.

Strand Lobben and Others v Norway [GC] (no. 37283/13) [2019] ECtHR (10 September).

Szot, A. (2016) 'The influence of European Court of Human Rights' jurisprudence on public administration governance processes', in M. Belov (ed), *Global Governance and its Effect on State and Law*, Peter Lang AG, pp 229–242.

Treib, O. (2014) 'Implementing and complying with EU governance outputs', *Living Reviews in European Governance*, 9: 1–47.

Tyler, T.R. (2006) 'Psychological perspectives on legitimacy and legitimation', *Annual Review of Psychology*, 57(1): 375–400.

Versluis, E. (2007) 'Even rules, uneven practices: Opening the "black box" of EU law in action', *West European Politics*, 30(1): 50–67.

Vinzant, J.D. and Crothers, L. (1998) *Street-level Leadership: Discretion and Legitimacy in Front-line Public Service*, Georgetown University Press.

Waltenburg, E.N., Grendstad, G. and Shaffer, W.R. (2015) *Policy Making in an Independent Judiciary: The Norwegian Supreme Court*, ECPR Press.

Winter, S.C. and Nielsen, V.L. (2008) *Implementering af Politik*, Hans Reitzels Forlag.

6

Representations of children in European Court of Human Rights judgments

Katrin Križ and Daniela Reimer

Introduction

This chapter examines how the European Court of Human Rights (henceforth 'ECtHR' or 'the Court') portrays children in 18 Chamber judgments about child protection-related cases from Norway that the Court decided between 2017 and 2022. In these cases, the parents lodged complaints with the ECtHR against the Norwegian government for violating Article 8 of the European Convention on Human Rights, which pertains to an individual's right to private and family life. The Norwegian child welfare authorities placed children into out-of-home care and determined parents' contact sessions with and adoption of the child; therefore, these cases represent an intriguing puzzle for studying how courts depict children because they are located at the crossroads between the rights of children and adults.

This chapter aims to contribute to the knowledge base about children's textual representations in judgments about international law, which is an under-researched topic. We are focusing on Norwegian cases because, as Marius Emberland shows in this book (see Chapter 2), the Court has judged a disproportionately high number of cases against Norway compared to other states. We analysed the Court's assessment of the applicants' complaints because these sections of the judgments comprise the Court's reasoning. It is important to examine these sections because, while the judgment texts contain language about children provided by the national courts in the sections describing the cases' facts, it is the ECtHR, in their assessment of the case, who decides what information to include and how to describe children when assessing whether the state's interference was 'in accordance with the law' and 'necessary in a democratic society', as per Article 8.

The conceptual framework that has guided our analysis of children's textual representation is a Child Equality Perspective (CEP) (Križ et al, in preparation). This perspective conceptualises children as equal to adults in decision-making by public administrations, assuming that, *in principle*, children of all ages are equal moral subjects in decisions about children's best interests. A CEP seeks to counter adultism in administrative decision-making and conceptualises children as capable individuals who should be visible, have a voice, and be viewed in their individuality in law, culture and organisational processes (Križ and Skivenes, in preparation).

European and international policy documents and guidelines about children's rights in administrative proceedings, like those in courts, establish children as subjects and promote children's views vis-à-vis the potential adultism of court proceedings (CRC, 1989; 2009; 2013; Council of Europe, 1996; 2011). These documents promote an understanding of children as individuals who can develop an informed opinion (depending on age and maturity) and should have a voice.

We will begin by providing some background information about the Norwegian child protection system and children's participation rights before synthesising prior research about the ECtHR and children's rights, discussing our findings, and describing our research methods. Lastly, we will discuss our study's limitations and implications for national courts and the ECtHR.

The Norwegian child protection system and children's participation rights

The Norwegian court system is a three-tier court system, with district courts, appeals courts and the Supreme Court. A judgment at the district court level can be directly appealed to the Supreme Court in cases where Norwegian statutory rules may be incompatible with human rights conventions that Norway ratified (Bruzelius, 2017). Unlike in other European countries, where parties present their arguments in written materials, the Norwegian courts hear parties and witnesses in direct, oral hearings (Ugelvik, nd). Decisions about involuntary child welfare services, such as care orders and contact visits with parents, are decided by Child Welfare Tribunals, specialist first-instance court-like bodies outside the three-tiered court system (called 'County Social Welfare Boards' in the judgments). The Child Welfare Tribunals normally consist of a lawyer (trained as a judge), a professional with expertise in child protection, and a layperson (Skivenes and Søvig, 2017; Child Welfare Tribunal, 2024). The United Nations Convention on the Rights of the Child (CRC) has been a national law in Norway since 2003, and children have had strong participation rights for over three decades. In child welfare cases, the views of children seven and older had to be considered at the time of the judgment decisions (Skivenes and Søvig, 2017). Today, all children have this right, per section 1.4 of the 2021 Child Welfare Act (2021), and a child 15 or older may appear as a party in a case (Child Welfare Act, 2021, section 12.3).

Prior literature

Prior literature about the ECtHR and children's rights suggests that the Court historically embraced an adult-centred, paternalistic approach (Fenton-Glynn, 2014) but that this tendency has changed in recent years. Helland's (2019) research on the balance between children's and parental rights in care order cases by the ECtHR concluded that the Court has increasingly embraced a 'child-centered focus' (Helland, 2019, p 228) with a more explicit focus on children's best interests (see also Breen et al, 2020).

Comparative scholarship on children's visibility, presence and voice in court judgments about child protection cases in European countries found that children remain largely invisible in these texts (Skivenes and Søvig, 2016; Križ et al, 2022). However, comparatively, judgments from Norway demonstrate a larger focus on the child in a case than in other European countries (Križ et al, 2022). Norwegian judgments' descriptions of children also stood out positively in a study comparing adoption judgments of the same seven European countries (Helland et al, 2023). However, McEwan-Strand and Skivenes (2020), who analysed 169 Norwegian County Boards' adoption judgments, concluded that young children are largely absent in the justifications.

Our expectations about what we would find in the data based on prior scholarship were not clear-cut. On the positive side of the child equality ledger lies the child-centrism of the Norwegian child welfare system (Hestbæk et al, 2023) and the court system, at least along some dimensions and compared to other European countries (Križ et al, 2022; Helland et al, 2023). As international and European institutions and policies promote children's participation in court proceedings and based on Helland's (2019) and Breen et al's (2020) analysis, we expected that the ECtHR judgments, which should revolve around the child's best interests, would portray children as subjects and discuss how children or their representatives were heard. Prior research has shown that a child's age is a predictor of children's participation in child welfare processes, with children younger than ten years typically experiencing lower levels of participation in meetings with caseworkers and participation in care order proceedings (Skivenes, 2015; Križ, 2020). Judging from this scholarship, we further assumed that the judgment texts would be more likely to depict children ten years and older as individuals with an opinion and voice.

Research methods

This chapter analyses how the ECtHR's assessments in 18 recent judgments about Norway depict children, as illustrated by Table 6.1.

Our colleagues at the University of Bergen located the judgments we analysed for this chapter in the HUDOC database. We analysed the Court's

Table 6.1: ECtHR judgments overview (Norway)

Judgment	Year finalised	Reason for complaint	Child is applicant	The child has a migrant background or is part of an ethnic minority	Age of child at first out-of-home placement	Age at application lodged with ECtHR	Age of the child at the Court's finalised decision	Violation of Article 8
M.L. v Norway (4370114)	2017	Placement of the child in a foster home and related procedures	No	No	4 months	2 years 4 months	5 years 10 months	No
Jansen v Norway	2018	Refusal to allow contact with the child. Relevant and sufficient reasons for the intervention and decision-making process	No	Yes	1 year	5 years (case communicated to ECtHR)	7 years	Yes
Mohamed Hasan v Norway	2018	Decisions about the removal and adoption of two children. Relevant and sufficient reasons for interventions and decision-making process	No	Yes	2 months 5 months	7 years and 4 months 5 years	10 years 5 months 8 years 1 month	No
Strand Lobben and Others v Norway	2017 (Chamber) 2019 (Grand Chamber)	Removal of parental authority over the child and the child's adoption. Relevant and sufficient reasons for state interference and fair process	Yes (2 children are applicants)	No	1 month	4 years 7 months	8 years (Chamber decision) and 10 years (Grand Chamber decision)	No
A.S. v Norway	2019	Severing parent-child ties without an adequate decision-making process. Refusal to terminate foster care and provide information about the child	No	Yes	2 years 3 months	6 years	10 years 3 months	Yes

(continued)

Table 6.1: ECtHR judgments overview (Norway) (continued)

Judgment	Year finalised	Reason for complaint	Child is applicant	The child has a migrant background or is part of an ethnic minority	Age of child at first out-of-home placement	Age at application lodged with ECtHR	Age of the child at the Court's finalised decision	Violation of Article 8
Hernehult v Norway	2020	Long-term placement of children into foster care and insufficient care procedures	No	Yes	6 years 8 years 13 years	9 years 11 years 16 years	13 years 15 years 20 years	Yes
K.O. and V.M. v Norway	2019	Relevant and sufficient reasons for the child's placement in public care and limited contact rights and proceedings	No	No	9 days	1 year 10 months	5 years 4 months	No violation regarding placement into care. Yes violation regarding contact restrictions
Pedersen and Others v Norway	2020	Replacement of foster care with an adoption	Yes	Yes	2.5 months	6 years 11 months	12 years	Yes
Abdi Ibrahim v Norway	2019 (Chamber) 2021 (Grand Chamber)	Removal of parental authority and child's adoption by the foster parents. Proportionality of measures. Inadequacy of the decision-making process	No	Yes	1 year	6 years 5 months	12 years 1 month (Grand Chamber decision)	Yes
E.H. v Norway	2021	Replacement of foster care with adoption and process	No	No	3 weeks	4 years 1 month	6 years 5 months	Yes

Table 6.1: ECtHR judgments overview (Norway) (continued)

Judgment	Year finalised	Reason for complaint	Child is applicant	The child has a migrant background or is part of an ethnic minority	Age of child at first out-of-home placement	Age at application lodged with ECtHR	Age of the child at the Court's finalised decision	Violation of Article 8
F.Z. v Norway	2021	Replacement of foster care with adoption and proceedings	No	No	At birth	5 years 11 months	9 years 10 months	Yes
K.E. and A.K. v Norway	2021	Proceedings about a care order and contact rights	No	No	1 month	1 year and 6 months	4 years 1 month	No violation regarding placement into care. Yes violation regarding contact restrictions
M.F. v Norway	2021	Child's placement in foster care and contact rights and procedure	No	No	6 months	2 years 1 month	4 years 11 months	No violation regarding the care order. Yes violation regarding contact limitations
M.L.v.Norway (6463916)	2021	Deprivation of parental responsibilities and child's adoption. Unfair trial (procedural)	No	No	9 days	5 years 7 months	10 years	Yes

(continued)

Table 6.1: ECtHR judgments overview (Norway) (continued)

Judgment	Year finalised	Reason for complaint	Child is applicant	The child has a migrant background or is part of an ethnic minority	Age of child at first out-of-home placement	Age at application lodged with ECtHR	Age of the child at the Court's finalised decision	Violation of Article 8
O.S. v Norway	2021	Child's placement in public care and contact restrictions	No	Yes	4 years 9 years	6 years 11 years	10 years 15 years	No
R.O. v Norway	2021	Child's placement in public care and contact restrictions and unfair decision-making process	No	No	At birth	1 year 4 months	4 years 1 month	No violation regarding the care order. Yes violation regarding contact limitations
A.L. and others v Norway	2022	Proceedings about care measures and limitations on contact rights. Art. 6: reasonable time requirement for decision-making	Yes	Yes	2 months	2 years 8 months	7 years 3 months	Yes
E.M. and others v Norway	2022	Proceedings about not lifting a care order, withdrawing parental responsibilities, and refuse contact rights	Yes	Yes	3 years 6 years	9 years 12 years	14 years 17 years	No

assessment sections in the judgments using standard qualitative coding techniques (Saldana, 2021) to determine patterns of themes in the data. The assessment sections are sections that follow, build on and cite the descriptions of the facts and relevant domestic and international law.

We coded phrases describing the child(ren) in the case, usually referred to as 'X'. Applying a CEP, we coded whether the Court's language portrays the children as subjects, that is, in their individuality and as agents with opinions and a voice, or as objects of other people's actions. We operationalised 'individuality' by examining whether the text contained demographic information about the child, described the child's abilities, development, needs, relationships with others, and the best interests of the specific child(ren) in the case. We operationalised 'the child's agency and voice' by looking at the child as doing something or expressing themselves with voice or (re)actions. We operationalised the 'child as object' as the child as an object of care by the state or adults and the child as a victim. Table 6.2 describes the codes for the categories 'the child as subject' and 'the child as object'.

Table 6.2: Categories, codes and code descriptions

Subject category The child as an individual and/or an agent	Object category The child as an object
An individual: • *Demographic information:* The text mentions the child's age, birth, cultural or ethnic background. • *Abilities, development, and needs:* The text describes the child's abilities, medical issues, vulnerability, positive or negative development, the child settling well into a foster home, and the child's needs. • *Relationships:* Statements about the child's relationship with others, including (a lack of) social ties with caregivers or foster parents. • *Best interests:* The text discusses the (best) interests of the child in the case (not the best interest principle in general).	*An object of the state or adult care:* The child in the case is described as an object of state intervention, expert assessment or adult caregivers' care, such as 'X was (to be) placed', 'X was taken into care', 'X's adoption', 'X's placement' or 'adopted him/her', 'the court withdrew parental authority over X', 'measures were adopted with respect to X', 'if X were returned to his mother', 'provide care for X' or 'care for X'.
An agent: • *Agency:* Statements about the child in the case doing something, such as 'living', 'moving' or 'returning' somewhere, or 'experiencing' something, such as 'losing contact'. • *Voice:* The text mentions the child expressing themselves through their actions or reactions to a situation, especially their interactions with their birth parent(s) or foster carer(s), or by expressing an opinion or wishes verbally.	*A victim:* The text represents the child as a victim or object of (potential) risk, harm and maltreatment; for example, 'X suffered neglect'.

Findings

We analysed how the ECtHR depicts the children in their assessments of child protection-related Article 8 cases, examining whether they portrayed children as subjects or objects. Table 6.3 provides an overview of our findings.

Table 6.3 shows variation across the judgments concerning the extent of the text segments describing the child(ren). Looking at the proportion of total coded text segments about the child, it is noteworthy that three judgments – Mohamed Hasan (2018), Strand Lobben (2019) and Hernehult (2020) – contain a high number of coded text segments with descriptions of the child (10 per cent or more of all coded text segments) compared to the other judgments. Nine judgments contain less than 5 per cent of the text segments describing the child. Six judgments fall in the middle (between 5 and 10 per cent).

Out of all the 539 coded text segments across all judgments, the descriptions of the child(ren) in the cases were relatively evenly divided between representations of children as subjects and objects. Overall, little over half of all text segments describing the child(ren) in the case (54 per cent or 290 text segments) depicted the child(ren) in the case as a subject, and a little less than half (46 per cent or 249 text segments) depicted the child(ren) as an object.

A look within the sample reveals that 13 of the 18 judgments portrayed the child(ren) in the case either equally as subjects and objects or the child's subjectivity dominated the depictions. Six judgments are pretty evenly matched in the percentage of the descriptions of the child(ren) as subjects (individuality and agency) and objects in the text: Jansen (2018), Pedersen and Others (2020), M.L. (2020), O.S. (2021), R.O. (2021) and A.L. and Others (2022). In seven texts (Mohamed Hasan, 2018; Strand Lobben, 2019; A.S., 2019; Abdi Ibrahim, 2021; E.H., 2021; F.Z., 2021; K.E. and A.K., 2021), depictions of the child(ren) in the case as subjects dominated. In five texts (M.L., 2017; Hernehult, 2020; K.O. and V.M., 2019; M.F., 2021; E.M. and Others, 2022), portrayals of the child(ren) as objects were more frequent.

The child as a subject

Tables 6.3 and 6.4 show that all the texts describe the child(ren) in a case as a subject to some degree – as people with individual characteristics and agency – but the judgments differ in the extent to which they do so. Out of all the text segments coded as 'the child as a subject', three texts, Mohamed Hasan (2018), Strand Lobben (2019), and Abdi Ibrahim (2021), contain the most numerous text segments describing the child as a subject. It is noteworthy that the child(ren) are described more frequently in their individuality than as agents, as Table 6.4 reveals: 211 text segments, or 73 per

Table 6.3: The child as a subject and object (number and percentage of all coded text segments)

Judgment	The child as a subject n = (%*)	The child as an object n = (%)	All coded text segments n = (%)
Totals (%)	290 (54%)	249 (46%)	539 (100%)
Strand Lobben dissenting	52 (9.6%)	22 (4%)	74 (14%)
Strand Lobben**	37 (6.9%)	21 (3.9%)	58 (11%)
Hernehult	11 (2%)	19 (3.5%)	30 (11%)
Mohamed Hasan	31 (5.7%)	24 (1%)	55 (10%)
Abdi Ibrahim	24 (4.4%)	19 (3.5%)	43 (8%)
E.M. and Others	16 (5%)	27 (11%)	43 (8%)
M.L. (64639)	17 (6%)	15 (6%)	32 (6%)
Jansen	15 (2.8%)	16 (3%)	31 (6%)
M.L. (43701)	11 (2%)	16 (3%)	27 (5%)
A.S.	17 (3.1%)	9 (1.7%)	26 (5%)
Pedersen and Others	12 (2.2%)	11 (2%)	23 (4%)
E.H.	13 (2.4%)	9 (1.7%)	22 (4%)
K.O. and V.M.	7 (1.3%)	12 (2.2%)	19 (3%)
F.Z.	9 (1.7%)	6 (1.1%)	15 (3%)
A.L. and Others	6 (2%)	7 (3%)	13 (2%)
M.F.	3 (1%)	10 (4%)	13 (2%)
K.E. and A.K.	6 (1.1%)	2 (0.4%)	8 (1%)
O.S.	1 (0.3%)	2 (0.8%)	3 (0.3%)
R.O.	2 (0.8%)	2 (0.8%)	4 (0.7%)

Note: * The percentages in all the tables are rounded. ** The tables divide the Strand Lobben (2019) judgment into two texts because the text contains a dissenting opinion.

cent of all the 290 coded text segments about subjectivity in all judgments describe the child's individual characteristics, while 79, or 27 per cent of all the 290 coded text segments (in 14 out of the 18 judgments), depict the child as an agent and someone who has a voice.

The most frequent subject-related descriptions contain information about the child's abilities, development and needs (25 per cent of all text segments in 17 judgments), followed by depictions of the child's relationships and ties with caregivers (19 per cent in 14 judgments), demographic information about the child's birth, age and cultural background (15 per cent in 13 judgments), the child doing something (14 per cent in 12 judgments), the best interests of the child in the case (13 per cent in 13 judgments) and the

Table 6.4: The child as a subject (number and percentage of all coded text segments)

Category	The child as an individual	The child as an individual	The child as an individual	The child as an individual	The child as an agent	The child as an individual	
Code	Demographic information	Abilities, development, needs	Relationships	Best interests	Agency	Voice	Total
Number of text segments in the judgments	43 (15%)	77 (25%)	54 (19%)	37 (13%)	40 (14%)	39 (14%)	290 (100%)
Number of judgments	13 (72%)	17 (94%)	14 (78%)	13 (72%)	12 (67%)	7 (39%)	18 (100%)
M.L. (43701)	1	4	2	1	3	0	11 (4%)
Jansen	2	3	2	2	6	0	15 (5%)
Mohamed Hasan	5	11	6	4	5	0	31 (11%)
Strand Lobben	4	10	4	9	7	3	37 (13%)
Strand Lobben diss.*	17	16	7	5	4	3	52 (18%)
A.S.	0	6	3	0	1	7	17 (6%)
Hernehult	0	3	2	2	3	1	11 (4%)
K.O. and V.M.	1	2	0	2	2	0	7 (2%)
Pedersen and Others	2	1	6	0	3	0	12 (4%)
Abdi Ibrahim	3	2	3	2	2	12	24 (8%)
E.H.	3	1	5	2	2	0	13 (4%)
F.Z.	1	1	5	1	1	0	9 (3%)
K.E. and A.K.	1	3	1	1	0	0	6 (2%)
M.F.	0	3	0	0	0	0	3 (1%)
M.L. (64639)	1	5	5	3	0	3	17 (6%)
O.S.	0	0	0	0	0	1	1 (0.3%)
R.O.	1	1	0	0	0	0	2 (0.7%)
A.L. and Others	1	2	2	1	0	0	6 (2%)
E.M. and Others	0	3	1	2	1	9	16 (6%)

Note: * This text is the dissenting/separate opinion by judges in the Strand Lobben (2019) case, but it is part of and counts as the Strand Lobben (2019) judgment.

child's voice (13 per cent in seven judgments). In the following, we will provide evidence for each subject code.

Seventeen judgments describe the child's abilities, health issues, vulnerability, (positive or negative) development, settling well into a foster home and the child's needs. The text segments on the needs of the child focus on the child's need for stability and security (through a stable caregiver) or refer to the child's 'caring needs' (E.H., 2021, p 8) or 'special care needs' (Strand Lobben and Others, 2019). Ten judgments depict the child(ren) as vulnerable, developmentally delayed or having a medical problem. For example, in A.L. and Others (2022), 'the Court takes note that the District Court essentially found that a care order was necessary because the child lagged behind in development, which was deemed to have a connection with insufficient parent-child interaction' (p 11). The child's vulnerability may originate from previous negative experiences, mainly with the birth family, such as neglect, frequent moves, abduction, chronic or other severe diseases, or relatives' neurodivergence. The descriptions underline the child's vulnerability with medicalised language that suggests objectivity and an indisputable medical diagnosis. This is evident in a section in Strand Lobben and Others (2019, p 38):

> Both the County Social Welfare Board and the City Court rejected the first applicant's appeal, referring to the report of the family centre which had considered that the mother was incapable of taking care of her child without support or follow up, as well as a psychological report, based on an evaluation of X between ten days old and two months, which had pointed to his early delayed development and the fact that he had been a child at high risk when first sent for evaluation.

Fourteen judgments depict the child(ren)'s relationships or social ties with caregivers, especially attachment to parents and foster carers. The child's attachment to the foster parents is highlighted as central to the further development of the child, as in M.L. no. 64639: 'In addition, the District Court found that the applicant's daughter had become so attached to her foster home and foster parents that removing her from them could lead to serious problems for her' (2020, p 22). Thirteen judgments mention some background information about the child, including the child's age at removal from the home, the child's birth or the child's ethnic background.

Twelve judgments describe the child as an agent – their action(s) or interaction(s) with others. Most of these text segments are short and refer to transitions in the child's life, such as 'staying' or 'remaining' with their parent(s), and 'moving to' or 'staying in' a foster home. Seven judgments describe the child expressing their views about their feelings and wishes, what is important to them,[1] and the child's reactions to interactions with parents of origin during contact visits. We coded the segments about children's reactions as 'voice' because children, especially when young, may consciously or unconsciously express their emotions through physical actions and reactions because they lack communicative skills, ability or alternatives to process and communicate their concerns and opinions.

The child as an object

Table 6.5 shows that all the texts describe the child(ren) in the case as an object, but here, too, the texts differ in the extent to which they do so. Five texts, Mohamed Hasan (2018), Strand Lobben (2019), Hernehult (2020), Abdi Ibrahim (2021) and E.M. and Others (2022), contain the most frequent text segments describing the child as an object.

Table 6.5: The child as an object (number and percentage of all coded text segments)

Code	Object of the state or adult care	Victim	Total
Number of text segments in the judgments	221 (89%)	28 (11%)	249 (100%)
Number of judgments	18 (100%)	7 (39%)	18 (100%)
E.M. and Others	19	8	27 (11%)
Mohamed Hasan	16	8	24 (10%)
Strand Lobben diss.	21	1	22 (9%)
Strand Lobben	21	0	21 (8%)
Hernehult	19	0	19 (8%)
Abdi Ibrahim	18	1	19 (8%)
M.L. (43701)	16	0	16 (6%)
Jansen	8	8	16 (6%)
M.L. (64639)	15	0	15 (6%)
K.O. and V.M.	12	0	12 (5%)
Pedersen and Others	11	0	11 (4%)
M.F.	9	1	10 (4%)
E.H.	9	0	9 (4%)
A.S.	9	0	9 (4%)
A.L. and Others	7	0	7 (3%)
F.Z.	6	0	6 (2%)
K.E. and A.K.	2	0	2 (1%)
O.S.	1	1	2 (1%)
R.O.	2	0	2 (1%)

Almost 90 per cent (or 221 out of 249) of the text segments describing the child as an object refers to the child(ren) in the case as an object of intervention measures by the state (an emergency removal, a care order or adoption), assessment by experts, or the care of parent(s) or foster parent(s). When these text segments construct the child as a passive client of the state, they evidence the passive voice of verbs or the use of nouns as a verb (nominal style) to emphasise that something is being done to the child. Examples are text segments such as 'the child was placed', 'was moved', 'was taken into care' or 'was adopted', or text using nominal style, such as 'X's placement' or 'X's adoption'.

Eleven per cent (or 28 out of 249) of the text segments depict the child as a victim of neglect or abuse or as a potential victim, as in this statement in M.F.: '[The District Court] looked into the emotional care provided to X and relied on the court-appointed expert's assessment of X's situation, which the expert considered had constituted neglect' (2021, p 9). Or as in E.M. and Others: 'the Court reiterates that when the children had first been placed in foster care, that was based on findings concerning violence and abuse in the home' (2022, p 15).

Discussion and conclusions

In this chapter, we analysed how the Court's assessments of 18 child protection-related Article 8 cases concerning Norway portray the child(ren) in a case, examining whether the judgment texts depicted children as subjects or objects. Our study was guided by a CEP, which assumes that children are morally equal to adults and should be subjects that have agency and voice in administrative and judicial proceedings (Križ and Skivenes, in preparation). Based on prior scholarship, we expected to find that children's subjectivity would emerge in the assessment sections of the judgments, which are the judgment parts that best represent the Court's voice.

The main takeaway of our analyses is the variation in judgment texts when it comes to descriptions of the child(ren) as subjects or objects: seven texts are subject-oriented, with a preponderance of text segments describing the child(ren) in the case as a subject. Six texts are subject-object-balanced, where the number of text segments describing the child(ren) in the case as a subject and object are even. These two types together – subject-oriented and the balanced type, comprise the majority (13) of the 18 judgments. Five of the 18 texts are object-oriented in that most of the coded text segments portray the child(ren) as an object. This variation in the Court's textual representations of the child(ren) in its case assessments resonates with Helland and Hollekim's findings about the variation in the Court's use of the CRC (2023).

It is noteworthy that only seven of the 18 texts we analysed for this chapter mention the child as someone expressing an opinion, either verbally or through their reactions to a situation. We wondered why this might be and then read the other parts of the judgment as well, not only the assessment section. We noticed that the 'Facts' section at the beginning of these seven judgment texts already mentioned the child's reactions or verbal statements. Therefore, it appears important that the original (national) judgments already conceptualise and portray the child as an agent with a voice – this makes it easier for the ECtHR to draw on an original description of the child as a subject with a voice.[2]

What the representations of the child(ren) as individuals with a voice also have in common is that at least one of the children in a case was at least four years old (and many were older) when the applicants lodged their complaint with the Court and at least ten years when the Court's final judgment was published. This observation appears to be consistent with prior literature suggesting that older children are more likely to be heard in child welfare processes and court proceedings (Skivenes, 2015; Križ, 2020). Yet, two judgments – Pedersen and Others (2020) and Mohamed Hasan (2018) – also involve older children, but they are not portrayed as having a voice in the Court's assessments.

We would like to conclude by emphasising that legal recognition for children as subjects with wishes, ideas and a voice is a central sphere of recognition as human beings (Honneth, 1992), which creates visibility and, according to Honneth, self-respect. If children's subjectivity is denied, personal integrity is violated (Nussbaum, 1995). If the ECtHR wants to take the realisation of children's participation seriously in the future, it must be assumed that all children will be granted subject status in the Court's proceedings. This means that their voice is documented in the proceedings and that their wishes, needs, and concerns regarding the proceedings are documented and taken seriously. In the proceedings we analysed, the children themselves were not systematically heard by the Court and did not have their own legal representation. Consistently hearing children and/or their legal representatives would be an important step towards strengthening the children's perspective and subject status regardless of their age.

Study limitations

This study has several limitations: First, it only covers a small number of judgments about Norway focusing on Article 8 in child protection cases, which limits their generalisability. Relatedly, the Court's language about the child is limited by the original judgment from Norway. If these judgments do not describe the child as an agent, the Court cannot 'conjure up' a child as a subject in its reasoning of a case. Future research will need to compare the descriptions of the child in the original Norwegian judgments to the judgment texts produced by the ECtHR.

Notes

1. One of the judgments – E.M. and Others (2022) – mentioned a 'representative' appointed for the children and represented their wishes in the Norwegian court system.
2. That being said, there are four judgments, A.L. (2022), Jansen (2018), K.E. and A.K. (2021) and M.F. (2021), that mention the child's reactions in the descriptions of the 'fact' section of the case, where the Court does not 'pick up' these descriptions in its case assessments.

Acknowledgements

We would like to thank our colleagues at the University of Bergen for their thorough reviews of this chapter. We would also like to thank our colleagues at Emmanuel College Boston who worked on preliminary analyses for this chapter: Loliana Morales, who contributed to creating the overview table about the judgments, and Mary Burns, Gabriela Serra, and Kerry Shea, who undertook a first round of coding of the descriptions of the child in the entire judgment texts.

References

Abdi Ibrahim v Norway (no. 15379/16) [2021] ECtHR (10 December).
A.L. and Others v Norway (no. 45889/18) [2022] ECtHR (20 January).
A.S. v Norway (no. 60371/15) [2020] ECtHR (17 December).
Breen, C., Krutzinna, J., Luhamaa, K. and Skivenes, M. (2020) 'Family life for children in state care: An analysis of the European court of human rights' reasoning on adoption without consent', *The International Journal of Children's Rights*, 28(4): 715–747.
Bruzelius, K.M. (2017) 'The Norwegian legal system, the work of the Appeals Committee and the role of precedent in Norwegian law', Norlam. Available from: https://files.nettsteder.regjeringen.no/wpuploads01/blogs.dir/223/files/2017/07/The_Norwegian_legal_system.pdf
Child Welfare Act (2021) *Lov om barnevern (barnevernloven)*, Barne- og familiedepartementet.
Child Welfare Tribunal (2024) 'About the Child Welfare Tribunal'. Available from: https://www.bvhn.no/home.565544.en.html
Council of Europe (1996) *European Convention on the Exercise of Children's Rights*, European Treaty Series No. 160.
Council of Europe (2011) 'Guidelines of the Committee of Ministers of the Council of Europe on child-friendly justice', *Council of Europe Publishing*. Available from: https://rm.coe.int/16804b2cf3
CRC (United Nations Committee on the Rights of the Child) (1989) 'Convention on the rights of the child'. Available from: https://www.ohchr.org/en/professionalinterest/pages/crc.aspx
CRC (2009) General Comment No. 12: The right of the child to be heard, 20 July 2009, CRC/C/GC/12. Available from: https://www.refworld.org/docid/4ae562c52.html

CRC (2013) General Comment No. 14 on the right of the child to have his or her best interests taken as a primary consideration (CRC /C/GC/ 14, 29 May 2013). Available from: https://www2.ohchr.org/english/bodies/crc/docs/gc/crc_c_gc_14

E.H. v Norway (no. 39717/19) [2021] ECtHR (25 November).

E.M. and Others v Norway (no. 53471/17) [2022] ECtHR (20 January).

Fenton-Glynn, C. (2014) 'The child's voice in adoption proceedings: A European perspective', *The International Journal of Children's Rights*, 22(1): 135–163.

F.Z. v Norway (no. 64789/17) [2021] ECtHR (1 July).

Helland, S.H., Križ, K. and Skivenes, M. (2023) 'Gauging the child's presence and voice in adoption proceedings of children from care in seven European countries: Applying a Child Equality Perspective', in N. Lowe and C. Fenton-Glynn (eds), *Research Handbook on Adoption Law*, Edward Elgar, pp 190–211.

Helland, T. (2019) 'Care order cases in the European Court of Human Rights: Parents' vs. children's rights', Master's thesis, The University of Bergen, Norway.

Helland, T. and Hollekim, R. (2023) 'The Convention on the Rights of the Child's imprint on judgments from the European Court of Human Rights: A negligible footprint?', *Nordic Journal of Human Rights*, 41(2): 213–233.

Hernehult v Norway (no. 14652/16) [2020] ECtHR (10 March).

Hestbæk, A.-D., Skivenes, M., Falch-Eriksen, A., Svendsen, I. and Bache-Hansen, E. (2023) 'The child protection system in Denmark and Norway', in J.D. Berrick, N. Gilbert and M. Skivenes (eds), *International Handbook on Child Protection Systems*, Oxford University Press, pp 113–134.

Honneth, A. (1992) *The Struggle for Recognition: The Moral Grammar of Social Conflicts*, MIT Press.

Jansen v Norway (no. 2822/16) [2018] ECtHR (6 September).

K.E. and A.K. v Norway (no. 57678/18) [2021] ECtHR (1 July).

K.O. and V.M. v Norway (no. 64808/16) [2019] ECtHR (19 November).

Križ, K. (2020) *Protecting Children, Creating Citizens: Participatory Child Protection Practice in Norway and the United States*, Policy Press.

Križ, K., Krutzinna, J., Skivenes, M. and Pösö, T. (2022) 'The invisible child: A comparative study of newborn removal judgments from a Child Equality Perspective (CEP)', *The International Journal of Children's Rights*, 30(3): 644–674.

Križ, K., Krutzinna, J., Pösö, T. and Skivenes, M. (in preparation) The Child Equality Perspective (CEP): Guideposts for protecting children's rights in decision-making in public organizations.

McEwan-Strand, A. and Skivenes, M. (2020) 'Children's capacities and role in matters of great significance for them: An analysis of the Norwegian county boards' decision-making in cases about adoption from care', *The International Journal of Children's Rights*, 28(3): 632–665.

M.F. v Norway (no. 5947/19) [2021] ECtHR (16 January).
M.L. v Norway (no. 43701/14) [2017] ECtHR (7 September).
M.L. v Norway (no. 2) (no. 64639/16) [2020] ECtHR (22 December).
Mohamed Hasan v Norway (no. 27496/15) [2018] ECtHR (26 April).
Nussbaum, M.C. (1995) 'Objectification', *Philosophy & Public Affairs*, 24(4): 249–291.
O.S. v Norway (no. 63295/17) [2021] ECtHR (30 September).
Pedersen and Others v Norway (no. 39710/15) [2020] ECtHR (6 August).
R.O. v Norway (no. 49452/18) [2021] ECtHR (1 July).
Saldana, J. (2021) *The Coding Manual for Qualitative Researchers*, SAGE.
Skivenes, M. (2015) 'The space for children's participation', *Tidsskrift for Velferdsforskning*, 1: 48–60.
Skivenes, M. and Søvig, H.H. (2016) 'Judicial discretion and the child's best interests: The European Court of Human Rights on adoptions in child protection cases', in E.E. Sutherland and L.A. Barnes MacFarlane (eds), *Implementing Article 3 of the United Nations Convention on the Rights of the Child*, Cambridge University Press, pp 341–357.
Skivenes, M. and Søvig, K.H. (2017) 'Norway: Child welfare decision-making in cases of removals of children', in K. Burns, T. Pösö and M. Skivenes (eds), *Child Welfare Removals by the State: A Cross-Country Analysis of Decision-Making Systems*, Oxford University Press, pp 40–64.
Strand Lobben and Others v Norway (no. 37283/13) [2019] ECtHR (10 September).
Ugelvik, S. (nd) *The Norwegian Legal System*, University of Oslo. Available from: https://www.uio.no › emner › iln › NORINT0500

7

Exploring ethnicity constructs in European Court of Human Rights judgments

Daniela Reimer, Katrin Križ, Mary Burns, Gabriela Serra and Kerry Shea

Introduction

European societies are ethnically heterogeneous (Bös, 2007), with different ethnic groups coexisting within nation-state boundaries.[1] This chapter explores how the language in judgment texts by the European Court of Human Rights (henceforth 'ECtHR' or 'the Court') portrays children's and families' 'ethnicity', that is, their language, cultural and religious beliefs and practices. We use qualitative text analysis of 18 recent child protection-related judgments from Norway[2] about the European Convention on Human Right (ECHR)'s Article 8 on the right to respect for private and family life. Nine of these texts involve families of minoritised ethnic (ME) backgrounds.[3] Nine concern families of non-minoritised ethnic (NME) backgrounds. This study is not concerned with racialised (or ethnicised) court *decision-making* (Muñiz, 2023) – we do not compare court decisions regarding different ethnic groups. Instead, we compare the words and phrases used by these 18 ECtHR judgment texts to describe the ethnicities of children and families with ME and NME backgrounds.

We were motivated to explore ethnicity-related terminology in these texts because language influences readers' perceptions of individuals and social groups, thus framing reality (Edelman, 1985). Language is particularly important in safeguarding human rights, which are universal, regardless of a person's ethnic background (Hunt, 2007). Words that devalue ME individuals by characterising or classifying them as less human or inferior to others based on stereotypical or essentialist classifications of their ME group, such as 'all members of this ME group behave like this because they are members of this group, and their behaviour is different from NME groups', create linguistic hierarchies that contradict the universality of human rights. By comparing the ME and NME judgment texts, this chapter aims to take an exploratory step in assessing court judgments in this way. We acknowledge that there are objective facts related to a court case. At the same time, we conceptualise the terminology the courts use when assessing the facts of a case as contributing to the linguistic construction of the family's ethnicity. As no prior analyses of the terminology used to describe the social construct of ethnicity exist for child protection-related ECtHR judgments, we aim to take the first step with this chapter. We cannot offer generalisable observations, and it is important to emphasise that these texts represent very specific types of discourse – legal discourse about child protection cases.

Human rights, children's rights and minoritised groups in Europe and Norway

Even though the ECHR protects the rights of minoritised groups, several European countries have recently systematically curtailed the human rights, including rights to family life, of people of minoritised ethnic and religious groups.[4] It is the task of the ECtHR to enforce the universalistic claim of human rights if European states turn human rights into particularistic rights by excluding certain groups in these ways. For our analysis, the right to family life (Article 8) and a fair trial (Article 6) are central for parents and children. The right to live as a family can be compromised if the well-being of the child in the family is at risk. In child protection cases, there is always a challenge of balancing and prioritising appropriately different rights, particularly the right of all family members to live as a family versus the child's best interest and its right to protection from violence, abuse, neglect and maltreatment (UNCRC, Articles 3 and 19) (Parkinson, 2003).

In child and youth welfare in European countries, the unequal distribution of power between majority and minoritised ethnic groups has various problematic effects, including family poverty and the over-representation of children of migrant backgrounds in out-of-home care (Del Valle and Bravo, 2013; Karlsson, 2021; NSPCC, 2021). In Norway, older children with a migrant background are over-represented in child protection cases (Skivenes, 2015; Juhasz, 2022). In recent decades, Norway has experienced an intense debate about the relationship between its child welfare services and ME families, especially families of migrant backgrounds. A few studies suggest that the Norwegian child welfare system has biases, including applying higher violence thresholds towards migrant children (Berggrav, 2013; Berg et al, 2017). Løvlie and Skivenes (2021) found that the county boards' justifications in child protection cases evidence only minor differences between migrant and non-migrant cases, including more evidence of direct severe violence, parents' denial of the violence and statements about children's opinions in migrant cases.

Ethnicity, culture and religion

Ethnicity and culture are terms often used in judgment texts and are central to the argumentation and justification of state intervention in families in some cases we analysed. In this chapter, we understand ethnicity as a social construct with the (narrative) power to define symbolic boundaries (Lamont et al, 2015) and establish hierarchies between social groups. Ethnicity as a social construct attributes group characteristics to a person or social group, such as language, diet, religious customs and other cultural traditions (Ford and Harawa, 2010). The judgments often use the word 'culture', which we avoid because we consider cultural attributions part of ethnicity as a social construct.

Methodological approach and data material

We conducted a textual analysis of 18 recent (2017–2022) ECtHR Chamber judgments about Norwegian child protection cases (Article 8). The cases are not about minority rights, but nine out of 18 involve ME families.

The data

The judgments consist of different sections. We focus on two parts of these sections. First, on the descriptions of the facts and history of the case as it winds itself through the Norwegian child protection and court system from the time the child and parents meet that system, henceforth called 'the national (Norwegian) case histories or descriptions'. These sections in the judgments include the parties' submissions and portray how child protection caseworkers, tribunals and courts portray the children and parents in the case.

Second, we focus on the section about the Court's assessment ('the Court's language') here. These are shorter than the national case histories and provide less material, but they are crucial for our analysis. When we first compared whether the nine ME judgments used different words and phrases to describe the ethnicity of children and parents from the nine NME judgments, we observed that the ethnicity-related language in the national case descriptions differed from the Court's language. This led us to add another dimension to our research and ask how ethnicity-related language in the national case descriptions compares to the Court's language. Figure 7.1 summarises our data.

Data analysis

We first read the entire 18 judgment texts several times and then identified and coded major recurring themes related to ethnicity and children's

Figure 7.1: The data about court cases

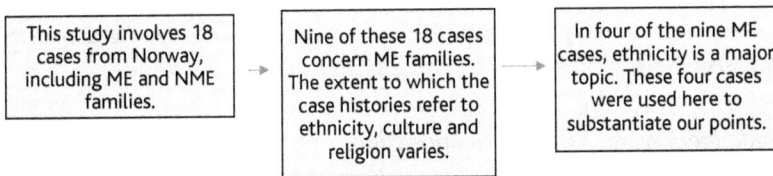

subjectivity (see Chapter 6 for the latter analysis). The code that was particularly important for this chapter was the code 'ethnicity'. This code encompassed statements about the child's or origin parents' or foster parents' culture, language, ethnicity, race, religion, nationality or country of origin.

We then reconstructed the cases as a whole by (1) creating a case history including the different perspectives from the judgment and (2) a table with the most important information about the case. In the next step, the text passages we coded with 'ethnicity' underwent a hermeneutic word-by-word analysis (Byrne, 2001). This two-pronged approach involving a contextual and word-for-word analysis allowed us to identify how the texts present the case linguistically and how the different actors frame their beliefs and conclusions argumentatively. However, our analysis and findings must be viewed in the context of the texts – these are legal texts assessing human rights violations, which include several layers from previous proceedings.

In Part 1 of the findings section that follows, we will summarise how the national case descriptions of all 18 judgments portray ethnicity among ME and NME families. To discuss all the judgments in detail would be beyond the scope of this chapter. We will use four of the nine ME cases, which offer a particularly rich language on ethnicity, to substantiate our points about the national case descriptions. In Part 2 of the findings, we will present the terminology the court uses for ethnicity in the same four ME cases.

Findings

The case histories

In the case histories referring to the (Norwegian) national context, ethnicity primarily refers to the parents of origin and their social environment. In some cases, the case histories might be read as placing ethnic labels on the children. Five constructs of ethnicity can be identified in the case histories in the 18 judgments overall. First, ethnic 'Norwegian' appears as a normative ethnic construct that is not questioned or problematised. Second, ethnicity is constructed as essentialist, universalised and demarcated. Third, certain ethnicities are constructed as acceptably similar to the norm, with the child needing to maintain a connection with their language and cultural 'roots'. The fourth construct of ethnicity is an ethnicity different from the norm and worthy of protection or preservation. The fifth category is related to a theme we call 'ethnic separation' – the child's separation from their ethnic background by the child protection system. This type is a construct emphasising ethnic differences, dangers and risks to the child.

'Ethnic Norwegian' as the normative ethnic construct

The 18 judgments can be understood as conceptualising an ethnicity constructed as 'ethnic Norwegian' as the norm. They could be viewed as not addressing, questioning or critically assessing cultural practices labelled as 'Norwegian'. In the case histories, 'Norwegian' could be read as appearing as an imprecise norm from which deviations are constructed. The behaviours of the parents who are described as Norwegian could be read as not requiring interpretation or ethnic or cultural justification.

The judgment terminology consistently assumes the children's whereabouts with a Norwegian background to be in Norway and can be read to assume that the child protection system's access to the children is secured. The terminology could be read as not addressing the risk of abduction by (Norwegian) birth parents who disagree with a child protection measure. For parents of all ethnicities to be treated equally, it would make sense for child protection agencies to assess the risk of a child's abduction in all cases, regardless of parents' cultural, religious or national background.

Partners in binational couples and intercountry adoptees are counted among the nine cases with minoritized backgrounds, but the terminology used mainly considered them assimilated into Norwegian ethnicity. In Pedersen v Norway (2020) and K.E. and A.K. v Norway (2021), biological parents appear together as applicants. One is Norwegian; the other parent was born in a different country and migrated. These judgments discuss the importance of the child knowing 'the other parent's culture' and 'roots' and having a connection to a different country. In the case involving a mother who was adopted from Costa Rica as a child (A.L. and Others v Norway, 2022), culture and ethnicity are not mentioned beyond the adoption from abroad and the 'disadvantaged' environment in which the mother grew up.

Ethnicity as essentialist and demarcated

The terminology on ethnicity can further be understood in a way that pictures ethnicity as inherent and universal across all individuals from an ethnic group, regardless of their social location. Case histories in which the family of origin and the child are described as having an unknown and 'foreign' culture portray ethnicity as non-changeable over time. These descriptions seem reductionist and draw symbolic boundaries (Lamont et al, 2015) between Norway's culture and 'other' cultures.

In the judgment texts, Norwegian nationals with Norwegian roots are just mentioned as 'Norwegian nationals'. The cross-section of all case stories attributes Norwegian society as cultivating non-violence, especially in the domestic and family environment, and assumes egalitarian gender relations as central norms. The 'different and potentially dangerous' ethnic groups are assumed to have deficits in this respect. This appears particularly evident in the case of Mohamed Hasan v Norway (2018), where both parents are Kurdish. This judgment refers to serious violence inflicted by a father to a mother and the child in the case. The children are not allowed to have any contact with their biological mother, who is separated from their biological father. In their minds, following the terminology used, readers of this judgment could potentially link the father's culture of origin to the danger posed to the child rather than conceptualising the father as an individual who behaves violently (regardless of his cultural background). The first part of this passage illustrates this point:

> It is very important to the father that the *children grow up in accordance with their Kurdish background*, and he is clearly *willing to go to great lengths to achieve this*, possibly also by *using violent methods*. He has stated that the purpose of the abduction was to take them to Iraq. ... After the presentation of the evidence, the High Court is in no doubt that the father is violent and represents a threat to the mother. ... Among other things, [the Court] points out *that the expert witness J.W., who has assessed the violence described in the case in a cultural context, believes that the mother's 'life probably was [or] is in serious danger'*. The mother and father are divorced, and the mother wants no further contact with the father. His behaviour ... shows that he is not willing to respect the mother's wish to break off contact [with him]. ... There can be little doubt that the father's further contact with the mother will be harmful to the children and constitute a significant deficiency in relation to the children's safety if the care order is revoked. (Mohamed Hasan v Norway, 2018, p 10; emphasis added)

In another passage, in the same judgment, the children's severance of contact with the mother is justified by the parents' 'cultural background' because both parents grew up in the same place in Kurdistan and had a 'strong' social network there. This aspect is again justified ethnically and attributed to the local culture. According to the attribution, even if she wanted to, the mother would not succeed in avoiding contact with the children's biological father in the long run. The 'culturally conditioned' ties to the shared social environment are considered so strong that the biological father could always find the mother. If she were in contact with the two children, the father could have access to the children, too.

The terminology used in this case history suggests that, regardless of their personal lives, social environments in Norway, economic situations, professional and educational careers, and dynamics of personal development, parents of origin, through their ethnicity, appear to be defined with unchangeable characteristics. One possible interpretation of this text might be that the static, essentialist conceptualisation of ethnicity might ultimately affect the parents' chance to have a relationship with their children. Of course, other interpretations of the text are possible, and future research should analyse how judgment texts like these are received by readers.

Ethnicity as acceptably similar to the norm

A third category of ethnic descriptions can be identified, but does not receive greater attention due to its attributed ethnic characteristics. It appears close to Norwegian ethnicity and can best be described as 'similar and different'. This type of ethnicity is evident in A.S. v Norway (2019), where the child has a mother of Polish origin. The 'cultural'/ethnic background is only mentioned a few times. In the judgment's terminology the mother is a 'speaker of a minority language'. The child's grandfather lives in Poland and is ready to move to Norway to support the applicant (the mother). Nevertheless, the importance of the child knowing 'his roots' is discussed. The judgment further notes a 'risk of kidnapping', and it remains unclear why this risk is mentioned at all. According to the responsible Norwegian City Court, it was not substantiated (A.S. v Norway, 2019, p 9).

Perhaps the 'risk of kidnapping' was considered due to the transnational character of the case, which could be seen as problematic because kidnapping could also take place in a national context. However, in the further text and the City Court's assessment, the Polish – and hence Christian, European 'culture' – does not seem to cause particular risk considerations despite its transnational character. Similar terminologies can be found in the case of Hernehult v Norway (2020), where the birth parents are Swedish and Romanian nationals, and the case of E.M. and Others v Norway (2022), with birth parents originating in Czechia. The national case histories in these judgments discuss the child's connection to 'cultural roots'. They also show that language may be critical to the Court's decisions. For example, in Hernehult v Norway (2020), the authorities oblige birth parents and children to speak a Scandinavian language in visiting contacts and prohibit the use of Romanian.

Ethnicity as different and worthy of protection

The fourth category of construction of ethnicity in the texts might be described as 'different and worthy'. This category refers to ethnic groups that traditionally coexist in Europe but to whom their own customs and traditions are attributed. Roma people, in particular, belong in this category. Their cultural heritage is considered worthy of protection, and the children should know 'their culture', even if they do not live with their parents. This attitude seems to meet with agreement in Europe due to the Roma people's marginalisation, the removal of their children and the attempt by Germans to exterminate them in the Holocaust (Sridhar, 2006). In our sample, there is one case involving a family with a Roma background, Jansen v Norway (2018). The terminology used in the case history might indicate that the Roma can still be understood as a marginalised ethnicity today. The Norwegian authorities could be read as 'othering' the Roma people with the judgment terminology by attributing the label of 'foreign' to them. In the case of the Roma family, the risk of abduction by the biological mother is also discussed. The birth family is described as violent and criminal in many respects and harmful to the child and the applicant, and the text mentions 'a statistical overrepresentation of Roma in abduction cases' (Jansen v Norway, 2018).

Ethnicity as different and potentially dangerous and ethnic separation as a solution

And finally, a fifth category of constructs of ethnicity in the judgment's terminology can be identified. These constructs can be described as 'different and potentially dangerous'. There is little information about these ethnicities in the judgments, and they appear to be potentially dangerous and harmful to children. They are ascribed harsh opposites to several values of Norwegian and European 'culture' and society. Thereby, the texts might be read as constructing an overall group identity that, as an entity, appears incompatible with Norwegian norms and that children need to be protected from. This ethnic identity represents a counter-design to the norms of the Norwegian child protection system. The cases Mohamed Hasan v Norway (2018) and, in part, Abdi Ibrahim v Norway (2019; 2021) are the only two examples of this category of this construct of ethnicity in our sample.

Parents' cultural values and practices are described as posing a primary risk to the child, and the child's ethnic community in Norway is described as posing a secondary risk. The Mohamed Hasan v Norway (2018) text, which we already discussed earlier, widely discusses present and future risks and ascribes them to the parents, especially the father – not the father as an individual but the father as a member of his culture. The children in the case have already experienced an abduction, and they are considered to be at constant risk of abduction. The judgment wordily describes the risk of violence and threat to the mother's and children's lives. It discusses the resulting developmental risks to the children and the risk of being raised in opposition to egalitarian gender norms. The terminology emphasises the father's cultural values, especially the honour code and forced marriage, as part of the birth parents' ethnicity. It conceptualises them as future risks for the children when they are teenagers.

Other ethnic groups do not appear to be as much of a risk to the children, even though the risk is discussed, too, but less related to ethnicity.[5] The Abdi Ibrahim case points towards the meaning of religion and the right to religious education. The 'risk to the child' can be seen almost reversely. The case experts explain the child's out-of-home placement with the mother's psychological disorders. They justify the child's placement in a practicing Christian foster family who wants to baptise the child by citing the lack of ethnic Somali foster carers in Norway. The Muslim faith is not mentioned as a risk to the child. However, the Norwegian authorities portray the placement in a Christian family as being in the child's best interest and particularly positive. The so-called 'calm' and 'friendly environment' in that family is considered more critical to the child than the ties with the birth mother's religion.

In the context of ethnicity, the judgment texts regularly refer to 'religion' and routinely attribute certain religious practices to 'cultures' and ethnicities. This is an interesting observation, as religious affiliation only plays a marginal role for most of the European population and does not apply to a part of the population. Norway is often considered one of the most secular countries in the world, although strongly culturally influenced by the Christian tradition.[6] However, as might be read into the judgment texts, a common conception of Europe is still based on it being a 'Christian continent' because of its cultural origins and Christianity's impact on European identity (Bös, 2007). This is the case even though Europe has never been an entirely Christian continent, and members of other religions, especially Jews and Muslims, have always been part of it (Greble, 2021).

To summarise Part 1 of the findings, in the Norwegian case histories, it appears as if the principles of Articles 20 (on the protection of children without parental care) and 30 (on the rights of children from minorities and indigenous origin) of the Convention on the Rights of the Child, to which the ECtHR refers, are not always shared and applied by the Norwegian child protection system. Some case histories create symbolic tension between 'the best interest of the child' and the child's knowledge of their ethnic group and biological family's religious affiliation. In some cases, the Norwegian child protection system seems to give more weight to various interests related to the child than the proximity to the family of origin and their ethnic group and the opportunity to bring the children closer to the values and traditions ascribed to their ethnicity. The aspects weighted more heavily include the child's bond with the foster parents, peace and stability for the child, belonging to the foster family, protection against abduction, and avoidance of stressful situations due to contact visitations.

In the case of Jansen v Norway (2018), this practice and the prioritisation of the child's (supposed) needs other than knowing and belonging to the birth family's ethnic group seems to be particularly evident. The text refers to the child's contact sessions with their parent, who is of Roma background:

> A psychologist, F., had testified before the City Court that the child showed signs of having suffered neglect at an early age. She was still a vulnerable child with attachment problems. She needed a calm life, extra security and therapy. She would probably be subjected to more neglect if she were abducted. ... Other than the general assumption that it was a good thing for a child to get to know its culture and background, there was little to indicate that contact sessions would be beneficial if they were to take place. Contact would be quite limited and the possibility for the child to get to know her background and Roma culture would thus in any case be significantly reduced. (Jansen v Norway, 2018, p 16)

The texts reveal that some ethnic minoritised children have minimal visitations with their parents of origin after entering out-of-home care. In the judgments' terminology, the child is depicted as vulnerable, and the family of origin's contact with the child threatens the vulnerable child. In the case of Jansen v Norway (2018), the risk of abduction is discussed (without any indication of a de facto risk of abduction) and presented as a developmental risk for the child. Because of the presented risks, contact is limited to a few short meetings per year (Jansen v Norway, 2018, p 9).

The judgments also included decisions for adoptions justified with breaks in contact with the parents of origin and ethnic separations against the birth parents' will: M.L. v Norway (2020), Abdi Ibrahim v Norway (2019; 2021) and Mohamed Hasan v Norway (2018), respectively, and very low-frequency post-adoption contact granted in Pedersen v Norway (2020).

The European Court of Human Rights' stance

Compared with the case histories that we just discussed, the judgments of the ECtHR distinguish themselves by the fact that in all 18 cases we analysed, the Court refrains in its terminology from culturally minoritising attributions or labels of individuals that reduce them to ethnicity or religion. It appears that this renunciation is not merely rhetorical but goes hand in hand with a clear stance on the universality of human rights irrespective of ethnicity and background and a clear commitment to individuals' fundamental rights to family life and a connection to an individual's roots.

In Jansen v Norway, where the Norwegian authorities intensively highlighted the Roma background of the mother of origin and her family and even concluded from this that the child was at risk of abduction, the ECtHR consistently rejected such attributions as racism and explicitly tied its own decision solely to the facts in the case:

> The authorities had presented old cases mentioning people from the Roma population, even though these people had had no connection whatsoever to the applicant or her family, including her father. This way of handling the case had emerged as racist and had not at all been suited to clarifying the applicant's situation. The High Court had, furthermore, spoken of a statistical overrepresentation of Roma in abduction cases, even though there had been no connection between the random criminal cases that had been presented and the applicant and her family. (Jansen v Norway, 2018, p 22)

The demand of the Norwegian authorities that the child should be brought closer to her roots, for example, through books, is also rejected by the ECtHR as untenable: 'As to A's cultural background, it was clear that a girl of her age could not take responsibility for learning about her culture from books or pictures' (Jansen v Norway, 2018, p 23).

In Hernehult v Norway (2020), where Norwegian authorities obliged parents and children to speak a Scandinavian language at supervised visiting contacts to control communication, the ECtHR also takes a clear stand for the family and their language in contacts:

> If they wanted to control communication, the local authorities should have ensured a Romanian speaking person is present instead of prohibiting speaking Romanian ... the decision that the family could not speak Romanian together during the contact sessions (see the information concerning the Board's decision, paragraph 16 above) would appear to have made these few sessions less likely to facilitate the children's return. (Hernehult v Norway, 2020, p 14)

In Abdi Ibrahim v Norway (2019), where a child with a Somali Muslim mother had been placed in a Christian family and was baptised, the ECtHR rules that the right to family life and freedom of religion was violated despite the claims of the Norwegian authorities that not enough Muslim foster families were available:

> X had been placed in a Christian family with a background very different from the applicant's and X's as to origin, language and ethnicity. Thus, the authorities could not have had reunification of the family as an aim. By placing X in a Christian home where the family, including X, went to church and ate pork, the respondent State had

also systematically violated the applicant's right to freedom of religion. (Abdi Ibrahim v Norway, 2019, p 9)

In Mohamed Hasan v Norway (2018), where Norwegian authorities and third-party interventions emphasise the impact of the parents and especially the father's cultural and ethnic background, the ECtHR does not advance any cultural arguments. The Court rules that there has not been a violation of the right to family life but argues solely on the grounds of the case's facts, its exceptionality, the risk of violence, the vulnerability of the children and their need for security (Mohamed Hasan v Norway, 2018, p 38).

Discussion and conclusions

Our analysis of the judgments detected some terminology furthering ethnocentrism and othering in the national case histories (the sections of the judgments explaining the facts of a case) on the one hand, and terminology representing universalism in the ECtHR's representation of minoritised children and families on the other hand. In the case histories' terminologies, certain ethnicities and religions – Norwegian, European and cultural Christian – seem to be (re)presented as an imprecise norm or standard. As a norm, the behaviours of members of these ethnicities are not framed as requiring cultural or religious justification or explanation. Their ethnicity is not explicitly mentioned. In contrast, the actions of members of other religions and ethnicities are culturally and religiously explained and questioned. These other ethnicities could be interpreted as being presented as inferior to the European ones regarding fundamental values of gender equality and freedom of religion.

The case histories we studied place some (but not all) minoritised ethnicities and religious groups in a narrowly constructed frame. These ethnicities and their members appear essentialist and unchangeable with time. They are described as representing a risk to the child in a certain situation and the future. These cases are characterised by an explicit linguistic dichotomy between the child's best interests and 'culture' or 'religion'. The Norwegian state agencies prioritise the child's best interests if in doubt. The knowledge of the child's 'roots' and 'religion' appears to be subordinated and, in some cases, sacrificed.

These practices might be interpreted as referring to a deep-seated European understanding of the essentialist character of so-called cultural differences and hegemonies and the narrative of Europe as a 'Christian continent'.[7] Ethnic groups to whom a different culture and/or religion is attributed tend to be marginalised or 'othered', a process that implies hierarchisation into inferiors and superiors (Foucault, 1982). This is particularly true of Muslims (Statham and Tillie, 2019).

Symbolic classifications are a means of power over a social group (Bourdieu and Passeron, 1977; Foucault, 1982). When the nine case histories involving minoritised families seem to adopt stigmatising and stereotyping linguistic representations of minoritised ethnic children and parents, this might highlight the *symbolic* power of states, which can turn into 'othering' (Foucault, 1982) and 'symbolic violence' (Bourdieu and Passeron, 1977) when fundamental human rights are questioned for members of certain ethnic groups.

The ECtHR's linguistic representation of minoritised children and families differs from these case histories. The Court takes a clear human rights-based stance against minoritising perspectives based on cultural, ethnic or religious background. No culturally minoritising attributions, othering labels or generalisations exist in the sections containing the Court's judgments. One text even rejects them as racist. The ECtHR makes decisions based on case-based facts, factual risk situations and resources of the families of origin, regardless of their ethnic background, thus applying human rights as universal rights. The case histories are not legal proceedings but are based on social work with families that end up in court over the years. In the context of growing ethnic diversity in Europe, one of the Court's major tasks might be to defend the universalism of human rights against the odds of particularistic ethnocentrism. In their distinct rejection of culturally minoritising attributions, the Court's judgments could foster a reflective approach to European countries' terminology and public discourse about ethnicity.

Limitations

Our analysis requires several caveats: The textual material itself has limitations. The judgment texts are based on layers of proceedings and written material. In all cases, the different layers refer to different decisions by different agencies at different moments in time, often with many years in between. The study is not a legal discourse analysis. It must be understood as an examination of how the texts might marginalise minoritised ethnic groups through classifications and conceptualisations. It is based on very specific cases, so it is impossible to generalise from our analysis. In addition, it is important to note that the judgments are legal documents that focus on human rights violations by child protection agencies and national courts against the right to family life and not violations of religious or ethnic discrimination. Another limitation is the small number of cases available to us that contain rich material for questions regarding ethnicity, culture and religion. Another limitation is that the cases that were most fruitful for the topic might produce bias in the sample: These cases can probably be considered the most 'challenging' cases in terms of ethnicity. We did our best to balance this issue in the text by avoiding generalisations.

Notes

1. For example, in 2020, 87 million international migrants resided in Europe (IOM, 2024).
2. We chose cases from Norway because, as Chapter 2 by Marius Emberland shows, child protection cases from Norway have been over-represented at the ECtHR in recent years.
3. We use the term 'minoritised ethnic' (and not 'minority ethnic') to emphasise that we understand ethnicity as a social construct. Minoritised ethnic individuals and groups have historically not held power in the society in which they live and have been subject to systematic marginalisation based on their race, religious creed and nation of origin (EU Agency for Fundamental Rights, 2017; Sotto-Santiago, 2019). The term encompasses newcomers to a country and indigenous minoritised ethnic groups.
4. For example, Switzerland prohibited people with the status of 'guest workers' (*saisonniers*) from bringing their children into the country until 2002, resulting in half a million children growing up separated from their parents (Nardone et al, 2022).
5. As in the Jansen v Norway (2018) case we mentioned before.
6. In Norway, about two-thirds of the population are officially affiliated with a Christian church, with a considerable decrease during the last years and a low commitment to religious practices like attendance of church services (Statistics Norway, 2023).
7. The narrative is significant in Europe's external representation and symbolic demarcation. Christianity – as diverse, contested and controversial as it is currently in Europe – thus represents an ethnic norm and identity, even if many (or in some countries: the majority of) individuals do not share it.

References

Abdi Ibrahim v Norway (no. 5379/16) [2019] ECtHR (17 December).
Abdi Ibrahim v Norway [GC] (no. 15379/16) [2021] ECtHR (10 December).
A.L. and Others v Norway (no. 45889/18) [2022] ECtHR (20 January).
A.S. v Norway (no. 60371/15) [2019] ECtHR (17 December).
Berg, B., Paulsen, V., Midjo, T. and Haugen, G.M.D. (2017) 'Myter og realiteter. Om møtet mellom innvandrere og Barnevernet [Myths and realities. About the encounter between immigrants and child welfare services]', NTNU Samfunnsforskning.
Berggrav, S. (2013) 'Tåler noen barn mer juling? [Can some children tolerate more beatings?]', *En kartlegging av hjelpeapparatets håndtering av vold mot barn i minoritetsfamilier [A Survey of the Support System's Handling of Violence in Minority Families]*, Redd Barna.
Bös, M. (2007) 'Ethnizität und grenzen in Europa [Ethnicity and boundaries in Europe]', in P. Deger and R. Hettlage (eds), *Der Europäische Raum: Die Konstruktion Europäischer Grenzen [European Space: The Construction of European Boundaries]*, VS Verl. für Sozialwiss, pp 49–69.
Bourdieu, P. and Passeron, J.C. (1977) *Reproduction in Education, Society, and Culture*, SAGE.
Byrne, M. (2001) 'Hermeneutics as a methodology for textual analysis', *AORN Journal*, 73(5): 968–970.

Del Valle, J.F. and Bravo, A. (2013) 'Current trends, figures and challenges in out of home child care: An international comparative analysis', *Psychosocial Intervention*, 22(3): 251–257.

Edelman, M. (1985) *Political Language and Political Reality*, Cambridge University Press.

E.M. and Others v Norway (no. 3471/17) [2022] ECtHR (20 January).

European Union Agency for Fundamental Rights (2017) 'Second European Union minorities and discrimination survey'. Available from: http://fra.europa.eu/en/publication/2017/second-european-union-minorities-and-discrimination-survey-main-results

Ford, C. and Harawa, N.T. (2010) 'A new conceptualization of ethnicity for social epidemiologic and health equity research', *Social Science and Medicine*, 71(2): 251–258.

Foucault, M. (1982) 'The subject and power', *Critical Inquiry*, 8(4): 777–795.

Greble, E. (2021) *Muslims and the Making of Modern Europe*, Oxford University Press.

Hernehult v Norway (no. 14652/16) [2020] ECtHR (10 March).

Hunt, L. (2007) *Inventing Human Rights: A History*, Norton.

IOM (International Office of Migration) (2024) 'World migration report 2024'. Available from: https://worldmigrationreport.iom.int/what-we-do/world-migration-report-2024-chapter-3/europe

Jansen v Norway (no. 2822/16) [2018] ECtHR (6 September).

Juhasz, I. (2022) 'Parenthood in the (child) welfare state: Legitimation of care orders and care rights in Norway', PhD dissertation, University of Bergen, Norway.

Karlsson, H. (2021) 'Is discrimination a driving force behind the overrepresentation of children with an immigrant background in Swedish out-of-home care? A quantitative study from Stockholm City', *European Journal of Social Work*, 24(4): 629–641.

K.E. and A.K. v Norway (no. 57678/18) [2021] ECtHR (1 July).

Lamont, M., Pendergrass, S. and Pachucki, M. (2015) 'Symbolic boundaries', *International Encyclopedia of the Social and Behavioral Sciences*, 23: 850–855.

Løvlie, A.G. and Skivenes, M. (2021) 'Justifying interventions in Norwegian child protection: An analysis of cases of violence in migrant and non-migrant families', *Nordic Journal on Law and Society*, 4(2): 1–41.

M.L. v Norway (no. 64639/16) [2020] ECtHR (20 December).

Mohamed Hasan v Norway (no. 27496/15) [2018] ECtHR (26 April).

Muñiz, R. (2023) 'A theory of racialized judicial decision-making', *Michigan Journal of Race & Law*, 28(2): 345–415.

Nardone, M., Cattacin, S., Riocciardi, T. and Stowcklin, D. (2022) 'Recommandations pour améliorer l'expérience du placement extrafamilial [Recommendations to improve out-of-home placements]', *NFP 76 Bulletin*, 9(2): 55–61.

NSPCC (2021) 'Statistics briefing: Looked after children 2021', NSPCC. Available from: https://learning.nspcc.org.uk/media/1622/statistics-briefing-looked-after-children.pdf

Parkinson, P. (2003) 'Child protection, permanency planning and children's right to family life', *International Journal of Law, Policy and the Family*, 17(2): 147–172.

Pedersen v Norway (no. 39710/15) [2020] ECtHR (10 March).

Skivenes, M. (2015) 'How the Norwegian child welfare system approaches migrant children', in M. Skivenes, R. Barn, K. Križ and T. Pösö (eds), *Child Welfare Systems and Migrant Children: Policies and Practice*, Oxford University Press, pp 39–61.

Sotto-Santiago, S. (2019) 'Time to reconsider the word minority in academic medicine', *Journal of Best Practices in Health Professions Diversity*, 12(1): 72–78.

Sridhar, C.R. (2006) 'Historical amnesia: the Romani holocaust', *Economic and Political Weekly*, 41(33): 3569–3571.

Statham, P. and Tillie, J. (eds) (2019) *Muslims in Europe: Comparative Perspectives on Socio-Cultural Integration*, Routledge.

Statistics Norway (2023) 'Church of Norway'. Available from: https://www.ssb.no/en/kultur-og-fritid/religion-og-livssyn/statistikk/den-norske-kirke

UNCRC (United Nations Convention on the Rights of the Child) (1989) 'Convention on the rights of the child'. Available from: https://www.ohchr.org/en/instruments-mechanisms/instruments/convention-rights-child

PART II

Transnational influence of the European Court of Human Rights

8

Prioritising the child's best interests: mixed messages in the international human rights arena

Elaine E. Sutherland

Introduction

All European jurisdictions accept that the state has a role in protecting children where their parents or other family members are unable or unwilling to do so. The optimum way for the state to fulfil that obligation is by means of prevention, something that can be attempted by providing universal services, coupled with effective and robust additional support for families that need it.

It is when the state steps beyond the voluntary and into mandatory intervention in a particular family that its role may become contentious. The issues are manifold. What constitutes child abuse and neglect? When is it legitimate for the state to intervene in responses to – often alleged or suspected – child abuse and neglect? Can the child's right to be cared for in his or her own family be reconciled with the right to protection? What of the rights of the child's parents and others, like siblings and substitute carers?

Individual jurisdictions take different approaches in their efforts to protect children, of course (Luhamaa et al, 2022), and there are numerous classifications of these efforts (Gilbert, 1997; Connolly and Katz, 2019; Berrick et al, 2023). Yet it remains the eternal dilemma of those charged with child protection that they will be 'damned if they do and damned if they don't'. On the one hand, they will be condemned for a failure to act timeously and appropriately, particularly where a child is injured or dies. On the other hand, they will be criticised for over-zealous intervention where their actions are perceived to be unwarranted or excessive.

One way to test the legitimacy of state action aimed at protecting children is to measure it against international human rights norms and there is no shortage of treaty provisions and further guidance available to the state. In Europe, the two main sources of these norms are the European Convention on Human Rights (ECHR) and the United Nations Convention on the Rights of the Child (UNCRC). All European states are parties to the CRC and the same was true of the ECHR until the Russian Federation ceased to be a party in 2022 (Council of Europe Newsroom, 2022). Each instrument has evolved over time and has been subject to extensive interpretation and amplification. Decisions of the European Court of Human Rights (ECtHR) have added flesh to the bare bones of the ECHR. Similarly, the United Nations Committee on the Rights of the Child (CRC Committee) has amplified the basic provisions of that instrument through its General Comments (GCs), Concluding Observations on State party reports, the case law under the Complaints Procedure and its Days of General Discussion (DGDs).

A difficulty arises, however, if the treaty provisions themselves – or the way in which they are interpreted and amplified – are inconsistent, since states may be left unclear about what is required of them, and it may be impossible for them to comply with all of the norms simultaneously.

This chapter examines the priority accorded to the child's best interests in the child protection context when weighed against the rights and interests of others, particularly the child's parents. Focussing on the ECHR and the CRC, it will drill down into their interpretation and amplification by the ECtHR and CRC Committee, respectively, in order to evaluate whether states are, indeed, being sent mixed messages and, if so, how that might be addressed.

The best interests of the child

At the outset, it is worth remembering that the best interests test itself has long been criticised as vague and indeterminate, resulting in unpredictability or inconsistency when it is used by public authorities or courts in decision-making (Mnookin, 1975). This may give the decision-maker the opportunity to apply his or her preferred values (Reece, 1996; Kohm, 2008). There is the further danger that, by emphasising the child's 'interests', the test undermines the advances made in recognising children as rights-holders (Bainham, 2002; Fenton-Glynn, 2019). In the light of this persistent criticism of the best interests test, it is legitimate to ask why it continues to be used. One answer was provided many years ago by Robert Mnookin, the arch-critic of the test, when he said, 'While the indeterminate best interests standard may not be good, there is no available alternative that is plainly less detrimental' (Mnookin, 1975, p 282).

European Convention on Human Rights

Some familiar observations can be made about the ECHR. Drafted, as it was, in the aftermath of the Second World War and designed to protect individuals from authoritarian regimes, it is unsurprising, perhaps, that it is adult-centric in nature, making scant reference to children.[1] That, however, does not make it inapplicable to children for the obvious reason that they are human beings, and the ECtHR has found violations of the rights of children, often in conjunction with finding violations of the rights of their parents (Marckx v Belgium, 1979; Johnston v Ireland, 1986; X v Austria, 2013).[2] Applications to the ECtHR relating to child protection are made by parents, with the child sometimes featuring as a co-applicant, something that has led commentators to observe that this focus on the parents' rights can result in the child's perspective being 'virtually invisible' (Breen et al, 2020, p 717).

The majority of child protection cases that come before the ECtHR found on Article 8 (right to respect for private and family life) of the ECHR, with Articles 5 (right to liberty and security), 6 (right to a fair trial), 9 (right to freedom of thought, conscience and religion) and 13 (right to an effective remedy) sometimes being founded upon as well (Fenton-Glynn, 2021, p 304).

In order to withstand a challenge under Article 8, the action of the state party designed to protect a child must be lawful, in pursuit of a legitimate aim and necessary. The lawfulness of state action is rarely challenged, since the state will usually be acting in accordance with domestic law, and child protection is regarded as a legitimate aim under Article 8(2). Thus, it is the necessity of the state's intervention that is usually at issue: that is, whether its response was proportionate.

The evolution of European Court thinking on child protection

Early ECtHR decisions on cases involving children reflected the adult-centric nature of the ECHR itself, something demonstrated by the now-notorious decision in Nielsen v Denmark in 1988, when the Court found no violation of the child's Article 5 rights in his mother's decision to authorise his detention in a mental health facility. Happily, its thinking has evolved (Fortin, 2009, p 555; Fenton-Glynn, 2021, p 305: Taylor, 2024, pp 364–365). In the child protection context, the Court initially emphasised parental rights, noting, in L v Sweden (1984), that interference with these rights 'cannot be justified simply on the basis that it would be better for the child to be taken care of by certain foster parents' (para 151) and opining, in Olsson v Sweden (No. 1), that interference could only be justified 'if it is clearly shown that the parents' exercise their rights 'in a manner contrary to the child's interests' (Olsson v Sweden, 1988, para 149).

Towards the end of the last century, with the heightened appreciation of children's rights occasioned by the adoption by the UNCRC, the Court shifted its focus to emphasising the need to strike a 'fair balance' between parental rights and the interests of the child (Olsson v Sweden (2), 1992, para 90; Hokkanen v Finland, 1994, para 146; Abdi Ibrahim v Norway, 2021, para 151). The possibility that applying this balancing test might result in the child's interests prevailing was acknowledged by the Court in Johansen v Norway (1996) when it said: 'a fair balance must be struck in the interests of the child and those of the parent and, in striking such a balance, particular importance must be attached to the welfare of the child which, depending on their nature and seriousness, *may override those of the parent*' (para 78; emphasis added).

The drafters of the CRC expended considerable energy debating whether the child's best interests should be the paramount or a primary consideration in decision-making, eventually settling on the latter, save in adoption cases where the former governs (Sutherland, 2016, p 27). Thus, it was less surprising than it might have been that, in R. and H. v United Kingdom, where the child had been adopted in the face of parental opposition, the ECtHR opined that, 'in all decisions concerning children, their best interests must be paramount' (R. and H. v the United Kingdom, 2011, para 73). It drew support for that position from the then-recent Grand Chamber judgment in Neulinger and Shuruk v Switzerland (2010, para 135), a case addressing the wrongful removal of a child and application of the relevant Hague Convention which, in its preamble, accords 'paramount importance' to the interests of children in custody matters (Hague Convention on the Civil Aspects of International Child Abduction, 1980, H.C. No. 25). There, the Court had noted 'that there is currently a broad consensus – including in international law – in support of the idea that in all decisions concerning children, their best interests must be paramount'. While these decisions must be understood in the context of international instruments that accorded paramountcy to the child's best interests in the particular context, for a brief period, they raised the tantalising prospect that there might be further elevation of the child's best interests across the board in decisions of the ECtHR (Simmonds, 2012). That period was brought to an end by the judgment of the Grand Chamber in Strand Lobben v Norway (2019).

Strand Lobben and its progeny

Discussions of Strand Lobben permeate this volume so the myriad facts and domestic court proceeding will not be explored again here (see, particularly, Emberland, Chapter 2; Archard and Skivenes, Chapter 13). In brief, Ms Strand Lobben's infant son, X, had been removed from her care and placed in foster care under an emergency care order due to serious concerns over her ability to look after him. Ultimately – and following numerous domestic court proceedings – her parental authority was removed and the foster parents, who had cared for X since he was three weeks old, were permitted to adopt him.

Ms Strand Lobben turned to the ECtHR for assistance, founding on Article 8 of the Convention. Noting the extensive enquiry undertaken by the child welfare authorities and the domestic courts which highlighted X's psychological vulnerability and his mother's continuing inability to care for him, the Chamber concluded, by four votes to three, that the decision-making process had been fair, that it had been motivated by an overriding concern for the child's best interests and that there were exceptional circumstances that warranted the termination of his mother's parental responsibilities and X's adoption by his foster parents. Thus, that there had been no violation of Article 8 (Strand Lobben and Others v Norway, 2017).

The stage was set for the case to go to the Grand Chamber and the controversy in Europe over the issue of child protection is reflected in the level of third-party involvement, with seven states and a number of organisations being granted leave to intervene in the case (see Cichowski and Crun, Chapter 11). Signalling the importance they attached to their decision and the division among them, no fewer than 11 of the 17 judges wrote (often joint) separate opinions, six concurring with the majority and five dissenting (see Emberland, Chapter 2).

The majority began by recognising that 'the mutual enjoyment by parent and child of each other's company constitutes a fundamental element of family life' and the familiar test that any interference with it will violate Article 8 unless it is in accordance with law, in pursuit of a legitimate aim and proportionate (Strand Lobben and Others v Norway, 2019, paras 202, 207). Signalling what was to prove central to its decision, it noted that, in assessing proportionality, regard must be had to the extent to which a 'fair balance' had been struck between 'the relevant competing interests' (Strand Lobben and Others v Norway, 2019, para 203).

More specifically, the Court set out the following basic principles to be applied in child protection cases: a care order should be regarded as a temporary measure, to be discontinued as soon as circumstances permit; the authorities are under a positive obligation to take measures to facilitate family reunification as soon as reasonably feasible; and, in the meantime, everything must be done to preserve personal relations (Strand Lobben and Others v Norway, 2019, paras 205–208). More far-reaching measures, like the termination of parental responsibilities or adoption, 'should only be applied in exceptional circumstances' and only where they can be justified by 'an overriding requirement pertaining to the child's best interests' (Strand Lobben and Others v Norway, 2019, para 209). In all of this, the Court was conscious of the danger that the 'effluxion of time' due to procedural or other delays could 'result in the de facto determination of the issue submitted to the court before it has held its hearing' (Strand Lobben and Others v Norway, 2019, para 212).

When it applied these principles to the instant case, it found a number of shortcomings in the decision-making process. In particular, it noted the limited opportunities for contact between the mother and the child, the failure to seek updated expert reports, the limited assessment of how the mother's situation had changed and the lack of detailed and up-to-date assessment of the child's continuing vulnerability (Strand Lobben and Others v Norway, 2019, paras 220–225). In concluding that there had been a violation of Article 8, it found that

> [T]he domestic authorities did not attempt to perform a genuine balancing exercise between the interests of the child and his biological family, but focused on the child's interests instead of trying to combine both sets of interests, and moreover did not seriously contemplate any possibility of the child's reunification with his biological family. (Strand Lobben and Others v Norway, 2019, para 220)

Decisions of the ECtHR have been criticised for a lack of clarity and consistency (Fenton-Glynn, 2019; O'Mahony, 2019) and the Court's approach to the importance to be attached to the child's best interests provides another example of that problem. It referred to the 'broad consensus, including in international law' that in all decisions concerning children the best interests of the child are 'of paramount importance' and 'must come before all other considerations' (Strand Lobben and Others v Norway, 2019, para 204). With respect, that is not entirely accurate. As we have seen, while the Hague Convention on Child Abduction, for example, accords paramountcy to these interests, the CRC treats the child's best interests as a primary consideration, save in adoption cases where paramountcy is the order of the day.

In any event, the Court departed from its position on paramountcy. Having emphasised that 'regard for family unity and for family reunification in the event of separation are inherent considerations in the right to respect for family life under Art.8' (Strand Lobben and Others v Norway, 2019, para 205), it concluded that 'where the respective interests of a child and those of the parents come into conflict, art.8 requires that the domestic authorities should *strike a fair balance* between those interests', albeit, it conceded that 'in the balancing process, particular importance should be attached to the best interests of the child which, depending on their nature and seriousness, may override those of the parents' (Strand Lobben and Others v Norway, 2019, para 206; emphasis added).

In their dissenting opinion, Judges Kjølbro, Poláčková, Koskelo and Nordén criticised the approach of their fellows in the majority as being 'riddled not only with some inevitable ambiguities but also with some undeniable tensions and outright contradictions, "internally" as well as in relation to the relevant specialised legal instruments, particularly the International Convention on the Rights of the Child' (Strand Lobben and Others v Norway, 2019, OIII-5). As they noted, the difficulty stems from 'how to reconcile the "sanctity" of the biological family with the best interests of the child' (Strand Lobben and Others v Norway, 2019, OIII-6) and, where reconciliation it not possible, to determine which takes precedence (Strand Lobben and Others v Norway, 2019, OIII-9). As they rightly pointed out, the ECHR and the CRC may give very different answers.

The decision in Strand Lobben had been followed in numerous Chamber judgments on child protection (see Emberland, Chapter 2) when the Grand Chamber returned to the matter of child protection, in 2021, in Abdi Ibrahim v Norway (2021). There, the authorities had authorised the adoption of the son of a young, Muslim, Somali woman by a Christian couple in the face of her opposition. The fascinating cultural and religious dimensions of that case are a matter for discussion another day. For our present purpose, two points should be noted. First, the Grand Chamber quoted in full – and endorsed – 'the general principles relevant to child welfare measures' that it had set out in Strand Lobben (2019, para 145). Second, it found that there had been violation of the mother's Article 8 rights and the Court repeated the criticism that the domestic authorities had not attempted 'to perform a genuine balancing exercise between the interests of the child and those of his biological family, but focused on the child's interests instead of trying to combine both sets of interests' (Abdi Ibrahim v Norway, 2021, para 151). It is clear, then, that the European Court now takes the view in child protection cases that, while the child's best interests are important, they must be balanced against respect for the rights of the child's parents.

United Nations Convention on the Rights of the Child

It is familiar territory that the CRC, adopted by the UN General Assembly in 1989, came into force more quickly than any other human rights treaty, becoming the most widely ratified international human rights instrument (Lopatka, 2007, p xli; Tobin, 2019, p 1). While the CRC is much younger than the ECHR, it has now featured in the human rights firmament for well over 30 years and there has been ample opportunity for it to be founded upon in domestic and international courts (Liefaard and Doek, 2015) and explored extensively in the academic literature.

In contrast to the ECHR, the CRC is unambiguously focused on children's rights. As is made clear in the preamble to the CRC, however, these rights are premised on a view of the family as 'the fundamental group of society and the natural environment for the growth and wellbeing of all its members and particularly children' and the centrality of the family is reinforced throughout the CRC. So, for example, there is the Article 9 injunction against separation of a child from his or her parents save where that is necessary in the child's best interests, while Article 16(1), protects against arbitrary or unlawful interference in the child's family.

Alongside this emphasis on the importance of the family, the CRC recognises that families alone may not always be relied upon to provide all children with adequate protection and, indeed, that family members may be the source of potential or actual harm (Sandberg, 2018). Thus, for example, Article 3(2) places an obligation on states parties 'to ensure the child such protection and care as is necessary for his or her well-being', while Article 19 addresses the state obligation to protect the child from abuse and neglect.

The focus here is on the priority accorded to the child's best interests in the child protection context when weighed against the rights and interest of others. Since Article 3(1) of the CRC provides that the child's best interests are 'a primary consideration in all actins concerning the child', these interests start from a strong position, something reinforced by the fact that Article 3(1) itself has long been regarded as one of the four general principles of the convention (UN, 2022, para 12).

The CRC Committee plays a crucial role in amplifying the content of the rights and obligations under the CRC. In the following sections, its contributions through Concluding Observations on state party reports and decisions under the Communications Procedure will be explored first since they are of limited assistance in addressing our concern. We then turn to the Committee's GCs, which do more to clarify the priority to be accorded to best interests, and the DGDs, which, arguably, point to a way forward.

Concluding Observations

The CRC requires each state party to submit an initial report to the CRC Committee on its progress in implementing the convention within two years of it entering into force in the country and periodic reports every five years thereafter (Article 44(1)). In 2022 – and in line with other treaty bodies – the CRC Committee extended the reporting cycle to eight years (UN, 2022, para 58). After a process of dialogue with the state party and deliberation, the CRC Committee publishes its Concluding Observations – essentially, a report card on the state party's performance – acknowledging progress made, highlighting matters that are cause for concern and making recommendations for action. Concluding Observations are important in assessing and recording the performance of the state under review, but they also serve a valuable function as an interpretative tool in respect of the CRC itself (O'Flaherty, 2006, p 51).

This opportunity for the CRC Committee to monitor the state party's compliance with its convention obligations and to amplify what CRC obligations entail is constrained, however, by the Committee's very part-time status. In 2014, the General Assembly introduced a further limitation when, as part of its efforts aimed at operating more efficiently, it encouraged treaty bodies to adopt a simplified reporting procedure, 'short, focused and concrete concluding observations' and to limit them to 10,700 words (UNGA, 2014).

The CRC Committee responded the following year, issuing new reporting guidelines (UN Committee on the Rights of the Child, 2015). States parties are directed to structure their reports using the model provided which groups cognate articles in the convention together in 'clusters' (para 17). There are 11 clusters in all, most having further sub-divisions, but of particular relevance for our present purpose are those dealing with general principles (taking in Article 3), violence against children, family environment and alternative care, and special protection measures.

Concluding Observations mirror the clusters in the guidelines, often addressing the various sub-divisions specifically. Unsurprisingly, there is always a discussion of the state party's progress in implementing Article 3(1), with the Committee emphasising its importance and reminding states parties of the need to apply it comprehensively and to train the relevant professionals in its application. Similarly, Concluding Observations address child protection, often making detailed recommendations in respect of the state party.

What is absent, however, is in-depth exploration of the priority to be accorded to the child's best interests when weighed against parental rights in the child protection context. Given that Concluding Observations deal with a wide range of topics and are subject to a word limit, that is no criticism of the Committee. It does suggest, however, that it might take the opportunity to address that matter in greater depth elsewhere.

Communications Procedure

The Optional Protocol to the Convention on the Rights of the Child on a Communications Procedure (OPIC) provides the CRC Committee with another opportunity to amplify the convention (UNGA, 2011). Since OPIC came into force in 2014, the Committee has been empowered to receive 'individual communications' – essentially, complaints – from, or on behalf of, a particular child or group of children that a state party has violated rights set out in the CRC or the First or Second Optional Protocols thereto and to make determinations on them (Article 5). Communications may only be received in respect of a state party that has ratified OPIC and, where the complaint concerns the First or Second Optional Protocols, the relevant instrument (Article 1) and a range of fairly standard admissibility criteria impose further limitations (Article 7). Echoing the CRC itself, the Committee is directed that, in dealing with communications, it 'shall be guided by the principle of the best interests of the child', having regard to the rights and views of the child (Article 2), and this approach is repeated in the Committee's own Rules of Procedure (2021).

The promise of the Committee's determinations under OPIC is that, unlike GCs and Concluding Observations, they will provide insights into its thinking in a case-specific context that more closely parallels judgments of the ECtHR. For our present purpose, that promise has yet to be fulfilled since the Committee's decisions on the merits to date have largely addressed migration-related issues (age determination, deportation and asylum), with a small number of cases dealing with access to education and intra-family disputes. In its only decision on the merits to date that dealt squarely with child protection, B.J. and P.J. v Czech Republic (2023), the Committee found such clear violation of the rights of two siblings, aged 13 and 15, under Articles 3(1), 9, 12 and 37(b) that it did not discuss the matter of balancing parental rights with those of the young people.[3]

Why OPIC has been used so rarely in respect of child protection is a matter for speculation. One explanation is that relatively few states – only 52 at the time of writing – have ratified it and some countries whose child protection procedures have given rise to cases before the ECtHR, including Norway and the United Kingdom, are not among them. It may simply be due to the fact that OPIC has only been in force for a relatively short time and using it is still feeding into litigators' thinking, an explanation made all the more persuasive by the fact that a number of cases raising child protection issues are pending. The Committee's determinations in these cases may provide a wealth of material for future analysis providing insights into the priority to be accorded to the child's best interests when weighed against the rights of others.

General Comments

In its Rules of Procedure, the CRC Committee describes the GCs it publishes periodically as being designed to promote the 'further implementation' of the Convention and to 'assist States parties in fulfilling their reporting obligations' (UN Committee on the Rights of the Child, 2019, r. 77). That modest statement underplays the immense importance of the GCs in fleshing out CRC obligations, in amplifying their application in particular contexts and the reliance placed on them by states parties, courts and commentators.

Numerous GCs address the obligation to protect children and young people in the many situations where their rights may be compromised (see UNCRC, 2005a, 2006, 2009, 2016, 2017), but of particular relevance for our present purpose is GC No. 13: The right of the child to freedom from all forms of violence (UNCRC, 2011). There, the Committee makes clear that, while 'in common parlance the term violence is often understood to mean only physical harm and/or intentional harm', Article 19 is designed to protect children from 'all forms of physical or mental violence, injury or abuse, neglect or negligent treatment, maltreatment or exploitation, including sexual abuse' (UNCRC, 2011).[4] Thus, the protection afforded by the Convention addresses the totality of the child's situation.

The CRC Committee had long signalled the importance of according to primacy to the best interests of the child in all actions concerning children, designating it one of the general principles of the CRC, when it turned its attentions to Article 3(1) again, in GC No. 14 (UNCRC, 2013). There, it provided the iconic description of the child's best interests as 'a threefold concept', being 'a substantive right … a fundamental interpretive principle and … a rule of procedure' (para 6).

Conscious of the criticism levelled at the concept of the child's best interests – that it is vague and indeterminate (see the discussion of 'The best interests of the child' earlier) – the Committee sought to clarify what was involved in making what it described as a 'best interests assessment and determination' using 'a non-exhaustive and non-hierarchical list of elements' that would provide decision-makers with 'concrete guidance, yet flexibility' (para 50). It emphasised that assessment should be undertaken by 'balancing all the elements necessary to make a decision in a specific situation for a specific individual child or group of children' (para 48). The elements it identified are as follows: the child's views; the child's identity; preservation of family environment and maintaining relations; care, protection and safety; situations of vulnerability; the child's right to health; and the child's right to education (paras 52–79).

These elements echo the CRC itself. So, for example, 'preservation of family environment and maintaining relations' has its roots in the Convention's preambular reference to the importance of the family as the fundamental group in society and to the numerous articles that acknowledge its importance. Similarly, by highlighting 'care, protection and safety' as a facet of best interests, the Committee was reiterating the state party's obligations to ensure protection for children. Addressing the situation where protecting the child might indicate intervention in the family, GC 14 drew on the UN Guidelines for the Alternative Care of Children (UNGA, 2010), emphasising that states parties should provide support to parents to enable them to fulfil their responsibilities; that separation of a child from his or her family should be a measure of last resort; that it should be accompanied by assessment, preferably by a multidisciplinary team of well-trained professionals with appropriate judicial involvement; and that the child should maintain links with the parents and family unless that is not in the child's best interests (paras 61–65).

Thus far, the approach of the CRC Committee has much in common with that of the ECtHR. It is when we turn to the priority to be accorded to the child's best interests that divergence emerges. Acknowledging that a particular child's rights might conflict with those of other people, whether children or adults, the Committee recommended balancing the interests of all concerned and seeking to find a compromise. However, it recognised that will not always be possible and, where conflicting rights cannot be harmonised, it was quite clear that the child's best interests 'have high priority', that they are 'not just one of several considerations' and, consequently, that 'a larger weight must be attached to what serves the child best' (para 39). That is a long way from the simple balancing test advocated by the ECtHR.

Days of General Discussion

In order to enhance a deeper understanding of the content and implications of the Convention, the CRC Committee devotes one or more meetings of its regular sessions to a general discussion of a specific topic or article of the Convention (2019).[5] These DGDs bring together a wide range of government representatives, organisations and individuals, including children and young people, and, following in-depth discussion, make recommendations for action by states and stakeholders.

That DGDs can have considerable impact is illustrated by the fact it was the recommendations from the Day of General Discussion in September 2005 on Children without Parental Care (UNCRC, 2005b, para 688) that led, ultimately, to the United Nations adopting the highly influential Guidelines for the Alternative Care of Children (UNGA, 2010).

In September 2021, the topic was Children's Rights and Alternative Care and the resulting Outcome Report (2022) set out comprehensive recommendations that were endorsed by the CRC Committee. Constraints of space do not permit in-depth exploration of the many excellent recommendations, but they repeat familiar themes, often echoing the Guidelines for the Alternative Care of Children and the General Assembly resolution of 2019. For our present purpose, the following recommendation is of particular interest:

> The Committee should, through its monitoring role, provide explicit guidance to States parties on practical steps to be taken to implement international human rights frameworks and commitments, including measures to strengthen prevention of family separation, building integrated systems for child protection and strategies for deinstitutionalization with specific time frames and adequate budgets. (UNGA, 2019, p 36)

It might be a stretch to interpret that recommendation as a call for the CRC Committee to issue a GC on child protection since it refers expressly to the Committee's 'monitoring role', something that was probably a reference to Concluding Observations directed to individual states parties. Yet it will be recalled that the Committee's own Rules of Procedure view promoting further implementation of the CRC as one of the goals of GCs (r. 77) and there is recent precedent for a GC to follow on from a DGD.[6]

Conclusion

The goal of this chapter was to explore whether the ECtHR, interpreting the ECHR, and the CRC Committee, amplifying the CRC, were sending states parties different messages about what is required of them in the priority to be accorded to the child's best interests when weighed against the rights and interests of other family members, particularly their parents.

Examination of the Court's judgments and the work of the CRC Committee reveals much common ground between the two in the child protection context. Each recognises the importance of the family to its individual members – be they children or adults – and to society as a whole. Accordingly, both emphasise the desirability of supporting families to enable parents to care for their children, while recognising that there may be circumstances in which protecting the child will involve removing him or her from parental care. Both require that the decision to take a child into care should be based on clear criteria and that separation should be for as short a period as possible. Provided it is consistent with the child's best interest, both support child–parent contact being maintained during any period of separation and the goal of family reunification.

Both the ECtHR and the CRC Committee recognise that the child's best interests are important when decisions that affect children are being taken. Where the two part company is on the issue of the priority to be accorded to these interests when they conflict with the rights and interests of others, particularly those of the child's parents. As demonstrated by its recent decisions, the Grand Chamber of the ECtHR requires the application of a balancing test: that is, that the decision-maker should 'perform a genuine balancing exercise between the interests of the child and his [or her] biological family' (Strand Lobben v Norway, 2019) It is in the nature of balancing competing interests that one or other might prevail in a given case.

In contrast, in GC 14 (UNCRC, 2013), the CRC Committee makes clear that, where a conflict arises between the child's best interest and the rights of another person, the child's best interests are 'not just one of several considerations' and that 'a larger weight must be attached to what serves the child best' (para 39). Thus, for the Committee, this is not a competition between two equal factors. As we have seen, the limitations placed on Concluding Observations curtails the scope for the CRC Committee to develop this theme further there. Similarly, the dearth of child protection cases coming before it under OPIC to date has denied it the opportunity to apply its approach to prioritising the child's best interests in specific cases. That, however, is likely to be a temporary deficit since a number of such cases are pending and it may be that the Committee will reiterate what it said in GC 14 in them.

In any event, for the time being, states parties are being sent conflicting messages about the priority to be accorded to the child's best interests where they conflict with parental rights and interests. As a theoretical proposition, a lack of coherence in the human rights arena is undesirable, but there are also practical consequences that place jurisdictions that seek to comply with their human rights obligations in an unenviable position. Should states parties draft laws and apply them in line with the approach of the ECtHR or should they seek to comply with that of the CRC Committee? How their actions are judged might well depend on whether any challenge to them is taken to the ECtHR or under OPIC.

How might this difficulty be resolved? It will be recalled that two decades ago, the Grand Chamber famously declared: 'The human rights of children and the standards to which all governments must aspire in realising these rights for all children are set out in the Convention on the Rights of the Child' (Sommerfeld v Germany, 2003).

Recent research confirms that the ECtHR continues to set great store by the CRC (Helland and Hollekim, 2023). Given this favourable climate, one avenue that might be worth pursuing would be for the CRC Committee to draft a new GC, dedicated to child protection, in which it takes the opportunity to explore all aspects of the subject, including the priority to be accorded to the child's best interests where they conflict with parental rights and interests.[7] Were it to adhere to the position it took in GC 14 – that is to say, that greater weight should be attached to the child's best interests – it might cause the ECtHR to revisit the matter and revise its own position.

Notes

[1] There is reference to minors in Article 5 and to juveniles in Article 6, with children being mentioned in Protocol 7, Article 5.

[2] Marckx v Belgium, no. 6833/74; (inheritance rights of child born outside of marriage); Johnston v Ireland no. 9697/82; (impact on child of father's inability to divorce); and X v Austria no. 19010/07; (impact on child of parent's same-sex partner being prevented from adopting the child).

[3] An earlier case, K.S.G. v Spain (2020), fell at the admissibility hurdle; CRC/C/85/D/92/2019 (inadmissible under OPIC, Article 7(f); communication manifestly ill-founded or not sufficiently substantiated).

[4] CRC/C/GC/13 (2011), para 4. It had already condemned corporal punishment and other abusive treatment in General Comment No. 8: The right of the child to protection from corporal punishment and other cruel or degrading forms of punishment, CRC/C/GC/8 (2006).

[5] Rules of procedure: CRC/C/4/Rev.5 (2019), r.79. Since 2012, these have been scheduled biennially.

[6] General Comment No. 26 on children's rights and the environment with a special focus on climate change, CRC/C/GC/26 (2023), has its origins in the 2016 DGD on Children's Rights and the Environment.

[7] Instead, the Committee might elect to issue a Statement, as it did in respect of Article 5: Statement of the Committee on the Rights of the Child on article 5 of the Convention on the Rights of the Child, 11 October 2023.

References

Abdi Ibrahim v Norway [GC] (no. 15379/16) [2021] ECtHR (10 December).

Bainham, A. (2002) 'Can we protect children and protect their rights?', *Family Law*, 32: 279–289.

Berrick, J.D., Gilbert, N. and Skivenes, M. (2023) 'Child protection systems across the world', in J.D. Berrick, N. Gilbert and M. Skivenes (eds), *Oxford Handbook of Child Protection Systems*, Oxford University Press, pp 943–969.

B.J. and P.J. v Czech Republic (no. 139/2021) [2023] CRC Committee (15 May).

Breen, C. Krutzinna, J., Luhamaa K. and Skivenes, M. (2020) 'Family life for children in state care: An analysis of the European Court of Human Rights' reasoning on adoption without consent', *International Journal of Children's Rights*, 28(4): 715–747.

Committee on the Rights of the Child (2019) Rules of procedure: CRC/C/4/Rev.5. Available from: https://tbinternet.ohchr.org/_layouts/15/treatybodyexternal/Download.aspx?symbolno=CRC/C/4/Rev.5&Lang=en

Committee on the Rights of the Child (2022) 'Day of general discussion: Children's rights and alternative care: outcome report'. Available from: https://www.ohchr.org/sites/default/files/2022-06/13Jun2022-DGD-Outcome-report-and-Recommendations.pdf

Connolly, M. and Katz, I. (2019) 'Typologies of child protection systems: An international approach', *Child Abuse Review*, 28(5): 381–394.

Council of Europe Newsroom (2022) 'Russia ceases to be party to the European Convention on Human Rights'. Available from: https://www.coe.int/en/web/portal/-/russia-ceases-to-be-party-to-the-european-convention-on-human-rights

Fenton-Glynn, C. (2019) 'Children, parents, and the European Court of Human Rights', *European Human Rights Law Review*, 6: 643–653.

Fenton-Glynn, C. (2021) *Children and the European Court of Human Rights*, Oxford University Press.

Fortin, J. (2009) *Children's Rights and the Developing Law* (3rd edn), Butterworths.

Gilbert, N. (ed) (1997) *Combatting Child Abuse: International Perspectives and Trends*, Oxford University Press.

Hague Convention on the Civil Aspects of International Child Abduction (1980) H.C. No. 25. Judgment of the Grand Chamber of 10 September 2019.

Helland, T. and Hollekim, R. (2023) 'The Convention on the Rights of the Child's imprint on judgments from the European Court of Human Rights: A negligible footprint?', *Nordic Journal of Human Rights*, 41(2): 213–233.

Hokkanen v Finland (no. 19823/92) [1994] ECtHR (23 September).
Johansen v Norway (no. 17383/90) [1996] ECtHR (7 August).
Johnston v Ireland (no. 9697/82) [1986] ECtHR (18 December).
Kohm, L.M. (2008) 'Tracing the foundations of the best interests of the child standard in American jurisprudence', *Journal of Law and Family Studies*, 10(2): 337–378.
L v Sweden (no. 10141/82) [1984] ECtHR (3 October).
Liefaard, T. and Doek, J.E. (eds) (2015) *Litigating the Rights of the Child: The UN Convention on the Rights of the Child in Domestic and International Jurisprudence*, Springer.
Lopatka, A. (2007) 'Introduction', *Legislative History of the Convention on the Rights of the Child*, Office of the United Nations High Commissioner for Human Rights, pp xxxvii–xliii.
Luhamaa, K., Krutzinna, J. and Skivenes, M. (2022) 'Child's best interest in child protection legislation of 44 jurisdictions', Centre for Research on Discretion and Paternalism, University of Bergen. Available from: https://discretion.uib.no/wp-content/uploads/2022/03/CBI-Report.pdf
Marckx v Belgium (no. 6833/74) [1979] ECtHR (13 June).
Mnookin, R.H. (1975) 'Child-custody adjudication: Judicial functions in the face of indeterminacy', *Law and Contemporary Problems*, 39(3): 226–294.
Neulinger and Shuruk v Switzerland (no. 41615/07) [2010] ECtHR (6 July).
Nielsen v Denmark (no. 10929/84) [1988] ECtHR (28 November).
O'Flaherty, M. (2006) 'The concluding observations of United Nations human rights treaty bodies', *Human Rights Law Review*, 6(1): 27–52.
Olsson v Sweden (No. 1) (no. 10465/83) [1988] ECtHR (24 March).
Olsson v Sweden (No. 2) (no. 13441/87) [1992] ECtHR (27 November).
O'Mahony, C. (2019) 'Child protection and the ECHR: Making sense of positive and procedural obligations', *International Journal of Children's Rights*, 27(4): 660–693.
R. and H. v the United Kingdom (no. 35348/06) [2011] ECtHR (31 May, final 15 September).
Reece, H. (1996) 'The paramountcy principle: Consensus or construct?', *Current Legal Problems*, 49(1): 267–304.
Sandberg, K. (2018) 'Children's right to protection under the CRC', in A. Falch-Eriksen and E. Backe-Hansen (eds), *Human Rights in Child Protection: Implications for Professional Practice and Policy*, Springer, pp 13–38.
Simmonds, C. (2012) 'Paramountcy and the ECHR: A conflict resolved?' *Cambridge Law Journal*, 71(3): 498–501.
Sommerfeld v Germany (no. 31871/96) [2003] ECtHR (8 July).
Strand Lobben and Others v Norway (no. 37283/13) [2017] ECtHR (30 November).
Strand Lobben and Others v Norway [GC] (no. 37283/13) [2019] ECtHR (10 September).

Sutherland, E.E. (2016) 'Article 3 of the United Nations Convention on the Rights of the Child: The challenges of vagueness and priorities', in E.E. Sutherland and L.A. Barnes Macfarlane (eds), *Implementing Article 3 of the United Nations Convention on the Rights of the Child*, Cambridge University Press, pp 21–50.

Taylor, R.E. (2024) *Fortin's Children's Rights and the Developing Law* (4th edn), Cambridge University Press.

Tobin, J. (2019) *The UN Convention on the Rights of the Child: A Commentary*, Oxford University Press.

UN (United Nations) (2019) Convention on the Rights of the Child: CRC/C/85/D/92/2019. Available from: https://documents.un.org/doc/undoc/gen/g20/275/77/pdf/g2027577.pdf

UN (United Nations) (2022) Report of the Committee on the Rights of the Child, A/77/41, General Assembly Official Records, Seventy-seventh Session, Supplement No. 41. Available from: https://documents.un.org/access.nsf/get?OpenAgent&DS=A/79/41&Lang=E

UNCRC (United Nations Committee on the Rights of the Child) (2003) General Comment No. 5: General measures of implementation of the Convention on the Rights of the Child, CRC/GC/2003/5 (27 November). Available from: https://www.refworld.org/legal/general/crc/2003/en/36435

UNCRC (United Nations Committee on the Rights of the Child) (2005a) General Comment No. 7: Implementing child rights in early childhood, CRC/C/GC/7/Rev.1.

UNCRC (United Nations Committee on the Rights of the Child) (2005b) Day of General Discussion on Children Without Parental Care, CRC/C/153, September 2005.

UNCRC (United Nations Committee on the Rights of the Child) (2006) General Comment No. 9: The rights of children with disabilities, CRC/C/GC/9/Corr.1.

UNCRC (United Nations Committee on the Rights of the Child) (2009) General Comment No. 11: Indigenous children and their rights under the Convention, CRC/C/GC/11.

UNCRC (United Nations Committee on the Rights of the Child) (2011) General comment No. 13: The right of the child to freedom from all forms of violence, CRC/C/GC/13 (18 April).

UNCRC (United Nations Committee on the Rights of the Child) (2013) General Comment No. 14 on the rights of the child to have his or her best interests taken as a primary consideration, CRC/C/GC/14.

UNCRC (United Nations Committee on the Rights of the Child) (2015) Treaty-specific guidelines regarding the form and content of periodic reports to be submitted by States parties under article 44, paragraph 1 (b), of the Convention on the Rights of the Child, CRC/C/58/Rev.3.

UNCRC (United Nations Committee on the Rights of the Child) (2016) General Comment No. 20: The implementation of the rights of the child during adolescence, CRC/C/GC/20.

UNCRC (United Nations Committee on the Rights of the Child) (2017) General Comment No. 21: Children in street situations, CRC/C/GC/21.

UNCRC (United Nations Committee on the Rights of the Child) (2019) Rules of Procedure: CRC/C/4/Rev.5. Available from: https://tbinternet.ohchr.org/_layouts/15/treatybodyexternal/Download.aspx?symbolno=CRC%2FC%2F4%2FRev.5&Lang=en

UNCRC (United Nations Committee on the Rights of the Child) (2023) Statement of the Committee on the Rights of the Child on article 5 of the Convention on the Rights of the Child, 11 October 2023. Available from: https://www.ohchr.org/sites/default/files/documents/hrbodies/crc/statements/CRC-Article-5-statement.pdf

UNGA (United Nations General Assembly) (2010) Guidelines for the Alternative Care of Children: resolution / adopted by the General Assembly, A/RES/64/142. Available from: https://www.refworld.org/legal/resolution/unga/2010/en/73661

UNGA (United Nations General Assembly)(2011) Rules of procedure under the Optional Protocol to the Convention on the Rights of the Child on a communications procedure, A/RES/66/138. Available from: https://violenceagainstchildren.un.org/content/ares66138

UNGA (United Nations General Assembly)(2014) Strengthening and Enhancing the Effective Functioning of the Human Rights Treaty Body System, GA/RES/68/268. Resolution adopted by the General Assembly on 9 April 2014. Available from: https://documents.un.org/doc/undoc/gen/n13/455/53/pdf/n1345553.pdf

UNGA (United Nations General Assembly)(2019) Resolution on the Rights of the Child, A/RES/74/133, adopted 18 December.

UNGA (United Nations General Assembly)(2021) Rules of procedure under the Optional Protocol to the Convention on the Rights of the Child on a communications procedure, CRC/C/158, 2021, r.1(1).

X v Austria [GC] (no. 19010/07) [2013] ECtHR (19 February).

9

Think of the children! Children's rights as the new frontier in anti-gender contestation

Neil Datta

Introduction

In December 2020, the Norwegian Human Rights Institution published a report on the contestation surrounding Norway's child protection system entitled 'Why is Norway convicted in the European Court of Human Rights? A status report on the child protection field' (Norges institusjon for menneskerettigheter, 2020) detailing how the European Court of Human Rights (ECtHR) had taken up 39 cases involving Norway's child protection service, Barnevernet. Indeed, contestation of Norway's Barnevernet has led not only to a plethora of cases before the ECtHR, but also to campaigns involving grassroots activism in both Norway and internationally, in political advocacy at the United Nations and the Parliamentary Assembly of the Council of Europe and even to a Bollywood film negatively portraying Barnevernet. This chapter will explore the contestation around Barnevernet specifically, and similar cases in other Nordic countries, from the perspective of the transnational civil society organisations which have a track record for anti-gender activism proactively engaged in activism on these cases.

This chapter will focus specifically on the role that anti-gender actors play in this form of contestation. Most of the research on anti-gender activism has focused on the traditional hot button issues of anti-gender contestation, namely sexual and reproductive health and rights (SRHR), and specifically abortion, as well as LGBTQIA+ rights and increasingly gender-based violence. What has not yet been explored is whether children's rights, and specifically the role of child protective services, feature in this anti-gender contestation, and if so, how. While contestation around child protective services based on Nordic models has increased, there has not yet been an analysis of this phenomenon from the perspective of gender ideology contestation. The chapter explores the role of anti-gender actors in contesting issues related to children's rights, highlighting their strategies, areas of focus and prominence within this arena.

There has been a blossoming of literature on anti-gender movements in Europe, with the most recent comparative example being the book released in 2024: *The Christian Right in Europe: Movements, Networks and Denominations* (Lo Mascolo, 2023) which explores this question in 20 European states, plus the European Union Institutions. The Norway chapter of *The Christian Right in Europe* does not address the contestation surrounding Barnevernet as part of the anti-gender landscape in the country. Separately, there exist some limited studies into the role of anti-gender actors and their contestation in specific areas of children's rights. Among these is the Colombian non-governmental organisation Sentiido in their report 'Manufacturing moral panic: Weaponizing children to undermine gender justice and human rights' (Sentiido, 2021).

This chapter is structured to explore the disinformation universe which has arisen around child protection; the categories of anti-gender actors involved in child protection contestation; the ideological origins of anti-gender contestation on children's rights; and the key anti-gender actors and how they engage in children's rights contestation. The chapter will focus specifically on four prominent anti-gender actors and their role in contesting child protection in general, and the Nordic model and Barnevernet more specifically. References to the sources used as data material for the analysis are found in the Appendix to the chapter.

Disinformation universe

Child protection cases are understandably often fraught with contestation as they may involve the forcible removal of a child from the custody of their parents by the government. Such cases may be extremely emotional for the parties involved, and for the child protective services, they often fall into a grey area of deciding to intervene for the best interests of the child before it is deemed too late for the child's safety. With such a backdrop, the very nature of the intervention of child protection services can lead to one-sided and emotional portrayals of specific cases, thus leading to misrepresentation and further to disinformation.

Thus, a first aspect to understand is the widespread disinformation which exists around the Norwegian child protective service, Barnevernet, specifically and by association, the child protective services of neighbouring Nordic countries. The Nordic Observatory for Digital Media and Information Disorder (NORDIS), a coalition of fact-checkers covering Denmark, Finland, Norway and Sweden, explored this disinformation universe in 2023 (Akerbæk, 2023) and how it is situated both within the Nordic countries concerned and internationally. The disinformation combines several different elements. A foundational element is the sincere critique against Barnevernet existing locally within Norway with NORDIS finding that 'there are at least 25 Norwegian groups, pages and personal profiles that have the same goal: To radically change the Norwegian child protection system. Together, these have over 140,000 followers' (Akerbæk, 2023). These local actors in Norway may seek external allies for their cause (see the section on 'Multi-pronged advocacy: how anti-gender actors engage in children's rights' in this chapter).

However, there are other components. One is the perception that Barnevernet is inherently racist and/or xenophobic in its approach, often drawing on specific cases of child custody involving immigrant families, thus providing the fodder for an international dimension to contesting the legitimacy of Barnevernet as the cases may gain notoriety in the countries of origin of the immigrant families concerned. One early example involved a case of an Indian family living in Norway, which later became popularised in a Bollywood film, *Ms Chatterjee vs Norway* (NDTV, 2023), also contributing to diplomatic tensions between the two countries. There have also been high-profile cases involving families with roots in the Czech Republic, Poland and Romania, in some cases leading to public rebuke by heads of state (Lohne et al, 2015) and to coordinated mass protests against Barnevernet in multiple countries (Johansen and Hansen, 2023).

These very real cases of child protection involving third-country nationals then generated attention and investigation into the Norwegian child protection system, paving the way for actors to engage in proactive disinformation efforts on Barnevernet specifically, and more broadly the Norwegian model and/or the Nordic models of child protective services. For example, NORDIS found that misinformation was circulating in Arabic-language social media platforms concerning child protective services in Denmark and Finland (Nordis Hub, 2023). The disinformation often misrepresents ongoing critiques of the child protective services – for example, in Finland misrepresenting the cost of child placement with trafficking in children (Liski and Gråsten-Lahtinen, 2023) – along with emotional portrayals of families affected. In the Czech Republic, this led to a 2017 documentary, *Děti státu*[1] (*Children of the State*), which strives to 'gives the public response to virtually everything you needed to know about Barnevernet and you were afraid to ask' (Zdechovský, 2020). In some cases, local actors from Nordic countries have used the international critiques of the child protective systems as validation for their domestic critiques of child protection systems and more broadly the progressive, often social democratic inspired models of society by supporting counter-models, by engaging in anti-liberal, and pro-Russian, conservative advocacy (Salovaara, 2014).

Beyond Nordic countries, local actors have found that demonising Barnevernet at an international level can then serve domestic purposes to advocate against social progress in their own countries. This was the case in Bulgaria, where Sentiido documents how the 'Norwegian model' of child protection, for example, was subject to 'a conspiracy theory that claims children will be taken from their families and given to same-sex couples in Norway'. In 2018 and 2019, the 'Norwegian model' was portrayed as a 'neocolonial and moral threat' to counter policies under consideration. For example, local anti-gender actors used a depiction of the 'Norwegian model' to counter Bulgaria's ratification of the Istanbul Convention as well as the Social Services Act (meant to ensure state responsibility to provide for vulnerable segments of the Bulgarian population, including children) (National Network for Children, 2020).

Separately, a 2017 report from the North Atlantic Treaty Organization (NATO), states that 'narrative about child welfare issues was identified in stories concerning Denmark, Norway, and Sweden' and constituted a major pillar of Russian disinformation efforts in the Nordic-Baltic region. This perspective often portrays the Nordic model of child protective services as an 'anti-model' and highlights it as a representation of the alleged decay of the Western world.

Notwithstanding the critiques of the child protection systems in each country, it is important to state that research into the practices of Nordic countries' child protection systems has not found any distinct, systemic bias against immigrant or racialised communities. Moreover, an analysis of the media coverage of Barnevernet found a tendency to 'portray the institution in a one-sided manner – using only the parents' reports, which emerge as emotional testimonials of their struggle'. Specifically, the objective of the media was 'not to mediate' between various interest groups or to help understand the problem better by providing information, but to sell more copies/subscriptions/ads by drawing readers' attention to an artificially sensationalised controversy. Thus, the very nature of the work of child protective services, whereby it may be forced to intervene within families, lends itself to possible misrepresentation and dramatisation should there be a difference of views between the individuals/family concerns and the child protection services.

Mobilising the troops: landscape of activism against children's rights

Anti-gender actors are extremely diverse and will have different entry points for engaging in contestation on child protection. The backdrop of intense disinformation and contestation at many levels of Barnevernet, specifically, and more broadly, child protection services in Nordic countries, provides a series of opportunities for a diverse set of actors to leverage to meet their own objectives and agendas. However, it is important to note that these different actors may have different motivations for their activism, different manners of engagement and, importantly, different desired outcomes, not all of which necessarily concern child protection systems as a primary concern. The following are five sets of actors, at times overlapping, which may cooperate or mutually reinforce each other, who are engaged in activism against children's rights and around child protection models. These are:

1. Anti-gender/Christian right advocates: This category opposes what they call 'gender ideology' (Paternotte, 2016) and are active in countering human rights claims in five interrelated areas: sexual and reproductive health and rights; LGBTQIA+ rights; children's rights; gender; and equality. This group will contest the authority of the state to intervene in what is considered the sacred space of the family, understood to be the traditional, heterosexual and patriarchal. This translates into contesting comprehensive sexuality education and using children's best interests as a discursive argument in other forms of contestation, for example, arguing that children have a right to a mother and a father in contesting LGBTQIA+ rights, or the life of unborn children in the case of abortion. This set of actors has the professional capacity to engage in sophisticated policy advocacy, including litigation.
2. Anti-trans activists: This group targets issues related to transgender rights as they may concern children (Amery, 2023). They emphasise parental rights over their children (to identify as transgender), express concerns about indoctrination of young people, and critique medical treatments for transgender individuals, particularly minors. For example, they may evoke the pseudo-scientific notion of Rapid Onset Gender Dysphoria (ROGD) (Broderick, 2023) to counter claims that minors may identify as transgender and mobilise against 'Drag Queen Story Hour', claiming that it constitutes indoctrination of children (Carbonaro and Mac Dougall, 2023). This group is able to provide real cases of individuals who feel aggrieved.
3. Fathers' rights groups: These groups concentrate on issues concerning fathers' rights, particularly within contexts of divorce and custody battles. Their focus is on ensuring equal parenting rights, which may stray into undermining women's rights, for example, in the case of gender-based violence (Keller, 2023). This has contributed to a legislative proposal in Italy in 2019 on divorce, which aimed to reinforce the position of the husband/father (Siviero, 2018). Like the the previous group, this group is able to provide real cases of individuals who feel aggrieved.
4. Ultra-nationalists: Some ultra-nationalist groups favour pro-children policies, hoping it will contribute to demographic growth. They emphasise the importance of maintaining or increasing the population to assert national strength and identity. In order to do this, human rights in

some areas or of certain communities must be compromised as they are deemed 'anti-children' and 'anti-family', such as abortion, contraception and LGBTQIA+ rights. Ultra-nationalists' role is to offer a platform for discussion and socialisation of this approach (Political Network for Values, 2023) and provide normative examples. Examples of ultra-nationalist policies concerning specifically children's rights include the Child Protection laws adopted in Hungary in 2022 (Kovács, 2023) and earlier in the Russian Federation in 2011 (Thoreson, 2015) which portray the need to protect children and minors as a justification to restrict the human rights of sexual minorities.

5. Libertarians: This ideological stance aligns with limited government intervention and small state principles. While not inherently anti-children's rights, they might oppose certain policies that they perceive as infringing on individual liberties or hindering market forces. This group promotes the privatisation of education and supports home-schooling through what they call educational choice and provide the intellectual framework for this approach as well as funding to engage in various forms of advocacy, specifically by the anti-gender actors mentioned earlier. Such lines of thinking are well developed by US right-wing think tanks such as the Heritage Foundation (Heritage Foundation, nd).

These diverse set of actors play different roles in the contestation of children's rights; some serve as a reservoir of support through their grassroots activism for the actors leading political initiatives or specific litigation. Some, such as the libertarian think tanks, offer intellectual support, while others can create conducive background noise, such as Russian disinformation efforts. Others can offer legitimacy such as the fathers' rights groups and the anti-trans movement by putting a human face on individual cases and personal stories. The contestations span a wide range of issues with children's rights at their core, but with vastly different entry points. However, the set of actors which have been the most involved in children's rights contestation has been the anti-gender actors.

Contesting children's rights: ideological origins and discursive use

An important area to explore is how specific anti-gender actors have addressed issues related to children's rights in their recent activism in Europe. This chapter looked at the over 100 anti-gender organisations (see Datta, 2018; Vision Network, nd)[2] active in the European region and found that all of them are active in children's rights. These actors all include advocacy on children's rights in some manner, usually coming to it from two main perspectives, the first being 'pro-life', that is anti-abortion, and the other being 'pro-family', namely anti-LGBTQIA+ rights. This form of activism will usually reference 'human dignity' as a primary motivation. However, looking further, the engagement of anti-gender actors within the realm of children's rights issues falls within two main categories; first are those who use children's rights as an entry point to justify contestation into broader issues, including SRHR, LGBTQIA+ rights and the overall role of the state within the sacred space of the traditional family or other political or geo-political motivation. A second, much smaller, group is involved in real cases involving children, families and their relationships with state authorities.

Human dignity

The primary motivation for anti-gender actors' activism on children's rights is grounded in their understanding of what they refer to as human dignity. While it appears as a secular concept often used in political and legal settings (Pastor, 2023), for anti-gender actors, human dignity actually refers to the Dignitatis Humanae Declaration (Vatican, nd) of 1965, a document of the Catholic Church concerning religious freedom. Anti-gender actors then further delineate human dignity into three core aspects: safeguarding life (from conception to natural death), preserving the traditional family structure (heterosexual and patriarchal) and protecting religious freedom (the right to deviate from laws and policies that contradict religious beliefs) (Datta and Paternotte, 2023).

These principles form the rationale for their involvement in children's rights issues. For instance, the principle of protecting life drives campaigns against abortion by framing it as denying life to the unborn fetus. Similarly, upholding the traditional family and religious freedom forms the basis for opposing comprehensive sexuality education (CSE), which is deemed to sexualise children (Ruse, 2020). However, these principles also underpin positions supporting parental rights in education, favouring parents over the state's involvement, and offering grounds for opting out of obligations such as public education through the assertion of religious freedom and advocating for the right to home-school. The concept of the traditional family additionally influences stances on custodial rights post-separation/divorce, favouring fathers' claims and limiting state interference through child protective services within the family sphere.

However, there are contradictions in this approach. For example, activism contesting abortion rights, specifically arguing that the unborn child is a bearer of rights, contradicts the same actors' claims that children do not have a right to education when contesting CSE, arguing that parents should have exclusive control over their children's upbringing. A separate set of arguments concerns protecting children from perceived dangers, specifically the dangers of 'gender ideology' and marriage equality and assisted reproduction, arguing that every child has the right to a mother and father and that parents should have the right and/or freedom to protect their children from what they perceive as dangerous influences.

Think of the children!

A feature anti-gender actors share is employing a similar rhetorical strategy, namely appealing to the sentiment of 'think of the children', arguing that children are the unintended victims of the human rights progress made in other areas. This approach serves as a discursive tool to impede progressive advancements in various areas, such as LGBTQIA+ rights, assisted reproduction, CSE and abortion. This discursive approach criticises the progressive approaches to gender and children's rights adopted by Nordic countries, with the objective of undermining these ideas and casting doubt upon their effectiveness. By opposing certain progressive policies related to children's rights and gender equality, anti-gender actors seek to rally support among conservative constituents and consolidate their influence within the political landscape. In addition, these actors actively work to delegitimise international norms and institutions that advocate for gender equality and children's rights. They endeavour to discredit these international bodies, portraying them as proponents of ideologies they vehemently oppose, thereby challenging the legitimacy and authority of such entities.

This is reflected in several strategy documents of anti-gender actors. The 2014 manifesto Restoring the Natural Order (Datta, 2018) warns that the International Convention on the Rights of the Child poses 'an inherent risk that it could be used to supersede the natural rights of parents (because what corresponds, or does not correspond, to "the best interests of the child" is ultimately to be answered by state authorities rather than by parents)' (Restoring the Natural Order, 2014, cited in Datta, 2018). In 2016, the Political Network for Values (IPAS, 2023)[3] identified language and legislative proposals on 'parents' rights on children's education' as a priority area. Most recently, the same Political Network for Values adopted its New York Statement at its October 2023 Trans-Atlantic Summit where it affirmed that 'parents have the right to choose the kind of education that shall be provided to their children' and 'to respect the liberty of parents and legal guardians to ensure the religious and moral education of their children in conformity with their own convictions' (Political Network for Values, 2023).

Key anti-gender actors mobilising on state intervention on child protection

While all anti-gender actors use children's rights as a discursive element in their contestations, a much smaller subset of these organisations is active on the broader issues of children's rights, specifically in areas of conflict between parents' rights and the state's duty to ensure the best interests of the child. These areas have tended to focus on home-schooling, emphasising parental rights and upholding religious freedom, contesting the state intervention in the family, and some specifically targeted the Nordic model of child protective services. Of those anti-gender organisations which share the same philosophical grounding in operationalising human dignity as described earlier and with the technical capacity and track record of engaging in campaigning in legal settings, four organisations specifically stand out: Alliance Defending Freedom International (ADFI), CitizenGO, the European Centre for Law and Justice (ECLJ), and Ordo Iuris Institute for Legal Culture (Ordo Iuris).

The four key organisations then leverage support from the wider community mentioned earlier when engaging in individual cases. These four actors have the professional capacity to become active actors in legal battles, often referred to as 'lawfare' (Yamin et al, 2018). Recent articles exploring the concept of lawfare and its implications, particularly within the context of the ECtHR, provide further insight. Notably, Van den Eynde in 2013 and Relaño Pastor in 2023 offer a comprehensive exploration of these themes and outline how the increase in third-party interventions can be attributed largely to the increased activism of Christian faith-based organisations, particularly several of the prominent actors mentioned.

The four mentioned organisations play significant roles in advancing their agendas within the realm of children's rights and beyond. Ordo Iuris[4] emerges as the most significant anti-gender actor with a pronounced focus on issues related to children's rights and beyond. Ordo Iuris is a think tank situated within the wider Tradition, Family and Property network (a far-right, pseudo-Catholic lay movement) (Datta, 2020) based in Warsaw, Poland, but also active at European and international levels (Curanović, 2023).

Over the span of eight years covering 2015–2022, Ordo Iuris has been engaged in more than 160 activities centered around 'children's rights', and over 40 just regarding Norway. Their primary concerns include issues such as abortion and CSE. When it comes to religious freedom and homeschooling, Ordo Iuris emphasises the rights of religious families to uphold their religious beliefs in the education of their children and for parental rights to provide religious education. Ordo Iuris goes further on children's issues by making them an important part of their activism in relation to paedophilia, communications about the Nordic protection system, including the Nordic approach to child protection, and even into the realm of geo-politics.

The next most important organisation is ADFI,[5] which describes itself as a 'faith-based legal advocacy organisation that protects fundamental freedoms and promotes the inherent dignity of all people'. It is the international arm of the US-based Alliance Defending Freedom (ADF) and in Europe claims to have offices in Brussels, Geneva, London, Strasbourg and Vienna. ADFI is actively engaged in legal cases before international and national courts and in Europe are active at the ECtHR, Council of Europe, European Union and EU Fundamental Rights Agency. ADFI specialises in advocating for religious freedom, family and traditional values. This translates into arguing that LGBTQIA+ couples could be harmful to a child's development (Peters, 2014) and using child protection narratives to halt consideration of the rights of transgendered persons (Pauly, 2023). Moreover, ADFI states that its works to 'protect the choice of parents to provide their children with faith-based or home education and halt the promotion of inappropriate "sexuality education" and other radical agendas at the national and international level that harm children' (ADFI, nda). ADFI consolidated its positions into a series of documents including a Charter on Parental Rights (ADFI, ndb), a booklet on parental rights, 'Your rights and duties as parents' (Du Plessis, 2023) and a White Paper on parental rights (Du Plessis, 2024) which states that 'the "best interest of the child" is binding upon states, not parents'.

While ADFI devotes significant effort to contestation around children's rights as such, for CitizenGO and the ECLJ it is a minor area of work. CitizenGO[6] is a petitions-based social media organisation based in Madrid, Spain which claims to be 'Defending life, family, and freedom across the world' through its 18 million active citizens who sign petitions in ten languages circulating across over 50 countries. CitizenGO is involved in various campaigns on contentious issues such as abortion, pornography and LGBTQIA+ rights. Its campaigns often include petitions and advocacy efforts aimed at influencing public opinion and policy, such as a petition to 'boycott the Barbie movies' (CitizenGO, 2023a) or to 'stop naked drag marches in front of children' (CitizenGO, 2023b). It is also connected to the Home School Legal Defense Association (CitizenGO, 2018a; 2018b; Home School Legal Defense Association, nd), emphasising support for home-schooling as part of its broader activism. Its efforts extend to international petitions concerning issues such as home-schooling and child protective services in countries like Brazil (CitizenGO, 2017a), Germany (home-schooling Wunderlich case) (CitizenGO, 2017b), Iceland (home-schooling) (CitizenGO, 2018b), Norway (home-schooling/Barnevernet) (CitizenGO, 2018a) and Romania (religious freedom/Barnevernet and the Bodnariu family) (CitizenGO, 2015).

The ECLJ[7] is the Strasbourg-based, European arm of the American Centre for Law and Justice,[8] which is itself based in Washington, DC. The ECLJ claims that it 'advocates in particular for the protection of religious freedoms and the dignity of the person' and focuses on defending religious freedom and parental rights, particularly in the context of home-schooling and is active at the Council of Europe, ECtHR, the UN system in Geneva and Vienna as well as the European Union. The ECLJ asserts the right of parents to educate their children according to their beliefs. Its involvement in home-schooling (Puppinck, nd) and parental rights advocacy showcase its commitment to preserving traditional family values and countering perceived state intervention. For example, through its involvement in a Danish case in 2018, which involved the intervention of child protective services when parents decided to home-school their teenage children (Foltzenlogel, nd).

Multi-pronged advocacy: how anti-gender actors engage in children's rights

The four prominent organisations engaged on countering children's rights employ a range of strategies to exert influence on the discourse surrounding children's rights, seeking to advance their specific objectives. These approaches include litigation and lawfare in individual cases before the ECtHR, public awareness campaigns, targeting Norway and the 'Nordic model', and influencing international norms.

Lawfare in individual cases

ADFI and Ordo Iuris have engaged directly in the litigation taking place before the ECtHR on several child protection cases involving Barnevernet (see Table 9.1.) leading Cichowski and Chrun to characterise them as 'repeat players' in their analysis (see Chapter 11). As Cichowski and Chrun describe, ADFI intervened in Strand Lobben and Others v Norway (2019) and Marius Bodnariu and Others against Norway (2020). Ordo Iuris for its part also intervened in the Bodnariu case as well as R.O. v Norway (2021), K.E. and A.K. v Norway (2021) and F.Z. v Norway (2021). Ordo Iuris also stated that the 'ECHR issued a further three judgments in which it directly referred to the "amicus curiae" opinions sent by the Institute' (2021b), referring specifically to the R.O. v Norway, the K.E. and A.K. v Norway and the F.Z. v Norway cases. In these three cases, the only civil society third-party intervention came from Ordo Iuris and in the case of Bodnariu v Norway, the only civil society third-party interventions were from ADFI and Ordo Iuris.

They have also been involved in similar cases against other countries, the first of which was in Wunderlich v Germany (2019), which concerned the state's authority to intervene in a case involving home-schooling, both ADFI and the ECLJ intervened. The ECLJ submitted written observations (Puppinck, 2016) to the court where it 'recalled the liberal principle of natural law according to which "the family takes precedence over the state", in particular in the field of education and teaching' while lawyers from ADFI served as the legal representatives of the Wunderlich family for six years (ADF Legal, ndb). This intensity of engagement, coupled with the fact the

Table 9.1: Anti-gender organisation involvement in ECtHR cases about child protection

Organisation	ADFI	CitizenGO	ECLJ	Ordo Iuris
Engagement in child protection/ custody	Strand Lobben v Norway Bodnariu v Norway Wunderlich v Germany	Bodnariu v Norway Shutakova v Norway	Wunderlich v Germany –	R.O. v Norway K.E. and A.K. v Norway F.Z. v Norway

ADFI and Ordo Iuris are often among the only third-party interveners in such cases, strongly suggest that child protection has become a priority area of legal action.

Public awareness campaigns

On the heels of the formal engagement as third parties in the litigation before the ECHR, the anti-gender actors engaged in public awareness campaigns, strategically designed to garner visibility and public support for their viewpoints. These campaigns may target specific issues cases, portraying the parents and children as unwitting victims of the state's authority, leveraging emotional appeals to elicit sympathy and sway public opinion in their favour. For example, ADFI created a video on its YouTube channel on the Strand Lobben v Norway case (ADFI, 2019a) and actively engaged with primarily Christian media outlets on the Bodnariu case (Clark, 2019; Hurd, 2023). CitizenGO, which is specialised in social media mobilisation, generated online petitions gathering tens of thousands of signatures asking a range of public authorities, including then US Vice-President Mike Pence, to intervene in the cases of the Bodnariu family (CitizenGO, 2015) and Natalya Shutakova (CitizenGO, 2019) which both encountered difficulties with Barnevernet (Hurd, 2019).

Ordo Iuris has engaged in extensive campaigning and media efforts targeting Barnevernet, for example, see the tag 'Barnevernet' on the Ordo Iuris website.[9] In a strange turn of events, Ordo Iuris was able to leverage the public outcry concerning the Catholic Church paedophilia scandals which erupted in Poland in 2018 (Snyder, 2018) to deflect attention from the responsibility of the Catholic clergy perpetrators and instead blamed the abuse of the prevalence of homosexuality and asserting that children were of the victims of gender and LGBTQIA+ ideology. Building on this connection it established between paedophilia and 'LGBTQIA+ ideology', Ordo Iuris then targeted CSE, arguing that the 2020 Stop Paedophilia Bill under consideration in the Polish Sejm would be an important step in 'protecting children against demoralizing sex education' (Ordo Iuris, 2020c).

Furthermore, public campaigning on child protection cases serves as a means of fundraising for these actors. Anti-gender actors capitalise on concerns surrounding the well-being of children and related parental rights to attract financial support from their followers, allowing them to sustain their advocacy efforts. Examples include Ordo Iuris' efforts to fundraise for the Silje Garmo (a Norwegian woman seeking to flee to Poland to escape Barnevernet) (*Visegrád Post*, 2019) case through its email and social media newsletter. Acting as Silje Garmo's legal counsel, these publicity efforts in Poland contributed to Ordo Iuris' victory in securing asylum in Poland for Silje Garmo in 2019 (Ordo Iuris, 2018), making her the first Norwegian to be granted asylum in a European country since the end of the Second World War. Similarly, ADFI has engaged in fundraising efforts for overall parental rights (ADF Legal, ndb) and specifically for the Wunderlich v Germany case, stating, 'And that's why, with the help of ADF International, the Wunderlichs have spent the last six years fighting this gross violation of their human rights' (ADF Legal, ndb).

Targeting Norway and the 'Nordic model'

Another area of engagement has been Ordo Iuris' activism against Nordic countries' child protective systems. In addition to the involvement in the Silje Garmo case described earlier, Ordo Iuris has an extensive track record of involvement with Barnevernet, reaching 42 engagements (Ordo Iuris, nd). In 2020, Ordo Iuris released a report entitled 'Children's rights pitted against children? The legal framework and practice of Barnevernet functioning in the perspective of international legal standards' (Ordo Iuris, 2020a), which was used as training material at an Ordo Iuris organised meeting in Oslo with representatives of Norwegian Ministry of Foreign Affairs and Bufdir, the government agency responsible for Barnevernet (Ordo Iuris, 2020b).

Ordo Iuris also contest the 'Nordic model' of social welfare, for example by challenging Sweden's Child Protection Services (Ordo Iuris, 2019) and the financial relationship between Poland and Norway. This involves Ordo Iuris strongly critiquing Norwegian concerns about the erosion of the rule of law in Poland and the restrictions Norway imposed on the use of its funding in Poland through the European Economic Area (EEA) funds. In response, Ordo Iuris accused the Norway Fund of being biased as it asserted a 'disproportionately high support for projects with left-wing or liberal ideological overtones' (Ordo Iuris, 2017) and published its own analysis of Norway's financial support to Polish civil society in a report 'Citizens for democracy: Assessment of the correctness of the allocation of the Mechanism's funds financial EEA (so-called 'Norwegian funds') by the Foundation Stefan Batory and description of the proposed changes to the current model' (Jabłoński et al, 2017). These examples from Ordo Iuris, as well as those of

ADFI in relation to parental rights mentioned earlier, reflect the willingness to shape public and political discourse on child protection and children's rights more generally, with the aim of advancing their anti-gender objectives.

Influencing international norms

Beyond engagement in specific legal cases, anti-gender actors attempt to shape international norms as they concern children's rights and parental rights by engaging with international institutions. For example, in 2021 Ordo Iuris submitted to the 88th session of the UN Committee on the Rights of the Child a report entitled 'Caring for the welfare of the youngest' (Bernaciński and Zych, 2020), which was aimed at 'improving the situation of children with disabilities and their families' by recommending extension of the Polish Constitutional Tribunal's decision to prohibit abortion for foetal anomaly of October 2020 (Ordo Iuris, 2021a). Another example of an attempt to influence international norms was ADFI's submission to the 33rd session of the Human Rights Council's Universal Periodic Review Working Group concerning Norway in 2019 (ADFI, 2019b). In its submission concerning Norway, ADFI specifically references the Strand Lobben and Bodnariu cases as well as the 2018 parliamentary report on the subject. According to ADFI, its submission 'focuses on Norway's failure to respect the rights of parents and children to private and family life'.

However, arguably the greatest success in influencing international soft norms on child rights and Barnevernet's international reputation was at the Parliamentary Assembly of the Council of Europe (PACE) in 2018 with the adoption of the PACE report 'Striking a balance between the best interest of the child and the need to keep families together' (Doc. 14568) (2018) for the Committee on Social Affairs, Health and Sustainable Development Report. This report emerged in the context of widespread disinformation campaigns targeting Barnevernet, particularly those related to cases with transnational implications. PACE's involvement aimed to provide an impartial assessment of these controversies, offering a balanced perspective that could guide not only Barnevernet but also other bodies, such as the ECtHR, in understanding the nuanced challenges faced. While the PACE reports are not legally binding, they wield considerable influence due to their ability to shape international opinion and inform policy discussions, thus demonstrating the significant soft power they hold in the realm of child rights and family reunification debates.

Originating from Romanian parliamentarian members of the PACE concerning the Bodnariu case, the report explored child protection systems generally but included a specific case study on Norway and Barnevernet's performance in the rapporteur's explanatory memorandum. In exploring the dynamics which led to this report and its main protagonists, it appears to be a case of an anti-gender success targeting children's rights.

For example, the rapporteur Valeriu Ghiletchi is a conservative Moldovan parliamentarian member of the European People's Party. Ghiltechi was one of the main anti-gender actors in the PACE during his mandate and was personally involved in anti-gender organisations and had forged partnerships with anti-gender actors, such as ECLJ (Datta, 2018). Ghiletchi was also highly ranked in the PACE and served as the Chair of the PACE's Social Affairs Committee, thus enabling him to secure the position of rapporteur on this portfolio.

As part of the preparations for the report, Ghiletchi led a fact-finding mission to Norway (a standard practice in preparing PACE reports) and met with local concerned parties, including representatives of Barnevernet. Ghiletchi also included in his Council of Europe mission a meeting and media appearance on TV Visjon Norge with Norwegian apostolic pastor Jan-Aage Torp, who also chairs the Kristen Koalisjon Norge (KKN) (EAL Media, 2016). Torp and the KKN have been outspoken critics of Barnevernet (Stortinget, 2021) and have engaged in campaigning activities concerning the Bodnariu case and Silje Garmo (Barns Beste, 2023). While Professor Hans Morten Haugen in *The Christian Right in Norway* describes Torp as 'currently irrelevant in Norway' (Haugen, 2024), it appears that Torp had influential friends abroad and served as a local ally and a source of legitimation for the transnational activism against Barnevernet. Indeed, Torp and the KKN have had long-term and close relations with several of the main anti-gender actors, and the source of their friendship was the contestation of Barnevernet. These relationships are revealed in KKN's annual Family Defense Award, in 2017 being attributed to the Bodnariu family (Ordo Iuris, 2021c), in 2018 to Ordo Iuris (Ordo Iuris, 2021c), in 2019 to Valeriu Ghiletchi (Kristen Koalisjon Norge, 2019), and in 2021 to ADFI (OSLO TV, 2021). In 2020, Torp was thanked for his contribution in the preface of Ordo Iuris' report 'Children's rights pitted against children?' (Ordo Iuris, 2020a) and in 2023 hosted Ghiletchi on TV Vision Norway (IDAG, nd). Thus, Torp found external allies to support his cause, while the transnational actors such as ADFI and Ordo Iuris found a local who provided an insider's view into the critique of Barnevernet. The successful adoption and dissemination of the PACE report was made possible thanks in part to anti-gender political allies, including PACE members Pavlo Ungurian, MP from Ukraine and Ronan Mullen, Senator from Ireland,[10] then relayed further thanks to ADFI, Ordo Iuris as well as other anti-gender networks such as the European Christian Political Movement which Ghiletchi presided at the time (ECPM, 2018).

Lifting the veil on the four prominent organisations

However, looking further into the prominent actors of ADFI, CitizenGO, the ECLJ and Ordo Iuris, another feature becomes apparent. All organisations have a contested reputation within mainstream civil society and are regularly considered 'extremist'. For example, both ADFI and ECLJ failed to obtain Participatory Status with the Council of Europe because they did not share the Institution's adherence to democracy and human rights (Committee of Ministers, nd). However, it appears that both are given leave to submit amicus briefs to the ECtHR and other courts. In their home country of the United States, the ADF is considered a hate group by the Southern Poverty Law Group (SPLC, nd) alongside the Ku Klux Klan and the Proud Boys. At the same time, ADF is an influential organisation having brought the Dobbs v Jackson Women's Health Organization to the US Supreme Court which overturned the long-established right to abortion in the United States (ADF Legal, nda). CitizenGO, for its part, regularly faces allegations of not being a genuine citizens' platform and instead being an astroturfing operation funded by largely foreign social and economic elites with far-right political motivations (Norris, 2021). In 2024, CitizenGO was also active in campaigning against the World Health Organization's draft pandemic treaty (CitizenGO, 2023c). Ordo Iuris has been established as the public face of a pseudo-Catholic lay movement with a far-right and paramilitary history called Tradition, Family and Property, which has faced contestation within the Catholic Church and by public authorities in several countries (Datta, 2020).

Thus, the perspective of the scholar Carlo Ruzzo (2021) and the notion of a conservative 'uncivil society' becomes relevant in understanding conservative contestation of children's rights. Given the wider context of these actors' involvement in a range of human rights issues, and their approach to the international institutions which uphold these rights, Ruzzo puts forward the concept of 'inimicus curiae' (that is, 'enemy of the court' in opposition to amicus curiae, 'friend of the court') and how these play into this broader context. These ideas suggest that anti-gender actors position themselves in opposition to the traditional role of amicus curiae, working to undermine progressive norms and challenge the values upheld by civil society. In doing so, they contribute to a complex and contentious discourse surrounding children's rights, one that is deeply intertwined with political, cultural and ideological dimensions. In sum, the engagement of anti-gender actors in children's rights goes beyond a singular focus. It is intertwined with challenges to state authority, anti-Nordic narratives, domestic political agendas, and a broader effort to contest international norms and institutions.

Conclusions: Anti-gender contestation of child protection as a blind spot

Several conclusions emerge from the present analysis of the contestation around children's rights and specifically Barnevernet. A first conclusion is that the engagement of anti-gender actors in the areas of children's protection has gone largely unnoticed. There are several possible explanations. One being that the traditional actors who monitor the usually contested areas of gender equality (SRHR and LGBTQIA+ rights) were not monitoring children's rights issues. This likely explains how the 2018 resolution at the PACE was adopted, but other anti-gender initiatives at the PACE in the same period were successfully blocked. In parallel, children's rights actors are likely equally unfamiliar with anti-gender activism and actors and therefore did not recognise the activism of the four main organisations, leading, in one extreme example, to a training session by Ordo Iuris with Norwegian state officials. Another reason may be that the children's rights actors are not equipped to engage in the multifaceted contestation which anti-gender actors are able to deploy simultaneously in a range of different settings and at multiple levels of decision-making.

Second, a specific set of four anti-gender actors has specialised in contesting children's rights and specifically the child protection model of which Barnevernet has become emblematic. These four organisations, ADFI, CitizenGO, ECLJ and Ordo Iuris, have led the charge in contestation ranging from grassroots activism, political and parliamentary advocacy, and various forms of lawfare, including litigation. Two of them, ADFI and Ordo Iuris, are often the only civil society organisations engaged in submitting third-party interventions in cases before the ECtHR. Indeed, it is anti-gender actors who are engaged in formulating the intellectual framework for this contestation, organising public campaigns around specific cases, generating policy documents that support their arguments, and engaging in litigation and other forms of lawfare on specific cases. To achieve this, they found a local ally in Norway through the KKN, which may have limited influence in Norway, but is compensated thanks to powerful transnational allies.

A third conclusion is that the debates surrounding children's rights and, specifically, Barnevernet fit into a larger pattern of anti-gender and anti-liberal value contestation. Opposition to child protection models like Barnevernet often serves additional objectives, such as limiting state intervention in family life and opposing human rights claims of sexual and gender minorities. Domestic criticism of child protection services, along with the highly publicised tragedies of certain cases, has created fertile ground for disinformation, which is then leveraged by various actors to push their agendas. While these actors often operate through democratic processes, they frequently do so in ways that undermine the rule of law and human rights principles. The complex and often grey areas inherent in child protection interventions make them easy targets for those seeking to promote distrust in public institutions. Anti-gender groups are increasingly using these contestations as a tool to erode confidence in democratic systems, a trend that is further fuelled by anti-democratic forces. This points to a broader issue: how easily democratic procedures can be manipulated by those with ulterior motives, highlighting a growing challenge for maintaining the integrity of public debate and policy making and, most importantly, the best interests of the child in a specific contested child protection case.

Appendix 9.1
List of data materials used for analysis

ADF Legal (nda) 'Dobbs v. Jackson Women's Health Organization'. Available from: https://adflegal.org/case/dobbs-v-jackson-womens-health-organization

ADF Legal (ndb) 'Wunderlich family'. Available from: https://adflegal.org/client/wunderlich-family

ADFI (nda) 'Parental rights are guaranteed'. Available from: https://adfinternational.org/our-focus/parental-rights

ADFI (ndb) 'Parental rights charter'. Available from: https://adfinternational.org/resources/parental-rights-charter

ADFI (2019a) 'Strand Lobben v Norway', YouTube video, added by Brynjar Østgård. Available from: https://www.youtube.com/watch?v=YzgV0tz3YZ0

ADFI (2019b) 'ADFI submission to the 33rd session of the Human Rights Council's Universal Periodic Review Working Group', April, Geneva, Switzerland. Available from: https://upr-info.org/sites/default/files/documents/2019-04/adf_international_upr33_nor_e_main.pdf

Barns Beste (2023) 'Silje Garmo – flyktning fra Norge [Silje Garmo – refugee from Norway]'. Available from: https://barns-beste.no/perspektiver/les1/siljegarmo-flyktning

Bernaciński, Ł. and Zych, T. (2020) 'Jak systemowo wspierać osoby z niepełnosprawnościami? Propozycje i kierunki zmian [How to support people with disabilities in a systemic way? Proposals and directions of change]', *Ordo Iuris*. Available from: https://ordoiuris.pl/sites/default/files/inline-files/Jak_systemowo_wspierac%CC%81_osoby_z_niepe%C5%82nosprawnos%CC%81ciami_0.pdf

CitizenGO (2015) 'Norway's child welfare services: Stop religious persecution of Christian family'. Available from: https://citizengo.org/en/pr/31645-norways-child-welfare-services-stop-religious-persecution-christian-family

CitizenGO (2023a) 'New Barbie movie and transgenderism'. Available from: https://www.citizengo.org/en-us/fm/211507-new-barbie-movie-and-transgenderism

CitizenGO (2023b) 'Stop naked drag marches in front of children'. Available from: https://www.citizengo.org/en-us/fm/211310-stop-naked-drag-marches-front-children

CitizenGO (2023c) 'Stop the UN's desperate pandemic treaty push'. Available from: https://citizengo.org/en-us/ot/211837-stop-uns-desperate-pandemic-treaty-push

CitizenGO (2017a) 'Petition to protect freedom of education in Brazil'. Available from: https://citizengo.org/en/ed/95534-petition-protect-freedom-education-brazil

CitizenGO (2017b) 'Sign now: Homeschooling family terrorized in Germany'. Available from: https://citizengo.org/en/ed/47779-sign-now-homeschooling-family-terrorized-germany

CitizenGO (2018a) 'Homeschooled twelve-year-old tackled by police in Norway'. Available from: https://citizengo.org/en-us/ed/156976-homeschooled-twelve-year-old-tackled-police-norway

CitizenGO (2018b) 'Sign support for freedom of education and homeschooling in Iceland'. Available from: https://citizengo.org/en/ed/165953-sign-support-freedom-education-and-homeschooling-iceland

CitizenGO (2019) 'Helfen Sie diesen Kindern'. Available from: https://citizengo.org/de/fm/174935-Helfen-Sie-diesen-Kindern

Committee of Ministers (nd) Search of Council of Europe. Available from: https://search.coe.int/cm#{%22CoEObjectId%22:[%2209000016808b8645%22],%22sort%22:[%22CoEValidationDate%20Descending%22].}

Český žurnál: Děti státu [Czech Journal: Children of the State] (2016) 'Česká televize'. Available from: https://www.ceskatelevize.cz/porady/10408111009-cesky-zurnal/216562262600004/

Du Plessis, G. (2023) 'Parental rights booklet', *ADF International*. Available from: https://adfinternational.org/resources/parental-rights-booklet

Du Plessis, G. (2024) 'ADF International white paper: Parental rights, protecting parents, empowering generations', *ADF International*. Available from: https://adfinternational.org/resources/white-paper/parental-rights

EAL Media (2016) 'We will win for the Bodnariu's the War against Barnevernet! 29 January'. Available from: https://e-a-l.eu/leadership/president-blog/read1/winning-for-bodnariu-family

ECPM (European Christian Political Movement) (2018) 'The Council of Europe asks for better protection for children and their families'. Available from: https://ecpm.info/news/the-council-of-europe-asks-for-better-protection-for-children-and-their-families.html

Foltzenlogel, C. (nd) 'Kafkaesque family nightmare in Denmark', ECLJ. Available from: https://eclj.org/family/eu/kafkaesque-family-nightmare-in-denmark

Heritage Foundation (nd) 'Education choice'. Available from: https://www.heritage.org/education-choice

Home School Legal Defense Association (nd) Available from: https://hslda.org/

IDAG (nd) 'Valeriu Ghile Chi: Statsmannen fra Moldova [Valeriu Ghile Chi: The Statesman from Moldova]', IDAG. Available from: https://idag.no/valeriu-ghile-chi-statsmannen-fra-moldova/19.41833

IPAS (2023) 'The political network for values: Global far-right at the United Nations'. Available from: https://www.ipas.org/resource/the-political-network-for-values-global-far-right-at-the-united-nations/

Jabłoński, P., Olszówka, M., Zych, T. and Dziubicki, S. (2017) 'Obywatele dla demokracji. Ocena prawidłowości alokacji środków Mechanizmu Finansowego EOG (tzw. "funduszy norweskich") przez Fundację im. Stefana Batorego oraz opis postulowanych zmian obecnego modelu [Citizens for democracy: Assessment of the correctness of the allocation of the Mechanism's funds financial EEA (so-called "Norwegian funds") by the Foundation Stefan Batory and description of the proposed changes to the current model]'.

Johansen, A.H. and Hansen, A. (2023) 'Norsk-rumensk familie ble fratatt alle sine fem barn: I dag demonstreres det mot norsk barnevern i 63 byer i 20 land [Norwegian-Romanian family was deprived of all five of their children: Today there are demonstrations against Norwegian child welfare in 63 cities in 20 countries]', *Dagbladet*. Available from: https://www.dagbladet.no/nyheter/norsk-rumensk-familie-ble-fratatt-alle-sine-fem-barn-i-dag-demonstreres-det-mot-norsk-barnevern-i-63-byer-i-20-land/60452851

Keller, G. (2023) 'Väterrechtler auf dem Vormarsch [Fathers' rights activists on the rise]', *Correctiv.org*, 19 September. Available from: https://correctiv.org/aktuelles/haeusliche-gewalt/2023/09/19/die-netzwerke-der-vaeterrechtler/

Kovács, Z. (2023) 'Child protection law: They just don't get it, do they?', *About Hungary*, 24 March. Available from: https://abouthungary.hu/blog/child-protection-law-they-just-dont-get-it-do-they

Kristen Koalisjon Norge (2019) 'Family Defense Award 2019'. Available from: https://web.archive.org/web/20230204001437/https://kristenkoalisjon.world/familydefenseaward/family-defense-award2019

Liski, J. and Gråsten-Lahtinen, H. (2023) 'Näin lapsia kaupataan ympäri Suomen kiskurihinnoilla [This is how children are trafficked around Finland at exorbitant prices]', *Iltalehti*. Available from: https://www.iltalehti.fi/politiikka/a/007a40ed-62b8-4ab3-90e8-44a5e9238c04

Lohne, J., Norman, M.G. and Ege, R.T (2015) 'Tsjekkias president sammenligner norsk barnevern med nazi-program [Czech President compares Norwegian child welfare to Nazi program]', *VG*, 9 February. Available from: https://www.vg.no/nyheter/i/o0zkK/tsjekkias-president-sammenligner-norsk-barnevern-med-nazi-program

National Network for Children (2020) 'Conspiracy theories and misinformation: How they affect children's lives and children's policies'. Available from: https://nmd.bg/en/conspiracy-theories-and-misinformation-how-they-affect-childrens-lives-and-childrens-policies

NDTV (2023) 'Child welfare not driven by profit: Norway Embassy on Rani Mukherjee film'. Available from: https://www.ndtv.com/india-news/child-welfare-not-driven-by-profit-norway-embassy-on-rani-mukherjee-film-3869031

Nordis Hub (2023) 'Misinformation about social services abducting children spreads across Nordic region, joint Nordis investigation shows'. Available from: https://www.nordishub.eu/misinformation-about-social-services-abducting-children-spreads-across-nordic-region-joint-nordis-investigation-shows/

Norges institusjon for menneskerettigheter (NIM) (2020) 'Hvorfor dømmes Norge i EMD? En statusrapport om barnevernsfeltet [Why is Norway being judged in the ECHR? A status report on the field of child welfare]'. Available from: https://www.nhri.no/rapport/barnevern/

Norris, S. (2021) 'The money men behind CitizenGO's anti-rights agenda', *Bylinetimes*. Available from: https://bylinetimes.com/2021/06/21/the-money-men-behind-citizengos-anti-rights-agenda

Ordo Iuris (2017) 'Fundacja Batorego po raz kolejny odmawia informacji o procedurze podziału 37 mln euro z funduszy norweskich [The Batory Foundation once again refuses to provide information on the procedure for dividing EUR 37 million from Norwegian funds]'. Available from: https://ordoiuris.pl/wolnosci-obywatelskie/fundacja-batorego-po-raz-kolejny-odmawia-informacji-o-procedurze-podzialu-37

Ordo Iuris (2018) 'Silje Garmo gets asylum: Success for Ordo Iuris'. Available from: https://en.ordoiuris.pl/family-and-marriage/silje-garmo-gets-asylum-success-ordo-iuris

Ordo Iuris (2019) 'Polish court supports family. Denis Lisow is allowed to stay in Poland'. Available from: https://en.ordoiuris.pl/family-and-marriage/polish-court-supports-family-denis-lisow-allowed-stay-poland

Ordo Iuris (2020a) 'Report: Children's rights pitted against children's legal framework and practice'. Available from: https://en.ordoiuris.pl/family-and-marriage/report-childrens-rights-pitted-against-children-legal-framework-and-practice

Ordo Iuris (2020b) 'Barnevernet: Human rights violations mechanism'. Available from: https://en.ordoiuris.pl/family-and-marriage/barnevernet-human-rights-violations-mechanism-ordo-iuris-report-presented-oslo

Ordo Iuris (2020c) 'The civic project "Stop pedophilia" will help protect children'. Available from: https://en.ordoiuris.pl/education/civic-project-stop-pedophilia-will-help-protect-children

Ordo Iuris (2021a) 'Caring for the welfare of the youngest – Ordo Iuris report for the UN', 25 August. Available from: https://en.ordoiuris.pl/family-and-marriage/caring-welfare-youngest-ordo-iuris-report-un

Ordo Iuris (2021b) 'European Court of Human Rights takes into account Ordo Iuris opinions on family matters'. Available from: https://en.ordoiuris.pl/family-and-marriage/european-court-human-rights-takes-account-ordo-iuris-opinions-family-matters

Ordo Iuris (2021c) 'Kristen Koalisjon Norge "Family Defense Award" Panel 2021', YouTube video. Available from: https://www.youtube.com/watch?v=T-xcDY6j-Lw

Ordo Iuris (nd) 'Barnevernet'. Available from: https://en.ordoiuris.pl/barnevernet

OSLO TV (2021) 'Award to Paul Coleman of ADF International'. Available from: https://oslo-tv.eu/newsworthy/read1/kkn-award-paulcoleman-adf

PACE (2018) 'Striking a balance between the best interest of the child and the need to keep families together', Rapporteur: Mr Valeriu Ghiletchi, Republic of Moldova, EPP/CD. *Committee on Social Affairs, Health and Sustainable Development Report*, Doc. 14568. Available from: https://assembly.coe.int/nw/xml/XRef/Xref-XML2HTML-en.asp?fileid=24770&lang=en

Pauly, M. (2023) 'Inside the secret working group that helped push anti-trans laws across the country', *Mother Jones*, 8 March. Available from: https://www.motherjones.com/politics/2023/03/anti-trans-transgender-health-care-ban-legislation-bill-minors-children-lgbtq

Peters, S. (2014) '10 shocking facts about the Alliance Defending Freedom', *HRC*. Available from: https://www.hrc.org/press-releases/10-shocking-facts-about-the-alliance-defending-freedom

Political Network for Values (2023) 'Transatlantic Summit V: New York 2023'. Available from: https://politicalnetworkforvalues.org/en/what-we-do/transatlantic-summit/v-transatlatic-summit-new-york-2023/

Political Network for Values (nd) Available from: https://politicalnetworkforvalues.org

Puppinck, G. (2016) Written observations submitted to the European Court of Human Rights in the case Wunderlich v Germany (no. 18925/15). Available from: http://media.aclj.org/pdf/EN-Observations-ECLJ-Wunderlich-v-Germany.pdf

Puppinck, G. (nd) 'Nouvelle étude de fond: Liberté éducative et droits de l'homme [New background study: Educational Freedom and Human Rights]', *ECLJ*. Available from: https://eclj.org/family/french-institutions/nouvelle-etude-de-fond---liberte-educative-et-droits-de-lhomme-

Ruse, C. (2020) 'Sex education in public schools: Sexualization of children and LGBT indoctrination', Family Research Council, Washington, DC. Available from: https://www.frc.org/brochure/sex-education-in-public-schools-sexualization-of-children-and-lgbt-indoctrination

Salovaara, O. (2022) 'Venäjän uskollinen mediasoturi [Russia's loyal media warrior]', *Helsingin Sanomat*. Available from: https://www.hs.fi/feature/art-2000008893252.html

Siviero, G. (2018) 'L'ONU sul DDL Pillon: Grave regression [The UN on DDL Pillon: Serious regression]', *Il Manifesto*. Available from: https://ilmanifesto.it/lonu-sul-ddl-pillon-grave-regressione

Snyder, D. (2018) 'Warsaw protest to demand investigation of pedophilia in Poland's church', *National Catholic Reporter*. Available from: https://www.ncronline.org/news/warsaw-protest-demand-investigation-pedophilia-polands-church

SPLC (nd) 'Extremist files: Alliance Defending Freedom'. Available from: https://www.splcenter.org/fighting-hate/extremist-files/group/alliance-defending-freedom

Stortinget (2021) 'Høringsinnspill fra Kristen Koalisjon Norge (KKN): Høring: Videokonferansehøring: Prop. 133 L (2020-2021) Lov om barnevern og lov om endringer i barnevernloven [Hearing input from the Christian Coalition Norway (KKN): Hearing: Video conference hearing: Prop. 133 L (2020–2021) Child Welfare Act and Act on Amendments to the Child Welfare Act]', Kristen Koalisjon Norge (KKN), *Høringsnotat*, 22 April. Available from: https://www.stortinget.no/no/Hva-skjer-pa-Stortinget/Horing/horingsinnspill/?dnid=16445&h=10004335

Vatican (nd) 'Dignitatis Humanae [Declaration on Religious Freedom]'. Available from: https://www.vatican.va/archive/hist_councils/ii_vatican_council/documents/vat-ii_decl_19651207_dignitatis-humanae_en.html

Visegrád Post (2019) 'Poland, land of asylum for Norwegian families', *Visegrád Post*, 12 January. Available from: https://visegradpost.com/en/2019/01/12/poland-land-of-asylum-for-norwegian-families/

Vision Network (nd) Available from: https://visionnetwork.online/

Zdechovský, T. (2020) 'Everything you wanted to know about Norwegian CPS Barnevernet and you were afraid to ask'. Available from: https://www.zdechovsky.eu/en/news/everything-you-wanted-to-know-about-norwegian-cps-barnevernet-and-you-were-afraid-to-ask

Notes

[1] Český žurnál: Děti státu (2016) Česká televize.
[2] These organisations are members of an anti-gender network called Agenda Europe which existed from 2013 to 2019 and then rebranded as the Vision Network as it still operates today. The Agenda Europe/Vision Network consisted of a loose community of over 300 organisations and individuals working together to counter certain evolutions in society which they found harmful and advance their own alternative vision. It consisted of three key pillars: an annual summit gathering the main protagonists, a common manifesto entitled Restoring the Natural Order, and a blog entitled Agenda Europe Blogspot (now private). This network contributed over 15 policy initiatives to counter claims mainly in sexual and reproductive health and rights and LGBTQIA+ rights. See Datta (2018).
[3] Political Network for Values (nd): for more information, see IPAS (2023).
[4] https://en.ordoiuris.pl/
[5] https://adfinternational.org/
[6] https://citizengo.org/en-us
[7] https://eclj.org/
[8] https://aclj.org/
[9] https://en.ordoiuris.pl/barnevernet
[10] Pavlo Ungurian and MP Senator Ronan Mullen are two parliamentarians who have a long track-record of anti-gender activism and affiliation with anti-gender networks. Pavlo Ungurian is a Baptist Pastor and was a parliamentarian until 2019. In 2012, he proposed a

homophobic bill in the Ukrainian parliament. Ronan Mullen was an Irish Senator, who previously worked for the Catholic Archdiocese of Dublin. Mullen specialised in anti-gender issues in his political life, opposing abortion and LGBTQIA+ rights. In 2018, he founded the Human Dignity Alliance, a political party dedicated to anti-gender causes, created in the aftermath of the abortion referendum.

References

Akerbæk, E. (2023) 'Desinformasjon om barnevern sprer seg i Norden [Disinformation about child welfare is spreading in the Nordic countries]', Faktisk. Available from: https://www.faktisk.no/artikler/zml9r/desinformasjon-om-barnevern-spres-i-nordenng

Amery, F. (2023) 'Protecting children in "gender critical" rhetoric and strategy: Regulating childhood for cisgender outcomes', *DiGeSt – Journal of Diversity and Gender Studies*, 10(2): 97–114.

Broderick, T. (2023) 'Evidence undermines rapid onset gender dysphoria claims', *Scientific American*. Available from: https://www.scientificamerican.com/article/evidence-undermines-rapid-onset-gender-dysphoria-claims/

Carbonaro, G. and Mac Dougall, D. (2023) 'Lipstick and heels: Stockholm deputy mayor protests far-right opposition to drag queen story time', *Euronews*. Available from: https://www.euronews.com/2023/06/15/lipstick-and-heels-stockholm-deputy-mayor-protests-far-right-opposition-to-drag-queen-stor

Clark, H. (2019) 'Court of Human Rights to hear case of Norwegian family whose children were seized over Christian upbringing', *Christian News Network*, 5 July. Available from: https://christiannews.net/2019/07/05/european-court-of-human-rights-to-hear-case-of-norwegian-family-whose-children-were-seized-over-christian-upbringing/

Curanović, A. (2023) 'The international activity of Ordo Iuris: The Central European actor and the global Christian right', *Politicization of Religion from a Global Perspective*, 12(12): 1038.

Datta, N. (2018) '"Restoring the natural order": The religious extremists' vision to mobilize European societies against human rights on sexuality and reproduction', *EPF*. Available from: https://www.epfweb.org/node/175

Datta, N. (2020) 'Modern-day crusaders in Europe. Tradition, family and property: Analysis of a transnational, ultra-conservative, Catholic-inspired influence network', *European Parliamentary Forum for Sexual and Reproductive Rights*, Brussels.

Datta, N. and Paternotte, D. (2023) '"Gender ideology": Battles in the European bubble', in G.L. Mascolo (ed), *The Christian Right in Europe: Movements, Networks and Denominations*, Transcript Verlag, pp 43–60.

F.Z. v Norway (no. 64789/17) [2021] ECHR (1 July).

Haugen, H.M. (2024) 'The Christian right in Norway', in G.L. Mascolo (ed), *The Christian Right in Europe: Movements, Networks, and Denominations*, Transcript Verlag, pp 293–305.

Hurd, D. (2019) 'Norwegian nightmare: 'Barnevernet' preys on children and parents', *Christian Broadcasting Network*. Available from: https://cbn.com/news/world/norwegian-nightmare-barnevernet-preys-children-and-parents

Hurd, D. (2023) 'Christian family takes Norway's notorious child welfare agency to court', *Christian Broadcasting Network*. Available from: https://www2.cbn.com/news/world/christian-family-takes-norways-notorious-child-welfare-agency-court

K.E. and A.K. v Norway (no. 57678/18) [2021] ECtHR 1 (1 July).

Lo Mascolo, G. (2023) *The Christian Right in Europe: Movements, Networks, and Denominations*, Transcript Verlag. Available from: https://library.oapen.org/handle/20.500.12657/85717

Marius Bodnariu and Others v Norway (no. 73890/16) [2020] ECtHR (26 November).

Pastor, E.R. (2023) 'A multi-approach to human dignity in the European Court of Human Rights (ECtHR)', in B.G. Scharffs, A. Pin and D. Vovk (eds), *Human Dignity, Judicial Reasoning and the Law: Comparative Perspectives on a Key Constitutional Concept*, Routledge, pp 115–139.

Paternotte, D. (2016) 'Habemus gender! The Catholic church and "gender ideology"', *Religion & Gender*, 6(2): 143–338.

R.O. v Norway (no. 49452/18) [2021] ECtHR (1 July).

Ruzzo, C. (2021) 'The institutionalisation of populist political discourse and consrvative uncivil society in the European Union', *Nordicom Review*, 42(s1): 119–133.

Sentiido (2021) 'Manufacturing moral panic: Weaponizing children to undermine gender justice and human rights'. Available from: https://globalphilanthropyproject.org/2021/03/24/manufacturing-moral-panic/

Strand Lobben and Others v Norway [GC] (no. 37283/13) [2019] ECtHR (10 September).

Thoreson, R. (2015) 'From child protection to children's rights: Rethinking homosexual propaganda bans in human rights law', *The Yale Journal of Law*, 124(4): 1327–1344.

Van den Eynde, L. (2013) 'An empirical look at the amicus curiae practice of human rights NGOs before the European Court of Human Rights', *Netherlands Quarterly of Human Rights*, 31(3): 271–313.

Wunderlich v Germany (no. 18925/15) [2019] ECtHR (10 January, final 24 June).

Yamin, A., Datta, N. and Andion, X. (2018) 'Behind the drama: The roles of transnational actors in legal mobilization over sexual and reproductive rights', *Georgetown Journal of Gender and the Law*, 19(533): 553–569.

10

When 'bad friends' lobby the court against human rights

Asgeir Falch-Eriksen

Introduction

Through the 1950s, the European Convention on Human Rights (ECHR) established a regional human rights catalogue and a court founded on the cosmopolitan normative ethos of the United Nations Universal Declaration to uphold that '[a]ll human beings are born free and equal in dignity and rights' (Cruft et al, 2015). The historically unique regional court, the European Court of Human Rights (ECtHR), and its law, the ECHR, were designed with a series of connections to each signatory country so that court decisions could carry legitimate authority and be socially accepted through country-based enforcement and implementation mechanisms.

The Court was designed so that its decisions would be influenced and informed through appealing cases from each country when legal remedies nationally were exhausted, and court decisions would reflect each country's legal and political progression towards aligning their practices with pan-European human rights standards. This approach would allow the Court to respect the diversity of European legal traditions across countries while progressively fostering a cohesive body of jurisprudence that upholds equal fundamental rights across the region. By examining cases within the specific contexts of individual member states, the Court could begin addressing unique national challenges and variations in interpreting and applying human rights principles. This iterative process ensured that the ECtHR evolved dynamically as if each signatory country accepted and enforced human rights, and where the Court sought out and strove towards an ideal of reflexive and integrative constitutionalism across Europe. Hence, the Court could connect each country's rule of law, their high courts' practices, and systems of democratic self-government and rule of law by enforcing a common ECHR across each signatory country. The lead design trait enabling this development is explicated in the preamble of the ECHR, specifically the legal doctrine known as the *margin of appreciation* (MoA). The doctrine was added to the preamble of the ECHR through the adoption of Protocol 15 in 2015 but has been part of ECtHR practice since its inception in the 1950s:

> Affirming that the High Contracting Parties, in accordance with the principle of subsidiarity, have the primary responsibility to secure the rights and freedoms defined in this Convention and the Protocols thereto, and that in doing so they enjoy a MoA, subject to the supervisory jurisdiction of the European Court of Human Rights established by this Convention. (ECHR, 1950)

The MoA has built a dynamic of democratically governed development of country-based ECHR practices combined with a supervisory court review function of the ECtHR set to uphold a common and evolving human rights standard at a supranational pan-European level (Smet, 2015). It implies that each country has kept their sovereignty and still has the authority to enforce human rights according to their respective democratic sentiments. Hence, a notable feature is the Court's dependency on each country's discretion and a lack of unitary enforcement of human rights and, thereby, a lack of pan-European authority of the Court. In this way, the ECtHR relies on each country through the MoA's inbuilt principle of subsidiarity to best know how to enforce the ECHR within their respective jurisdictions.

Although the MoA can practically be considered a post-Second World War invention that simultaneously maintains state sovereignty as well as international rights norms, it is important to move ahead and understand the various ways this so-called margin works. This implies identifying how different legal theories approach the doctrine and how it is incorporated into law and court practices, with consequences for the practice of human rights at nation-state level. There are multiple ways of interpreting and practising the MoA once it becomes an integral part of a legal theory. In the practical realm of jurisprudence, particularly in how it underpins judicial reasoning and decision-making in the courts, legal theory is not merely an academic exercise but becomes an integral part of professional courtroom decision-making by judges. This means that judges' rulings depend on what legal theory they subscribe to. It serves a crucial practical function by providing the foundational concepts and principles of rationality that guide the interpretation and application of the law. Hence, a robust legal theory equips judges with the philosophically based tools necessary to interpret laws in a way that aligns with broader principles of justice and rationality (Alexy, 2002).

Unless the MoA doctrine is embedded in a robust legal theory, courts risk engendering inconsistent or arbitrary judicial decision-making, thereby undermining the rule of law and the legitimacy of the Court itself. The already established inherent flexibility of the ECtHR through the MoA permits variations in the implementation and enforcement of human rights across different country jurisdictions, making it a necessity to identify and stabilise court practices and discern the underlying rationality of various approaches to the MoA. To elucidate this necessity, I will use the in-built challenge posed by judicial lobbying through third-party interventions or amicus curiae briefs (amicus briefs for short) as these interventions become included in judgments by the Court. Different approaches to the MoA, provided by different legal theories, would yield different solutions. Now, before we continue, it is worth noting that I cannot do justice to the multitude of legal theories out there and how they would respond to the challenge differently through their different approaches to the MoA, and so a key purpose of this chapter is to illustrate how the MoA is not a singularly determined doctrine.

Non-governmental organisations (NGOs), nation-states or other entities can claim to hold relevant and legitimate opinions on cases before the Court, and due to the MoA and how it works, the opinions can vary immensely across the ECtHR jurisdiction (cf ECHR Article 36(2)). These third-party interventions become illustrative of significant de facto variations in human rights interpretation and challenges to enforcement from one country's jurisdiction to the next, which can lead to substantial discrepancies in the strategic contestation across ECHR rights principles. Stabilising the approach to the MoA through legal theories provides a framework for understanding and managing these contestations. Judicial lobbying by third parties, ostensibly acting as 'amici curiae', exemplifies the potential for entities with ulterior motives to influence court decisions detrimentally. Neil Datta's chapter in this volume (see Chapter 9) highlights how some NGOs, masquerading as friends of the Court, seek to undermine human rights standards, acting not as amicus but as 'Inimicus curiae' – an enemy of the court. For the sake of argument, it should be stressed here that I will hold that bad amicus exists and that their efforts to eschew court practices are a part of their primary efforts, but bad amicus is not the empirical focus in and of themselves in this chapter. Despite the system's design to incorporate public engagement and discourse on ECtHR matters, bad amici can exploit the MoA's flexibility to attempt to sway the Court even if their third-party interventions are not formally accepted. Hence, the mechanism of third-party interventions is made into a tool levered by bad amici to engage with the Court no matter what. Bad amicus underscores the critical need to understand the MoA within different theoretical frameworks.

This chapter will explore how the MoA can be understood as an integral part of the legal theoretical schools of legal positivism and discourse theory and how they yield distinct, separate judicial outcomes, particularly in the context of third-party interventions by bad amicus. By examining these two theoretical approaches, the chapter aims to reveal each jurisprudence's inherent strengths and vulnerabilities facing bad amicus. In conclusion, it will be argued that a more complete and conscientious approach to a human rights standard must be invoked. However, it should be underlined that these discussions can be applied to any legal theory, potentially establishing a multitude of conceptions of the MoA to be understood and discussed.

The problem: third-party interventions by bad amicus

Within the ECtHR design, the right to put forth your opinion through invitation or being granted leave and then to inform the Court is a democratic mechanism built into the Court's design where those affected by the decision-making can inform the Court in specific cases to optimise decision-making. However, the third-party intervention comes from a place of special interests and motivations that arguably can and will contest human rights norms. Our problem with bad amicus, then, becomes exacerbated by special interests utilising a benevolent design trait of the Court to influence judgments by their special interests. Hence, judicial lobbying becomes directed at human rights jurisprudence and seeks to eschew the Court's practice away from human rights standards.

To illustrate the problem of bad amicus, we can use an ECtHR landmark case that involved a third-party intervention: The Strand Lobben and others v Norway judgment, where a US-based NGO called the Alliance Defending Freedom (ADF) International was granted leave to intervene as amicus and file an amicus brief. ADF stressed the need to raise the threshold of state intervention to a higher level of endangerment for the child and that the biological bond between parents and children had to be maintained unconditionally. These types of claims do not align with a human rights standard. A child's right to protection from violence begins long ahead of endangerment, and where biological bonds are secondary to the child's right to protection from violence. We do not know to what extent ADF influenced the case, but Norway lost the case and was held in violation of the right to respect for family life (ECHR Article 8).

At a European level, the amicus brief mechanism becomes a test case for the MoA doctrine when a bad amicus piggybacks the MoA's width to claim the variation of interpretation of human rights norms to its advantage, namely that the right to respect for family life could allow for detrimental care of children. By affording states an undefined level of discretion, the doctrine allows for contestations as a model of engagement and for judicial lobbying to push for specific agendas strategically on a case-by-case basis. The stage is thereby set for the problem of bad amicus.

Two theoretical approaches to the margin of appreciation: positivism and discourse theory

I have selected the theoretical strand of positivism and discourse theory not to pass judgment on them as prevailing schools of legal theories within the

ECtHR, but rather to emphasise that they represent two distinct schools. While legal realism, pragmatism or feminism could have been chosen as well, that is not the focus here. My intention is to illustrate that the Court's rulings will be shaped by the understanding and application of the MoA, and that judges will perceive the role of the ECtHR differently depending on which version of the MoA they endorse.

Legal positivism and the MoA

The modern positivist school in legal theory is widely held to be the scholarly offspring of Jeremy Bentham and John Austin. In particular, the focus has been on detaching legal theory from the natural law tradition and focusing on the authority of law which, for all practical purposes, is recognised as commands issued by a sovereign entity and backed by sanctions (Dworkin, 1986; Himma, 2002). To understand the positivist approach to the MoA, I will focus on three lead characteristics of positivist theories that the margin must respond to: The separation thesis, authoritative issuance of law, and legal rules as commands.

The *first* and most notable characteristic the MoA must conform to is the defence of the separation thesis, namely denying that there is a necessary connection between law and morality (Hart, 1994; 2009). It does not make positivist legal practices amoral, but that morality is not a part of legal practice per se. Scholars subscribing to a positivist legal theory address law as analytically decoupled from moral purpose. Holding this separation thesis implies that the positivist approach must also be able to defend that morality and law are conceptually separated (Alexy, 2002). What is implied is 'the content of the law can be anything whatsoever' (Kelsen, 1967). This involves neutralising any moral drive emanating from the normative underpinnings of human rights ethics. Substantially, the separation thesis dictates that the MoA cannot serve any 'higher purpose', as a push for constitutionalisation or a push for democracy while reaching judgments. As Hart argued, laws derive their potency not from any moral stance but from their recognition as commands within the community of the jurisdiction (Hart, 1994). When viewed from a positivist perspective, the MoA becomes a legal mechanism separate from moral considerations and instead gives precedence to legal structures and conventions that are accepted and recognised under the rule of law in each respective member state. National law-making thereby becomes a part of ECtHR's jurisprudence and vice versa through the MoA, bridging the national level to the supranational. MoA thereby couples a country's legal order to a supranational commitment.

Abiding by the separation thesis implies the margin's boundary becomes narrowed down to focus on the jurisdiction prescribed by law in a strict sense. This allows positivism to claim higher legal precision, but it also deems extra-legal factors and moral dimensions of law to be irrelevant or disruptive of legal certainty. A positivist approach to the ECtHR thereby means giving considerable weight to the interconnection between a country's constitutional practice and the ECHR as law. The questions guiding the positivist rationale would be: Is the signatory state's decision or practice in alignment with the stipulated provisions of the ECHR? Moreover, to what extent does a member country's constitutional settlement allow for compliance with decisions of the ECHR? As a notable contender in the tradition of legal positivism, Hans Kelsen would posit that the focus remains on adherence to the legal framework in its 'pure' form, detached from extraneous moral judgments (Kelsen, 1967). This means that a state's decision, as long as it adheres to the textual provisions of the ECHR in combination with each country's constitutional practice and which enforces its basic legal norms authoritatively, would be granted a substantial MoA by a positivist-influenced ECtHR. While this could lead to a broad interpretation of the ECHR, it also offers a shield against what is deemed as weak international rules (Hart, 1994), and also a shield against morally subjective judgments that could potentially cloud the clarity of legal rulings.

Let us now move to the *second* characteristic of the positivist approach, namely that it relies on law having authoritative issuance. As Hart emphasises, laws derive their essence from the fact that a recognised authority endorses them. This is often settled by the sovereign authority or, in many modern democracies, through constitutionally embedded popular sovereignty (Hart, 1994). This is not too distant from Kelsen's postulation that a legal system is a hierarchy of norms, and its validity originates from the *Grundnorm*, or basic norm, which is usually embodied in the constitution or even a norm the constitution itself, as the basic law, derives its authority from (Kelsen, 1967). Authoritative issuance of law, when we refer to the ECtHR and the MoA, underlines the precedence of the sovereignty of individual member states, where the authority of the rule of law is settled also for the ECtHR. While the ECHR establishes a supranational legal framework and a court, the interpretation and application of its provisions still need to be embedded into national law where the basic norm stipulating the authority of law is issued, and is backed by coercion.

The second characteristic has large consequences for how the MoA operates. The ECtHR would weigh the decisions of member states against the ECHR, deriving the authority from each country, and comes with a caveat. The authoritative norms and legal practices within a member country would be accorded due reverence, recognising that each country has its foundational legal authority hierarchically foundational to their commitments to the ECHR (Kelsen, 1967). This deference can be equated with legal relativism of ECtHR practices through the practice of the MoA along positivist lines, where each state's legal structure garners respect so long as it does not dramatically conflict with the ECHR. Accordingly, although the same rights are held by citizens living in each of the respective countries, their rights can mean different things according to their respective country's authoritative issuance of law.

However, as legal philosopher and positivist Joseph Raz points out, it is worth noting that the legal authority must be reasoned and not blind (Raz, 2009). Hence, while authoritative issuance can justify a country's position, the ECtHR, being an arbiter of human rights, must ensure that deference to authoritative issuance does not morph into tacit approval of rights violations or the distortion of the ECtHR's own law. Hence, the ECtHR must be true to its foundational purpose, although being hierarchically dependent on the basic norm of each country. In essence, when viewed through the prism of authoritative issuance, the margin becomes a balancing act between upholding the supranational doctrine of human rights and respecting the inherent legal authority of member countries.

The third characteristic of positivism is that legal rules are recognised as commands by legal subjects – the citizens (Hart, 1994; Raz, 2009). Accordingly, legal rules exist not merely as abstract guidelines or statements but as directives issued by an authority, demanding compliance from those they are addressing. This command-oriented characteristic has multiple implications within the framework provided by the ECtHR. For one, member countries, in the exercise of the MoA, are not only tasked with interpreting the ECHR in alignment with their legal code but also ensuring that their citizens recognise and respect these interpretations as authoritative directives once they have become sewn into the jurisprudence of each member country. Recognition of the Court's decisions to be aligned with the established authority of the law on the country level thereby becomes crucial for the effective implementation of the ECtHR's decisions on the national level, but also very risky as it depends on the infrastructure of each country's legal order being able to implement decisions optimally.

Along with the third characteristic, the margin serves as a buffer, while ensuring that the Court's judgments become embedded in the practice of legal rules within each country, making the judges adaptable and sensitive to the local legal context of each country. This flexibility, however, still upholds the authoritative nature of the Court's directive and emphasises the importance of country members translating these directives into actionable and recognisable commands for their citizenry. This, nevertheless, opens vastly different legal practices of human rights from one country to the next, although court decisions become recognised by citizens as binding commands that govern their behaviour (Kelsen, 1967).

Discourse theory and the margin of appreciation

Discourse theory provides a perspective on law that centres on rational argumentation. Instead of seeing law merely as a set of rigid rules or as entirely contingent on socio-political factors, discourse theorists regard law as agreements from collective deliberation and rational discourse through the democratic rule of law. Concerning the discourse theoretical approach, I will focus on four characteristics: Rational discourse as a foundation, universalisability, the prominence of rights and the interconnection between democracy and rule of law.

Starting with the first characteristic – rational discourse as the foundation of democratic legitimacy – discourse theory suggests that the MoA is not an arbitrary latitude granted to each country, but a discretionary space carved out for rigorous and rational discourse on the merits of the ECtHR legal domain. The 'public sphere's' inbuilt representation through the establishment of legitimate law and the subsequent decisions, rulings and norms formed within the margin can draw on the legitimacy of how each country has democratically accepted and continues to accept the ECHR as law. The margin becomes a portal for pooling democratic discourse to a supranational level, where arguments will be tested in the ECtHR against all other arguments of those affected by the Court's decision. Only in this manner will those affected and potentially affected by the Court's decisions be able to find decisions legitimate (Habermas, 1996).

The second characteristic is a Kantian universalisability test, which calls for any rights norm, to be valid, it must gain acceptance from all relevant parties in an ideal speech situation. Such a concept makes the margin narrower and more complex in that anyone affected by a decision must be able to accept it, and thereby, each case can open for arguments from anywhere across ECtHR's jurisdiction if arguments are relevant. The margin, thereby, needs to be elastic and flexible to include all relevant arguments. While working within the margin, countries should ensure that their interpretations and decisions are not parochial or coloured by local or nationalistic biases that could not withstand valid counterarguments. Instead, decisions should be framed so that, in an ideal discourse situation, they would be acceptable to a broader, potentially global audience. This does not mean a homogenisation of norms but rather a robust justification process where countries recognise the diverse, cosmopolitan human rights standards and aim to integrate corresponding legal cultures. In practical terms, the principle of universalisability thereby challenges certain country practices or interpretations that cannot withstand scrutiny (Habermas, 1996).

The third characteristic is the prominence of rights. To discourse theory, rights are not immutable endowments but are subject to a dynamic process of continuous implementation and justification, aiming to safeguard the dignity of the right-holder through a system of rights constantly developing in response to societal needs for protection (Habermas, 2010). The margin thereby serves as an avenue for legal-political discourse and, through public discourse, searches for commonalities to define how rights work and should be developed within an open discourse framework. When a state invokes its MoA to limit or define a particular right further, from the ECHR, discourse theory would demand that such a limitation is not arbitrary but emerges from a deliberative process wherein the legitimacy of that limitation is rigorously questioned and justified for and with those affected. Hence, the protection of individual dignity comes forth as a presupposition. Accordingly, the margin demands transparency, rigour and, most importantly, a deep respect for individual dignity tied to the purpose of rights, ensuring that their adaptation or limitation in different contexts emerges through open discourse.

The fourth and last characteristic is the interconnectedness between law and democracy, and democracy as a legitimating force. As Habermas (1996) elucidates, the legitimacy of laws is connected to the principle of popular sovereignty and the normativity of what *demos* wants through legislation. The discourse theoretical approach holds that the rule of law is not a mere instrument to secure order; it reflects the democratic will of collective coordination and decision-making. In this light, the rule of law is not a top-down command but a collective realisation of a society's principles and values. Every invocation of the MoA thereby becomes a democratic act. It is each country representing its people, interpreting and applying the law in line with its societal values and norms of those governed. The democratic process and the rule of law are not merely parallel structures but deeply intertwined through law-making and amendments. Thus, any legal decision made under the MoA inherently has democratic implications. It impacts not just the rights in question but also the broader democratic ethos of the country.

How the different theories cope with bad amicus

The discussions have now revealed that there is no single definitive answer to what constitutes the MoA – it is not a unitary doctrine. The two legal theories we have discussed only scratch the surface of its complexity. This highlights the importance of recognising that the MoA varies depending on the legal perspective of a legal scholar, judge, lawyer or politician. For instance, a judge following the positivist school may risk becoming moralistic if making rulings based on non-legal norms or prioritising the normative cosmopolitan foundation of human rights. In the following section, I will explore how these approaches address the issue of biased third-party interventions, particularly in cases where amicus briefs seek to sway the Court in ways that do not align with human rights.

One of the hallmarks of positivist legal theory is its insistence on the separation of law and morality (Hart, 2009). Bad amici actors blur the lines between personal or group moralities and legal reasoning – as they seek to infuse their morally driven interests onto others specifically. For a court evaluating amicus briefs, a positivist approach would strictly assess the arguments based on legal merits, involving methodically stripping away moral or ethical undertones as irrelevant for qualifying arguments. This clear demarcation ensures that court decisions remain influenced solely by codified ECHR law, case law or established precedent, drastically reducing the inroads for interest groups from bad intents (cf Kelsen, 1967).

If we then move over to the authoritative issuance of law, and that laws need to be derived from what Kelsen refers to as the authority of the basic norm (1967), we can translate this to a type of scrutiny of amicus briefs that implies that any legal argument must be traced and justified backwards to an authoritative source of law. Amicus briefs attempting to eschew a human rights standard without clear legal backing from law that carries authority, no matter how hidden or eloquently argued, would be disqualified as deviating from the basic norm. However, suppose a country has begun to provide legislation that downplays the ECHR from a constitutional viewpoint, which is more likely to be constitutional backsliding that is legitimate according to their basic norm; bad amicus could become a useful ally to continue such a process and push the ECtHR away from the country's own jurisdictional practices.

Finally, to positivism, legal rules are not mere guidelines – they are definitive commands to be recognised and obeyed by those governed. Suppose a decision within the ECtHR is an interpretation of the commands within the law and is recognised as such by citizens. In that case, decisions become implemented as authoritative, even if they clash with narratives advanced by particular amicus briefs. Hence, amicus briefs departing from the law will not be able to influence decisions as commands as they are unhelpful. Therefore, the supremacy of established judicial rulings of case law ensures that the ECtHR's decisions override potentially bad amici interpretations contained within amicus submissions. The positivist legal theory gives the judiciary a robust framework to critically assess and neutralise the influence of interests not conducive to human rights stipulated by the ECHR. By keeping law distinct from morality, rooting legal argumentation in authoritative sources and reiterating the binding nature of laws, positivism is a strong defence against the distortions that bad amici might seek to introduce.

However, although the positivist approach separates law from morality, morality is obviously still immersed in legislation, albeit held to be irrelevant to the Court itself. By disengaging from the moral implications of a ruling, the Court might inadvertently begin to sanction state actions that, while legally justifiable, may be morally or ethically questionable from a human rights point of view. Those who are bad amicus can thereby strategise on achieving their moral aims incrementally through a positivist approach to law that builds case law incrementally in their favour. Although such an approach is time-consuming and dependent on multi-layered court lobbying, it can gradually build a solid foundation for a legal culture that is not conducive to a human rights court in any moral sense. Alternatively, it might accept state practices that are morally questionable but legally justifiable. This can present a potential conflict between the objective pursuit of law and morality. In the end, if your agenda is to eschew the understanding of the law towards your interests, bad amicus can utilise the law as a 'neutral' tool to further your morally questionable agenda. The positivist approach to the MoA opens for such an approach.

Unlike the legal theory of positivism, the discourse theoretical approach begins at the opposite end, namely with a basic aim in safeguarding the dignity of the right-holder, and that a human rights court is equipped to reach legitimate decisions by itself and on the merits of its law alone. The Court must ensure that judgments are pursued on the merits of a human rights standard best recognised by its fundamental principle of dignity of the individual person (Habermas, 2010). Hence, the ECtHR's purpose becomes upholding and distributing rights equally to all citizens, and variable sociolegal contexts do not constitute valid restrictions on argumentation. What is held to be legitimate decision-making must align itself with the outcome best suited for protecting the dignity of those affected.

Discourse theory's focus on rational discourse as the foundation of procedurally establishing legitimacy of law shapes how bad amicus are identified and handled. As interest groups seek to pull the Court's decision-making towards their ends, it also becomes dependent on inhibiting others from launching counterarguments. The interests of bad amicus, provided their interests are contrary to the ethos of human rights, can only be fulfilled if not all interests can be represented in the process of argumentation through providing reasonable counterarguments. Hence, bad amicus breaches the call from discourse theory to participate in rational discourse, where non-coercive truth telling and mutual agreements are settled aims of discourse. The implication for a discourse theoretical approach is that bad amicus' contributions are permissible, indeed necessary, for the integrity of a communicative process where the interests of bad amicus is only one affected party among all affected parties. Hence, bad amicus will not be allowed dominance simply through their ability to participate. The contributions of bad amicus must thereby endure the rigour of discursive validation, where the only allowed outcome is those claims that are reached in agreement (Habermas, 1996). We can argue bad amicus' arguments become transmuted through the reflexive process of argumentation of the Court itself and thereby thrown out. This, however, calls for courts to be forthright with debunking arguments and providing reasons that, in our case, would conclude an amicus brief indeed came from a bad amicus.

The discourse theoretical approach aligns itself with a human rights ethos in the sense that protecting dignity is foundational to the interpretation and enforcement of rights, namely, a thin concept of ethical universalisability (Habermas, 2010). Through the MoA, it is not a democratic prerogative that is sought, but rather a constitutional and rights-based approach. From a discourse theoretical standpoint, the ECtHR's main objective will be to seek out the implementation of rights-based approaches first, and with a secondary aim of achieving societal objectives locally within each country. Hence, the prominence of rights through the discourse-theoretical approach binds the MoA to provide each country with far more restrictions on their discretionary practices in implementing and enforcing rights. The discourse theoretical approach thereby upholds the strong defence of individual dignity no matter what any country's socio-political positions might be.

Conclusion: Bad amicus and the threat towards individual dignity

The MoA ensures that human rights jurisprudence does not shut itself in within each country and becomes impervious to its need to progress and adapt to whatever time brings. How the MoA is enforced thereby becomes imperative for how human rights norms become integrated into the legal-political fabric of each country member separately and combined. Contestation and active contradiction are principled aspects of a court of law in liberal constitutional democracies, and the irony it must maintain is to reproduce contestation and never settle for interpretations that last into perpetuity. Actors with bad intent, where the contestation pushes the human rights discourse away from a human rights ethos and are bent on using judicial lobbying to seek to eschew the Court into bad practices, have become a challenge to the ECtHR. Depending on what legal theory judges lean towards, the success of bad amici will vary.

Judges who align with positivism, emphasising strict adherence to codified laws and the separation of law and moral reasoning, are more likely to disregard amicus briefs that introduce extra-legal arguments, especially those rooted in moral or ethical discourse rather than clear legal principles. In contrast, judges who lean towards discourse theory – grounded in the belief that law is shaped by ongoing rational dialogue and moral argumentation – may be more receptive to the broader implications and societal values that amici briefs attempt to introduce, even if they are weak or poorly constructed. The legal framework a judge follows – whether rooted in positivism's rigid structure or discourse theory's emphasis on rational consensus – plays a crucial role in determining the success or failure of such amici.

When filtered through different legal theories, the MoA allows signatory countries to adopt human rights standards and practices differently in fulfilling their human rights obligations. The margin does, however, not allow for different interpretations of the human rights standard itself, provided we choose a perspective that stipulates that the purpose of the ECtHR is to uphold human rights law as a human rights court proper. Hence, the MoA does not open up for unequal interpretations of what the human rights standard calls for, although MoA practices according to the positivist approach, say it can. Along the two approaches, equal cases may be treated factually and legally unequally depending on the country where a European citizen resides. However, this discrimination is only relative to the potential of equal enforcement of the human rights standard and not necessarily unequal protection in a normative sense. Although this inherent disparity raises concerns about the principle of law as citizens' rights and protections become contingent on geographical location, it nevertheless hinges instrumentally on the country's ability to enforce human rights according to a standard that aligns with a human rights ethos. Intended to account for legal, political, cultural and societal variations, the MoA introduces a paradoxical situation where equal cases can be subject to unequal treatment, undermining the essence of human rights to be distributed equally and universally.

References

Alexy, R. (2002) *The Argument from Injustice: A Reply to Legal Positivism*, Clarendon Press.

Cruft, R., Liao, S.M. and Renzo, M. (2015) *Philosophical Foundations of Human Rights*, Oxford University Press.

Dworkin, R. (1986) *Law's Empire*, Belknap Press.

ECHR (European Convention on Human Rights) (1950) *European Convention for the Protection of Human Rights and Fundamental Freedoms as amended by Protocol No. 11*, European Treaty Series, 5.

Habermas, J. (1996) *Between Facts and Norms: Contributions to a Discourse Theory of Law and Democracy*, Polity Press.

Habermas, J. (2010) 'The concept of human dignity and the realistic utopia of human rights', *Metaphilosophy*, 41(4): 464–480.

Hart, H.L.A. (1994) *The Concept of Law: With a Postscript Edited by Penelope A. Bulloch and Joseph Raz*, Clarendon Press.

Hart, H.L.A. (2009) 'Positivism and the separation of law and morals', *Law and Morality*, 71(4): 63–99.

Himma, K.E. (2002) 'Inclusive legal positivism', in J.L. Coleman and S. Shapiro (eds), *The Oxford Handbook of Jurisprudence and Philosophy of Law*, Oxford University Press, pp 353–430.

Kelsen, H. (1967) *Pure Theory of Law*, University of California Press.

Raz, J. (2009) *The Authority of Law: Essays on Law and Morality*, Oxford University Press.

Smet, S. (2015) 'When human rights clash in the age of subsidiarity: What role for the margin of appreciation?', in P. Agha (eds), *Human Rights Between Law and Politics: The Margin of Appreciation in Post-National Contexts*, Hart Publishing, pp 73–91.

11

Mobilised interests, the European Court of Human Rights and children's rights

Rachel Cichowski and Elizabeth Chrun

Introduction

International courts are increasingly a battleground for mobilised interests. While we might not expect the child protection services of a small European state to garner widespread political and legal attention, the 2019 Strand Lobben and Others v Norway case before the European Court of Human Rights (ECtHR) illustrated quite the opposite. With an unprecedented number of 11 amicus curiae (or friends of the courts briefs) participating in the case, from national governments to human rights organisations and religious lobbying groups, this legal mobilisation exemplifies a growing trend. International courts, while privileging state access, continue to facilitate and develop avenues for direct participation by a diversity of other interests in the work of developing and enforcing international law (for example, Cichowski, 2007; Squatrito, 2018; Kahraman, 2023; Van der Vet and McIntosh Sundstrom, 2023). Amicus curiae briefs are an increasingly popular form of participation and are filed by interested third parties providing comparative research, policy preferences and legal reasoning that can influence judicial outcomes (Collins, 2018). Our chapter examines this dynamic in the context of the European Convention system and asks how and why organisations, including national governments as well as advocacy groups, intervene as third parties in ECtHR litigation. In particular, we provide an in-depth case law analysis of ECtHR judgments to examine amicus curiae participation in the Norwegian children's rights cases.

Our chapter contributes to the following three goals of this edited volume. First, our analysis expands knowledge about patterns and processes of legal mobilisation by individuals, states, organisations and interest advocacy groups before an international court. The ECtHR children's rights cases become an excellent avenue to explore general patterns of mobilisation to gain a better understanding of whether there are countermobilisation motivations or just an enlarging net of actors seeking to shape important human rights developments. Second, our analysis enables us to examine the role that the ECtHR has in expanding access to legal processes, particularly by the inclusion of interests beyond the two parties directly involved with the case. There is considerable research on amicus curiae in the American context (for example, Collins, 2018), but much less is known about other domestic and international jurisdictions (for example, Cichowski, 2016; Collins and McCarthy, 2017). Finally, our chapter contributes to the larger goal of demystifying international litigation dynamics with a particular emphasis on the third-party intervention process. The Norwegian children's rights cases bring into stark relief a site for judicial politics, where a particularly contested set of fundamental rights collide in a legal and political terrain fraught with vague and competing principles (be it 'best interest of the of the child' or state discretion as embedded in the margin of appreciation doctrine). Our analysis will shed light on the varying interests and the ways the existing legal institutions both shape and are shaped by this legal mobilisation. The chapter will first introduce the conceptual approach and data, followed by an analysis of amicus participation in the Norwegian children's rights cases before the ECtHR.

Conceptual approach

The analysis adopts the assumption that in any system of governance with an independent judiciary, litigation provides a potential avenue for policy change (Shapiro, 1981). It is this potential for participating in legal discussions that can develop the law and shape policy, that helps explain why third parties mobilise and participate in litigation processes. Our approach adopts a framework that focuses on three theoretically significant institutional factors that help us understand how and why organisations (including states as well as advocacy groups) participate in ECtHR litigation (Cichowski, 2016).

First, the scope of rules and rights governing individual and group access to the ECtHR shape when and how organisations participate in international litigation process (Cichowski, 2016; Dzehtsiarou, 2023). The rules surrounding amicus curiae access evolved through the ECtHR's case law beginning with the Winterwerp v Netherlands judgment in 1979 as there was no clear process for third-party interventions in the original Convention. Yet by 1998, access was codified through the European Convention (Article 36§2) and the Rules of the Court (44§2) providing states, persons and organisations who were not parties to the case a mechanism to share their views with the Court (see also Emberland, Chapter 2).

Second, as is true more broadly with any court, the ECtHR's relative review power and scope of jurisdiction shapes its potential as a site of influence over significant public policy issues and thus an attractive venue for organised interests and rights claiming (Stone Sweet, 2000; Cichowski, 2006). Connected to this judicial power, scholars argue there are two general explanations for why entities file briefs: to influence judicial outcomes and to uphold their organisation's interests and that of its members (Collins and McCarthy, 2017; Collins, 2018). These key Protocol 11 institutional reforms in the late 1990s led to massive reform of Convention institutions, including an expansion in the Court's power through compulsory jurisdiction and compulsory rather than optional standing for individuals and groups. Expanding power enhanced the Court's appeal as a forum for third parties to provide information and influence the development of human rights. Finally, the degree of organisational strength, expertise and experience helps us better understand how and why particular organisations are successful at participating in ECtHR litigation (Conant et al, 2018). Together, we expect these factors to help us better understand how and why organisations participate as third party interveners in this case study of Norwegian children's rights cases.

Data and methods

Our analysis utilises the European Court of Human Rights Database (ECHRdb) (Cichowski and Chrun, 2024) to examine patterns of advocacy group participation. The database compiles judgment and legal mobilisation information from primary documents collected at the ECtHR as well as the Court's comprehensive full text online judicial decision database, HUDOC,[1] for the period 1961 to 2022 and includes a total of 23,809 judgments. For this chapter, we have extracted a series of datasets from the larger ECHRdb. First, a set of judgment data, including all third-party interventions from the first amicus in 1979 through 2022 (N= 2,121 amicus briefs), enables us to examine the Norwegian case study in a broader context and identify how key institutional variables shaped amicus participation. We study the main content of the third-party brief through the summaries included in the ECtHR judgment and code when the brief supports the applicant or the respondent state. Second, we extract data from the ECHRdb on all the ECtHR judgments against Norway from the first in 1990 through 2022 (N=72 judgments). These Norway judgments provide the backbone of this chapter enabling us to identify the children's rights cases (first ECtHR judgment in 1996, N= 33 judgments) and also those Norwegian children's rights judgments that included amicus briefs (first judgment in 2019, N=15 judgments, N=45 amicus briefs). Through case law analysis of these judgments and process tracing relying on primary and secondary sources we are better able to understand how and why organisations intervene in this ECtHR children's rights litigation involving Norway.

Analysis: the Norwegian case study

We begin by placing the Norwegian case study in a wider context of expanding access at the Court. Figure 11.1 details the annual number of third-party interventions in ECtHR judgments from the first intervention in 1979 to 2022. There are 2,121 and include 23 different types of organisations from state governments to corporations and human rights organisations. How did the key institutional reforms affect the general amicus curiae participation rates? The data clearly show an upward trend following the massive reforms in the Convention institutional machinery through Protocol 11 in 1998. This last reform also represented a major consolidation of the Court's power and legitimacy, establishing it as an important venue to shape policy on human rights in Europe. Standardised numbers that controlled for a growing number of Contracting States (including a massive growth in new membership in the early 1990s with the fall of the Soviet Union) show a steady annual 20 per cent increase in amicus briefs. Further, the top repeat players in this data are well-resourced international organisations such as the International Commission of Jurists, the Helsinki Foundation for Human Rights and Amnesty International. Together the data suggests that these institutional reforms helped shape this upward trajectory of participation by third parties.

Despite this evolving trend, the ECtHR judgments involving Norway only began to get the attention of organisations in 2008, with a total of 53 third-party interventions between the first in 2008 and 2022. If we focus specifically on children's rights cases, another interesting trend emerges. From the first judgment against Norway in 1990 to 2022, Norway was called before the Court in 33 cases[2] pertaining to children's rights. Notably, not a single amicus brief was filed in the 14 cases before 2019. A shift occurred with Strand Lobben and Others v Norway. The applicants – T. Strand Lobben, her two children X and Y, and her two parents – held that the decision by the Norwegian child protection authorities to allow the adoption of X by his foster parents had violated their right to respect for family life. The case attracted international attention, and for the first time in a child welfare case against Norway, parties sought to intervene in the proceedings. In total, there was a constellation of 11 different interveners, including state governments, non-governmental organisations and the child's adoptive parents.

In this analysis, we examine the ways in which a dispute between a claimant and the Norwegian government evolves into a much wider policy discussion regarding child welfare and rights between families, interest and advocacy groups, state governments and the ECtHR. Table 11.1 details all the Norwegian children's rights ECtHR judgments that included a third-party intervention by a state or interest group through 2022. After Strand Lobben there were 14 more ECtHR children's rights judgments through 2022 that included 34 third-party interventions by states or interest groups. The table

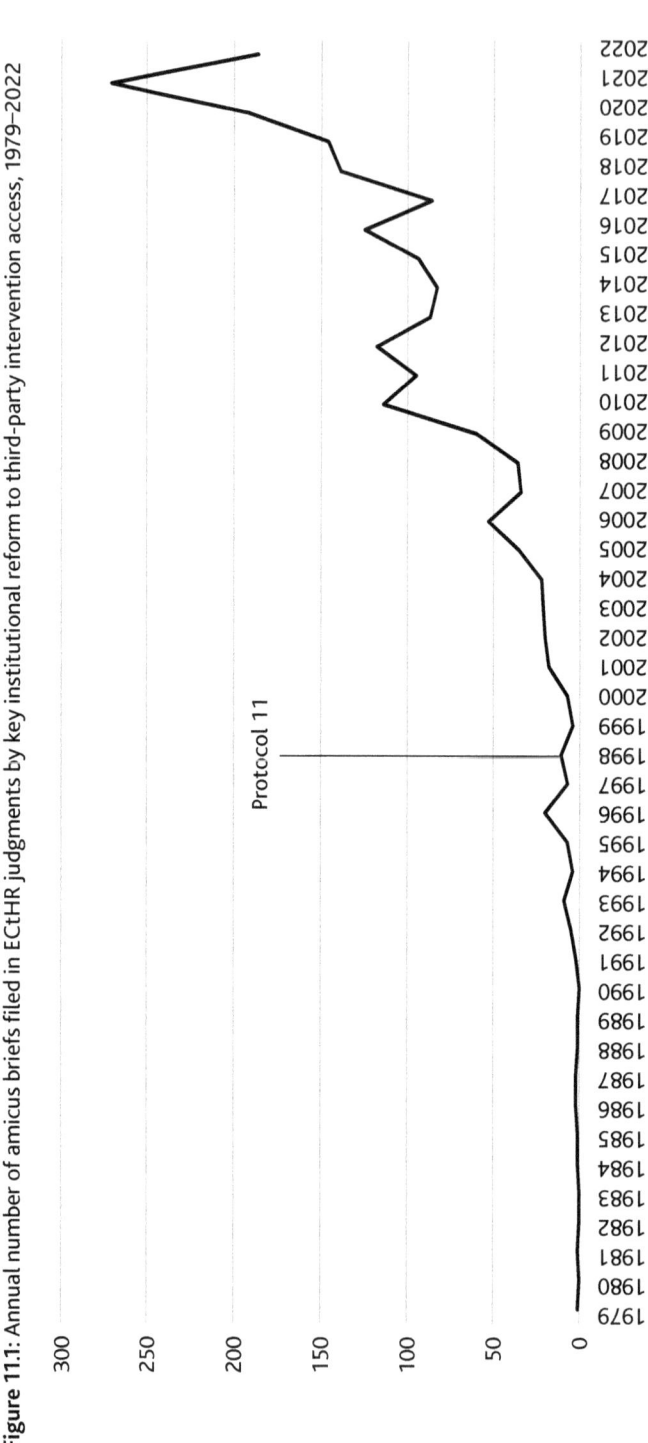

Figure 11.1: Annual number of amicus briefs filed in ECtHR judgments by key institutional reform to third-party intervention access, 1979–2022

Note: N=2,121. The figure includes aggregate annual numbers (since the first amicus brief in 1979) in order to identify the real growth in amicus participation and the Court's growing engagement with third-party interveners. Standardised numbers are not included, but they showed a steady 20 per cent average annual increase in amicus briefs. Key institutional reform: 1998: Protocol 11 adopted, granting the ECtHR compulsory jurisdiction, making compulsory standing for individuals and organisations to bring a claim and codifying individual and organisation access to the Court as a third-party intervener.
Source: Cichowski and Chrun (2024)

Mobilised interests and the ECtHR

Table 11.1: Norwegian children's rights ECtHR judgments and associated third-party interventions by state governments and interest groups from 2019 to 2022

Case	App #	Year	Interest groups: Ordo Iuris Institute	AIRE Centre	ADF	AIMMF	State governments: Czech Republic	Slovakia	Turkey	Poland	Belgium	Bulgaria	Denmark	Italy	United Kingdom
Alleleh and Others*	569/20	2022													
A.M.*	30254/18	2022		•											
E.M. and Others	53471/17	2022	•				•	X							
A.L. and Others	45889/18	2022	•				X	•							
Abdi Ibrahim	15379/16	2021		X			•		•						
Jallow	36516/19	2021													
M.F.	5947/19	2021	•				X	X							
E.H.	39717/19	2021					X								
O.S.	63295/17	2021	•				X	X							
R.O.	49452/18	2021	•				X	X							
F.Z.	64789/17	2021	•				X	X							

(continued)

197

Table 11.1: Norwegian children's rights ECtHR judgments and associated third-party interventions by state governments and interest groups from 2019 to 2022 (continued)

			Interest groups	Ordo Iuris Institute	AIRE Centre	ADF	AIMMF	State governments	Czech Republic	Slovakia	Turkey	Poland	Belgium	Bulgaria	Denmark	Italy	United Kingdom
K.E. and A.K.	57678/18	2021		•					X	X							
M.L.	64639/16	2020		•						•							
Pedersen and Others	39710/15	2020							•								
Hernehult	14652/16	2020								•							
A.S.	60371/15	2019										•					
Abdi Ibrahim	15379/16	2019			•				•								
K.O. and V.M.	64808/16	2019				○			•								
Strand Lobben	37283/13	2019		•					•	•			•		○		○
Total TPI			8	3	1	1		12	10	1	1	1	1	2	1	1

Note: N=43. * Denotes a case unrelated to a care order. ○ denotes that the third party supported Norway. • denotes that the third party supported the applicant. X denotes an unclear position due to insufficient information.

Source: Cichowski and Chrun (2024)

also details whether the third-party intervener supported the applicant or the Norwegian state. We discuss these cases in the analysis that follows.

State governments as amicus curiae

How did state governments intervene as third parties? Along with the sheer number of third parties participating in the Strand Lobben case, another distinguishing feature is the significant number of governments submitting briefs. Historically, there have been instances where multiple governments have intervened, effectively morphing an individual dispute into a European wide referendum on a particularly contentious public policy matter (see A v the United Kingdom, 2002; Lautsi v Italy, 2011; Tarakhel v Switzerland, 2014; A and B v Norway, 2016). The Strand Lobben case stands out because there was no clear consensus between the intervening state governments. Italy, Denmark and the United Kingdom each sided with the Norwegian authorities whereas Belgium, Bulgaria, the Czech Republic and Slovakia submitted observations that supported the applicants' case and biological family reunification.

In the Strand Lobben case, a central point of disagreement between the intervening states concerned the balancing of children's rights against those of their biological parents, and, relatedly, the question as to whether the state had a duty to preserve biological family ties when children were placed in public care (Strand Lobben v Norway, 2019, para 186). The Italian government submitted that ties should be maintained only in situations that benefit the child, effectively arguing that the best interests of children prevailed over biological parents' rights. Similarly, the United Kingdom suggested that the Norwegian state was not required by Article 8 of the Convention to make 'endless attempts at family reunification' (Strand Lobben v Norway, 2019, para 189). Interestingly, in the Court's summary of Denmark's submission, the state did not address the substance of the issue and instead argued that the Court's assessment of the case should be limited to the decision-making process instead of carrying out a 'forensic examination of the facts'. On the other end of the spectrum were the governments of Czech Republic and Slovakia, who stressed the importance of maintaining a bond between biological parents and their children. Both states held that the placement of a child into public care should be temporary, and that such measures should be followed by constant efforts to promote family reunification (Strand Lobben v Norway, 2019, paras 190 and 187). The Belgian and the Bulgarian governments both noted that states enjoyed a margin of appreciation in the manner they chose to intervene with respect to child welfare and placement in public care, but crucially, the latter stressed the importance of family reunification despite evidence that a child could benefit more from being placed in a different environment (Strand Lobben v Norway, 2019, paras

176–177). All in all, their positions were clearcut: one camp prioritised the child's rights and the other called for greater recognition of the rights of the biological parents and the importance of biological family reunification.

In subsequent judgments, while fewer state governments intervened, the Czech and Slovak authorities kept reappearing, submitting 12 and eight briefs respectively, maintaining their support for the reunification of children with their biological parents. Poland and Turkey each intervened once to similarly support applicants. After Strand Lobben, Denmark was the only state government that submitted observations to support the Norwegian authorities' actions by arguing in the Abdi Ibrahim (2021) case that the best interests of the child should be the guiding factor with regard to the choice of a foster home. Consistent with scholarship on amicus curiae, we found a pattern that suggests that states seek to intervene as third parties when they have a national interest in the development (or protection) of a certain set of rights and want domestic and international audiences to know they are a part of these policy discussions (Collins, 2018; Dzehtsiarou, 2023).

The trajectory of the top repeat player, the Czech Republic, fits this pattern. The Czech state's motivation to intervene can be traced back to the political and media frenzy surrounding the Michálková case, which peaked[3] years before it itself reached the ECtHR in 2017 (E.M. and Others v Norway, 2022). Eva Michálková, a Czech national who emigrated to Norway, first drew attention in 2013 when she sought to gain back custody of her two sons from the Norwegian Barnevernct in 2011 (Koukal, 2013). The private matter became political when Czech Members of Parliament, Members of the European Parliament, Prime Minister Bohuslav Sobotka and President Miloš Zeman got involved and pushed for the swift reunification of the biological family (Leinert, 2014; AP News, 2015; Mladá fronta DNES, 2015). Czech officials seemingly used every opportunity to provide the Court with a resolution that relied on an argument that privileges the rights of the biological mother.

Other interventions follow the same pattern. In 2006, the placement by Barnevernet of Turkish-Iranian children in a different ethno-religious foster family led to criticisms from Turkish politicians and media, and discussions on the importance of the intergenerational familial transmission of cultural and religious identities (Vassenden and Vedøy, 2019). The Abdi Ibrahim case, in which Turkey intervened in 2021, exemplifies this conflict as the Court grappled with the question of whether placing a child with a Christian foster family violates the freedom of religion rights of the applicant (the child's mother), a Somali Muslim woman. In 2011, Norway similarly became embroiled in diplomatic feuds with Poland, again as a result of foster home placements. The political conflict between both countries was reactivated as Oslo expelled the Polish consul Slawomir Kowalski over his conflicts with Barnevernet in 2019 (Czarnecki, 2019). Poland also intervened in A.S. v

Norway (2019) to support the applicant, a Polish national whose child was placed in foster care. In 2018, Cvetelina Oland asked representatives of the Bulgarian Foreign Ministry for the return of her children (Bulgarian News Agency, 2018) before her plea reached the European Parliament (European Parliament, 2018) and Bulgaria went on to intervene as a third party in the Strand Lobben case.

What explains the salience of these cases and the subsequent mobilisation that ensued is the potency of the underlying online campaigns of misinformation that have sought to demonise the Norwegian Barnevernet since as early as 2015. Under slogans such as 'Norway steals children' that were aimed at stoking fears among the general population, these campaigns circulated sensationalist narratives that suggested that the agency abducted children from immigrant parents for sex trafficking and other purposes, or to place them in LGBTQIA+ families (Whewell, 2016; Svatoňová, 2021). In 2015–2016, rallies involving religious groups among others took place simultaneously all over the world to protest the agency's interference in migrant families (Schönfelder and Holmgaard, 2019). Although protests were mainly organised in Eastern and Central Europe, they also took place in Western capitals such as London and Washington, DC. These sensationalist stories effectively amplified individual real-world cases such as those of Michálková and Oland and increased the pressure on state officials of Central and Eastern Europe to secure family reunification and signal their commitment to protect nationals' interests.

At the most general level, state governments intervene when they have an interest in the outcome of a case or of an issue that is being debated before the ECtHR. While it remains that some state governments intervened to defend the interests of their nationals in cases where they were the litigants (Czech Republic, Slovakia and Poland in the cases of E.M. and Others v Norway; A.L. and Others v Norway (2022); and A.S. v Norway (2019), respectively), this alone does not explain the bulk of state interventions neither in the cases under study nor in the rest of the Court's case-law.[4] Consistent with expectations, third-party activity, particularly those of repeat players, suggest that state officials follow ECtHR cases and are aware of the implications that judgments of similar children's rights cases could have on their own domestic affairs and policies and they utilise the third-party intervention mechanism as a way of asserting those interests and preferences.

Interest and advocacy groups as amicus curiae

How did interest groups intervene as third parties? Three interest groups intervened in the Strand Lobben case, far fewer than state governments. The Advice on Individual Rights in Europe Centre (AIRE) is a non-governmental organisation that specialises in legal advocacy in the field of human rights. The Associazione Italiana dei Magistrati per i Minorenni e per la Famiglia (AIMMF) is an Italian professional association of judges who seek to promote and protect juvenile and family rights through advocacy (AIMMF, 2019). The third intervener was the Alliance Defending Freedom (ADF) International, an American faith-based conservative group specialising in legal advocacy. While the participation by advocacy groups was not insignificant in Strand Lobben, there have been numerous cases in the history of the Court that have attracted greater mobilisation from such groups (see Orlandi and Others v Italy 2017; Big Brother Watch and Others v United Kingdom 2018; X v Poland 2021; H.F. and Others v France 2022). Referring back to Table 11.1, after Strand Lobben, only two interest groups intervened in Norway children's rights cases during the observed period: the AIRE Centre intervened twice and the Polish conservative advocacy group the Ordo Iuris Institute for Legal Culture (hereinafter Ordo Iuris), was the top repeat player with eight separate submitted briefs.

A remarkable feature of this group mobilisation in ECtHR children's rights cases is the unprecedented alignment of conservative interest groups and human rights groups. Through their interventions as third parties, conservative interest groups typically provide stark counterpoints to rights groups across a number of issues; both camps typically disagree on the preferred outcome of a case on abortion rights (see Tysiąc v Poland, 2007), reproductive rights (see S.H. and Others v Austria, 2011) and the right to die (see Pretty v United Kingdom, 2002), among others. In the Strand Lobben case, the AIMMF concluded that it was in the best interests of the child to strengthen his relations with his foster parents (Pretty v United Kingdom, 2002, para 195). While not necessarily disagreeing with the AIMMF, the AIRE Centre suggested it was in a child's best interests to retain contact with their birth parents and stressed the rights of parents with intellectual disabilities, citing the Convention on the Rights of the Child (Pretty v United Kingdom, 2002, para 198). ADF International agreed that Norway had a duty to maintain contact between parents and children but went further by advocating for family reunification as an end goal (Pretty v United Kingdom, 2002, para 192). Examining the larger dataset, including all judgments involving third-party interveners (1979–2022), to the best of our knowledge, there were only two other times a human rights advocacy group and a conservative interest group aligned on a similar legal position. The case of Bayatyan v Armenia (2011) had six different third-party interveners, including the Jehovah's Christian Witnesses, alongside well-known human rights groups such as Amnesty International, all supporting the applicant's right as a conscientious objector. Similarly, the case of F.G. v Sweden (2016) had seven interveners, including religious groups such as ADF and human rights defenders like the AIRE Centre and the UN Commissioner for Human Rights. All supported the applicant, an Iranian national who had converted to Christianity, whose asylum application was rejected in Sweden, and who feared religious persecution if returned to Iran.

Further, we note that the inclusion of conservative groups in court proceedings in cases pertaining to care and adoption orders effectively expanded the substance of the debates at hand. Looming underneath the difficulty of striking a balance between a child's interest and their biological parents' rights and circling back to the themes and narratives conveyed in the misinformation campaigns targeting the Norwegian Barnevernet policies, is the larger question of what constitutes a family. Ordo Iuris, in particular, espoused a narrow view of the definition of a family and emphasised that 'the most complete guarantee of children's good is education by biological parents who are married', adding that children are 'best served with his or her biological family – any doubts should therefore be resolved in favour of the parents'. Even in situations where there is substantial evidence that this presumption is false, 'the state shall continue to attempt to re-establish the sound relationship between the child and its parents' (M.L. v Norway, 2020).[5]

Why did interest groups intervene as third parties? We find that despite an ideological divide, interest and advocacy groups share the goal of intervening in a way that upholds the body of rights consistent with their policy agendas. Contrary to state governments, they do not necessarily have antecedents with Norway and Barnevernet.[6] They simply make strategic use of the ECtHR legal process to shape the outcome of cases in line with the rights of the communities they serve.

ADF International and the Ordo Iuris Institute are both conservative groups that aim to push the advancement of conservative ideas and policies at the ECtHR. By intervening in this subset of cases against Norway, they instrumentalise a debate centring on children's rights to push for the recognition and the protection of the traditional nuclear family. ADF International is a Christian legal advocacy organisation that calls itself the 'world's largest legal organisation committed to protecting religious freedom, free speech, marriage and family, parental rights, and the sanctity of life' (ADF International, 2024). Ordo Iuris Institute is a conservative lobbying group whose areas of intervention at the ECtHR considerably overlap with the ADF's, but whose stated mission is not, incidentally, faith-based. As a friend of the Court, the group has intervened in ECtHR cases against Norway but also Iceland, Germany, Austria, Poland, Ukraine and Denmark. Using a multi-pronged legal strategy, both organisations have intervened at the ECtHR to limit reproductive rights, LGBTQIA+ rights and women's rights in their capacity as legal representatives and third-party interveners (Cichowski and Chrun, 2024).

The scope of the activity of interest and advocacy groups who intervened in Norwegian children's rights cases suggest that these groups intervene at the ECtHR to provide comparative research and legal arguments that might shape the judicial outcome. Examining the ECHRdb data over time, the AIRE Centre is one of the top repeat players in the history of the ECtHR participating as third-party intervener and legal representative 71 times between 1961 and 2022. Since Ordo Iuris' first intervention at the ECtHR in 2017, the group has become a rising player, submitting observations in 35 judgments. Similarly, ADF International has a total of 28 interventions. The groups are acutely aware that their strategic legal mobilisation is amplified given the potential radiating effects of the ECtHR judgments. In a video produced by Ordo Iuris, its legal counsel Jennifer Lea speaks about the Strand Lobben case: 'whatever the outcome of the hearing today, this case will have a huge impact across Norway, for families in Norway, and other Member States as well'.

Conclusion

This analysis of third-party activity in children's rights cases against Norway showcases the expansion of the ECtHR's legal terrain and two concomitant phenomena: the willingness and sometimes eagerness of European governments to use the Court as a forum on issue matters that are especially relevant to them, and the formal recognition of international conservative voices in that same arena. On the matter of children's protection policies, the importance of the biological family reunification was emphasised using different reasonings. For states whose migrants claimed to have been deprived of their parental rights, advocating for biological family reunification was a means to protect states' margin of appreciation in the manner they intervened with respect to their nationals' child welfare. For interest groups, the importance of biological family reunification was supported by an ideological definition of what constitutes a family. All in all, the multiplication of third-party interventions in cases suggest that actors are well-aware of the ECtHR's review powers and understand that judgments can have direct implications on domestic policy.

The chapter also suggests avenues for future research. First, the case of Strand Lobben highlights the growing quantity of third-party interventions filed by states and subsequently suggests a promising research agenda that digs deeper into the motivations and effects of this type of participation in ECtHR litigation. Second, preliminary analyses from our database, the ECHRdb, suggest that this growing trend in third-party interventions by 23 different types of organisations raises a host of empirical questions surrounding mobilisation patterns across areas of law. Finally, when we step back from this analysis of Norway and European processes of international litigation, it clearly lays the groundwork for examining this dynamic interaction between interest and advocacy organisations, states and international courts and tribunals in jurisdictions beyond Europe, be it at the regional level (for example, Intra

American Court of Human Rights or African Court of Human Rights) or the international level (for example, United Nations Treaty Bodies). Mobilised interests will always seek out new venues to influence policy outcomes, and we would be remiss not to look long and hard at the growing role of amicus curiae in judicial decision-making around the globe.

Notes

1. HUDOC can be accessed at http://hudoc.echr.coe.int/
2. Inadmissible and communicated cases are not included in this count.
3. Searches in the Factiva news search engine using the terms 'Eva Michaláková' and 'Barnevern*' show that media interest peaked in 2015 and 2016 respectively in Czech newspapers.
4. Under Article 36§1 of the Convention, the Court invites the contracting state of the nationality of the applicant of a case to submit observations. Between 1961 and 2022, following such invitations state governments have declined to intervene in 86.53 per cent of cases that involved their own nationals (803 out of 928 opportunities) (Cichowski and Chrun, 2024).
5. Written observations for M.L. v Norway.
6. A notable exception is Ordo Iuris who has a history of concerning themselves with the child protection actions of the Norwegian Barnevernet, including assisting Norwegian nationals, a mother and 8 month old baby, seek asylum in Poland: https://en.ordoiuris.pl/family-and-marriage/ordo-iuris-lawyers-applied-asylum-norwegian-citizen-and-her-8-month-old

References

A v the United Kingdom (no. 25599/94) [2002] ECtHR (17 December).
A and B v Norway [GC] (no. 24130/11) [2016] ECtHR (15 November).
Abdi Ibrahim v Norway [GC] (no. 15379/16) [2021] ECtHR (10 December).
Abdi Ibrahim v Norway (no. 15379/16) [2019] ECtHR (17 December).
ADF International (2024) 'Who we are', *ADF International*. Available from: https://adflegal.org/about-us
AIMMF (2019) 'Who we are', *Associazione Italiana dei Magistrati per i Minorenni e per la Famiglia*. Available from: https://www.minoriefamiglia.org/index.php/component/content/article/27-associazione/720-associazione-italiana-dei-magistrati-per-i-minorenni-e-per-la-famiglia-2?Itemid=101
A.L. and Others v Norway (no. 36130/11) [2022] ECtHR (20 January).
Alleleh and Others v Norway (no. 23394/16) [2022] ECtHR (23 June).
A.M. v Norway (no. 30254/18) [2022] ECtHR (24 March).
AP News (2015) 'Norwegian ambassador not welcomed at Czech presidential seat', *AP News*, 8 October. Available from: https://apnews.com/article/1b972427dbb0420b84c7b03c44d54528
A.S. v Norway (no. 60371/15) [2019] ECtHR (17 December).
Bayatyan v Armenia [GC] (no. 23459/03) [2011] ECtHR (7 July).
Big Brother Watch and Others v United Kingdom [GC] (no. 58170/13) [2018] ECtHR (13 September).

Bulgarian News Agency (2018) 'Press – review', *Bulgarian News Agency*, 6 June. Retrieved from Factiva database.

Cichowski, R.A. (2006) 'Courts, democracy and governance', *Comparative Political Studies*, 39(1): 3–21.

Cichowski, R.A. (2007) *The European Court and Civil Society*, Cambridge University Press.

Cichowski, R.A. (2016) 'The European Court of Human Rights, amicus curiae, and violence against women', *Law & Society Review*, 50(4): 890–919.

Cichowski, R. and Chrun, E. (2024) *European Court of Human Rights Database (ECHRdb), Version 2.0*. Available from: http://echrdb.org

Collins, P.M., Jr. (2018) 'The use of amicus briefs', *Annual Review of Law and Social Science*, 14: 219–237.

Collins, P.M., Jr. and McCarthy, L.A. (2017) 'Friends and interveners: Interest group litigation in a comparative context', *Journal of Law and Courts*, 5: 55–80.

Conant, L., Hofmann, A., Soennecken, D. and Vanhala, L. (2018) 'Mobilizing European law', *Journal of European Public Policy*, 25(9): 1376–1389.

Czarnecki, M. (2019) 'MSZ: polski konsul zostanie w Oslo. Polska odrzuca wezwanie Norwegii do jego odwołania [MFA: Polish consul to stay in Oslo. Poland rejects Norway's call for his recall]', *Gazeta Wyborcza*, 23 January. Available from: https://wyborcza.pl/7,75399,24390455,polski-konsul-zostanie-w-oslo-msz-odrzucil-wezwanie-norwegii.html

Dzehtsiarou, K. (2023) 'Conversations with friends: "Friends of the Court" interventions of the state parties to the European Convention on Human Rights', *Legal Studies*, 43(3): 381–401.

E.H. v Norway (no. 23024/16) [2021] ECtHR (25 November).

E.M. and Others v Norway (no. 53482/13) [2022] ECtHR (20 January).

European Parliament (2018) Ilhan Kyuchyuk (ALDE) Question to the Commission (E-003810/2018). Available from: https://www.europarl.europa.eu/doceo/document/P-8-2018-004624_EN.html

F.G. v Sweden [GC] (no. 43611/11) [2016] ECtHR (23 March).

F.Z. v Norway (no. 23700/16) [2021] ECtHR (1 July).

Hernehult v Norway (no. 14652/16) [2020] ECtHR (10 March).

H.F. and Others v France [GC] (no. 24384/19) [2022] ECtHR (14 September).

Jallow v Norway (no. 36516/19) [2021] ECtHR (2 December).

Kahraman, F. (2023) 'What makes an international institution work for labor activists? Shaping international law through strategic litigation', *Law & Society Review*, 57(1): 61–82.

K.E. and A.K. v Norway (no. 31045/16) [2021] ECtHR (1 July).

K.O. and V.M. v Norway (no. 64808/16) [2019] ECtHR (19 November).

Koukal, J. (2013) 'Czech mother fights for her life', *Právo*, 18 November. Retrieved from Factiva database.

Lautsi and Others v Italy (no. 30814/06) [2011] ECtHR (18 March).

Leinert, O. (2014) 'Why does the Czech mother keep her sons? writes Sobotka to the Finnish Prime Minister', *Mladá fronta DNES*, 10 December. Retrieved from Factiva database.

M.F. v Norway (no. 64875/16) [2021] ECtHR (25 November).

M.L. v Norway (no. 64639/16) [2020] ECtHR (22 December).

Mladá fronta DNES (2015) 'Norway is "denationalising" children like the Nazis, Zeman was surprised', *Mladá fronta DNES*, 9 February. Retrieved from Factiva database.

Orlandi and Others v Italy (no. 26431/12) [2017] ECtHR (14 December).

O.S. v Norway (no. 28570/17) [2021] ECtHR (30 September).

Pedersen and Others v Norway (no. 39710/15) [2020] ECtHR (10 March).

Pretty v United Kingdom (no. 2346/02) [2002] ECtHR (29 April).

R.O. v Norway (no. 40183/19) [2021] ECtHR (1 July).

Schönfelder, W. and Holmgaard, S. (2019) 'Representations of child welfare services in Norwegian, Danish and German newspapers', *Children and Youth Services Review*, 100: 89–97.

S.H. and Others v Austria [GC] (no. 57813/00) [2011] ECtHR (3 November).

Shapiro, M. (1981) *Courts: A Comparative and Political Analysis*, Chicago University Press.

Squatrito, T. (2018) 'Access to international courts: Democratising international law-making', *Global Governance*, 24(4): 595–613.

Stone Sweet, A. (2000) *Governing with Judges*, Oxford University Press.

Strand Lobben v Norway [GC] (no. 37283/13) [2019] ECtHR (10 September).

Svatoňová, E. (2021) '"Gender activists will kidnap your kids": The construction of feminist and LGBT+ rights activists as modern folk devils in Czech anti-gender campaigns', in M.D. Frederiksen and I. Harboe Knudsen (eds), *Modern Folk Devils: Contemporary Constructions of Evil*, Helsinki University Press, pp 135–155.

Tarakhel v Switzerland [GC] (no. 29217/12) [2014] ECtHR (4 November).

Tysiąc v Poland (no. 5410/03) [2007] ECtHR (20 March).

van der Vet, F. and L. McIntosh Sundstrom (2023) 'Activists in international courts: Backlash, funding, and strategy in international legal mobilization', *Law & Society Review*, 57(1): 6–11.

Vassenden, A. and Vedøy, G. (2019) 'Recurrence, eruptions, and a transnational turn: Three decades of strained relations between migrants to Norway and the child welfare services', *Child & Family Social Work*, 24(4): 582–591.

Whewell, T. (2016) 'Norway's Barnevernet: They took our four children ... then the baby', *BBC News*, 14 April. Available from: https://www.bbc.com/news/magazine-36026458

X v Poland (no. 20741/10) [2021] ECtHR (16 September).

PART III

The European Court of Human Rights and its jurisprudence

12

Children and rights to identity at the European Court of Human Rights

Jill Marshall

Introduction

This chapter explores how the European Court of Human Rights' (ECtHR) development of a right to personal identity has already, and could in future, be interpreted in relation to *children's* lives and their sense of *identity*. It reveals tensions between personal identity rights and child protection at the ECtHR. Helland, Gloppen and Skivenes state, in Chapter 1, that children have the same rights to protection of their fundamental rights and freedom as adults under Article 1 of the European Convention on Human Rights (ECHR), yet such explicit provisions are largely absent within its text (Chapter 1).[1] Do children enjoy the same rights to identity as adults? Tensions are evident in ECtHR jurisprudence interpreting children's rights from general non-child-specific provisions (Chapter 1). This comes to the fore in children's protection arguments justifying state interventions into family life, restricting parents' rights, with gendered implications particularly for women and *their* rights, to seemingly secure a child's interests and well-being.

The preamble to the Convention on the Rights of the Child (CRC) (1989) states:

> [T]he family, as the fundamental group of society and the natural environment for the growth and well-being of all its members and particularly children, should be afforded the necessary protection and assistance so that it can fully assume its responsibilities within the community,
> Recognizing that the child, for the full and harmonious development of his or her personality, should grow up in a family environment, in an atmosphere of happiness, love and understanding.

Yet, potential tensions are revealed, and are indicative of children's rights more generally, because, we are told, this child ought to be 'fully prepared to live an individual life in society [and be] brought up in the spirit of the ideals proclaimed in the Charter of the United Nations, and in particular in the spirit of peace, dignity, tolerance, freedom, equality and solidarity' (CRC, 1989, preamble). The creation of this sense of one's own identity, becoming this individual person in a democratic society, requires such a framing of childhood. Yet it is the very state and human rights institutions which may require the child to be removed from their biological parent(s) to enable such a life to exist, this identity to be formed and continued, to become an individual adult with a mind of one's own.

The chapter does not purport to set out a detailed analysis of children's or family rights at the ECtHR (see Kilkelly, 1999; 2010; Van Bueren, 2007; Choudhry and Herring, 2010; Council of Europe, European Agency for Fundamental Rights, 2015; Fenton-Glynn, 2020) or to examine the category of 'the child' at the ECtHR (see Trotter, 2018). Rather, it examines how European human rights law seeks to protect and permit constructions of identity formation *from birth* through creating coherent understandings consistent with cohesion, tolerance, broadmindedness and pluralism, words repeatedly used by the ECtHR jurisprudence as hallmarks of democratic societies (see Handyside v the United Kingdom, 1976; Dudgeon v the United Kingdom, 1981; Bédat v Switzerland, 2016; Macate v Lithuania, 2023). In my analysis, it matters how identity is constructed in human rights law as law frames and is part of the social structures framing permissible forms of agency and identity. As previously argued (see, for example, Marshall, 2009), some interpretations of identity present a fixed and restrictive version, others seem fluid and flexible, allowing us to become seemingly independent persons with, at least some form of, agency and ability to craft our own identity through a lived life. The latter is, in my view, more consistent with the underlying principles or 'very essence' of the ECHR 'respect for human dignity and human freedom' (Goodwin v UK, 2002; I v UK, 2002) and in line with global human rights' stated aims of securing individual human dignity and freedom (see, for example, the preamble to the International Covenant on Civil and Political Rights 1966), although, these can be in tension with the aims of the CRC and the rights and freedoms of others, including parents, as will be explored in this chapter.

In previous publications, I have explored the development of the right to autonomy and identity in human rights law and specifically at the ECtHR (see, in particular, Marshall, 2009; 2014; 2022). This chapter differs from this previous work by focusing on children's lives, their sense of identity, tensions between children's and adults' identity rights, and child protection's moral assumptions. The chapter is structured in four parts. First, it examines the concept of the human with a personal identity in human rights law, linking this to childhood development. Second, it provides a brief overview of the development of a legal right to personal identity at the ECtHR, drawing on a framework from my previous work on the development of this right. Third, it develops this framework to explore relevant ECtHR case law examples on children and markers of one's personal identity. Fourth, it highlights some pointers to future interpretations by the ECtHR in relation to children's lives and their sense of identity for this largely undeveloped aspect of children's rights.

The human of human rights who has a personal identity

Human rights law is often interpreted as protecting existing pre-legal pre-social inherent rights that we possess because we are born human. Consequently, these rights will be protected when we are left alone, including by the government or state. This version presents humans – normatively and empirically – as detached, self-centred and self-interested, containing a core of pre-social freedom with an innate capacity to enable and act on one's own free choices and life plans (see critiques by Jaggar, 1983; West, 1997; Glendon, 1999; Marshall, 2005). Such a view of the human has its normative attractions, when seemingly independent, powerful and strong, but is unattractive if uncaring and selfish. It is an empirically flawed account, not least because it must assume humans come into the world already existing as fully formed adults with an independent personality or identity in a vacuum of one's own self-assuredness (Lacey, 1998). It fails to account for the intersubjective way we become those seemingly independent persons. Human rights law is more expansive, potentially transformative and meaningful when based on a version of the human who is universally real, particular, unique and situated, formed in a communal, intersubjective world (Honneth, 1992; Benhabib, 2002). Together with abstract notions of peace, harmony, equality and universal solidarity, the international framework of human rights law emphasises the human family, community, religion and culture, networks of relationships without which there would be no person capable of making any informed choices (for example, the Universal Declaration of Human Rights [UN General Assembly, 1948]). It is a scientific fact that no one can be born or survive beyond birth without at least some care from, attachment to, and relationships with, at least one other. This is a version of the human as a social animal or person, who needs to be *enabled* to develop and express their personal sense of self, their freedom, personality, persona and personal identity in and to the world. This 'enabling' happens in and through our social conditions; within groups, spaces, places, geographical settings, structures and institutions, nation-states, class systems, ethnicities, races, genders, cultural traditions and religions in our families, communities and affiliations. These may or may not be chosen by one's family, but they cannot be chosen by a newborn baby, toddler or small child. Babies need care, safety and resources provided to them to be able to survive, live and, ideally, flourish. Such care is required to instil a sense of empathy and respect (Slote, 2004), being linked to the development of our capabilities and a sense of self: basic needs must be met with support and recognition. As Herring observes, care – in feeding, bathing and so on – is crucial to survival, emotional well-being and psychological identity (Herring, 2013, p 2). We need others to provide these acts at birth, and at times of dependency, including growing up. It is this sense of the formation of love and trust with others that creates and forms identity through childhood and beyond.

In his recognition theory, Honneth argues that if infants have a good start in their first relationships with others, 'they gradually acquire a fundamental faith in their environment and a sense of trust in their own bodies as reliable sources of signals as to their own needs' (Honneth, 1992, p xii; see further Marshall, 2014, pp 226–230). This view of *building self-confidence* concerns the underlying capacity to express needs and desires without fear of being abandoned. The presence or absence of parental love affects a child's self-esteem and self-love as well as on the capacity to form loving attachments to other persons in adulthood (Blustein, 1991). The child acquires their sense of value as individuals as they respond to their parents, and other carers, with love and trust, because they connect with their sense of their own worth with a need to perceive of themselves as uniquely precious and irreplaceable (Blustein, 1991, pp 180, 194–198; Raz, 2001). This provides children with a solid psychological foundation on which to build intimate relations of love and trust with persons outside the family. This shared history, what we have done for each other and what we have done together, informs relationships, with intimacy and love being personalised, and *self-esteem*, *self-confidence* and *belonging* in identity formed (Honneth, 1992). These theories point to love and care being the foundation of identity with other relational factors shaping it. This has clear implications for how children develop a sense of their own identity and how the state interprets protecting a child through its intervention.

A right to personal identity at the European Court of Human Rights

This section explains the development of a right to personal identity at the ECtHR, summarising aspects of my existing work that are relevant to the framing and development of a child's identity and protection in this chapter. The right is not explicitly mentioned in the ECHR but arises from the ECtHR's interpretation of provisions in the ECHR's text to provide rights to autonomy, identity and integrity. These arise from a range of case law, largely through Article 8's right to respect for one's private life, and to a certain extent from the right to freedom of religion and its expression in Article 9, the right to freedom of expression in Article 10, the right to be free from discrimination in Article 14, and the right to education in Article 2 of Protocol 1. These rights are qualified rights: they provide protection as set out in the first subparagraph to each article but are subject to restrictions set out in the second subparagraph. Although the wording differs, the ECtHR balances applicants' rights in a societal context, asking if any restrictions serve 'a legitimate aim' and are 'necessary in a democratic society'. All these qualified rights are said by the ECtHR to constitute essential foundations of a democratic society and basic conditions for its progress and self-fulfilment of each individual. Article 10, for example, applies not only to information or ideas favourably received or regarded as inoffensive, or as a matter of indifference, but also to those which offend, shock or disturb. The ECtHR continually states, 'such are the demands of pluralism, tolerance, and broadmindedness without which there is no democratic society' (see Dudgeon v the United Kingdom, 1981; Bédat v Switzerland, 2016; Macate v Lithuania, 2023).

Article 8's respect for private life, and to an extent Article 3's absolute right to be free from torture, inhuman and degrading treatment or punishment as interpreted into a right to bodily integrity, protects against unwanted intrusions into people's lives, protecting our ability to have our own personal inner space of our mind and our bounded body in and through which our identity forms and develops. Although Article 3 jurisprudence does not refer to identity rights on a standalone basis, the right to bodily integrity is interconnected to a right to psychological identity mentioned in developing ECtHR case law on Article 8 so the two provisions work together to form a right to integrity – described by the ECtHR as bodily and psychological (see X v Iceland, 1974; Bruggemann and Scheuten v Germany, 1976; X and Y v Belgium, 1982; Niemietz v Germany, 1992; Burghartz v Switzerland, 1994; Friedl v Austria, 1995; Goodwin v UK, 2002; I v UK, 2002; Pretty v UK, 2002; Von Hannover v Germany, 2004).[2] Further, a communal, intersubjective understanding of private life, and subsequently personality development or identity, is evident from the ECtHR's case law since the 1970s, with Article 8 interpreted to protect the personal sphere of each individual including their right to establish details of their identity as individual human beings and in relationships with other people, other things and the outside world.[3] This version of the human, with identity forming because of, and in relation to, other people, links to economic, social and cultural rights. The ECtHR has developed aspects of such rights through its interpretation of Articles 8 to 10 and Article 2 of Protocol 1. There is developed case law concerning: national bans on homosexuality (Dudgeon v the UK, 1981); gender identity (Goodwin v the UK, 2002, para 90); access to information on origins (Odièvre v France, 2004);[4] and identity expressed through dress or clothing (Şahin v Turkey, 2005). I have argued elsewhere that some case law points to a self-determined fluid identity (Marshall, 2008a; 2008b; 2009). In sexual orientation and gender identity case law, for example, interpretation began with a sense of personal ownership of control over identity in Judge Martens' dissenting opinion in Cossey v the UK that persons should be free to shape themselves and their fate in ways that person deems best fits his or her personality/identity. This is later confirmed and restated in Goodwin and I v the UK, the Court finding an Article 8 violation for lack of legal recognition of the applicants' gender identity. This interpretation points to a self-created, fluid version of identity, permitting future new versions of ourselves as we deem fit for our free expression of identities. Other case law on knowledge of origins, which are usually equated to children's identity rights, appears to equate identity to a pre-determined self or internal essence waiting to be discovered as will be explored in my next section. Other case law on Islamic and religious dress, for example, is not generally sympathetic to women who wear the headscarf. Elsewhere I have argued that criminally banning clothing in the name of the rights and freedoms of others because the majority find it difficult to communicate with someone veiled fails to recognise a member of a minority as a person worthy to be listened to, with an identity to be valued, and fundamental rights to be protected (Marshall, 2015). This is counterproductive and inconsistent with other case law on tolerance, which indicates the fundamental quality of the value of any choices being made by, belonging to, constitutive of that particular person and having those legally recognised. I return to these points in the final part of my chapter. For now, I explore aspects of case law from the ECtHR on how this identity is formed in babies, children and young persons, with the development of personal inner space to contemplate and make one's own decisions, in a body that functions and reacts in the social environment in which they, by chance, happen to exist. This is a formation of identity, of preparing for 'an individual life in society' to be created in an atmosphere of 'peace, dignity, tolerance, freedom, equality and solidarity' (CRC, 1989, preamble). How, if at all, has the ECtHR engaged such notions in relation to children and their identity rights?

European Court of Human Rights case law on children and personal identity

As the ECtHR explains, the starting point in cases involving children is the broad consensus in national laws and in broader international law, that their best interests are a primary consideration (Neulinger and Shuruk v Switzerland, 2010; X v Latvia, 2013; Paradiso and Campanelli v Italy, 2017; Vavřička and Others v the Czech Republic, 2021; Macate v Lithuania, 2023, para 204). These are largely cases heard under the 'family' life right rather than 'identity' arising from 'private life'. How the ECtHR understands 'family unit', 'family life', and what circumstances can allow for the justifiable interference of that right under Article 8 have been analysed by other scholars, and that is not the purpose of this chapter (see Breen et al, 2020). What follows analyses selected ECtHR case law on a construction of identity as the development of personality during childhood years.[5]

Identity is listed as one factor in international human rights law, including the ECtHR and the UN Committee on the Rights of the Child, when considering a child's best interests, but what does a child's identity mean in this context? In much literature, it equates to accessing information concerning knowledge of the identity of one's biological parents, with special emphasis on one's mother or birth giver (for the distinction, see O'Donovan and Marshall, 2006). This definition of identity has largely arisen from the CRC provisions in Article's 7 on name, nationality, official recognition and 'whenever possible' that 'children should know their parents and be looked after by them'. CRC's Article 8 states that children have the right to their own identity set out as an official record of who they are, which includes their name, nationality and family relations, and which should not be taken from them, or, if this happens, governments must help children to quickly get their identity back (see O'Donovan, 2002). Identity rights sometimes appear to be narrowly interpreted equating to genes or biology. However, I have argued that a more expansive, wider, interpretation will enable freedom and dignity of the person to develop, which is in keeping with the underlying principles of human rights law, including that set out in the preamble to the CRC (1989), and to the development of a sense of becoming one's own unique person. This is a view of the human formed holistically in our biological and psychological body through care, dependence and living in the already existing world on our arrival into it, and in our becoming our own person in and through this world. This is in line with the stated aim of the CRC, and in tune with the ECHR's purpose: that children ought to have a childhood that fully prepares them to live a fully individual life in society, and human rights law needs to protect children to enable them to do so including providing for situations where such a life may not be possible within one's biological family. A child's right to identity therefore, in my view, covers more than pre-birth origins. Given that origins, genes or biology are often equated to children's identity rights, it is to those that I turn first.

Knowledge of origins

In a line of cases involving grown-up children, identity is presented in terms of knowledge of one's parentage, particularly one's mother, as equated to identity. In Odièvre v France (2004), the French government was successful, and no violation of Article 8 was found in a case brought by the applicant, a daughter born of secret or anonymous birth – a system in France permitting this legally. It was a divided court, and the decision rested on a balance of mothers' rights to confidentiality and the applicant's rights to identity, expressed as knowledge of their mother's identity, and a distinction between a right to life/safety and a right to identity for a child – the argument being the child may not have been born if this policy did not exist. The French mechanism was recently reconsidered by the ECtHR and found suitable as it ensured a fair and reasonable balance between the rights and interests at stake (Cherrier v France, 2024). In Jäggi v Switzerland (2008) a majority of five to two found violations of Article 8. For the Jäggi court, the right to 'uncover the truth about an important aspect of their personal identity' (establishing the identity of ascendants) needed to be balanced with protecting third persons from being compelled to make themselves available for medical DNA testing. The ECtHR noted that the third party – the putative biological father of the elderly applicant born in 1939 – was dead and the court equated this to him having no right to private life under Article 8. Further, it was impossible for the applicant to obtain DNA analysis of the remains in the system in question. In Godelli v Italy (2012), the majority of six to one decided that the Italian law, permitting a mother the right not to be named on the birth certificate when she expressed this wish to the hospital at birth, violated Article 8 because the now 69-year-old adult applicant could not discover knowledge of her mother. The applicant's birth certificate recorded the date and time of birth to 'a woman, who did not consent to being named'. The ECtHR noted that even though the applicant had

> been able to develop her personality even in the absence of certainty as to the identity of her birth mother, it must be acknowledged that an individual's interest in discovering his or her parentage does not disappear with age, quite the reverse. Moreover, the applicant has shown a genuine interest in ascertaining her mother's identity, since she has tried to obtain conclusive information on the subject. Such conduct implies mental and psychological suffering, even if this has not been medically attested. (Godelli v Italy, 2012)[6]

It was a lack of access to non-identifying information concerning the child's origins or the disclosure of the mother's identity in Italian law which led the ECtHR to decide that the Italian authorities failed to strike a proportionate balance between the interests at stake. Related but different issues arise in relation to the retention of birth family ties, birth registration and access to related identity documents.

Birth family ties and cultural identity

A line of cases touch upon children's identity rights when children are involuntarily removed from biological parents by the state, taken into state care, fostering and/or adoption. Although these are 'family life' cases, they concern a child's identity through a focus on biology and parental cultural and religious identity and it is Norwegian examples that are prominent in the ECtHR's jurisprudence. The paramount case here is Strand Lobben v Norway (2019), which focuses on the need to keep the family preserved in relation to adoption. The ECtHR, confirming previous case law, stated that protecting biological family ties was fundamental, except when a family has proved particularly unfit. In this instance, the Court decided that the domestic authorities had not attempted to perform a genuine balancing exercise between the interests of the child and those of his biological family as required by European human right law. Instead, it decided that the decision-making process that had led to the authorisation of adoption had not been conducted to ensure that all the views and interests of the applicants had been fully considered. The process did not have the safeguards required for such a grave interference and the seriousness of the interests at stake, and therefore breached Article 8.

Abdi Ibrahim v Norway (2021) develops this with a focus on the interests of the parents to allow the child to retain ties to their cultural and religious origins. Abdi Ibrahim references the CRC's Article 20 – a provision consistent with CRC's preamble (1989) regarding staying with one's biological family, and its Article 7 right, as far as possible, to know and be looked after by one's biological parents. Article 20 states that 'due regard shall be paid to the desirability of continuity in a child's upbringing and to the child's ethnic, religious, cultural and linguistic background'. In Abdi Ibrahim, the Somali Muslim applicant was successful because she raised this issue early. The foster parents were described as 'active Christians who wished to baptise the foster child and to change his name', and this involved permanent adoption. The ECtHR states that when public care is imposed, restricting family life, a positive duty lies on the authorities to take measures to facilitate family reunification as soon as reasonably feasible, guided by the principle that a care order should be regarded as a temporary measure, and the best interests of the child generally mean that the child's ties with its biological family be maintained, but not always. In Kilic v Austria (2023, para 150), where no violation was found, the ECtHR accepted that the Austrian authorities had made efforts to place the children with families corresponding to the applicants' cultural, linguistic and religious background, even though the birth family raised this late in the process, but that no such family had been available. In Kilic, the ECtHR noted the broad consensus, including in international law, that in all such decisions, paramount importance is given to the best interests of the child (para 120). The child's best interests must come before all other considerations. Evidence produced appeared to demonstrate that the children were often afraid of their parents with the consequence that it was in the children's best interests to be placed elsewhere.

As well as trying to find culturally similar families, Austrian law and foster care practice included information on the importance of 'biography work', of the biological family's origins, and a child's search for his or her identity.

In my view, these cases are consistent with the ECtHR's development of the right to personal identity and children's identity rights and children's protection under international law. They are based on the child's best interests to ensure their development in a 'sound environment, and a parent cannot be entitled under Article 8 to have such measures taken as would harm the child's health and development' (Strand Lobben, 2019, paras 207–208; Kilic v Austria, 2023, paras 207–208). While origins, background and cultural heritage are important to identity, what is in the child's best interests will not always include the maintenance of biological ties, including the cultural, religious and linguistic heritage of one's biological parents. Any decisions will be based on the facts of each case.

Identity documents

In G.T.B. v Spain (2023), the ECtHR found a violation of Article 8 through delays in birth registration and related documents. It interpreted Article 8's right to respect for private life to include a right to birth registration with 'obstacles in obtaining birth registration and lack of access to identity documents resulting from those obstacles' having 'a serious impact on a person's sense of identity as an individual human being' with the effect of 'not being able to establish details of a person's identity' (G.T.B. v Spain, 2023, para 118). The ECtHR considered that 'the right to respect for private life … should be seen as including, in principle, an individual's right to have one's birth registered and as a consequence, where relevant, to have access to other identity documents' (G.T.B. v Spain, 2023, para 118). The ECtHR stated that requirements for registration and access to identity documents were a matter for domestic law with their margin of appreciation. However, providing the requirements were met, the state was obliged to issue birth certificates and to enable access to associated identity documents (G.T.B. v Spain, 2023, note 24, para 119). This case concerned a minor with psychological disorders since the age of 11. The child's parent, his mother, was described as 'failing to act diligently' in securing registration of his birth. Not having the documents impacted his ability to pursue academic studies, made him unable to secure stable job contracts, affected his ability to organise his private and family life and contributed to his feelings of anxiety and distress (G.T.B. v Spain, 2023, para 123). As such 'it was incumbent on the authorities to act in the best interests of the child whose birth registration was being sought in order to compensate for the mother's failings and to prevent the child from being left unregistered and hence, without identity documents'. There was a positive obligation on the authorities to act with due diligence to assist the applicant to obtain his documents to ensure effective respect for his private life (G.T.B. v Spain, 2023).[7]

Children's access to information and education

There are many cases on children's right to education, and it is not my intention to cover this in my chapter. I will only focus on one recent case concerning children and education that relate to the formation of certain types of individuals in society. This relates to sex education.

Macate v Lithuania (2023) concerns a Lithuanian ban on a children's book of fairytales with same-sex relationships as part of the content. The ECtHR found a violation of Article 10 and set out general principles regarding the legitimacy of the aim pursued by state restrictions on literature about same-sex relationships aimed directly at children and written in a style and language easily accessible to them. The ECtHR made clear that *equal and mutual respect for persons of different sexual orientations is inherent in the whole fabric of the ECHR*. It follows that insulting, degrading or belittling persons on account of their sexual orientation or promoting one type of family at the expense of another is never acceptable under the ECHR. Contrary to Lithuanian government arguments, the ECtHR found that the book sought to foster acceptance of different family types, encouraging tolerance and acceptance of various marginalised social groups. It contained characters of diverse ethnicities, with different levels of physical and mental ability, and living in various social and material circumstances, who were all depicted as caring and deserving of love (Macate v Lithuania, 2023, paras 13, 15, 19 and 26).

The ECtHR began with the best interests of the child. It then proceeded to consider that children are more impressionable and more easily influenced than older people (Dahlab v Switzerland, 2001). Education is explained as being fundamental, and needs to be objective, critical and contain pluralistic content appropriate to age (Kjeldsen, Busk Madsen and Pedersen v Denmark, 1976; Jiménez Alonso and Jiménez Merino v Spain, 2000; Folgerø and Others v Norway, 2007; Dojan and Others v Germany 2011; A.R. and L.R. v Switzerland, 2017). Limitations are permitted if the content is encouraging harmful or criminal behaviour (Handyside, 1976, paras 52–58), including hate speech (Vejdeland and Others v Sweden, 2012, para 54). Differences based on sex and sexual orientation require 'particularly convincing and weighty reasons' as justification: differences based solely on considerations of sexual orientation are unacceptable under the ECHR (Salgueiro da Silva Mouta v Portugal, 1999; E.B. v France, 2008; Vallianatos and Others v Greece, 2013; Bayev and Others v Russia, 2017). There was no scientific evidence or sociological data suggesting that the mere mention of homosexuality, or open public debate about sexual minorities' social status, would adversely affect children (Alekseyev v Russia, 2010, para

210). Instead, it was conducive to social cohesion for minors to be exposed to ideas of diversity, equality and tolerance. Restricting children's access to information about same-sex relationships solely on the basis of sexual orientation has wider social implications, demonstrating that the authorities have a preference for some types of relationships and families over others, continuing stigmatisation. Such restrictions are stated by the ECtHR to be incompatible with the notions of equality, pluralism and tolerance inherent in a democratic society. This case illustrates how it is essential for children to learn about these notions which bring about social cohesion, respect for others, equality and pluralism, aspects in my view that are core to becoming an independent person, developing one's own identity within society.

Girls, young women and Islamic headscarves

One obvious way of presenting or expressing identity is through clothing, especially for young people. In Europe this legally impacts mostly minorities who more often outwardly express their religious and cultural backgrounds and beliefs. The ECtHR's case law on Islamic headscarf illustrates this.

When it comes to young women still in full-time education at university, as in Şahin v Turkey (2005), or in school, as in the recent case of Mikyas and Others v Belgium (2024), this is particularly poignant. In both cases, the headscarf-wearing applicants were unsuccessful and bans were said to comply with the ECHR (on Şahin, see Marshall, 2008b). In Mikyas, the applicant pupils were prohibited from wearing the Islamic headscarves by state schools' regulations because of a ban on wearing visible symbols of belief in the official education system of the Flemish community in Belgium. Their claim for violation of Article 9 was declared inadmissible as manifestly ill-founded. The ECtHR stated that the relevant regulations were provided by law. As to whether they served a legitimate aim, the Court said it had already found that measures prohibiting pupils or students from wearing the headscarf in a school or university environment could pursue the legitimate aims of protecting rights and freedoms of others and public order and could therefore accept that the interference pursued these same aims and that, in a democratic society, the Court could limit or even prohibit the wearing of religious symbols by pupils or students in the school or university environment, without violating the right to freedom of religious expression. The official education system here had to be constitutionally neutral. Belgium had a margin of appreciation, and the ECtHR considered that the concept of neutrality, understood as prohibiting pupils wearing visible symbols of belief, did not in itself run counter to Article 9 of the Convention and its underlying values. Even if a different interpretation of neutrality could have been implemented by the authorities, it did not imply that the option selected and accepted by the Belgian courts was contrary to

Article 9. The ECtHR noted that the ban was not confined to the Islamic veil but applied to all visible symbols of one's beliefs and the applicants had freely chosen to attend schools and could not have been unaware that the governing bodies required neutrality. The applicants had agreed to abide by the rules in advance. In terms of the ban's intention to protect pupils from any form of social pressure and proselytisation, the ECtHR stated that underage pupils were more vulnerable than teachers and prohibitions on pupils wearing religious symbols could correspond to concerns to prevent exclusion or pressure, while respecting pluralism and the freedom of others. The court had emphasised on several occasions that pluralism and democracy were to be based on dialogue and a spirit of compromise, necessarily entailing compromises justified to maintain and promote the ideals and values of a democratic society. The restriction could therefore be regarded as proportionate to the aims pursued, that is, the protection of the rights and freedoms of others and of public order, and thus necessary in a democratic society.

Social conditions for children's identity: living together in equality and broadmindedness

The phrase 'living together' used in recent Islamic headscarves jurisprudence at the ECtHR, arising from Islamic (and other) dress which covers the face (S.A.S. v France, 2014; Belcacemi and Oussar v Belgium, 2017; Dakir v Belgium, 2017) and calls for compromises to assist social cohesion in the ECtHR jurisprudence, are in keeping with tolerance, broadmindedness and pluralism in the long line of ECtHR's jurisprudence. However, it depends what interpretation is given to these phrases currently and in future. Using these terms to impose a majority, popular or fashionable view, at least represented as such by the governments involved, is not, in my view, conducive to supporting harmonious societies. 'Living together' can consistently be interpreted to mean accepting each person's individuality and the uniqueness of each person, giving each person dignity and enabling each to be free to live together on equal terms: pluralism, tolerance and broadmindedness. This is empowering and emancipating because it permits and encourages self-development, social inclusion, belonging, through living together, respecting cultural and other types of diversity. Living together with mutual respect, never mind with cohesion and harmony, will not occur if 'people are forced to live together in resentment' (Adenitire, 2015). How does and may this translate to children's lives? Living together with each of us being able to develop our own personal identities from birth requires a social environment, including structural institutions and legal systems, that fosters an atmosphere of tolerance, pluralism, broadmindedness, allowing the development of one's unique sense of self, personality, building and retaining an ability and capacity that is each person's domain to enable them to think reflectively to develop critical thinking and to be enabled to live a life equally with others (see further Marshall, 2008b; 2009). This provides the conditions which give meaning to children's lives as they become their own person, forged in an atmosphere of belonging and care for them to successfully become competent, during their formative years, and capable of making meaningful informed choices as young adults and beyond. It is from this position that children, young people and adults decide what value to attach to goods that may bring meaning to one's life.

There are many implications for future changes impacting on children's development and becoming full persons. For example, newly emerging and manipulative technologies, their effect on mental stability and psychological continuity (Ligthart, 2024), their abuse and use by and on young people, have problematic implications for freedom of one's own inner space to think for oneself and to develop into a freethinking adult, their freedom of expression, safety and privacy. Donor conception, surrogacy and other reproductive medical developments arguably affect one's sense of identity if knowledge of origins, genes and biology continue to be prominent in meanings of identity. The very threat to future generations coming into existence because of climate change needs further examination in terms of children's identity (Duarte Agostinho and Others v Portugal and 32 Others, 2024).[8] Pollution and socio-economic circumstances, race, religion, culture and ethnicity, gender identity, including any requirements for medical treatments to satisfy legal gender recognition and conflicts between competent young people and their parents in that regard (Haas v Switzerland, 2011; P and S v Poland, 2012; A.P., Garçon and Nicot v France, 2017; Semenya v Switzerland, 2023),[9] will likely be subject to future rulings with implications for children's identities.

Conclusion

Love, care, a safe environment, education, access to information, participation, inclusion and recognition are all important in the context of developing a sense of autonomy, agency, and therefore one's own sense of identity: crucially important in formative childhood years. Young people who live in free, democratic, multicultural societies should be afforded increasing autonomy and respect in how they ultimately choose to express and define themselves. At the same time, it is important to actively foster improved social conditions through human rights law and other means to protect, without suffocating, the encouragement of individuality and empowerment of young people. This supportive architecture of care will develop critical minds in places and spaces of equality and belonging. This interpretation of identity formation and its protection acknowledges children's impressionability and vulnerability, that they are still forming their own sense of identity, and guards against brainwashing. Childhood is the time for this development – physically, psychologically, emotionally – of personality, for attachments and relationships to be forged, for the importance of the state ensuring the provision of accurate factual education and knowledge as a form of protecting children. It is therefore crucial that the ECtHR continues to develop any construction of children's identity rights to reflect the development of personality in a liberating way with understandings of social cohesion fair to all. How the ECtHR develop their jurisprudence regarding children and identity rights will be an important issue deserving further research in the years to come.

Acknowledgements

I would like to thank the University of Bergen, in particular Professor Marit Skivenes, for their generosity and hospitality in hosting me as Visiting Fellow at their Centre for Research on Discretion and Paternalism during 2024–2025. This provided the space to carry out my research including writing this chapter. Thanks also to the editors and reviewers of this volume for their helpful comments.

Notes

1. Highlighting that children (minors or juveniles) are specifically mentioned in the main body of the ECHR's Articles 5 and 6.
2. See, for example, M.C. v Bulgaria ECtHR 4 March 2003, in which the ECtHR found violations of Articles 3 and 8 for failures in relation to the rape of a 14-year-old girl. Further details on matters relating to children's safety from harm, including gender-based violence, are beyond the scope of this chapter.
3. See, for example, X v Iceland Application no. 6825/74, Decisions and Reports of the European Commission Vol 5 p 86, Bruggemann and Scheuten v Germany Yearbook XIX [1976] at p 382; (1981) EHRR 244, X and Y v Belgium, D&R 28 (1982) p 112 (124), Niemietz v Germany (1992) 16 EHRR 244; Burghartz v Switzerland [1994] Application no. 16213/90; Friedl v Austria 31 Jan 1995 Series A no 305 B Commission; Goodwin v UK (2002) 35 EHRR 18; I v UK Judgment 11 July 2002; Pretty v UK (2002) 35 EHRR 1, Von Hannover v Germany ECtHR 24 June 2004.
4. Odièvre v France (2004) 38 EHRR 43.
5. Cases have been selected with themed case law based on my previous listed publications and more recent ECtHR registry guides summaries on children's rights, LGBTQIA+ rights, together with searches of the HUDOC database on Article 8 and identity.
6. Godelli at para 56 citing Jäggi note 16 at para 40.
7. G.T.B. v Spain (2023, para 124). This obligation had arisen on the authorities in 2002 which was a delay of four years.
8. Compare Duarte Agostinho and Others v Portugal and 32 Others ECtHR 9 April 2024.
9. Compare A.P., Garçon and Nicot v France ECtHR 6 April 2017, Semenya v Switzerland ECtHR 11 July 2023, Haas v Switzerland ECtHR 20 January 2011, P and S v Poland ECtHR 30 October 2012.

References

Abdi Ibrahim v Norway [GC] (no. 15379/16) [2021] ECtHR (10 December).
Adenitire, J. (2015) 'Has the ECHR recognised a legal right to glance at a smile?', *Law Quarterly Review*, 131: 43–48.

Alekseyev v Russia (no. 4916/07) [2010] ECtHR (21 October).
A.P., Garçon and Nicot v France (nos. 79885/12, 52471/13 and 52596/13) [2017] ECtHR (6 April).
A.R. and L.R. v Switzerland (no. 22338/15) [2017] ECtHR (19 December).
Bayev and Others v Russia (nos. 67667/09, 44092/12 and 56717/12) [2017] ECtHR (20 June).
Bédat v Switzerland (no.56925/08) [2016] ECtHR (29 March).
Belcacemi and Oussar v Belgium (no. 37798/13) [2017] ECtHR (11 December).
Benhabib, S. (2002) 'Sexual difference and collective identities: The new global constellation', in S. James and S. Palmer (eds), *Visible Women: Essays on Feminist Legal Theory and Political Philosophy*, Hart Publishing, pp 335–361.
Blustein, J. (1991) *Care and Commitment: Taking the Personal Point of View*, Oxford University Press.
Breen, C., Krutzinna, J., Luhamaa, K., and Skivenes, M. (2020) 'Family life for children in state care. An analysis of the European Court of Human Rights' reasoning on adoption without consent', *International Journal of Children's Rights*, 28(4): 715–747.
Bruggemann and Scheuten v Germany (no. 6989/75) [1976] ECtHR (7 December).
Burghartz v Switzerland (no. 16213/90) [1994] ECtHR (22 February).
Cherrier v France (no. 18843/20) [2024] ECtHR (24 June).
Choudhry, S. and Herring, J. (2010) *European Human Rights and Family Law*, Hart.
Council of Europe, European Agency for Fundamental Rights (2015) *Handbook on European Law Relating to Children's Rights*.
CRC (United Nations Convention on the Rights of the Child) (1989) Treaty Series, vol 1577: 3.
Dahlab v Switzerland (no. 42393/98) [2001] ECtHR (15 February).
Dakir v Belgium (no. 4619/12) [2017] ECtHR (11 July).
Dojan and Others v Germany (no. 31966/07) [2011] ECtHR (13 September).
Duarte Agostinho and Others v Portugal and 32 Others (GC) (no. 39371/20) [2024] ECtHR (9 April).
Dudgeon v the United Kingdom (no. 7525/76) [1981] ECtHR (22 October).
E.B. v France [GC] (no. 43546/02) [2008] ECtHR (22 January).
Fenton-Glynn, C. (2020) *Children and the European Court of Human Rights*, Oxford University Press.
Folgerø and Others v Norway (no. 15472/02) [2007] ECtHR (28 June).
Friedl v Austria (no. 15233/89) [1995] ECtHR (31 January).
Glendon, M.A. (1999) *Rights Talk: The Impoverishment of Political Discourse*, The Free Press.
Godelli v Italy (no. 33783/09) [2012] ECtHR (25 September).

Goodwin v the United Kingdom (no 28957/95) [2002] ECtHR (11 July).
G.T.B. v Spain (no. 3041/19) [2023] ECtHR (16 February).
Haas v Switzerland (no. 31322/07) [2011] ECtHR (20 January).
Handyside v the United Kingdom (no. 5493/72) [1976] ECtHR (7 December).
Herring, J. (2013) *Caring and the Law*, Hart Publishing.
Honneth, A. (1992) *The Struggle for Recognition: The Moral of Grammar of Social Conflicts*, Polity Press.
I v the United Kingdom (no. 25680/94) [2002] ECtHR (11 July).
Jaggar, A. (1983) *Feminist Politics and Human Nature*, Rowman and Allanheld.
Jäggi v Switzerland (no 58757/00) [2008] ECtHR (13 July).
Jiménez Alonso and Jiménez Merino v Spain (no. 27279/97) [2000] ECtHR (25 May).
Kilic v Austria (no. 27700/15) [2023] ECtHR (12 April).
Kilkelly, U. (1999) *The Child and the European Convention on Human Rights*, Oxford University Press.
Kilkelly, U. (2010) 'Protecting children's rights under the ECHR: The role of positive obligations', *NILQ*, 61(3): 245–246.
Kjeldsen, Busk Madsen and Pedersen v Denmark (no. 5095/71) [1976] ECtHR (7 December).
Lacey, N. (1998) *Unspeakable Subjects: Feminist Essays in Legal and Social Theory*, Hart Publishing.
Ligthart, S. (2024) 'Towards a human right to psychological continuity? Reflections on the rights to personal identity, self-determination, and personal integrity', *European Convention on Human Rights Law Review*, 5(2): 199–229.
Macate v Lithuania (GC) (no. 61435/19) [2023] ECtHR (23 January).
Marshall, J. (2005) *Humanity, Freedom and Feminism*, Ashgate.
Marshall, J. (2008a) 'Giving birth but refusing motherhood: Inauthentic choice or self-determining identity?', *International Journal of Law in Context*, 4(2): 169–185.
Marshall, J. (2008b) 'Conditions for freedom? European Human Rights Law and the Islamic headscarf debate', *Human Rights Quarterly*, 30(3): 631–679.
Marshall, J. (2009) *Personal Freedom Through Human Rights Law? Autonomy, Identity and Integrity under the European Convention on Human Rights*, Martinus Nijhoff.
Marshall, J. (2014) *Human Rights Law and Personal Identity*, Routledge.
Marshall, J. (2015) '*S.A.S. v France*: Burqa bans and the control or empowerment of identities', *Human Rights Law Review*, 15(2): 377–389.
Marshall, J. (ed) (2022) *Personal Identity and the European Court of Human Rights*, Routledge.
M.C. v Bulgaria (no. 39272/98) [2003] ECtHR (4 December).
Mikyas and Others v Belgium (no. 50681/20) [2024] ECtHR (9 April).

Neulinger and Shuruk v Switzerland (no. 41615/07) [2010] ECtHR (6 July).
Niemietz v Germany (no. 13710/88) [1992] ECtHR (16 December).
Odièvre v France (no. 42326/98) [2004] ECtHR (13 February).
O'Donovan, K. (2002) '"Real" mothers for abandoned children', *Law and Society Review*, 36(2): 347–378.
O'Donovan, K. and Marshall, J. (2006) 'Afterbirth: Decisions about becoming a mother', in K. O'Donovan and A. Diduck (eds), *Feminist Perspectives on Family Law*, Cavendish, pp 101–122.
P and S v Poland (no. 57375/08) [2012] ECtHR (30 October).
Paradiso and Campanelli v Italy (no. 25358/12) [2017] ECtHR (24 January).
Pretty v the United Kingdom (no. 2346/02) [2002] ECtHR (29 April).
Raz, J. (2001) *Value, Respect and Attachment*, Cambridge University Press.
Şahin v Turkey (no. 44774/98) [2005] ECtHR (10 November).
Salgueiro da Silva Mouta v Portugal (no. 33290/96) [1999] ECtHR (9 December).
S.A.S. v France (GC) (no. 43835/11) [2014] ECtHR (1 July).
Semenya v Switzerland, 2023 (no. 10934/21) [2023] ECtHR (11 July).
Slote, M. (2004) 'Moral sentimentalism', *Ethical Theory and Moral Practice*, 7(1): 3–14.
Strand Lobben and Others v Norway [GC] (no. 37283/13) [2019] ECtHR (10 September).
Trotter, S. (2018) 'The child in European human rights law', *Modern Law Review*, 81(3): 452–479.
UN General Assembly (1948) *Universal Declaration of Human Rights*, 217 A (III), 10 December 1948. Available from: https://www.refworld.org/legal/resolution/unga/1948/en/11563
Vallianatos and Others v Greece (GC) (nos. 29381/09 and 32684/09) [2013] ECtHR (7 November).
Van Bueren, G. (2007) *Child Rights in Europe: Convergence and Divergence in Judicial Protection*, Council of Europe.
Vavřička and Others v the Czech Republic (GC) (nos. 47621/13, 3867/14, 73094/14, 19298/15, 19306/15, 43883/15) [2021] ECtHR (8 April).
Vejdeland and Others v Sweden (no. 1813/07) [2012] ECtHR (9 February).
Von Hannover v Germany (no. 59320/00) [2004] ECtHR (24 June).
West, R. (1997) *Caring for Justice*, New York University Press.
X v Iceland (no. 6825/74) [1974] ECtHR (7 December).
X v Latvia [GC] (no. 27853/09) [2013] ECtHR (26 November).
X and Y v Belgium (no. N/A) [1982] ECtHR (7 December).

13

Normative considerations about the guiding principles for the European Court of Human Rights allocating custody in child protection

David Archard and Marit Skivenes

Introduction

How do, and how should, we determine the custody of children in situations where children are in the care of the child protection system? Countries have different policies, laws and practices on this matter, and these differences may reflect contrasts in public or cultural attitudes as well as political priorities and resource availability (Archard and Skivenes, in preparation). Any policy on custody in child protection situations, along with its underlying justification, will be underpinned by various normative considerations. All jurisdictions take some account of these considerations but accord them different degrees of importance (Berrick et al, 2023).

A seminal decision on child protection was published on 10 September 2019, by the European Court of Human Rights (ECtHR) (Strand Lobben and Others v Norway [GC], 2019). The ECtHR concluded that there had been a violation of Article 8 of the European Convention on Human Rights (ECHR). This Grand Chamber judgment, hereafter referred to as GC Strand Lobben, has already been established as key case law in child protection cases (Helland and Skivenes, in preparation; Emberland, Chapter 2) and is also considered a setback for children's rights (Fenton-Glynn, 2021; Mørk et al, 2022): 'This judgment, coming as it does from the Grand Chamber, sets a new and concerning precedent. To criticise a state for focusing too much on the interests of the child is an astounding position, turning the clock back on the position of children before the Court' (Fenton-Glynn, 2021, p 307).

The Grand Chamber judgment is not unanimous. Four dissenting judges argue that the government's actions are not a violation of Article 8 and thus showcase a conflict in interpretations and weighting of principles by the ECtHR. Yet, the judgment still has a seemingly huge impact on ECtHR case law and European child protection.

In this chapter we examine core principles within child protection as laid out by the majority judges and minority judges in the ECtHR GC Strand Lobben. We are not conducting a detailed review and evaluation of this judgment nor of the Court's case law around Article 8. We also include a contrasting example on custody in a case of surrogacy from the United States to showcase how arguments for parenthood may be changed. In the following we broaden the scope and discuss some key dimensions about custody, thereafter considerations on allocation of custody, a discussion section, and ending the chapter with concluding remarks.

Considerations on custody and caring for children

What then is meant by custody? By custody we mean the exclusive care of some child by designated adults. The sense of 'exclusive' is that of excluding other adults from that caring relationship, although not of course from being otherwise in associative relations with the child. The parent of a schoolfriend of another parent's child may, for instance, entertain the child for meals, have them join their family events, and stay over. But it is the designated parent or parents who, in the instance, are accorded the primary and exclusive role of custodial care. We can leave to one side for now the question of whether we understand this exclusive care as a right or as a responsibility. In effect, we mean by a custodial role, parenthood in its social sense (who society allocates such a caring role to) or legal sense (who the law determines shall have such a role). These senses of parenthood are distinguished from physical or biological parenthood as defining who caused the child to come into being. Determining who is the parent or custodian of a child will also serve to designate what counts as a particular instance of a family. We need only use a minimal definition of 'family' as a group of adults and children in which the former take continuing primary responsibility for the care of the former (Archard, 2010). This bare definition allows that some forms of the family should be morally preferred to others. We can thus define the family as a social institution by affirming the generally agreed presumption that children need custody, being dependent during their minority, and benefiting from continuous, committed care from some adults. Such a definition also permits acknowledgement that there are better or worse ways to provide such care, as is typically at stake in child protection situations (Skivenes, 2023).

Questions of who should have custody of any child arise at least in the following circumstances: birth, surrogacy, the use of artificial reproductive technology, familial breakdown and child protection. In each case it is in principle an open question as to who should have custody, however, legally and in practice we allow as a general rule those who created the child to have custody.[1] Although, as in some cases one may determine *ex ante* that a pregnant woman is an unfit parent and make arrangements for the transfer of her baby at birth to a foster or adoptive parent. The law on surrogacy might allow or disallow custody of the child of a surrogate mother to be given to the adults who have commissioned the surrogacy. Artificial reproductive technology will be regulated in such a way as to allocate custodial roles for the child that is the outcome of successful fertility treatment. In the wake of a breakdown in the relationship of a couple the law may be required to award custody of any child of that relationship to one of the two adults or fix the terms in which such custody is shared. And, finally, where it is determined that a child is at risk of or has suffered serious harm at the hands of a parent, child protection authorities may transfer custodial care of that child to the state by foster care/residential homes, or to another adult by adoption.

Considerations that underpin any allocation of custody

At the outset in custody cases there are three sets of interests: those of the child, those of prospective parents and the state (or the public or the society) (Archard, 2003). Briefly, each set of interests is as follows.

The United Nations Convention on the Rights of the Child (CRC), which all nations bar one have ratified, provides children with individual rights. This means that children have political, civil and social rights that should be protected on equal footing as adults' rights. Article 3 of the CRC requires that in 'all actions concerning children, whether undertaken by public or private social welfare institutions, courts of law, administrative authorities or legislative bodies, the best interests of the child shall be a primary consideration'. This Article is generally regarded as expressing a key principle, and all jurisdictions follow it in giving the best interests of the child central importance in the design of law, regulations and policy. How we should understand the interests of any child, what it might mean to promote their *best* interests, and whether these should be 'primary' (as the CRC insists) or 'paramount' (as some have argued) are difficult questions, ones that different courts have sought to clarify and answer. Our aim is to discuss some key principles for custody in child protection situations as laid out in the GC Strand Lobben judgment.

The interest of a prospective parent is that of being in an enduring and exclusive custodial relation with a child. It is important to distinguish an interest in being the parent of *a* child (that is, any child) and that of being the parent of *this* child (an identifiable child to whom the prospective parent bears some relation, most obviously for instance that child which the parent has procreated). Article 8 of the ECHR is securing this specific interest.

Lastly, there are state or public interests. Any society has an interest in ensuring, for its own sustained and viable reproduction over time, that children are brought up to be good members of that society, as workers, law-abiding citizens, administrators and parents, to mention some roles individuals have.

Child protection and child health measures were introduced in England at the beginning of the 20th century upon discovery of the significant number of young men failing the medical tests for service in the army, this at a time when England was engaged in critical military ventures. A society whose children do not grow up in sufficient numbers to be eligible to serve in its armies will not survive. In Norway, having a child protection act already in 1896, the aim was primarily to ensure societal safety and prevent children from committing criminal acts (Dahl, 1974). Shortly after, in 1915, the Castbergs Act was shifting the focus to child welfare and social reform for children that were in difficult and vulnerable situations (for example, Graver, 2000).

In taking account of these different kinds of interests we present six arguments or positions on how to consider custody.

Property argument

It is important to distinguish between a non-derivative and a derivative moral consideration. Let us take a critical and important example. An adult might claim an interest in parenting the child they have created. They are the child's biological parent. We could envisage them supporting this claim by saying something like, 'This is my child – I am responsible for its being brought into existence, it is my flesh and blood, it carries my genes – and I should be the one to have custody of it and bring it up.' Here there is an appeal to a basic consideration, one that simply appeals to the simple, non-derivative fact of the child being 'mine'.

Evidence for its prevalence and force is well illustrated by the slogan employed by parents in some high-profile cases who disputed the decisions made for their child's care by doctors: 'My child, my choice.' It should immediately be added that – for all its appeal and widespread use in common discourse – there is, for many, something unclear or mysterious in this claim. What exactly is doing the moral work in such a refrain? Why does a biological fact – this is my flesh and blood – serve to justify a custodial relation? It is standard to deprecate a 'proprietarian' view that was once a standard presumption of family jurisprudence, namely that the parent-creator has rights of ownership over the created child. A child is obviously an object that can be owned, and, as such, treated like any other owned object, namely given away, sold or destroyed. Yet, as is frequently noted, the view that a child is 'mine' in the sense of my property casts a long shadow over much thinking about parental rights and a view in conflict with children as individual rights bearers, as is set out in the CRC.

Commitment–identity argument

The procreative parent could argue differently and as follows, 'It is best for the child to be brought up by its biological parent, both because such a parent has the greatest commitment to care for the child they have created, and because the child benefits in significant ways from the relation it can establish with the adult who, by creating the child, gives that child its essential identity or nature' (see also Marshall, Chapter 12). Here, it is the interests of the *child* that support the claim of the parent to custody. The biological relation of the adult to the child supports a claim or interest of the former in being the social or legal parent by virtue of an interest of the child (in having a parent who promotes their best interests). The parent's claim is derivative and based upon the child's interest.

Attachment argument

Provided that the child has been cared for by loving and considerate parents who have been consistently meeting their physical, emotional and psychological needs, a child has likely formed a strong attachment to their primary caregivers. With increasing age, children also have a more developed understanding of their relationships and surroundings, and they have formed a sense of security and trust based on their attachment experiences. Attachment theory also postulates that experiences of neglect or maltreatment may disrupt developments of secure and organised attachment (for example, Baer and Martinez, 2006; Cyr et al, 2010; Madigan and Korczak, 2023; Madigan et al, 2023). Attachment theory is widely influential, and a literature review reveals a wealth of studies and meta studies on the empirical relevance of the theory (for example, Deneault et al, 2023; Madigan et al, 2024), including cross-cultural relevance (for example, Van Ijzendoorn and Kroonenberg, 1988).

Competency argument

The argument for requiring parents to demonstrate minimal skills and be able to provide basic necessities for their child can be derived from the provision pillar in the CRC. Creating a safe environment is crucial for a child's well-being and development. Parents should have the capacities to prioritise the child's best interests, leaving a wide space for various ways of living conditions and preferences of what is a good life. Parents who can't provide basic standards for raising a child could harm the child's long-term development and well-being. The CRC Article 19 provides the absolute minimum standards for what parents cannot do, which includes abuse, neglect and mistreatment of their child.

Balancing various interests

The question then is how these various interests are balanced when we determine who should have, and who should retain, the custody of any child.

In doing so, we should recognise that the different interests may reinforce and also delimit one another. Thus, it may be, as is argued in a 'dual interest' theory of parenthood (defended by Brighouse and Swift, 2006), that both the child's and the adult's interests serve to justify the allocation of custody. Moreover, it is in the interests of the prospective parent to have the kind of relation – intimate, exclusive and enduring – with a child that is in the child's interest. Moreover, the exercise of that custodial relation should be constrained by the child's interests. A parent does not always and in every instance have to do what is in the child's best interest. Apart from anything else, such a requirement would severely stunt and harm the interests of any parent, however a parent should never do anything that significantly damages the interests of their child. In this latter regard, the CRC set very clear boundaries for what any adult or state can do towards a child or towards children as a group.

The fiduciary role

The orthodox view of parenthood on this kind of account, one that takes proper account of both the child's and parent's interests, is that it is a fiduciary role, one of caretaking and stewardship. It endures during the child's minority and ceases when the child has become an adult. Throughout that period of the child's dependence the adult can enjoy parenthood and exclude others from the custodial role, but only so far as the parent is guided by a concern to do what is in the child's interests (see also Archard and Skivenes, 2009). It should be added that such an account of who should have custody also serves the state or a public interest. It can be argued that families, minimally defined and in which the parents act as trustees for the developing interests of their dependent children, ensure that normally children grow up to be healthy adults who can contribute as appropriate to society. Talk of temporal duration and an enduring relation broaches one very difficult question. This concerns the significance of the permanence of the parent–child relationship. It should be clear, and is confirmed by all relevant studies, that what matters to the child, what is valuable to it, what contributes to the child's healthy development, is an enduring relationship with a parent.

Discussion

When custody must be determined – at the outset (birth) or subsequently (when there is reason, for instance because of familial breakdown or serious failings of parental care, to re-allocate custody) what account should be given, and what weight accorded, to the history of and to the future prospects of sustained parenthood? These considerations must be weighed alongside other distinct considerations, deriving from the interests of any existing parents, those of the child, and public interests. When the state has intervened due to neglect, abuse and/or maltreatment, as CRC Article 19 requires, questions around custody are raised, including: Should the child be reunified with birth parents? Do foster parents, having custody for the child on assignment of the state, have a right to custody? What role does the interests and rights of the child play in these processes? How about the interests of other family members, for example the child's siblings, either by biology or by relations in for example the foster home?

Strand Lobben and Others v Norway

In GC Strand Lobben (2019) the central parties in the case were the birth mother (who brought the case to the ECtHR, and she included the child as applicant), the child and the Norwegian state. The latter, by its child protection system and its judicial system, had evoked Article 19 of the CRC and had decided a care order was necessary and to move the child into a foster home. It was later also decided an adoption of the child was in the child's best interest, and in the Norwegian system it is only the foster parents that can become adoption parents when an adoption from care is conducted (Pösö et al, 2021). The adoptive parents were not considered central in the GC Strand Lobben case (2019), but they were given the opportunity to provide a third-party intervention (see also Falch-Eriksen, Chapter 14).

Without going into details of the applicants' arguments, the birth mother claimed her rights after ECHR Article 8 were violated – and as mentioned, the majority (13–4) in the Grand Chamber of the ECtHR concluded that there had been a violation of Article 8 by the Norwegian state.[2] In the following, we focus on the justifications that are provided by the majority and the minority related to the general principles, and we examine the reasons they provide for custody and parenthood for the child.

The majority: 13 judges

The majority in GC Strand Lobben (2019) lay out three main principles for their considerations, which include *temporary state interventions*, *child's best interest* and *de facto family life*. The temporarily principle is considered a guiding principle for the ECtHR in child protection cases and is by the GC Strand Lobben (2019) formulated in the following way:

> A care order should be regarded as a temporary measure, to be discontinued as soon as circumstances permit, and that any measures implementing temporary care should be consistent with the ultimate aim of reuniting the natural parents and the child. ... In this type of case the adequacy of a measure is to be judged by the swiftness

of its implementation, as the passage of time can have irremediable consequences for relations between the child and the parent with whom it does not live. ... Furthermore, the ties between members of a family and the prospects of their successful reunification will perforce be weakened if impediments are placed in the way of their having easy and regular access to each other. (Strand Lobben and Others v Norway 2019, Court's assessment, p 67, (a) general principles #208)

The ECtHR majority in the Strand Lobben judgment may be understood to affiliate its reasoning around the principle of temporary measure with the *property argument*. The reasoning expresses that birth parents are the 'natural parent' and as such are seemingly the 'owner' of the child. It is due to this reason the child should be returned to birth parents as soon as possible. The focus on time and swift implementation may also be understood as an *attachment argument*, because if too much time passes without birth parents caring for the child their relational bounds may not be built and/or developed.

The majority also introduces the *child's best interest principle*, and the importance that the temporary principle is always 'being balanced against the duty to consider the best interests of the child' (Strand Lobben and Others v Norway, 2019, Court's assessment, p 67, (a) general principles #208). The reference to the best interest principle comes from previous case law. In terms of the role the best interest principles should play, the majority only points out that it should be 'considered', whereas the CRC and case law would say the principle should be paramount or primary. The majority neither provide any specification of what might be meant with the principle of a child's best interest, and as such is leaving it open to decision-makers and others to determine how to fill this principle with content. Within child protection legislation across Europe, there are some common components that decision-makers are obligated to take regard of when making a child's best interest decision (Skivenes and Sørsdal, 2018; Tobin, 2019; Luhamaa et al, 2022). The one component that almost all child protection legislation requires decision-makers to consider is the child's opinion – this is an important instruction from national legislators to the judiciaries across Europe when they are considering a child's best interest in child protection. The majority in the GC Strand Lobben does not have the child's opinion as a consideration in their reasoning and justifications (see also Helland and Skivenes, in preparation).

The majority also mentions the child's de facto family, which is the family that foster the child. This may be understood as affiliated with the argument of the child's *attachment*, although not to the foster/adoption family. However, the majority does not include this argument as a consideration in their assessment: 'when a considerable period of time has passed since the child was originally taken into public care, the interest of a child not to have his or her *de facto* family situation changed again may override the interests of the parents to have their family reunited' (Strand Lobben and Others v Norway, 2019, Court's assessment, p 67, (a) general principles #208). In sum, the majority in this Grand Chamber judgment are laying out three principles, in which the main principle is that any removal of a child is temporary, and the underlying argument seem to be that the child is a *property* of the parent with a leaning to include the *attachment* to the birth parents.

The minority: dissenting four judges

The minority in the Strand Lobben judgment, four judges, laid out their arguments on page 87 and onwards, and we are here particularly interested in their views and interpretations of the three general principles. The minority points out that the presentation of principles is ambiguous:

> At present, the general principles as set out by the Court are riddled not only with some inevitable ambiguities but also with some undeniable tensions and outright contradictions, 'internally' as well as in relation to the relevant specialised legal instruments, particularly the International Convention on the Rights of the Child (CRC). (Strand Lobben and Others v Norway [GC], 2019, p 87)

The minority discuss the guiding principles and take an issue with the position and understanding of the child and the child's best interest principle that the majority lay out. Their concern, as we understand it, seems to rest on the arguments that the child has individual rights and is a moral subject, which resonates with a *fiduciary argument*. Also, they are of the opinion that the best interest principle as a guiding norm is given too little weight in the majority's understanding of principles, pointing to the argument of *balancing interests*. The minority are thus true to previous ECtHR case law (Breen et al, 2020) and the CRC in which the principle should be paramount or primary (see Mørk et al, 2022). Furthermore, the minority also presents the argument that a singular focus on temporary care and biological family in child protection situations disregard other arguments for custody, which indicate a different understanding of parenthood and consideration of other arguments for custody to consider.

> The dilemma is well illustrated by the above rendition of the position in the Chamber judgment. Under this approach, reuniting the natural parent(s) and the child is the 'inherent' and 'ultimate' aim and the 'guiding principle' to be followed. This guiding principle is 'subject to' the proviso that the 'ultimate aim' (of reuniting the biological family)

must be 'balanced against' the duty to 'consider' the best interests of the child. This gives the impression that the 'ultimate aim' of reuniting the biological family might override the best interests of the child. Under the CRC, and similar constitutional or other provisions in many domestic legal orders, however, the position has evolved to one where the best interests of the child are recognized as a primary, or paramount, consideration – based on children's particular need for protection as dependent and vulnerable human beings. This in turn implies that the best interests of the child may, where the circumstances so demand, override the aim of reuniting the child with the biological parent(s). (Strand Lobben and Others v Norway, 2019, p 88)

The minority reasoning about family life and custody rests on arguments about *attachment*, that a child may establish with carers such as a foster family. Furthermore, they emphasise the child's needs which may be related to the *competency* arguments. They especially take issue with the argument of custody and parenthood as property which is embedded in the reasoning on biology and the child as something owned by the parents:

Yet another manifestation of the tensions mentioned above is the fact that the Court has held that it is 'in principle in a child's interests to preserve family ties, save where weighty reasons exist to justify severing those ties' (see paragraph 157 of the present judgment). However, especially in situations where it has been necessary to adopt care measures in respect of an infant and to maintain placement with a foster family for a long period, the child's *de facto* family life and family ties may be almost exclusively with the foster family rather than the biological parent(s). In this sense, too, the ultimate question may be which perspective, namely that of the child or that of the biological parent(s), and (accordingly) which family life, should take precedence. (Strand Lobben and Others v Norway, 2019, p 89)

Taking issue with the property argument, the minority also enhances the relevance of attachment the child and foster/adoptive parents have developed as a de facto family. They question a narrow understanding of family as only consisting of biological bonds and also call for a balancing of interests by asking which perspective should prevail (see also Mørk et al, 2022). This line of reasoning is included in what may be a main issue by the minority, and that is that the ECtHR with this Grand Chamber judgment does not make clear what the guiding principles are. The minority is of the opinion that the problem with a lack of clarifying the principles is to be found in what must be characterised as the key issue in child protection cases, namely how important key principles should be weighted in matters of custody and thus consequences of obscuring the contradictory considerations. Their reasoning is as follows:

> In this sense, it does make a difference whether the determinative precept is that reuniting the biological family can take precedence over the best interests of the child, or whether the determinative precept is that the best interests of the child may take precedence even where this entails renouncing the child's reunification with his or her biological parent(s). It appears undeniable that this remains a point of principle on which the Court is struggling. As a result, it has difficulty formulating general principles with all the desirable clarity and coherence. (Strand Lobben and Others v Norway, 2019, p 89)

The case of Baby M

Another legal case which illustrates what weight is accorded to custody arguments, to the history of and to the future prospects of sustained parenthood – and more – is that of Baby M in the United States (Baby M, 1988). A couple unable to have a child of their own contracted with a surrogate who, using the semen of the commissioning husband, became pregnant and gave birth to Baby M in 1986. The surrogate changed her mind after M's birth, and having initially surrendered the child to the commissioning couple, kidnapped and fled with Baby M, caring for the child for several months before a final judgment awarded custody to the couple. The judgment invoked the best interests of the child as the key determinant of who should have custody. Nevertheless, the court also recognised the validity of the surrogacy contract whereby the birthmother surrendered her custodial rights prior to conception and/or birth (see Feldman [2018] for a 30-year follow-up review).

At the heart of the debate about the *ethics* of surrogacy is a question as to whether a birth parent can in this fashion, by contract, transfer her parental rights over the child she gives birth to, to others. The custodial argument rests on a premise of property. Did she have rights as the birthmother, if so, why, and can these rights be transferred to another without regard to what might be in the interests of the child?

What significance should have been given to the fact that the birthmother did care for the baby for some period and as attachment developed might have been, in prospect, a permanent custodian? If that consideration has weight, how do we adjudicate in cases we can imagine where someone kidnaps and provides good care for an infant over a significant period of time? The argument of parenthood as attachment will then be relevant. If sustained care has moral weight, how is it to be balanced against the claim of the biological parent when the kidnapped child is discovered?

Less fanciful than such kidnapping cases are those deeply tragic cases where parents take home the wrong baby from the hospital, the mistake being discovered or apparent only after some time, and at which point the parents are unwilling to hand over the child to the natural and, for some, the 'real' parents.[3] How at that later point – and how much later – should we resolve these disputes?

Concluding remarks

In sum, in examining what justifies any custodial policy or case law we should try to discern the underlying normative considerations about parenthood and their respective weights: how do we balance the various interests of the child, parent(s) and public? The rudimentary analysis of the majority and minority in GC Strand Lobben show that parenthood and the understanding of the weight of principles are understood distinctly different. Where the majority emphasise parenthood as property and biological parenthood as the child's best interest, with seemingly little regard to parenthood as attachment (with de facto family) nor to arguments of a balancing interests, the minority have a somewhat different approach. First, parenthood for them seem to a much stronger degree being related to attachment and to the child's best interest. They call for a wider concept of family in questions of custody. Second, they directly include the specific child protection situations in their consideration of custody, which often do not happen in discussions on custody. Third, a call for a stronger focus on the balancing of interests is also clearly evident in the minority's considerations. Finally, the minority emphasise the negative implications of not clarifying the role and content of the principles and interests at stake in child protection cases.

Spelling out the normative considerations in discussions about custody and care for children helps to make clearer the differences in law, policy and practice. At the same time these considerations can be appraised with a view to determine the best possible policies. For example, if a policy or attitude appeals to considerations that are problematic, either in themselves or in how they are combined, then that provides a good basis for its generally unfavourable evaluation. Such an evaluation matters because there can be reasons to ensure a convergence of law and policies across different jurisdictions, and the case law from ECtHR is one type of convergence. We call for more clarity and transparency in the guiding principle for custody matters in child protection.

Notes

[1] Birth parents may decide to transfer parental rights to another adult and/or the state, and it varies across countries if and to which degree the state would be involved in such decisions (Burns et al, 2017).

2   See also Emberland, Chapter 2, and Sandberg, Chapter 4, in this volume, and Søvig and Tjelmeland (2019) for more on GC Strand Lobben judgment. Furthermore, see the Norwegian Supreme Court (2020).
3   In a recent Norwegian case, which involved two babies being switched in 1965 only to be discovered in the 1980s, the children (now adults) and the mothers raised a human right and tort case against the municipality and the state, and it was decided that it was not a violation. See: https://www.advokatbladet.no/oslo-tingrett/staten-med-full-seier-i-erstatningssoksmal-om-to-babyer-som-ble-forbyttet-ved-fodsel/220521. For examples of babies being switched throughout history, see: https://en.wikipedia.org/wiki/Babies_switched_at_birth#:~:text=In%201945%2C%20Denice%20Juneski%20and,Kay%20McDonald%20were%20accidentally%20switched

Acknowledgements

Many thanks to Hege S. Helland and Mathea Loen for insightful feedback.

References

Archard, D. (2003) *Children, Family, and the State*, Ashgate.
Archard, D. (2010) *The Family: A Liberal Defence*, Palgrave Macmillan.
Archard, D. and Skivenes, M. (2009) 'Balancing a child's best interests and a child's views', *The International Journal of Children's Rights*, 17(1): 1–21.
Archard, D. and Skivenes, M. (in preparation) 'Parenthood'.
Baby M (1988) re Baby M, 537 A.2d 1227, 109 N.J. 396 (N.J.).
Baer, J.C. and Martinez, C.D. (2006) 'Child maltreatment and insecure attachment: A meta-analysis', *Journal of Reproductive and Infant Psychology*, 24(3): 187–197.
Berrick, J.D., Skivenes, M. and Roscoe, J.N. (2023) 'Public perceptions of child protection, children's rights, and personal values: An assessment of two states', *Children and Youth Services Review*, 150: 1–8.
Breen, C., Krutzinna, J., Luhamaa, K. and Skivenes, M. (2020) 'Family life for children in state care: An analysis of the European Court of Human Rights' reasoning on adoption without consent', *The International Journal of Children's Rights*, 28(4): 715–747.
Brighouse, H. and Swift, A. (2006) 'Equality, priority, and positional goods', *Ethics*, 116(3): 471–497.
Burns, K., Pösö, T. and Skivenes, M. (eds) (2017) *Child Welfare Removals by the State: A Cross-Country Analysis of Decision-Making Systems*, Oxford University Press.
Cyr, C., Euser, E.M., Bakermans-Kranenburg, M.J. and Van Ijzendoorn, M.H. (2010) 'Attachment security and disorganization in maltreating and high-risk families: A series of meta-analyses', *Developmental Psychopathology*, 22(1): 87–108.
Dahl, T.S. (1974) 'The emergence of the Norwegian child welfare law', *Scandinavian Studies in Criminology*, 5: 83–98.
Deneault, A.S., Hammond, I. and Madigan, S. (2023) 'A meta-analysis of child–parent attachment in early childhood and prosociality', *Developmental Psychology*, 59(2): 236–255.

Feldman, E.A. (2018) 'Baby M turns 30: The law and policy of surrogate motherhood', *American Journal of Law & Medicine*, 44(1): 7–22.

Fenton-Glynn, C. (2021) *Children and the European Court of Human Rights*, Oxford University Press.

Graver, H.P. (2000) 'Mellom individualisme og kollektivisme – forvaltningsretten ved inngangen til et nytt århundre [Between individualism and collectivism – administrative law at the beginning of a new century]', *Lov og Rett*, 39(8): 451–482.

Helland, H.S. and Skivenes, M. (in preparation) 'Fair trial for children in the ECtHR? An analysis of all child protection judgements from 1959–2022', unpublished manuscript.

Luhamaa, K., Krutzinna, J. and Skivenes, M. (2022) 'Child's best interest in child protection legislation of 44 jurisdictions', Centre for Research on Discretion and Paternalism, University of Bergen.

Madigan, S. and Korczak, D.J. (2023) 'Is it time to reconsider the diagnostic construct validity of depressive disorders for young children?', *JAMA Pediatrics*, 177(10): 1008–1010.

Madigan, S., Deneault, A.A., Racine, N., Park, J., Thiemann, R., Zhu, J., et al (2023) 'Adverse childhood experiences: A meta-analysis of prevalence and moderators among half a million adults in 206 studies', *World Psychiatry*, 22(3): 463–471.

Madigan, S., Deneault, A.A., Duschinsky, R., Bakermans-Kranenburg, M.J., Schuengel, C., Van Ijzendoorn, M.H., et al (2024) 'Maternal and paternal sensitivity: Key determinants of child attachment security examined through meta-analysis', *Psychological Bulletin*, 150(7): 839–872.

Mørk, A., Sandberg, K., Schultz, T. and Hartoft, H. (2022) 'A conflict between the best interests of the child and the right to respect for family life? Non-consensual adoption in Denmark and Norway as an example of the difficulties in balancing different considerations', *International Journal of Law, Policy and the Family*, 36(1): ebac019.

Norwegian Supreme Court (2020) HR 2020–661-S.

Pösö, T., Thoburn, J. and Skivenes, M. (eds) (2021) *Adoption from Care: International Perspectives on Children's Rights, Family Preservation and State Intervention*, Policy Press.

Skivenes, M. (2023) 'Principles of public policy for child protection: Cross national perspectives', in M. Daly, N. Gilbert, B. Pfau-Effinger and D. Besharov (eds), *International Handbook of Family Policy: A Life-Course Perspective*, Oxford University Press, pp 824–836.

Skivenes, M. and Sørsdal, L. (2018) 'The child's best interest principle across child protection jurisdictions', in E. Backe-Hansen and A. Falch-Eriksen (eds), *Child Protection and Human Rights: Implementing the CRC in Policy and Professional Practice*, Springer, pp 59–88.

Søvig, K.H. and Tjelmeland, M.E. (2019) 'Strand Lobben mot Norge – noen refleksjoner [Strand Lobben against Norway – some reflections]', *Tidsskrift for Familierett, Arverett og Barnevernrettslige Spørsmål*, 17(4): 345–352.

Strand Lobben and Others v Norway [GC] (no. 37283/13) [2019] ECtHR (30 November).

Tobin, J. (2019) 'Introduction: The foundation for children's rights', in J. Tobin (eds), *The UN Convention on the Rights of the Child: A Commentary*, Oxford University Press, pp 1–20.

Van Ijzendoorn, M.H. and Kroonenberg, P.M. (1988) 'Cross-cultural patterns of attachment: A meta-analysis of the strange situation', *Child Development*, 59(1): 147–156.

14

The relationship between the UN Convention on the Rights of the Child and the European Court of Human Rights in numbers

Claire Fenton-Glynn

Introduction

Through its seven decades of existence, the European Court of Human Rights (ECtHR) has slowly but surely developed a strong body of jurisprudence in the area of children's rights. While it is by no means without its flaws (see Fenton-Glynn, 2019), the Court has nevertheless been able to build on the scarce text of the European Convention on Human Rights (ECHR) to carve out strong protection for children, at least in certain areas.

Child protection is one of these areas in which the ECtHR has shown particular strength, using the right to respect for private and family life under Article 8, as well as the protection from inhuman and degrading treatment under Article 3, to create both positive and negative obligations on which the state must act. On the one hand, the authorities have an obligation to step in to protect a child who is in danger of abuse or neglect, where they know or ought to know that this is occurring (see Z v the United Kingdom, 2001). On the other hand, the protection that is provided must be strictly proportionate to the danger that has arisen, and the child may not be removed from their family unless this is necessary for the child's well-being. At every stage of the proceedings – from investigation to intervention, from removal to reunification – the state must show that they have balanced the child's need for physical and emotional integrity with the right of the family to be free from state interference. This is a difficult line to draw, and the balance between the two competing obligations is a delicate one. This is made more difficult by the fact that, as will be discussed later in this chapter, the ECHR was not drafted with children's rights in mind, nor is it ideally suited to deciding on difficult child rights issues.

All member states of the ECHR have also ratified the UN Convention on the Rights of the Child (CRC), meaning that they are all bound equally by international law to implement both of their obligations. Of course, the primary job of the ECtHR is to implement the ECHR, and it is not its role to enforce the CRC directly. However, there is also no doubt that in order to interpret the ECHR in a way that is effective for children, the ECtHR needs to be able to narrow down the wide provisions of that Convention to identify appropriate standards, and the Court has repeatedly stated that the CRC should be used for this purpose – making clear that ECHR rights must be interpreted in light of the CRC.

The aim of this chapter is to consider how the ECtHR refers to the CRC, as well as the guidance of the UN Committee on the Rights of the Child (CRC Committee) through General Comments and Concluding Observations (associated materials). While the focus of this edited collection is to consider law and practice surrounding child protection, this chapter will cast its net wider, considering all cases before the Court in all subject areas. It is hoped, however, that it will help inform how those focusing on child protection consider the decision-making of the ECtHR, and areas where further strategic litigation could be directed.

This will be a descriptive numerical overview of the Court's jurisprudence: it will analyse how frequently the CRC is used, in what subject areas, and in what part of the decision-making process. This has the advantage of showing the foothold that the CRC has in the ECHR system, and in particular, highlighting the progress (or lack thereof) in the engagement of the Court with children's rights (Helland and Hollekim, 2023).[1]

Having said this, it will not examine how the CRC has substantially impacted on the outcomes of cases. As such, it only gives a partial picture, and it has limitations. First, an examination of the text of the ECtHR judgments only gives one insight into the decision-making process – albeit an important one. What is written in the judgment does not necessarily reflect all aspects which have been taken into account, or that have influenced, the decision of the Court. The second limitation with respect to this approach is the fact that the ECtHR adopts a very concentrated style of decision-making. Unlike many common law jurisdictions, it does not incorporate significant amounts of outside material into its judgments, preferring instead to focus only on the Convention and its jurisprudence.

Having said this, the fact that the ECtHR *does* in fact make reference to the UN Convention and UN Committee guidance in some judgments demonstrates that where it is judged sufficiently relevant or important, then it is included. As such, even though it is not a perfect analytical tool, I believe that this examination of the use of these materials provides interesting insight into the way in which child rights are incorporated into ECtHR judgments, and a useful starting point – even if not the end point – for discussion of the relationship between the two instruments.

The UN Convention on the Rights of the Child and the European Convention on Human Rights: uneasy bedfellows?

The CRC and the ECHR came into being at very different times in the human rights landscape. While the CRC is one of the most recent international conventions – coming into force in 1990 – the ECHR is one of the earliest, as part of the first wave of international instruments following the Second World War. This has led not only to very different texts in general, but also very different implications for child rights, especially in the sphere of family law.

At the time of drafting of the ECHR, there was limited recognition of children's rights at either domestic or international law. The only international child rights instrument in existence at that time, the 1924 League of Nations Geneva Declaration on the Rights of the Child, largely focused on special protection that should be given to children, including the 'the right to be among the first to receive relief', and the 'right to understanding and love by parents and society'. As such, children were still seen in an essentially paternalistic way, reinforcing the notion that children are objects of benevolence rather than subjects of rights and holders of individual agency.

This can be seen in the construction of Article 8 – the right to respect for private and family life – which is the primary article under which children's rights have been considered by the ECtHR. It is clear from the drafting of the ECHR that family life under Article 8 was considered as an adjunct to private life, with the *travaux preparatoires* emphasising: 'the father of a family cannot be an independent citizen, cannot feel free within his own country, if he is menaced in his own home and if, every day, the State steals from him his soul, or the conscience of his children' (Teitgen, 1975, pp 76, 78). This deference to the family unit reflects the historical social importance placed on the autonomy of the family under which parents are granted the liberty to make decisions as to how best raise their child (Appell and Boyer, 1995). In this way, the ECHR takes a very conservative approach to family life, upholding the power structure within this unit, insulating it from state interference. This can be advantageous where children's rights correspond to parental rights – especially as parents have the ability to advocate before the ECtHR in a way children do not (see Fenton-Glynn, 2019). However, where children want to assert a right against their parents, or where their rights conflict – for example, in cases of child protection[2] – it leaves children in a position where their rights are suppressed within the wider recognition of the family as a whole (Charlesworth et al, 1991).

The tension between the two instruments was highlighted by the separate opinion of Judges Kjølbro, Poláčková, Koskelo and Nordén in the Grand Chamber judgment of Strand Lobben v Norway. There, they stated: 'The

ECHR is rooted in the protection, and balancing, of the rights of everyone within a State's jurisdiction, including those who have formed a family, whereas the CRC is focused on strengthening and protecting children as holders of distinct individual rights' (Strand Lobben and Others v Norway, 2019, para 9). Despite these fundamental differences, we can still see that the ECtHR has progressively begun to call on the CRC, as well as General Comments and Concluding Observations by the CRC Committee.

Methodology

The cases analysed in this chapter were collected by undertaking a search of the HUDOC database which contains all decisions and judgments of the ECtHR, and its precursor, the European Commission on Human Rights. Cases that mentioned the CRC, or which referred to a General Comment regarding that Convention were identified, as well as those which referred to a Concluding Observation by the CRC Committee, using search terms 'United Nations Convention on the Rights of the Child'; 'UN Convention on the Rights of the Child'; 'Convention on the Rights of the Child'; 'UNCRC'; 'UNCROC'; 'child rights convention'; '1989 Convention'; 'New York Convention'; 'Committee on the Rights of the Child'; 'General Comment' + 'child'; 'Concluding observation' + 'child'.

Each of the cases were then read in their entirety, before being examined as to the subject matter of the complaint; the type of decision (admissibility decision; chamber decision; Grand Chamber decision); and the article or part of the CRC mentioned (in relation to Concluding Observations, they were catalogued according to the country which the observations referred to; while General Comments were divided according to topic).

Separately, the cases were analysed according to where in the judgment the CRC was mentioned – in relation to the domestic proceedings; in discussing the relevant law; in the submissions by parties (including third parties); or the decision of the Court itself. Where the CRC was mentioned in the decision of the Court, the cases were further analysed according to whether it was in the majority opinion, or in a (partly) concurring or dissenting opinion. Finally, these cases were then examined as to *how* the CRC was used by the Court: in a substantive way; as standard referred to (but not engaged with); or in passing, in a way that did not relate to the case itself.[3]

General findings

The CRC or its associated materials[4] have been referred to in the text of 161 judgments of the ECtHR.[5] This number includes 17 admissibility decisions and 29 Grand Chamber judgments – the remaining 115 being Chamber judgments. While this may seem like a large number, it is only a fraction

Table 14.1: Number of cases mentioning the CRC

Year	Average number of cases per year (total over period in brackets)
1991–2000	1.5 (15)
2001–2010	4.2 (42)
2011–2020	7.7 (77)
2021	14
2022	13

of child law cases which have come before the Court, and an even smaller fraction of the over 24,500 cases decided by the Court from its inception. Although it is true that the Court was making decisions for almost 40 years before the CRC came into existence, the majority of its jurisprudence comes from 1991 onwards – that is, concurrent with the CRC.

Indeed, if we look at the way in which the CRC and associated materials have been used following the UN Convention's coming into force in September 1991, we see a sharp increase from its initial decade, where it was only mentioned once or twice a year, to its current use in almost every case (see Table 14.1).

The first time the CRC was mentioned in an ECtHR judgment was in 1992, in the child protection case of Olsson v Sweden (No 2). Rather than it being used by the majority to come to a decision, however, the UN Convention was instead called upon by the partly dissenting opinion of Judge Pettiti (joined by Judges Matscher and Russo). Judge Pettiti 'regretted that reference was not made to the [CRC]' and argued that it was 'paradoxical that in the year of the implementation of the United Nations Convention on the Rights of the Child, which stresses the importance of parent-child relations, there should have been such a failure in the application of Article 8 (art. 8) of the European Convention' (Olsson v Sweden, 1992).[6] The fact that the UN Convention was not mentioned by the majority, or even included as a relevant 'international text', is not surprising. When analysing the judgments of the ECtHR, even in the 161 cases in which the CRC has been mentioned, in the majority of cases this has not led to any substantive engagement with its standards.

For example, in 20 of the 161 judgments, the CRC was raised in the submissions of one of the parties – be that the applicant, the government or a third party intervenor – but not by the Court; and in six it was mentioned in relation to the domestic proceedings, but not engaged with in the ECtHR decision (see Table 14.2). Moreover, in a further 34 cases, provisions of the CRC were set out in the section of the judgment which presents 'Relevant International Law' (or similar title), but not mentioned in the content of the judgment. These cases highlight fact scenarios where the CRC *was* applicable

Table 14.2: Part of the judgment in which the CRC was mentioned

Domestic proceedings only	6
Relevant law only	34
Submissions by parties only	20
Decision of the Court	101

Table 14.3: Level of engagement with Convention materials

Level of engagement	Number of cases
Relevant standard only	39
Substantive engagement by majority only	23
Substantive engagement in concurring or dissenting opinions only	26
Substantive engagement by majority and concurring/dissent	5
Mentioned in passing only	8

to the case in hand, but that the Court itself failed to engage with how it might inform their decisions.

In only 101 of the 161 cases were the CRC and associated materials discussed in the text of the judgment itself – either by the majority, or in dissenting or concurring opinions.

When we turn to the level of engagement with the Convention materials, as is set out in Table 14.3, in eight of the judgments, the CRC was mentioned in passing, but not in a way that was relevant to the decision – for example, a reference to the CRC not yet having been implemented in the jurisdiction in question (Burghartz v Switzerland, 1994; Bajrami v Albania, 2006);[7] or that the CRC does not in fact refer to the subject matter (Bajrami v Albania, 2006). In a further 39, the CRC was referred to as a relevant standard that informs the decision – for example, where the judgment refers to the CRC as a standard which aligns with the Court's case law (ABC v Latvia, 2016; Abdi Ibrahim v Norway, 2021), or where it is noted that the obligations of the ECHR must be interpreted in light of the CRC (Eskinazi and Chelouche v Turkey, 2005; Emonet and Others v Switzerland, 2007; Ferrari v Romania, 2015). There is no doubt that these references are important: they raise the visibility of the CRC and demonstrate the significant role it plays in the interpretation of the ECHR. However, in these judgments there was no further discussion of the CRC past setting out its relevant provision(s), leaving the engagement somewhat empty. As discussed earlier, it is not the role of the ECtHR to implement the CRC: nevertheless, when the Court itself states that obligations must be interpreted in its light, it seems odd that it would not more fully engage with what such interpretation leads to.

As discussed in the introduction, there are limitations to this analysis, and simply because the CRC was not mentioned does not mean it was not influential, or at least considered. However, it does show a pattern of paying lip service to the CRC, emphasising its importance and relevance, and then failing to follow through with that potential.

This leaves only 54 cases in which there was any substantive engagement with the CRC: 23 where the engagement was by the majority only; 26 by the judges in concurring or dissenting opinions only; and five in both. When you look at the text of ECtHR judgments, you can clearly see that judges have more flexibility in what is included in a concurring or dissenting opinion, and it is therefore not surprising that there is greater substantive discussion of the CRC in that space than by the majority. However, when we consider that it is only in 28 judgments in the history of the Court that the majority decision has engaged substantively with the CRC, we can see that there is a huge potential for deeper consideration.

There is insufficient space in this chapter to go into further detail concerning how this substantive engagement occurred, and the extent to which it actually influenced or dictated the outcomes of the individual cases. Nevertheless, this numerical analysis provides a snapshot of the way in which the Convention has been used, and more importantly, where it has not been used. In doing so, it highlights significant room for further improvement.

Subject areas

When we look at the 161 cases that the CRC or its associated materials have been mentioned in, we can see that it has been heavily used in areas such as immigration (17), juvenile justice (15), the private law issues of custody/contact and child abduction (14 and 19 respectively), as well as child protection (16), adoption (17) and protection from abuse (12) (see Table 14.4).

What is particularly interesting is the CRC articles which were used in these decisions (see Table 14.5). However, before we analyse these articles, it is interesting to note that in 21 cases, the CRC was only referred to in general terms, and no specific article was mentioned. As discussed earlier, even a passing reference to the CRC without further engagement can be important – and likewise, even a mention of this Convention in general without a specific provision can have the effect of further entrenching it in the ECtHR system. Having said this, at the same time, it represents a missed opportunity, where the Convention is clearly relevant, but the ECtHR has failed to delve deeper.

We can see that a wide range of rights are mentioned, covering nearly every article in the CRC. This is commendable, showing the ECtHR is willing to look to the CRC on the whole range of topics covered by that

Table 14.4: Areas of law where the CRC has been cited

Area of law	Number of cases
Child abduction	19
Immigration	17
Adoption	17
Child protection	16
Juvenile justice	15
Custody/contact	14
Protection from abuse	12
Education	7
Surrogacy	5
Parenthood (excluding surrogacy)	3
Anonymous birth	3
International relocation	2
Freedom of expression	2
Freedom of association	2
Freedom of religion	2
Slavery/trafficking	2
Other*	23

Note: * Including subjects such as domestic violence; medical treatment; inheritance; child support; vaccinations; abortion; property rights; privacy; protest; and freedom from torture.

Convention. Of the three articles that are not mentioned, it is not surprising that this includes Article 31, the right to rest and leisure, as this does not fall within the scope of issues which have been considered by the Court. However, it is more surprisingly that Articles 25 and 26 have been ignored. Article 25 recognises the right to a child who has been placed into state care to periodic review of this placement – something that is of significant importance in terms of child protection. Likewise, Article 26 relates to the right of the child to benefit from social security – an issue that falls under Article 1, Protocol 1.

The CRC articles that have been used most extensively correlate with the case law subject matters as set out earlier: Articles 9 and 20 (child protection); Article 21 (adoption); Article 19 (protection from abuse); and Articles 37 and 40 (juvenile justice). What is perhaps most telling, however, is the way in which the four 'key principles' of the CRC have been relied on. The CRC Committee has designated four articles as the cornerstones of the Convention, which must be used to interpret all other rights: Article 2 (non-discrimination); Article 3 (best interests principle); Article 6 (right

Table 14.5: CRC Articles used in decisions

Article	Subject	Number of times used
3	Best interests	71
9	Separation from parents	36
37	Inhuman treatment and detention	27
19	Protection from violence, abuse and neglect	19
21	Adoption	15
7	Birth registration, name and nationality	13
12	Participation	13
18	Parental responsibilities and state assistance	11
40	Juvenile justice	11
Preamble	General	10
20	Alternative care	10
8	Protection of identity	9
1	Definition of the child	8
10	Family reunification	8
28	Education	6
34	Protection from sexual exploitation	6
2	Non-discrimination	4
5	Parental guidance and evolving capacities	4
14	Freedom of thought, belief and religion	4
6	Life, survival and development	3
16	Privacy	3
30	Children from minority or indigenous groups	3
35	Protection from abduction, sale and trafficking	3
39	Recovery from trauma and reintegration	3
4	Implementation of the Convention	2
11	Child abduction	2
17	Access to information	2
22	Refugee children	2
24	Health	2
27	Adequate standard of living	2
29	Goals of education	2
32	Protection from economic exploitation	2
36	Protection from other forms of exploitation	2
13	Freedom of expression	1
15	Freedom of association	1
23	Children with a disability	1
33	Protection from drugs	1
Total		322

to life, survival and development); and Article 12 (participation). Yet despite these four articles being of equal importance, only one – the best interests principle – really seems to have been incorporated into the Court's decision-making in any real way. Article 3 was mentioned almost twice as many times as the next most cited article, showing just how deeply it has become ingrained in the ECtHR's case law. This can be particularly seen in cases concerning Article 8 ECHR, where Article 8(2) allows for the balancing of the right to respect for private and family life against certain considerations, including the 'rights and freedoms of others'. This has been interpreted by the Court to include the justification that the government took the action 'in the child's best interests'.

Interestingly, in the seminal case that established this principle, Johansen v Norway (1996), although the CRC was mentioned, this was not by the ECtHR itself. Instead, it was the government of Norway which argued that when conducting a review of the proportionality of a measure under Article 8 ECHR, the Court should give special weight to the child's interests when balancing it against the rights of others, drawing on Article 3 of the CRC. The government's reasoning was accepted, and largely reproduced, by the Court, though it made no reference to the CRC as the source of this principle. Later judgments have, however, engaged with Article 3 on a more substantive level, in particular Neulinger and Shuruk v Switzerland (2010), and Strand Lobben and Others v Norway GC (2019).

It is not the purpose of this chapter to consider in more detail how the best interests principle has been used in the ECtHR case law: not only is there not enough space, this has been done elsewhere by other authors (Sormunen, 2020; Zamperini, 2024). Nevertheless, it is telling that this principle has been cited over five times as frequently as the right to participation in Article 12 – the next most frequently cited key principle. This distinction is important, as these two rights emphasise contrasting needs of children – on the one hand, protection and paternalism, and on the other, participation and autonomy. While the Court is comfortable with the former, it is less keen to recognise the latter.

It is understandable that Articles 2 and 6 are not mentioned frequently – after all, the ECHR itself has its own non-discrimination clause and right to life (if not to development). It is disappointing, however, to see how infrequently Article 12 has been called on. When it has been called on – for example, in the context of child participation in private law disputes – it has been particularly effective. In M and M v Croatia, the ECtHR used Article 12 CRC to find that although Article 8 ECHR does not contain any explicit procedural obligations, it nevertheless requires that the child be adequately involved in the decision-making process. The ECtHR noted that the concept of 'private life' in Article 8 includes the right to personal autonomy, and in particular, the right to self-fulfillment, which is exercised through their right to be consulted and heard. However, this recognition of the right to participation has not been mirrored in other areas of the ECtHR's case law such as child protection and adoption; and too often, the child's interests are subsumed within the rights of the parents or family as a whole (see Fenton-Glynn, 2019). As such, while this shows the impact that Article 12 could have, it is limited to isolated cases, rather than being integrated throughout the case law of the Court.

General Comments of the Committee on the Rights of the Child

The final two substantive sections of this chapter move away from the CRC itself and focus on the guidance for its interpretation and implementation, as set out by the CRC Committee. In its decision-making process, the ECtHR has referred to both General Comments by the UN Committee on how the Convention should be interpreted, as well as Concluding Observations on state compliance with the CRC.

The use of General Comments has been much less frequent than the CRC itself – a General Comment from the CRC Committee has only been referred to in 39 judgments. In only two cases was a General Comment mentioned where a CRC article itself was not also referred to – though in each case, a reference was made to the Convention in general.

Table 14.6 sets out the General Comments that have been used, their subject matter, and in how many cases they have been referred to. Unsurprisingly, and consistently with the analysis of the CRC articles discussed in judgments, the most frequently cited General Comment is on the best interests of the child. This is followed closely by the guidance on implementing child rights in early childhood, and on right of the child to freedom from all forms of violence.

When we look at where and how these General Comments have been used in the Court's decision-making, in 17 of the 39 judgments, they were mentioned in the section on 'Relevant Law', and not elsewhere in the decision. In two cases there was a reference in the explanation of domestic proceedings, and in a further two, in the submissions by the third-party intervenors, but not in the ECtHR judgment itself.

In the 16 cases where a General Comment was referred to in the substantive decision-making, there were eight citations by the majority, and four in dissenting or concurring opinions, without further engagement. This left only three cases where the majority engaged with a General Comment in any substantive way; and four dissenting or concurring judgments.

This analysis of the use of General Comments is in line with what was seen in the use of the UN Convention itself – a willingness to refer to it as a relevant source of law, but less enthusiasm for substantive discussion of the ways in which it might impact on the interpretation of the ECHR.

Table 14.6: UN Committee General Comments

	Subject	Number of times used
General Comment No. 14 of the Committee on the Rights of the Child (2013)	The right of the child to have his or her best interests taken as a primary consideration	14
General Comment No. 7 of the Committee on the Rights of the Child (2005)	Implementing child rights in early childhood	10
General Comment No. 13 of the Committee on the Rights of the Child (2011)	The right of the child to freedom from all forms of violence	7
General Comment No. 10 of the Committee on the Rights of the Child (2007)	Children's rights in juvenile justice	4
General Comment No. 6 of the Committee on the Rights of the Child (2005)	Treatment of Unaccompanied and Separated Children Outside Their Country of Origin	3
General Comment No. 12 of the Committee on the Rights of the Child (2009)	The right of the child to be heard	3
Joint General Comment No. 3 of the Committee on Migrant Workers and No. 22 of the Committee on the Rights of the Child (2017)	In the context of international migration: General principles	3
Joint General Comment No. 4 of the Committee on Migrant Workers and No. 23 of the Committee on the Rights of the Child (2017)	In the context of International Migration: States parties' obligations in particular with respect to countries of transit and destination	3
General Comment No. 5 of the Committee on the Rights of the Child (2003)	General Measures of Implementation of the Convention on the Rights of the Child	2
General Comment No. 9 of the Committee on the Rights of the Child (2006)	The rights of children with disabilities	2
General Comment No. 11 of the Committee on the Rights of the Child (2009)	Indigenous children and their rights under the Convention	2
General Comment No. 20 of the Committee on the Rights of the Child (2016)	The implementation of the rights of the child during adolescence	2
General Comment No. 8 of the Committee on the Rights of the Child (2006)	The right of the child to protection from corporal punishment and other cruel or degrading forms of punishment	1
General Comment No. 15 of the Committee on the Rights of the Child (2013)	The right of the child to the enjoyment of the highest attainable standard of health	1
General Comment No. 24 of the Committee on the Rights of the Child (2019)	Children's rights in the child justice system	1
Total		58

Concluding Observations of the UN Committee on the Rights of the Child

Under the CRC, countries are subject to periodic review, where the CRC Committee examines the child rights practices in the jurisdiction in question, and makes recommendations accordingly. These recommendations – referred to as 'Concluding Observations' – provide not only a snapshot of how children's rights are protected and promoted in the country in question, but also provide more general guidance as to best practice in particular areas. As such, they are a useful tool for governments, non-governmental organisations, and indeed, for a court, looking to determine whether a child's right has been breached in a particular instance.

Having said this, the ECtHR has appeared reluctant to consider Concluding Observations in coming to their decisions, only having referred to recommendations from the CRC Committee in 19 cases across its whole jurisprudence. Of these 19, eight were cases concerning juvenile justice; two on private child law (vaccinations, residence and contact); two on immigration; and two on surrogacy. Five cases were focused on child protection, adoption or protection from abuse.

Even in these 19 cases where the Concluding Observations were mentioned, they were not engaged with in any real way. In 16 of the 19 cases which referred to Concluding Observations, they were set out under the heading of 'Relevant law' (or equivalent) but then not again referred to by the Court. In the remaining three cases, two mentioned the Concluding Observations in a footnote, and only one in the text. Even in these three, the references came from concurring or dissenting opinions, rather than being part of the reasoning of the court.

It is interesting to note that the Concluding Observations in these three cases – that is, the only ones that were engaged with in any way – the Concluding Observations referred to states other than that which were before the court. In Söderman v Sweden (2013), the Court referred to Concluding Observations on Costa Rica; in Paradiso and Campanelli v Italy (2017), Concluding Observations on the United States were referred to; while in KK and Others v Denmark (2022), the United States, India, Mexico and Israel were all mentioned – countries that not only were not involved in the dispute, but who are not part of the Council of Europe system. It is also significant that the latter two judgments were focused on the ethics of international surrogacy – something that has caused great controversy across Europe (and indeed, across the world), and an issue with which many countries are struggling to determine how to appropriate legislate.

It is not surprising that Concluding Observations are used less frequently, and less widely, than the other documents examined in this chapter. Concluding Observations focus on domestic legal framework and practice, in contrast to the UN Convention itself, and General Comments, which provide more general guidance as to how children's rights should be interpreted. As such, Concluding Observations are much more narrowly applicable, and therefore of less use to the Court. Nevertheless, their use in relation to surrogacy demonstrates that they can be of wider relevance – not only relevant to the state in question, but also where there is similar law or practice. Concluding Observations are also produced on a much more frequent basis than General Comments (approximately 20 per year) and cover a much broader range of topics than the more specific focus of General Comments. As such, this may be an untapped resource which could be of greater use to the Court going forward, if they are brought to the Court's attention by the parties.

Conclusion

This chapter has attempted to provide a snapshot of the relationship between the ECHR and the CRC through the lens of the decision-making of the European Court. As discussed, it only provides a partial picture, and the methodology has its limitations in what it can actually demonstrate. Nevertheless, this numerical analysis provides an important insight into how the Court uses the CRC, and the guidance of the CRC Committee through General Comments and Concluding Observations. Overall, we can see that although the Court clearly states that the ECHR must be interpreted in light of the CRC, most of its engagement with the UN Convention is superficial – in the form of a reference, rather than substantive discussion. There are clearly areas in which the Court is more comfortable – most notably the best interests principle – but overall there is a disappointing lack of deeper consideration of how the specialised UN framework on child rights could inform the decision-making of the European Court.

It is to be hoped that this analysis will pave the way for further research, in particular looking at the impact of the CRC on decision-making, rather than just its presence in it. But equally importantly, it is to be hoped that it prompts reflection on the part of applicants, third parties and indeed judges themselves, about how this existing expertise and knowledge on child rights – by a Convention and Committee recognised by all European states – could help the European human rights system become more child rights friendly.

Notes

[1] Since first undertaking this analysis, I have had the opportunity to see the excellent work of Trond Helland and Ragnhild Hollekim (2023), which undertakes a similar analysis. This article is worth reading in conjunction with this chapter.

[2] Children's rights in child protection do not necessarily conflict with parental rights – for example, where the state has removed a child from their family prematurely, a recognition

of a parental right can also benefit the child. However, this will not necessarily be the case, and they should nevertheless be treated as separate concerns.
3   For further on this, see 'General findings' section in this chapter.
4   This section refers to the general analysis of all materials relating to the CRC, General Comments and Concluding Observations. The different sources will be considered separately further in this chapter.
5   To March 2023.
6   Olsson v Sweden (No 2) (Appl. No. 13441/87) 27.11.1992 (Ch), partly dissenting opinion of Judge Pettiti joined by Judges Matscher and Russo.
7   For example, in Bajrami v Albania (Appl. No. 35853/04) 12.12.2006 (Ch), the Court mentioned that Albania had not yet implemented the CRC; while in Burghartz v Switzerland (Appl. No. 16213/90) 22.02.1994 (Ch), it was noted that the CRC does not have any explicit provisions which relate to the naming of individuals (the subject of the case).

References

ABC v Latvia (no. 30808/11) [2016] ECtHR (31 March).
Abdi Ibrahim v Norway [GC] (no. 15379/16) [2021] ECtHR (10 December).
Appell, A.R. and Boyer, B.A. (1995) 'Parental rights vs. best interests of the child: A false dichotomy in the context of adoption', *Duke Journal of Gender Law and Policy*, 2(1): 63–84.
Bajrami v Albania (no. 35853/04) [2006] ECtHR (12 December).
Burghartz v Switzerland (no. 16213/90) [1994] ECtHR (22 February).
Charlesworth, H., Chinkin, C. and Wright, S. (1991) 'Feminist approaches to international law', *American Journal of International Law*, 85: 613–636.
Emonet and Others v Switzerland (no. 39051/03) [2007] ECtHR (13 December).
Eskinazi and Chelouche v Turkey (no. 14600/05) [2005] ECtHR (6 December).
Fenton-Glynn, C. (2019) 'Children, parents and the European Court of Human Rights', *European Human Rights Law Review*, 6: 643–653.
Ferrari v Romania (no. 1714/10) [2015] ECtHR (28 April).
Helland, T. and Hollekim, R. (2023) 'The Convention on the Rights of the Child's imprint on judgments from the European Court of Human Rights: A negligible footprint?', *Nordic Journal of Human Rights*, 41(2): 213–233.
Johansen v Norway [GC] (no. 17383/90) [1996] ECtHR (27 June).
KK and Others v Denmark (no. 25212/21) [2022] ECtHR (6 December).
Neulinger and Shuruk v Switzerland (no. 41615/07) [2010] ECtHR (6 July).
Olsson v Sweden (No. 2) (no. 13441/87) [1992] ECtHR (27 November).
Paradiso and Campanelli v Italy [GC] (no. 25358/12) [2017] ECtHR (24 January).
Söderman v Sweden (no. 5786/08) [2013] ECtHR (12 November).
Sormunen, M. (2020) 'Understanding the best interests of the child as a procedural obligation', *Human Rights Law Review*, 20(4): 745–768.
Strand Lobben and Others v Norway [GC] (no. 37283/13) [2019] ECtHR (10 September).

Teitgen, P. (1975) 'Rapporteur of the Committee on Legal and Administrative Questions, Consultative Assembly', *Collected Edition of the Travaux Preparatoires*, Martinus Nijhoff.

Z v the United Kingdom (no. 29392/95) [2001] ECtHR (10 May).

Zamperini, R. (2024) 'Establishing parenthood through adoption and surrogacy: A test case for the ECtHR use of the best interests of the child principle', *Family and Law*.

15

The European Court of Human Rights: an untapped source for advancing child rights?

Hege Stein Helland, Marit Skivenes and Siri Gloppen

Introduction

Child protection systems sit at the intersection of family autonomy, state responsibility and children's rights – a tension amplified by international human rights litigation. This concluding chapter synthesises findings from an interdisciplinary exploration of how the European Court of Human Rights (ECtHR) shapes child protection policies, with Norway's contested system as a focal point. Through legal, sociological and political lenses, the authors interrogate the ECtHR's evolving jurisprudence and its implications for children's rights in an era of growing transnational advocacy and backlash.

The book chapters expand our knowledge about the vertical and horizontal influences of supranational human rights decision-making and litigation in matters concerning children and the family. The ECtHR is an undisputed authority in the development of human rights principles and the monitoring of states' enforcement of citizens' human rights, and its decisions have repercussions for the practice of member states beyond individual cases (Helfer and Voeten, 2014; Zysset, 2018). But there is a lack of knowledge about the ECtHR's decision-making and its role and functioning in relation to its surroundings in the areas of child protection and children's rights. For example, what are the top-down effects of the ECtHR's judgments: Are the principles developed by the ECtHR implemented in domestic legal systems, and what are the social and political implications at a national and transnational level? Through the study of the Court's jurisprudence, and particularly cases concerning Article 8 (right to family life) and the judgments concerning Norway, we dig into the potential repercussions these have or could have for Norway and other member states' activities and for children's rights in general. The Grand Chamber Strand Lobben and Others v Norway judgment (2019) serves as a pivotal case study. This Grand Chamber ruling, which found Norway in violation of Article 8, solicited the wave of litigation against the Norwegian model of child protection. While critics of the child protection system hailed the decision as validation of systemic flaws, domestic authorities faced a paradox: reforms aimed at complying with ECtHR rulings led to a sharp decline in care orders, adoptions and child protection services (Skivenes, 2023; Helland, Chapter 5), raising concerns that children's welfare was being subordinated to parental rights. By 2024, the Norwegian Ombudsperson for Children warned that misinterpretations of Strasbourg's judgments risked destabilising the child-centric ethos enshrined in national law (Children´s Ombudsperson, 2024).

The book situates these developments within broader debates about legitimacy and coherence in human rights frameworks. Tensions arise from conflicting interpretations of the 'best interests of the child' principle by the ECtHR and the UN Committee on the Rights of the Child (CRC Committee). Such inconsistencies leave states grappling with incompatible obligations, as seen in Norway's struggle to align its commitments to the Constitution and the UN Convention on the Rights of the Child (CRC) with ECtHR mandates. A striking theme is the ECtHR's role as a site of ideological contestation. Third-party interventions (amicus curiae), particularly those from conservative governments and advocacy groups, may be seen as exploiting the Court's 'margin of appreciation' (MoA) doctrine to advance agendas that oppose state intervention in family life. These actors frame Nordic child protection systems and the welfare state more broadly as threats to parental rights, often conflating critiques with resistance to gender equality and LGBTQIA+ rights. The discussion reveals how Norway's cases attracted unprecedented geo-political attention, with member states leveraging Strasbourg's platform to assert divergent family policy ideologies. According to the then state attorney Marius Emberland (2018), the process of selecting judges to sit on the Grand Chamber for the Strand Lobben (2019) case was carried out based on meticulously selected geo-political criteria to secure representation from states that have typically been found to vote in 'socio-culturally grouped' ways. Yet, the ECtHR's potential to advance children's rights remains underexploited. While the CRC increasingly informs the Court's jurisprudence, child protection cases – typically initiated by parents – rarely centre children's voices and rarely engage with children's rights in any substantive manner (Helland and Skivenes, in preparation). There are contributors who warn of stagnation and a backlash, driven by anti-liberal movements targeting the ECtHR's mechanisms.

Methodologically, the volume bridges gaps between legal scholarship and social sciences. Contributions from legal scholars, political scientists, philosophers, social workers and sociologists discuss the ECtHR's opaque and discretionary decision-making processes, the implications of the ECtHR's jurisprudence, and its relationship and role in relation to the broader society and other human rights institutions. Learning more about the activities and characteristics of the ECtHR by posing questions such as how the ECtHR employs the doctrine of the 'margin of appreciation', and how the rights of children are represented and subsequently balanced and interpreted in relation to other human rights treaties such as the CRC as well as the rights of parents, the state and the family unit, has contributed with valuable insight into the ECtHR's operations. This interdisciplinary approach, which also includes jurists with professional experience from the ECtHR proceedings, offers critical insights for policy makers and advocates navigating the complex interplay between international law and domestic child protection. By examining Norway's experience, the book underscores broader lessons for European states: sustaining legitimate child protection systems requires reconciling international human rights norms with democratic accountability, while ensuring that child rights are neither overlooked nor instrumentalised in ideological battles.

Although the driver for the questions posed in this book has been the critique of the Norwegian child protection system and the protection of children's rights, drawing on the case of Norway provides insights into broader themes concerning child protection, welfare state and the role of the ECtHR. As such, the book has relevance for a wider European audience and for readers from different professional fields. Readers from states with similar child protection systems to the Norwegian, 'family-service' and 'child rights oriented' (Burns et al, 2017; Berrick et al, 2023), will have a learning interest in this edited volume, and so will those interested in the ECtHR's role and functions. The book is anchored in the political science tradition, but its interdisciplinary approach is a key strength as it provides varied perspectives to guide the discussions addressed in the book.

The structure of this chapter is as follows: in the next section, the judgment against Norway is discussed. Thereafter, the legitimacy of ECtHR as a human rights instrument is examined, followed by an exploration of third-party interventions and a discussion of the ECtHR as a vehicle for child rights. The chapter concludes with an outline of future research.

The implications of European Court of Human Rights judgments for child protection and child rights

Several of the Nordic countries have, at different times, been under the scrutiny of the ECtHR, which have led to pervasive systemic changes (Helland, Chapter 5; Sandberg, Chapter 4), with lasting effects on how the mandate of child protection is interpreted in legislation and practice, such as in Finland (see Huhtanen and Pösö, Chapter 3). For Norwegian child protection, the ECtHR judgments have had a strong impact. The last ten years (2015–2025) marks a unprecedented high number of judgments where Norway is found to violate Article 8. In all child protection systems, frontline staff or the courts are in varying intensity criticised for their interventions, or lack of interventions (Gilbert et al, 2011; Burns et al, 2017; Berrick et al, 2023). This part of the public sector is said to be damned if they do and damned if they don't. At the same time, subjecting state institutions to the critical observation of citizens and independent authorities is necessary for a well-functioning democratic state (Habermas et al, 1974), as it enables the correction and adjustment of illegitimate or inefficient practices, and holds states accountable (Bessette, 2001). As such, states are expected to be responsive to critique to maintain democratic legitimacy and accountability (Gloppen, 2008). As both Helland and Sandberg demonstrate in their analysis, the Norwegian state initiated a range of actions to address the critique from the ECtHR, and the judgments also had immediate effects on domestic decision-making practices. Several of which have been found to improve the quality of decision-making and to change incorrect practices. However, rapid changes in child protection provisions have been a cause for concern. Between 2017 and 2021, the number of care orders dropped dramatically (Skivenes, 2023; Helland, Chapter 5). Helland (Chapter 5) asks whether domestic child protection authorities will achieve a state of equilibrium in their practice over time, as the judgments seem to have thrown the practice field for a loop. The Grand Chamber judgments Strand Lobben and Others (2019) and Abdi Ibrahim (2021) have been said to represent a turning point for children's rights in the ECtHR, as the children were not at the centre of the decision and the rights of parents were put above those of the child (Fenton-Glynn, 2021; Do Vale Alves, 2023). Researchers and jurists from the Ombudsperson for Children and the Norwegian Human Rights Institute expressed concern that the judgments from the ECtHR have led to a setback for Norwegian child protection, pushing towards a more restrictive practice at the expense of children's well-being (Nordmoen and Kvalø, 2023; Skivenes, 2023). A main challenge for the ECtHR and its member states is that little attention is given to children's right to a fair trial and to have their voices heard and given weight in decision-making. A study of all child protection judgments by the ECtHR (Helland and Skivenes, in preparation) reveals that the child's opinion is often invisible. The lack of children's voices is also criticised by Kriz and Reimer (Chapter 6), as they observe that children's voices in the analysed judgments are often overlooked. They remind the reader of the national obligations of the Norwegian government to respect the Constitution and the CRC on equal grounds as the judgments from the ECtHR. Similar sentiments are echoed by Helland (Chapter 5) and by Sandberg (Chapter 4) in their analyses of the effects of the judgments on Norwegian courts and jurisprudence.

The ECtHR appears to have reached a saturation point regarding Norwegian child protection in 2024. Of the cases originating after the Strand Lobben complaint, the Court has dismissed 49 Norwegian applications as inadmissible on merit or on procedural grounds (Emberland, Chapter 2).

Twenty of them were dismissed in 2024. The explanation for this remains to be discovered. According to Borud and Kvalø (2024), jurists at the Norwegian Human Rights Institution, this development is due to the ECtHR's satisfaction with the way Norwegian authorities balance the interests of the child with those of their parents and the reunification goal in the newer cases. They also highlight that the ECtHR places greater emphasis on the child's views in these cases than before, justifying its decisions with reference to the particular circumstances of the concerned parties. Whether this indicates that the ECtHR finds the adjusted national approach to balancing the rights and interest of children and their parents to be compatible with the ECHR, and whether domestic decision-makers have found some form of equilibrium in their adherence to the ECtHR with their mandated and autonomous discretion to make decisions in the best interest of the child, remains to be seen.

The parent focus in the European Court of Human Rights

The ECtHR has wide and strong discretionary power (Skivenes and Søvig, 2016). Sandberg (Chapter 4) questions the Court's ability or willingness to recognise the child's independent interests from those of their parents. In her analysis of the ECtHR's interpretation of the best interest of the child and the weighing of their interests with those of their parents, she identifies an inconsistency in the interpretation of the guiding norm on the best interest of the child at the transnational level. Such inconsistencies have been previously found in child protection cases by human rights lawyer Professor O´Mahony (2019). Similar concerns are raised by Sutherland (Chapter 8) as she examines how rights are articulated in the European Convention on Human Rights (ECHR) and the CRC. Her findings show that it can be problematic for states that are mandated to intervene in child protection situations, as it is 'unclear about what is required of them, and it may be impossible for them to comply with all of the norms simultaneously' (Sutherland, Chapter 8). The priority accorded to the child's best interests in the child protection context when weighed against the rights and interests of others (particularly the biological parents) is the topic of Sutherland's study. Through an examination of how the ECtHR and the CRC Committee interpret and amplify relevant human rights norms, she evaluates whether states are being sent mixed messages and how this might be addressed. As Sutherland highlights in her chapter, states are currently receiving mixed messages from the ECtHR and the CRC Committee regarding the priority to be accorded to the child's best interests when they conflict with parental rights and interests. She points out that such a lack of coherence is not only undesirable from a human rights perspective, but it also puts the states party to the ECHR and CRC in a challenging position. Incoherent human rights norms hinder the practical implementation of Convention rights for governments seeking to comply with their human rights obligations and undermine the concept of legal certainty. A primary concern is that this leads to an undercommunication of children's rights (Sutherland, Chapter 8; Sandberg, Chapter 4).

The analysis of the judges' reasoning in the Grand Chamber Strand Lobben judgment by Archard and Skivenes (Chapter 13) shows how arguments about children as parents' property and the strength of biological bonds prevail. The child's best interests and a broader concept of family, which includes foster families, are given less regard by the majority in this ruling. However, the fact that the Grand Chamber judgment was not unanimous is insufficiently emphasised. As Archard and Skivenes (Chapter 13) show, the judges in the minority question both the one-sided approach to custody for children that the majority expresses, and the lack of clarity of how principles are interpreted.

The broad nature of the ECHR nonetheless allows for children's rights to be read into the ECHR if we consider the Court's positive obligations to facilitate individuals' achievements of rights, the 'living instrument doctrine' and the margin of appreciation. If the Court is willing to exercise its discretion and adapt the provisions of the ECHR to incorporate children's needs and rights, the CRC can serve as an interpretative tool in its adjudication. This would be in line with the evolving nature of the ECHR, and an ambition to maintain social and legal relevance in today's world (Kilkelly, 1999).

Third-party interventions and contestation of children's rights and the Nordic model

Input from third-party intervenors has been highlighted as an important mechanism to promote dialogue between the ECtHR and civil society to anchor the human rights development more strongly in the member countries and thus facilitate broader democratic legitimacy (Council of Europe, 2018; Pastor, 2021). Emberland (Chapter 2), Falch-Eriksen (Chapter 10) and Cichowski and Chrun (Chapter 11) all address third-party interventions, or amicus curiae, before the ECtHR. Well-intended and well-advised amicus curiae briefs can be a valuable source of information and insights for the Court's decisions. There is potential to nudge the Court towards increased engagement with children's rights by raising their awareness of relevant child rights instruments and principles (Lawson et al, 2023). However, amicus curiae can also be used to counter child rights advancement by actors with ulterior motives. Falch-Eriksen (Chapter 10) explores this issue by linking it to the vulnerability of the doctrine of MoA to judicial lobbying by third-party intervenors. Through a critical exploration of legal theory, he discusses how although the ECtHR uses the MoA to balance national diversity with cohesive human rights jurisprudence (Arai-Takahashi, 2002), the MoA's flexibility can be exploited by 'bad amici' or 'bad friends of the court', that seeks to influence court decisions to align with interests that do not align with a human rights ethos. Falch-Eriksen raises the concern that, without a solid theoretical foundation, the ECtHR risks inconsistency in its decisions due to the influence of bad amici and calls for greater transparency in third-party interventions, as well as a conscientious approach to human rights standards, to maintain the court's legitimacy. He urges the ECtHR to adopt an integrated theoretical approach to the MoA, ensuring decisions align with justice and rationality while resisting manipulation by interest groups.

The Norwegian cases before the ECtHR have, as mentioned, attracted unprecedented attention by third-party interveners. Specifically regarding the attention from other Council of Europe member states. Emberland writes 'the child welfare cases against Norway attract home state intervention on an unprecedented scale' (Chapter 2). This suggests that there is something about child protection and the Norwegian or Nordic approach to organising child protection or enforcing children's rights that is evoking political urgency among other states that have no direct connection to the cases themselves. Cichowski and Chrun (Chapter 11) argue that third-party activity by other European governments appears motivated by an interest in asserting their own child rights preferences and communicating their stance on such policy discussions to the international audience. This indicates that the normative conflict lines concerning family policies and children's rights and interests, which are found between different groups and states, have also made their way to the ECtHR, where children's rights are currently being contested by governments with competing interests and policy agendas. Based on an analysis of amicus briefs in the Norwegian cases, Cichowski and Chrun identify two discourses: on the one hand, those seeking to influence the interpretation and development of human rights argue for greater prioritising of child's rights, and on the other hand, those that argue for greater recognition of the rights of the biological parents and the importance of biological family reunification.

These sentiments are visible in Neil Datta's (Chapter 9) analysis of interest and advocacy groups submitting briefs, for whom the ECtHR has also become a popular site for contestation of child rights. According to Datta, the contestation around child protective services based on Nordic models has increased and has moved into the ECtHR, where anti-liberal and anti-gender actors have specialised in the contestation of child rights and child protection. This type of advocacy presents a series of opportunities for conservative actors to leverage to meet their objectives and agendas. It is thus targeted by conservative actors that want to influence international norms concerning children's rights and parental rights. In his analysis, Datta showcases how opposition to Nordic child protection models is attractive as it often serves additional objectives, such as limiting state intervention in family life and opposing human rights claims of sexual and gender minorities. Datta echoes Falch-Eriksen's concern that these actors utilise democratic processes in a manner that undermines the rule of law and human rights principles.

The European Court of Human Rights as a vehicle for human rights development: also for children?

The ECtHR is one of the most influential supranational courts in the world, and although it does not have any obligations towards the CRC, it can still play a significant role in promoting children's rights. The ECtHR has the authority to interpret and uphold human rights and should, at a minimum, ensure that the rights of children under the ECHR are protected equally to those of adults. Several of the chapters in this volume have addressed the decision-making of the ECtHR. The book sheds light on the ECtHR proceedings and exercise of discretion in decisions concerning children and child protection.

Children's rights continue to be at the centre of contestation and controversy across Europe. This book has illustrated how the CRC is an increasingly important source of guidance for the ECtHR in cases concerning children (Fenton-Glynn, Chapter 14). There is potential in the Court's jurisprudence for advancing children's rights in areas such as identity development (Marshall, Chapter 12) and protecting them from discrimination (Reimer et al, Chapter 7). However, although the Court has used its discretion to accord rights to children and afford their protection in some areas of the Convention, its engagement with children's rights is still largely superficial or limited, as illustrated by several of the contributions in this book. As Sandberg (Chapter 4) notes, child protection cases are, in all essence, brought to the ECtHR by parents, causing the rights and interests of the child to not feature prominently. The authors highlight a lack of progress in the substantial engagement with children's rights (Fenton-Glynn, Chapter 14) and concerns about the standstill and potential backlash against children's rights in child protection matters (Huhtanen and Pösö, Chapter 3; Sandberg, Chapter 4; Helland, Chapter 5; Sutherland, Chapter 8).

As illustrated by the attention from third-party interveners (Emberland, Chapter 2; Cichowski and Chrun, Chapter 11) and transnational civil society organisations engagement in the contestation of children's rights and the 'Nordic model' of child protection (Datta, Chapter 9), it is clear that there are ideological and normative differences among different states and societal groups about the boundaries between the family and the state's responsibility for children. The lack of agreement among the judges in Strand Lobben and Others also add to this picture, in that the minority not only disagreed with the majority's decision to depart from its previous position on the paramountcy of children's best interests when weighed against the interests of others but criticised them for failing to consider the CRC in their assessment (Sutherland, Chapter 8; Archard and Skivenes, Chapter 13).

This book has, moreover, shown how children's rights are challenged and used as leverage by those seeking to undermine human rights standards and challenge children's independent rights (Datta, Chapter 9). Neil Datta suggests that children's rights have become the new frontier in the worldwide anti-gender contestation and points out how anti-liberal and conservative engagement in the areas of children's protection has gone unnoticed for a long time. The potential exploitation of the ECtHR democratic mechanism to counter children's rights has also been highlighted as a potential threat to the advancement of human rights and child rights in particular (Falch-Eriksen, Chapter 10; Cichowski and Chrun, Chapter 11).

Future research

The book has expanded our knowledge of welfare states and international law, as well as child protection and human rights. There are, however, still some critical gaps in knowledge regarding the intersection of international human rights law, child protection systems and children's rights advocacy across Europe. We will highlight some of the gaps that have emerged from this book. The succession of cases brought against the Norwegian state – and the subsequent judgments that found a violation of Article 8 – have garnered substantial attention in the legal community, academia and the public sphere. However, we have not explored the conditions and mechanisms that gave rise to and facilitated the Norwegian cases being admitted by the ECtHR from the point of view of individual applications and grassroots mobilisation. The forces and opportunity structures that allowed and encouraged this scenario to occur remain largely under-researched.

Generally, there is a lack of transparency into the processes of the ECtHR, and there are knowledge gaps about the mechanisms by which the Court operates. While discretionary decisions are found at all stages of the Court process, aspects of their decision-making are largely hidden from the public in areas such as admissibility decisions, assessments relating to third-party interventions and how the Court employs the doctrine of the 'margin of appreciation'. The inner workings of the Court may as such be described as a black box. Although the contributions in this book have shed light on the discretionary assessments of the Court in relation to how children are represented and how their rights and interests are understood and interpreted in relation to other stakeholders and to other human rights instruments, we urge others to pose questions about the Court's exercise of discretion in aspects that are yet to be addressed. Such as how the Court assesses which friends of the court are allowed to intervene in a case and what information to include in the judgments, how cases are filtered in the first instances when admissibility decisions are made on the merits rather than procedural grounds in order to address these important blind spots in the Court's inner workings.

The doctrine of the margin of appreciation appears to have some vulnerabilities, and analyses of how third-party interventions may potentially exploit the doctrine to influence ECtHR decisions are worth looking into. Hereunder, to explore strategies to safeguard against manipulation. This brings us over to the topic of third-party interventions in child protection cases, in particular, but also in general. Studies of the role of amicus curiae briefs in shaping ECtHR judgments are necessary and important to follow up on, and this should include an evaluation of their potential to advance or hinder, for example, child rights.

There is also a need to investigate how ECtHR rulings, particularly those of the Grand Chamber, such as the Strand Lobben and Abdi Ibrahim cases, have influenced child protection policies and practices in member states. One dimension is whether these rulings have led to practices where parental rights are prioritised over child rights and children's best interests. The inconsistencies between the ECtHR and CRC Committee in interpreting the 'best interests of the child' principle are opening an area of uncertainty about how states navigate conflicting obligations under different human rights frameworks. Following this, it will be essential to examine how member states strike a balance between children's rights and parental rights, as well as how this is addressed in international human rights law, particularly in the context of family law.

In relation to this, there is a need to know more about the role of children's rights to participation and to be part of, and have a say in, matters that concern them in the ECtHR and more broadly in the international human rights arena. An assessment of the extent to which children's perspectives are represented and considered in ECtHR child protection cases is well overdue. A key aspect of this should include an investigation into mechanisms to enhance their visibility and influence in judicial processes.

References

Abdi Ibrahim v Norway [GC] (no. 15379/16) [2021] ECtHR (10 December).
Arai-Takahashi, Y. (2002) *The Margin of Appreciation Doctrine and the Principle of Proportionality in the Jurisprudence of the ECHR*, Intersentia.
Berrick, J.D., Gilbert, N. and Skivenes, M. (eds) (2023) *Oxford Handbook of Child Protection Systems*, Oxford University Press.
Bessette, J.M. (2001) 'Accountability: Political', in N.J. Smelser and P.B. Baltes (eds), *International Encyclopedia of the Social & Behavioral Sciences*, Pergamon, pp 38–41.
Borud, P. and Kvalø, K.K. (2024) 'EMD og norsk barnevern: Flere frifinnelser enn domfellelser [ECHR and Norwegian child welfare: More acquittals than convictions]', *Fontene*. Available from: https://fontene.no/debatt/emd-og-norsk-barnevern-flere-frifinnelser-enn-domfellelser-6.47.1089728.a77bc97b26

Burns, K., Pösö, T. and Skivenes, M. (eds) (2017) *Child Welfare Removals by the State: A Cross-Country Analysis of Decision-Making Systems*, Oxford University Press.

Children's Ombudsperson (2024) 'Bekymring knyttet til store endringer på barnevernsfeltet og rapport om brudd på bistandsplikt [Concerns related to major changes in the child welfare field and report of violation of duty of assistance]'. Available from: https://www.barneombudet.no/vart-arbeid/brev-til-myndighetene/bekymring-knyttet-til-store-endringer-pa-barnevernsfeltet-og-rapport-om-brudd-pa-bistandsplikt

Council of Europe (2018) 'Copenhagen Declaration', para 40. Available from: https://www.echr.coe.int/Documents/Copenhagen_Declaration_ENG.pdf

Do Vale Alves, A. (2023) 'Children's religious identity in alternative care and adoption: The need to recentre the child's best interest in international human rights adjudication', *Human Rights Law Review*, 23(2): 1–22.

Emberland, M. (2018) 'Det norske barnevernet under lupen – del 3 [The Norwegian child welfare system under the microscope – part 3]', *Lov og Rett*, 57(10): 583–584.

Fenton-Glynn, C. (2021) *Children and the European Court of Human Rights*, Oxford University Press.

Gilbert, N., Parton, N. and Skivenes, M. (eds) (2011) *Child Protection Systems: International Trends and Orientations*, Oxford University Press.

Gloppen, S. (2008) 'Litigation as a strategy to hold governments accountable for implementing the right to health', *Health and Human Rights*, 10: 21–36.

Habermas, J., Lennox, S. and Lennox, F. (1974) 'The public sphere: An encyclopedia article (1964)', *New German Critique*, 3: 49–55.

Helfer, L.R. and Voeten, E. (2014) 'International courts as agents of legal change: Evidence from LGBT rights in Europe', *International Organization*, 68(1): 77–110.

Helland, H.S. and Skivenes, M. (in preparation) 'Fair trial for children in the ECtHR? An analysis of all child protection judgements from 1959–2022'. Unpublished manuscript.

Kilkelly, U. (1999) *The Child and the European Convention on Human Rights*, Ashgate/Dartmouth.

Lawson, D., Stalford, H. and Woodhouse, S. (2023) 'Promoting children's rights in the European Court of Human Rights: The role and potential of third-party interventions', *University of Liverpool, European Children's Rights Unit*. Available from: https://www.liverpool.ac.uk/media/livacuk/law/2-research/ecru/June,2023,-,Strategic,Litigation,-,ECRU.pdf

Nordmoen, M.L. and Kvalø, K. (2023) 'Barnevern i motsatt grøft? [Child welfare in the opposite ditch?]', *Fontene*. Available from: https://fontene.no/debatt/barnevern-i-motsatt-groft-6.47.938208.911e976930

O'Mahony, C. (2019) 'Child protection and the ECHR: Making sense of positive and procedural obligations', *The International Journal of Children's Rights*, 27(4): 660–693.

Pastor, E. (2021) 'Christian faith-based organizations as third-party interveners at the European Court of Human Rights', *BYU Law Review*, 46(5): 1329–1367.

Skivenes, M. (2023) 'Wrong direction for the Norwegian child protection?', *Centre for Research on Discretion and Paternalism*. Available from: https://discretion.w.uib.no/2023/04/04/concerns-about-changes-in-norwegian-child-protection/

Skivenes, M. and Søvig, K.H. (2016) 'Judicial discretion and the child's best interests: The European Court of Human Rights on adoptions in child protection cases', in E.E. Sutherland and L.-A. Barnes Macfarlane (eds), *Implementing Article 3 of the United Nations Convention on the Rights of the Child: Best Interests, Welfare and Well-being*, Cambridge University Press, pp 341–357.

Strand Lobben and Others v Norway [GC] (no. 37283/13) [2019] ECtHR (10 September).

Zysset, A. (2018) *The ECHR and Human Rights Theory: Reconciling the Moral and the Political Conceptions*, Routledge.

Index

References to figures appear in *italic* type; those in **bold** type refer to tables.
References to endnotes show both the page number and the note number (113n1).

A

Abdi Ibrahim v Norway 1, 30
  child's best interest 141
  ethnicity constructs 123, 124, 126–127
  implications for children's rights 263
  personal identity rights 219
  representation of children 106, 110
  third-party state intervention 33, 34, 200
abduction 120, 121, 123, 125, 126
  Hague Convention on Child Abduction 138, 140
abortion 159, 166, 168
activism *see* anti-gender activism
adoption 66, 92
  D.B. v United Kingdom 28–29
  and ethnic constructs 120
  R. and H. v United Kingdom 138
  Strand Lobben and Others v Norway 59, 138–139
  Strand Lobben group of cases 24, 30, 141
  see also custody allocation
Adoption Act, Finland 50–51
Advice on Individual Rights in Europe Centre (AIRE) 201–202, 204
advocacy groups 201–204, 266–267
  see also anti-gender activism
Agenda Europe 175n1
A.L. and Others v Norway 32, 109, 113n1, 120
Albania 258n7
Alliance Defending Freedom (ADF) 161, 168
Alliance Defending Freedom International (ADFI) 161–162, 169
  case interventions 163–164, 181, 202, 203, 204
  and Council of Europe (CoE) 168
  influence on international norms 166
  public awareness campaigns 164, 165
amicus curiae 180, 192, 193, 261
  annual increase 195, *196*
  bad amicus 181, 187–190, 266
    (*see also* inimicus curiae)
  interest and advocacy groups as 201–204
  state governments as 199–201
anti-gender activism 153–154, 156–158
  as blind spot 168–170
  ideological origins 158–160

key actors 160–163, 167–168
strategies 163–167
anti-trans activists 157
Armenia 32
A.S. v Norway 32, 122, 200–201
Associazione Italiana dei Magistrati per i Minorenni e per la Famiglia (AIMMF) 202
attachment argument 233, 236–237, 238
Aune v Norway 24
Austria 219–220
authoritative issuance of law 183–184

B

bad amicus 181, 187–190, 266
  see also inimicus curiae
Bajrami v Albania 258n7
balancing interests 233–234, 237–238
Barnevernet 1, 93, 153–156, 164–170, 200, 202–203
  activism against 156–158, 163–167
  as blind spot 168–170
  disinformation regarding 154–156
  third-party state intervention 200, 201
Bayatyan v Armenia 202
Belgium 34, 199, 222–223
best interest 68–71, 136, 253, 264–265
  and anti-gender activism 160
  Baby M 239
  balancing interests 233–234
  and cultural identity 219
  evolution of European Court thinking on 137–141, 147
  Strand Lobben and Others v Norway 59, 138–141, 236, 237, 238, 265, 267–268
  United Nations Convention on the Rights of the Child (CRC) 141–147, 147–148
birth family ties 218–220
B.J. and P.J. v Czech Republic 144
Bodnariu v Norway 34, 163, 164, 166
Bollywood films 155
Borud, P. and Kvalø, K.K. 264
Bosnia and Herzegovina 33
Bulgaria 34, 156, 199, 201, 225n1

C

Canon, B.C. and Johnson, C.A. 76, 77, 80
care 214
  exclusive 230

272

Index

care orders
  Finland 47, **48**, 49, 50, 51–55
  Norway 59, 89, 92, 139, 219, 235–236, 263
Castbergs Act, Norway 232
change
  practical 89
  theory of 90
child as object **107**, 110–111
child as subject 106–110, 111, 112
Child Equality Perspective (CEP) 98–99, 105, 111
Child Flourishing Index **8–9**
  survival indicators 17n8
child health measures 232
child protection
  demonstrations against 6
  dilemma of 135
  and ECtHR member states 9–11, **12**
  European Court of Human Rights (ECtHR)'s role and function 260–269
  evolution of European Court thinking on 137–141
  protests against *see* anti-gender activism
child protection agencies (CWS)
  judicial implementation of ECtHR judgements 76–78, 90–93
    adjustments to ECtHR judgements 87–89
    interpretation of ECtHR judgements 82–87
    reception of ECtHR judgements 82, 89–90
    research limitations 93
    research methods 80–81
Child Protection Boards, Norway 63, 65
child protection judgements 3
  Article 8 (ECHR) judgements **7**
  against Finland 45–49
    implications 49–55
  guidance from UN Committee on the Rights of the Child 254–257
  list of cases 35–42
  against Nordic countries **46**
  against Norway 1, 6, 16n1, 71–72, 75 (*see also* Strand Lobben and Others v Norway; Strand Lobben group of cases)
  and anti-gender activism 163–164
  and children's rights 267–268
  ethnicity constructs *see* ethnicity constructs
  implications for child protection and child rights 262–264
  judicial implementation *see* child protection agencies (CWS): judicial implementation of ECtHR judgements
  list of cases 35–39

overview **101–104**
parental focus 264–265
representation of children *see* children's representation
reunification goal *see* reunification goal
third-party interventions **197–198**, 265–267
references to United Nations Convention on the Rights of the Child (CRC) 247–250
  CRC Articles used in decisions **252**
  subject areas 250–254
summary by state **28**
child protection systems (CPS) 262–263
  Norway (*see also* Barnevernet)
    attacks on 1–2, 25
    and children's participation rights 99
  typology 11
child rights 3–6
  European Court of Human Rights (ECtHR)'s role and function 260–269
  see also children's participation rights; United Nations Convention on the Rights of the Child (CRC)
Child Welfare Act, Finland 46, 47, 49–50, 51, 53, 54
Child Welfare Act, Norway 59, 62, 65, 79, 99
Child Welfare Tribunals 99
children
  personal identity
    right to 211–212, 216–223, 224–225
    and social conditions 223–224
  self-esteem 214
children's participation rights 99, 100, 254
children's representation 98
  child as object **107**, 110–111
  child as subject 106–110, 111, 112
  prior literature 100
  research methods 100–105
  study limitations 112
children's rights activism *see* anti-gender activism
child's best interest 68–71, 136, 253, 264–265
  and anti-gender activism 160
  Baby M 239
  balancing interests 233–234
  and cultural identity 219
  evolution of European Court thinking on 137–141, 147
  Strand Lobben and Others v Norway 59, 138–141, 236, 237, 238, 265, 267–268
  United Nations Convention on the Rights of the Child (CRC) 141–147, 147–148
child's own view 69
Christian church 129n6

273

Christian Right in Europe, The
 (ed. Mascolo) 154, 167
Christianity 122, 124, 126–127,
 129n7, 203
CitizenGo 162, 168, 169
clothing 216, 222–223
commitment-identity argument 232–233
Committee of Ministers of the Council of
 Europe (CM) 25, 79
 Rule 4 §1 42n2
communication 77, 84
competency argument 233, 238
comprehensive sexuality education
 (CSE) 159, 164
Concluding Observation, CRC
 Committee 142–143, 256–257
contact 61, 62, 140
Cossey v the UK 216
Costa Rica 256
Council of Europe (CoE) 3, 16n3,
 45, 168
 Parliamentary Assembly of the Council
 of Europe (PACE) 166–167, 169
Croatia 253–254
cultural identity 218–220
culture 87–88, 118, 121
custody allocation 230–231, 240
 Baby M 239
 considerations underpinning 231–234
 Strand Lobben and Others v
 Norway 235–239
 see also adoption
Cyprus 34
Czech Republic 32, 33, 34, 144, 155,
 199, 200

D

Days for General Discussion (DGDs),
 CRC Committee 146–147
D.B. v United Kingdom 28–29
de facto family life 236–237, 238
democracy 223
 and law 186
democratic legitimacy 185
Denmark 33, 137, 199, 200, 256
dignity *see* human dignity;
 individual dignity
discourse theory 185–186
 and bad amici actors 188–189
disinformation 154–156
 see also misinformation
Dobbs v Jackson Women's Health
 Organization 168
domestic implementation, ECtHR
 judgements *see* child protection
 agencies (CWS): judicial
 implementation of ECtHR
 judgements

domestic signalling 77–78, 84–85, 90, 92
domestic violence 30

E

education *see* comprehensive sexuality
 education (CSE); homeschooling;
 schools; sex education
E.M. and Others v Norway 32, 110,
 113n1, 122
E.M. and T.A. v Norway 32
Emberland, M. 261
enemy of the court *see* bad amicus;
 inimicus curiae
England 232
ethnic separation 123–124
ethnicity 116, 118
ethnicity constructs
 case histories 119–125, 127–128
 European Court of Human Rights
 (ECtHR) stance 125–127, 128
 methodology and data material
 118–119
 study limitations 128–129
European Centre for Law and Justice
 (ECLJ) 162–163, 167, 168, 169
European Convention on Human Rights
 (ECHR) 135–136, 136–137
 Article 1 5, 211
 Article 2 214–215
 Article 3 215
 Article 8 3–4, 55n1, 60, 214, 215, 231,
 246, 253
 and Finish child protection 47–49
 violations against 1, 3, 24, 27, 30, 98,
 140, 141, 216
 Article 9 214, 222–223
 Article 10 214
 Article 14 214
 Article 36 25, 31
 Finnish ratification 45
 Nordic countries **46**
 relationship between United Nations
 Convention on the Rights of the Child
 (CRC) and 244–245, 246–247
European Court of Human Rights
 Database (ECHRdb) 194, 204
European Court of Human Rights
 (ECtHR) 178
 child protection judgements *see* child
 protection judgements
 and child rights 3–6
 evolution of thinking on child
 protection 137–141
 guidance from UN Committee on the
 Rights of the Child 254–257
 member states and child protection
 9–11, **12**
 references to United Nations Convention on
 the Rights of the Child (CRC) 247–250

CRC Articles used in decisions **252**
  subject areas 250–254
  role and function in relation to child protection 260–269
exclusive care 230
extremist groups 168

F

family 203, 211, 230
  de facto family life 236–237, 238
  see also birth family ties
family life, right to 67–68
  see also European Convention on Human Rights (ECHR): Article 8
family reunification 219
  Finland 47, 49, 50, 51–52
  reunification goal 60–61
    changes in practice 63–65
    and children's rights 65–69
    and child's best interest 70–71
    Supreme Court's interpretation and adaptation 61–63
    Strand Lobben and Others v Norway 60–61, 237–238
fathers' rights groups 157
Fenton-Glynn, C. 5
F.G. v Sweden 202–203
fiduciary argument 234, 237
Finland
  Adoption Act 50–51
  Child Welfare Act 46, 47, 49–50, 51, 53, 54
  disinformation 155
  ECtHR child protection judgements 45–49
    implications 49–55
  European Convention on Human Rights (ECHR) 45
  National Child Strategy Committee report 52–53
  Supreme Administrative Court 51–52
  United Nations Convention on the Rights of the Child (CRC) 45
France 217–218
friends of the court *see* amicus curiae
F.Z. v Norway 163

G

Garmo, C. 165
gender *see* anti-gender activism
gender identity 215–216
General Comments (GCs), CRC Committee 144–146, 254, **255**
Germany 30
Ghiletchi, V. 167
Godelli v Italy 218
Goodwin and I v the UK 216
G.T.B. v Spain 220–221

H

Habermas, J. 186
Hague Convention on Child Abduction 138, 140
Hart, H.L.A. 182
hate groups 168
Haugen, H.M. 167
headscarves / veils 216, 222–223
health 66–67, 72n6
health measures 232
Helland, H.S. 100
Hernehult v Norway 106, 110, 122, 126
Herring, J. 214
H.K. v Finland **48**, 49
home state intervention 31–32
homeschooling 158, 159, 161, 162–163
Honneth, A. 112, 214
HUDOC database 26, 194, 247
human dignity 159–160
  see also individual dignity
Human Dignity Alliance 175–176n10
'human' in human rights law 213–214
Human Rights Council 166
Hungary 158

I

identity *see* cultural identity; gender identity; personal identity
identity documents 220–201
India 256
individual dignity 186, 188, 189
  see also human dignity
inimicus curiae 168, 180
  see also bad amicus
interest groups 201–204, 266–267
  see also anti-gender activism
Islamic headscarves / veils 216, 222–223
Italy 33, 199, 218, 256

J

Jäggi v Switzerland 218
Jansen v Norway 24, 113n1, 123, 125–126
Johansen v Norway 16n1, 24, 138, 253
judicial implementation *see* street-level judicial implementation
judicial lobbying *see* amicus curiae; anti-gender activism; inimicus curiae; mobilised interest; third-party interventions

K

K. and T. v Finland 47, **48**, 49
K.A. v Finland **48**, 49
K.E. and A.K. v Norway 113n1, 120, 163
Kelsen, H. 183
Kilic v Austria 219–220
KK and Others v Denmark 256

knowledge of origins 217–218
Kristen Koalisjon Norge (KKN) 167, 169

L

L v Sweden 137
Lancet Child Flourishing Index **8–9**
  survival indicators 17n8
language 116, 122
Latvia 29–30, 34
law and democracy, interconnectedness between 186
League of Nations Geneva Declaration 246
legal positivism 182–184
  and bad amici actors 187–188
legal rules as commands 184
Lewin, K. 90
libertarians 158
Lithuania 221–222
'living together' 223–224
Løvlie, A.G. and Skivenes, M. 117

M

M and M v Croatia 253–254
Macate v Lithuania 221–222
margin of appreciation (MoA) 4, 178–180, 189–190, 261, 265–266
  and discourse theory 185–186, 188–189
  and legal positivism 182–184, 187–188
  Mikyas and Others v Belgium 222
M.C. v Bulgaria 225n1
McEwan-Strand, A. and Skivenes, M. 100
Mexico 256
M.F. v Norway 111, 113n1
Michálková, E. 200
migration 3
Mikyas and Others v Belgium 222–223
minoritised ethnic (ME) individuals 116
minoritised groups 117
misinformation 203
  see also disinformation
M.L. v Norway 24
Mnookin, R. 136
mobilised interest
  conceptual research approach 193–194
  data and research methods 194
  Strand Lobben and Others v Norway 195–205
    interest and advocacy groups as amicus curiae 201–204
    state governments as amicus curiae 199–201
  see also amicus curiae; anti-gender activism; third-party interventions
Mohamed Hasan v Norway 24
  domestic violence 30
  ethnicity constructs 121, 123
  representation of children 106, 110, 112
morality 182–183, 187–188
Ms Chatterjee vs Norway (film) 155
Mullen, R. 167, 175–176n10

N

National Child Strategy Committee report, Finland 52–53
Netherlands 28
Neulinger and Shuruk v Switzerland 138, 253
neutrality 222–223
Nielsen v Denmark 137
Nordic Observatory for Digital Media and Information Disorder (NORDIS) 154–155
North Atlantic Treaty Organization (NATO) 156
Norway
  Castbergs Act 232
  Child Protection Boards 63, 65
  child protection system (CPS) 1–2, 25 (see also Barnevernet)
  Child Welfare Act 59, 62, 65, 79, 99
  children's participation rights 99
  ECtHR child protection judgements 1, 6, 16n1, 71–72, 75 (see also Strand Lobben and Others v Norway; Strand Lobben group of cases)
  and anti-gender activism 163–164
  and children's rights 267–268
  ethnicity constructs see ethnicity constructs
  implications for child protection and child rights 262–264
  judicial implementation see street-level judicial implementation
  list of cases 35–39
  overview **101–104**
  parental focus 264–265
  representation of children see representation of children
  reunification goal see reunification goal
  third-party interventions **197–198**, 265–267
  minoritised ethnic (ME) individuals 117
  mobilised interest case study see Strand Lobben group of cases: mobilised interest
Norwegian Human Rights Institution 153

O

object, child as **107**, 110–111
Odièvre v France 217–218
Oland, C. 201
Olsson v Sweden 137, 248
Optional Protocol to the Convention on the Rights of the Child on a Communications Procedure (OPIC) 143–144

Ordo Iuris 25, 161, 168, 169, 205n6
  activism against Nordic child protection systems 165–166
  case intervention 163–164, 202, 203, 204
  influence on international norms 166, 167
  public awareness campaigns 164–165
origins, knowledge of 217–218
othering 123, 127, 128

P

Paradiso and Campanelli v Italy 256
parentage, knowledge of 217–218
parental contact 61, 62, 140
parental interests 264–265
parental rights 240n1, 246, 257–258n2
parenthood 230, 234, 240
  dual interest theory 234
Parliamentary Assembly of the Council of Europe (PACE) 166–167, 169
participation rights 99, 100, 254
Pastor, E.R. 161
Pedersen and Others v Norway 112, 120
personal identity, right to 214–216
  children 211–212, 216–223, 224–225
  and social conditions 223–224
  in human rights law 213–214
pluralism 223
Poland 32, 33, 122, 155, 165, 200–201
Political Network of Values 160
positivism, legal 182–184
  and bad amici actors 187–188
practical change 89
private life, right to *see* European Convention on Human Rights (ECHR): Article 8
procedures 88–89
prominence of rights 185–186
property argument 232, 236, 238
public awareness campaigns 164–165
public interests 231–232

Q

qualified rights 4, 215

R

R. and H. v United Kingdom 138
R. v Finland **48**, 49
rational discourse 185
Raz, J. 184
recognition theory 214
religion 124, 126–127, 141, 161, 200, 216, 219
  see also Christianity
religious symbols 222–223
representation of children 98
  child as object **107**, 110–111
  child as subject 106–110, 111, 112
  prior literature 100
  research methods 100–105
  study limitations 112
Restoring the Natural Order (Datta) 160
reunification goal 60–61
  changes in practice 63–65
  and children's rights 65–69
  and child's best interest 70–71
  Supreme Court's interpretation and adaptation 61–63
rights, prominence of 185–186
R.M. v Latvia 29–30
R.O. v Norway 163
Roma people 123, 125–126
Romania 155
rule of law 6–9
Russia 34, 136, 156, 158
Ruzzo, C. 168

S

schools 222–223
  see also comprehensive sexuality education (CSE); sex education
self-confidence 214
separation thesis 182–183
sex education 221–222
  see also comprehensive sexuality education (CSE)
sexual orientation 215–216, 221–222
signalling 77–78, 84–85, 90, 92
Silje Garmo case 165
Slovak Republic 32, 33–34, 199, 200
social cohesion 223
Söderman v Sweden 256
sovereignty 179, 183, 186
Spain 220–221
state interests 231–232
state intervention 160–163, 199–201
  temporary 235–236
  see also third-party state intervention
Strand Lobben and Others v Norway 246–247
  anti-gender activism 163, 164, 166, 181
  Article 8 (ECHR) violation 1, 5
  child's best interest 59, 138–141, 236, 237, 238, 265, 267–268
  custody allocation 229, 235–239
  family reunification 60–61, 237–238
  implications for child protection and child rights 260–261, 263
  mobilised interest 195–205
    interest and advocacy groups as amicus curiae 201–204
    state governments as amicus curiae 199–201
  personal identity rights 219

representation of children 106, 109, 110
street-level judicial implementation 86
Strand Lobben group of cases 23, 24–25
  interrogation of uniqueness 26–35
    comparison with judgements against other states 27–31
    research methodology 26–27
    third-party state intervention 31–34
  list of cases 35–39
  mobilised interest 192
  violations 79
street-level judicial implementation 76–80, 90–93
  adjustments to ECtHR judgements 87–89
  interpretation of ECtHR judgements 82–87
  reception of ECtHR judgements 82, 89–90
  research limitations 93
  research methods 80–81
subject, child as 106–110, 111, 112
Supreme Administrative Court, Finland 51–52
Supreme Court, Norway 61–63, 79, 84–85, 90, 92
surrogacy 239–240
survival indicators 9, 17n8
Sweden 137, 165, 202–203, 248, 256
Switzerland 129n4, 138, 218, 253
symbolic violence 128

T

temporary state intervention 235–236
theory of change 90
third-party intervention mechanism 25, 31
third-party interventions 163–164, 180, 181, 193, **197–198**, 261
  and contestation of children's rights 265–267
  key actors 160–163
  see also amicus curiae; anti-gender activism; inimicus curiae; mobilised interest
third-party state intervention 31–44, 199–201
Tlapak and Others v Germany 30
Torp, J.-A. 167
Turkey 34, 200

U

ultra-nationalists 157–158
uncivil society 168
Ungurian, P. 167, 175–176n10
United Kingdom 28–29, 33, 138, 199, 216
  see also England
United Nations Committee on the Rights of the Child (CRC Committee) 5, 66, 67, 68, 72n6, 136
  Concluding Observation 142–143, 256–257
  Days for General Discussion (DGDs) 146–147
  General Comments (GCs) 144–146, 254, **254**
  Optional Protocol to the Convention on the Rights of the Child on a Communications Procedure (OPIC) 143–144
United Nations Convention on the Rights of the Child (CRC) 5, 17n9, 60, 99, 135–6, 211–212
  Article 3 66, 142, 231–234
  Article 6 67
  Article 7 217, 219
  Article 8 217, 218
  Article 8 220
  Article 9 68, 141–142
  Article 12 50, 69
  Article 16 67–68, 142
  Article 19 10, 65, 144–145, 233
  Article 20 66, 124, 219
  Article 24 66–67
  Article 25 251
  Article 26 251
  Article 30 124
  Article 31 251
  European Court of Human Rights (ECtHR) references to 247–250
    CRC Articles used in decisions **252**
    subject areas 250–254
  Finish ratification 45
  relationship between European Convention on Human Rights (ECHR) and 244–245, 246–247
United Nations Guidelines for the Alternative Care of Children (UNGA) 145, 146
United States 161, 168, 239, 256
universalisability 185
utility theory 83

V

Van den Eynde, L. 161
van Slooten v Netherlands 28
veils / headscarves 216, 222–223
violence 65, 72, 117, 121, 123
  symbolic 128
Vision Network 175n1
vulnerability 61, 109, 125, 127, 139, 140, 223, 238

W

Wetjen and Others v Germany 30
World Health Organization (WHO) 168
World Justice Project (WJP), Rule of Law Index 6–7, **8–9**

www.ingramcontent.com/pod-product-compliance
Lightning Source LLC
Chambersburg PA
CBHW051530020426
42333CB00016B/1866